Valuing Your Customers

From quality information to quality relationships through database marketing

Angus Jenkinson

McGRAW-HILL BOOK COMPANY

London · New York · St Louis · San Francisco · Auckland
Bogotá · Caracas · Lisbon · Madrid · Mexico · Milan
Montreal · New Delhi · Panama · Paris · San Juan
São Paulo · Singapore · Sydney · Tokyo · Toronto

Published by
McGRAW–HILL Book Company Europe
Shoppenhangers Road, Maidenhead, Berkshire, SL6 2QL, England
Telephone 01628 23432
Fax 01628 770224

British Library Cataloguing in Publication Data
Jenkinson, Angus
   Valuing Your Customers: From Quality
   Information to Quality Relationships
   Through Database Marketing.
   I. Title
   658.80028574

   ISBN 0-07-707950-7

Library of Congress Cataloging-in-Publication Data
Jenkinson, Angus
   Valuing your customers: from quality information to quality
relationships through database marketing / Angus Jenkinson.
     p. cm.
   Includes bibliographical references and index.
   ISBN 0-07-707950-7 (alk. paper)
   1. Database marketing.   2. Total quality management.   I. Title.
HF5415.126.J46   1995
658.8–dc20   95-20988
            CIP

McGraw-Hill
A Division of The McGraw·Hill Companies

2345 BL 9876

Typeset by BookEns Ltd, Royston, Herts.
and printed and bound in Great Britain by Biddles Ltd., Guildford.
Printed on permanent paper in compliance with ISO Standard 9706.

Contents

Contents

Preface

In 1986 I was a director of Britain's top IBM midrange software business, JBA International, with a background in sales and marketing and looking for an opportunity to manage something with as much potential as accounting systems that was not already being developed by companies like JBA. John Watson, head of what became Britain's most successful direct marketing advertising agency (now WWAV Rapp and Collins), gave me the chance to lead a new independent database marketing branch and I had the good fortune to see that this was where the future lay.

The international target of today's blue riband companies is customer satisfaction and delight. This is perceived as the purpose of quality. Organizations are equally clear on the importance of information. Ignorance may be bliss, but not for long. The march of information technology into every corner of the organization has finally reached the sales and marketing community. A 1989 *Harvard Business Review* report ('Automation to boost sales and marketing', Moriarty and Swartz, Jan./Feb. 1989) concluded that this was the 'last frontier for IT'.

Linking the power of information to total quality sales and service in a new world is the subject of this book. A new world because it is not just the technological change that is profound, but the change in people. We are no longer as we were. This may sound trite, but the emancipation of the individual is a social trend significantly more profound than the current fads in technology, and it will reshape marketing.

Behind the book is a new way of thinking which shifts mass marketing from an impersonal war and direct marketing from a tactical junk mail tool – as many see it! – to a vision of enhanced value: profits from retained and delighted customers who feel personally valued, a responsive company which feels good to work for, a job worth doing. Every part of the company will be involved in the new methods.

The shift is replacing the marketing norms of the century. Mass marketing is as big as a brontosaurus, and just as vulnerable. It is time for the little warm-blooded creatures to come out to play.

The term 'database marketing' is used. As chapter one shows, this means much more than a set of computer systems, and maybe more than many database marketers expect. Relationship marketing, one-to-one marketing and other common terms might have been used, but because there is a central argument about the power of information-based marketing, knowing *who* you are talking with, and the addressability of the new marketing (although not always using the mail), the traditional term has been preferred. Furthermore, I wanted to emphasize that, essentially, database marketing is a *discipline* using TQM principles to focus in a new world on the customer threshold, how we engage with customers. This is also an interface to our salaries, our jobs and our feel-good factor. Eventually, all these various terms will disappear, because 'marketing' will have become a new amalgam of these elements and the epithets will be unnecessary.

This book is different in another respect: it sets out not just to describe the new marketing but to link it back to the organizational changes, systems building and creative and analytical skills involved.

In the new marketing paradigm of the next generation, business moves increasingly from an impersonal, amoral exercise in generating transactions to a sustained personal service and exchange relationship: good goods and fair value, I to I, one to one.

It has begun.

About this book

The ideas and cases in this book explain how:

- quality must evolve from product quality, to process quality to relationship quality to meet the needs of today's consumers and employees, and to achieve optimum potential (returning over the route in implementation);
- lifetime value becomes the key to both long- and short-term profitability;
- strategic application of knowledge and of communications changes products, transforming them into personalized and commodity-proof service brands;
- shifting from 'brand management' to 'account stewardship' preserves and nurtures the brand;
- 'moments of truth' crystalize service experience, organization development and relationship management in the 'archetypal moments' that make customers come back – and tell their friends;
- guarantee management thinking builds an end to end business devoted to acquiring and sustaining valued relationships;

as well as provide an introduction to the basics, mechanics and 'how-to' principles of database marketing.

Throughout, the word 'consumer' or 'customer' means a private individual, an individual within a company or a company quite interchangeably according to context or need. Where a distinction needs to be highlighted, it usually is.

Acknowledgements

There are many people to thank, including my clients, family, colleagues from past and present, friends who reviewed the text and McGraw-Hill. Forgive me if not all are mentioned. Without the support of my wife and children when I spent long periods away from them before and during the writing of this book, it simply could not have been produced. Thank you.

The genesis of the book began in 1990 when I was invited by the Direct Marketing Centre, now the Institute of Direct Marketing, to create a database marketing workshop, which has been operating regularly ever since. Over the years it forced me to think through and become conscious of issues I might otherwise have taken for granted. To Derek Holder, Caroline Robertson and the rest, thank you for all your help and encouragement.

Many colleagues at The Computing Group and WWAV – such as Judi Gehlcken, Paul Maynard, Ken Horler, Mike Thomas, Tony Reynolds, Tony Masters and John Watson – have, over the years, taught me much of what I know.

Thanks also to John Carlisle, Martin Leith and Mo Cohen, consultant friends who have assisted greatly, as well as to the members of the British Deming Association's Sales and Marketing Research Group working on quality in sales and The Association for Social Development, the international network of development consultants inspired by Bernard Lievegoed. John Carlisle is a leader in the developing world of buyer–supplier partnerships which mirrors the customer relationship. Mo Cohen talked to me about how marketers look at what creates the seams rather than what links the group. Martin Leith reminded me at the right time about Abraham Maslow. Deming startled me some years ago when I first read his work: he brought the obvious wisdom I had sensed into systemic form and Lievegoed is the wonderful architect of integrated development, and the sixty or so colleagues who meet together regularly reflect this.

There are many clients I should thank, including everyone who asked me a tough question on the workshops. Many are, of course, mentioned in the book.

Ogilvy & Mather Direct Europe needs a special mention for funding and encouraging research and development projects in association with their own corporate development, as well as involving me with a number of client projects. Their excellent ideas and the thinking opportunities greatly helped. In particular, I would like to thank Miles Young, Wim van Melick, Patty Lyons and Reimer Thedens of O&M Direct plus Nigel Howlett and Sarah Boussofiane of O&M Dataconsult. Their contribution was particularly relevant to the development of the economics of loyalty, service product benchmarking and the uses of database marketing.

When the book was first planned, a friend for 25 years and once a fellow director, Chris Last, had intended to be a co-author. Personal time commitments unfortunately meant he had to withdraw. We still do many workshops together, and without his encouragement this book may never have been started. My partner Jan Steward's tireless typing, editing and human support actually made it happen.

Valuing your customers recommends feedback and conversation and I, too, would welcome that from readers, so please write to:

Angus Jenkinson
c/o Stepping Stones Consultancy Ltd
16 High Street, Chesham, Bucks HP5 2PJ, UK
or fax +44 1494 775236

PART ONE
MARKETING TRANSFORMATION
The true potential of database marketing

'Database marketing' and its source 'direct marketing' are often seen as tactical tools and, at worst, purveyors of junk mail. The potential is very different. These are disciplines to transform organization and customer value by creating, sustaining and developing relationships of value. The evolution of quality from product performance to relationship performance is the critical step because this meets the new aspirations of customers and employees: it seems, amazingly enough, that more business is lost from poor service and poor customer care than from poor products.

If the transformation is successfully implemented, the result will sweep the old, impersonal, antagonistic mass marketing out as a learning phase. If not, companies will count the cost in declining margins.

Why and how has the junk mail image arisen, and how can this be transformed or avoided? Why has database marketing developed now, and so suddenly? It seems to be an idea whose time has come: two great social trends have met, like the Mississippi–Missouri, i.e. the evolution of information technology and the emancipation of the individual. (Implications for the organization and will be developed in later sections.)

Traditional bases of loyalty are no longer given. A new understanding of loyalty is essential to be able to develop it in the corporate customer community. Loyalty or retention of customers is demonstrated as the key to profitability; this depends not just on product quality but on service quality and knowledge of the customer – the strengths of database marketing. Tomorrow's marketers will need to build competences which move marketing from an impersonal, transaction focus powered by image to a personal, relationship focus built on substantial service in aid of the brand, not just one to one, but I to I (I∞I), using and mobilizing all the responsive company's resources in the promise, the guarantee of quality, delivered at the moment of truth to a recognized individual.

Case examples are given of how systems and ideas integrate in acquisition and retention of customers across the customer threshold, including brand development, sales productivity, service and trust building. How database marketing resources and disciplines enable marketers to develop loyalty using total corporate resources is a major theme of this part, developing elements of the model shown in Figure P1.1. This model indicates some of the ideas developed in the book: ideas centred around managing the flow of the relationship across the dynamic customer interface, the threshold between the company and its customer community.

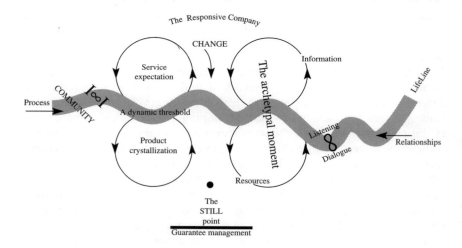

Figure P1.1   A model of models

1
The real mission of database marketing

Summary In this chapter, the key issues and opportunities that will drive the future of database marketing will be described. Database marketing and, its mother, direct marketing will be described not as grubby tactical tools to produce segmented mailings but as essential disciplines for the survival of tomorrow's companies and the basis of best practice in relationship and retention marketing, service development and total quality marketing. In fact, the old ways of marketing are increasingly inadequate for today's world and need to be supplemented and transformed.

The steps to success in this vital discipline then provide the body of the book.

Is not every meeting actually a critical moment in the world's evolution?

(Athys Floride)

Positioning database marketing

Database marketing, when made integral to the workings of the service-oriented business, is the learning discipline and toolkit which enables exceptional, personal and valued action to be implemented. It is the means of transforming the impersonal, unvalued noise of the modern marketplace into welcomed moments of truth, which become the basis for the cultivation of a reciprocal relationship between the individual members of the customer community and the responsive company.

Direct marketing was a response to a problem in marketing: fragmentation of media and the rise of individualism were two key reasons why it became popular. Furthermore, it worked, and was accountable! This meant that the marketers knew in detail the return on the marketing dollar and could justify spend to themselves as well as to colleagues, while getting better results than by broadcast techniques.

As a result, direct marketing made enormous strides during the 1980s and into the 1990s. In the United States, direct marketing generates at least $200 billion in revenues; in the UK, over £12 billion, with well over 2 billion

3

pieces of direct mail being generated each year. Other European countries have a similar developing investment in infrastructure and skills, although variation is considerable. There are flourishing worldwide agencies. New industries have been formed, such as direct insurance and direct computer sales. The Royal Bank of Scotland's subsidiary, Direct Line Insurance, continually hit the mainstream consumer headlines when its founder and managing director earned monster bonuses from the profits generated by Direct Line. Digital Equipment's US direct subsidiary is worth over $1 billion a year in revenues to its parent, and other subsidiaries or divisions operate around the globe. IBM has committed a significant part of its future to developing direct competences. In one survey of large European consumer product companies, 84 per cent claimed to be using direct marketing techniques and 67 per cent believed that promoting consumer loyalty was the main purpose of direct marketing. And surveys suggest that it will be even more important in five years.

Database marketing was a further refinement of direct techniques, emphasizing knowledge, continuous improvement, sustained customer relationship and more exact personalization of message and targeting. Database marketing developed as the marriage of the burgeoning consciousness of the power of information and information systems on the one hand, and the emphasis on customer-oriented businesses among quality and marketing professionals and executives on the other.

From around 1989, interest in relationship marketing began to develop. One stimulus was the seminal work of the consultancy Bain & Co., partly in conjunction with Earl Sasser of Harvard Business School, in retention economics. Another was the evolving awareness of what the database marketing community was doing. For example, the term 'relationship marketing' may first have been used by international nature charity, WWF, for its membership and fundraising activities. Retention economics is at the heart of database marketing through the concept of lifetime value, and existed for years in direct marketing and mail order before Bain & Co. first published.

However, it was neither conceptualized nor described in ways that reached the hearts and minds of the broad business community, partly because, for reasons to be explained, the direct business was busy killing its own reputation as fast as it created it: 'How can the "junk mail" people be serious about retention based on service quality?' came the question.

Yet, in reality, database marketing is the key to the successful implementation of relationship marketing. Not only did Bain & Co. describe the economics of retention, but they also gave impetus to root cause analysis as the means of understanding why we lose customers. Paradoxically, while this is a spur to improved database marketing, it is database marketing that is the key support tool for its implementation.

Relationship, database and direct marketing

How are relationship marketing, database marketing and direct marketing related? The description that follows seems to be justified by pragmatic observation, although others may have a different angle. Perhaps what matters is that the relationship (Figure 1.1) represents the perspective of the book and therefore orients the reader.

Using a narrow definition, *direct marketing* is essentially the art and psychology of communication dialogue and relationship building. It is focused on the creative process of crafting and delivering messages in response to known and anticipated customer groups to meet business goals. This is the world of image and copy, loyalty programmes and campaigns, brand development and sales propositions, and their evaluation; in other words, profitable, evolving selling. It is often used to emphasize creative mailing techniques, but it embraces the whole process of direct, one-to-one, targeted communication across all channels, including the salesforce, telephone and service representatives. All selling depends on communication and meeting. Indeed, selling is mostly communication and the organization of communication. Communication, of course, includes listening, takes place on verbal and non-verbal channels and is at least a direct, two-way meeting process.

When the word 'direct' is used later to characterize an activity, it will mean this personalized marketing dialogue, the two-way cycle of personalized, focused, relevant communication and response capture.

Relationship marketing is the discipline of organizing business resources to enhance each customer encounter as part of a long-term strategy of

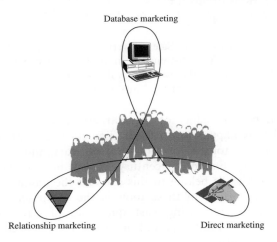

Figure 1.1   The positioning of database, direct and relationship marketing

profitable retention. It is concerned with process, culture, product and personnel development; ensuring that the skills, resources, people, service attitude and means to respond and act are in place. Culture, service and product development are described in some detail in later chapters, particularly Chapters 8 and 9. Many of the key issues of relationship marketing will simply be discussed when appropriate.

Database marketing is the development of information resources and the skill disciplines to take advantage of them. It is focused on developing the knowledge and subsequent decision making to enable the organization's resources and communication to be used with maximum effectiveness. Database marketing can be described as the cutting edge of direct marketing, with an emphasis on the *systematic process* of building and using information creatively.

The addition of marketing to the portfolio of information systems applications has been the most significant breakthrough of the last five years. According to Donnelley Marketing's 1994 survey of promotional practices, 56 per cent of US retailers and manufacturers have a marketing database and an additional 10 per cent are planning one; 85 per cent believe they will need one to be competitive at the end of the century; and more will no doubt realize that a database is necessary long before then. All this contrasts with a near-zero base in 1985!

All three 'marketings' are involved with what is widely called 'strategy making' and all three are involved in maximizing relationship value with customers, as will be demonstrated. The focus on database marketing arises because until an organization knows who its customers are, it is effectively operating with serious disadvantages.

In his book *Total Quality Marketing*, John Frazer Robinson argues:

> A revolution is about to begin. Sales, advertising and marketing people cannot escape this revolution. The customer is in control. He can take his business anywhere. The survivors, the winners, will be those who master the new techniques and learn the ways of total quality marketing.[1]

Being governed by the reality of the marketplace means responding to people and what is happening to them. Traders and entrepreneurs have known and served customers for thousands of years, and personal service was probably more common a century ago than now. However, new methods, tools and skills belong to this age and the unique challenges we face. The most important of these tools is the computer: the means of handling, organizing and using vast quantities of data. This enables companies to provide traditional and authentic personalized service on a scale never before realized.

The information system is the enabler of best practice. Until a company

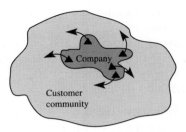

Figure 1.2   The company and its customers: a dynamic interface

has developed effective knowledge about the interaction of customers and company at the front line, and how communications, operations and activities affect customer attitudes and behaviour, it has little opportunity to optimize those encounters (Figure 1.2). Until it knows who its *individual* customers are and how they are behaving, it will find it difficult to break out of an impersonal and undifferentiated treatment of them.

There are, of course, other terms, such as 'one-to-one marketing', 'micromarketing', 'maximarketing', 'retention marketing' and, later in the book, 'individualized marketing', which seem to be variations on the same theme. They all recognize the new paradigm. Unless the organization commits to the inner disciplines of direct and relationship marketing, it will not be possible to develop powerful knowledge or take advantage of it.

The three competences of direct, relational and database marketing are therefore not alternatives but the essentials of modern business and will increasingly affect every part of every successful company, from the finance function to R&D and manufacturing. Together, they may be described as enabling the development of *the responsive company*.

This vision balances seven elements:

1. It engenders long-term thinking.
2. It places stress on quality, effectiveness *and* responsible ethics.
3. It is creative and people powered.
4. It focuses on individual, personal customers and cultivates relationships with them through service.
5. It depends on information technology as an enabling partner.
6. It is flexible, dynamic and responsive.
7. It is accountable; i.e. learning through measurement.

The vision of quality database marketing is therefore: *the effective use of information and information technology to support, at minimum cost for optimum effect, a creative and continuous ethical development of relationship value with a company's customer community by an informed, service-oriented and improving personal dialogue involving any relevant part of the company, sometimes responding to and sometimes initiating positive changes both in the company and among its customers.*

This implies marriages of technology and culture, process and goal, customer and company. As we shall see, database marketing is the most right-brained left-brain activity in commercial life.

Key points in this definition include:

- the effective use of information;
- elimination of waste (minimum cost) while focusing on results (optimum effect);
- continuous improvement of the key long-term asset of the business: customer lifetime value expressed as relationship value;
- the concept of a *customer community*; i.e. a group of customers as people who share something in common, namely a connection or interest in the brand or brands of the company;
- *two-way, personal communication*, mutually proactive and responsive, stimulating benefits and changes for each party – e.g. a customer's complaint or a customer's thanks; this dialogue recognizes individuals on both sides of the organization threshold, is informed by the computer-aided knowledge of the people, and uses all media at the company's disposal, including everyone in the company.

The community building concept is central to quality database marketing. Building loyal relationships with personal customers means building community. For example, Saga Holidays is a UK company that saw an opportunity to match the freedom of senior citizens to travel, their desire to find warmth in the winter cold, and the need to do so cheaply, with the availability of off-season, idle capacity in Mediterranean holiday resorts. Saga created the brand leader in a new market with a database of well over two million mature people. In their category they are well known, outside it they are relatively obscure because they focus their communications only where relevant. They also recognize that in serving their chosen community they have an opportunity to capitalize on the perception of Saga as lifestyle leaders.

A special interest consumer magazine not only expands their service, but also promotes other products and services. By asking questions about customer interest – e.g. 'Would you be interested in Home Security and if so what would be important?' – they have developed a range of services from knitting patterns to specially designed apartments for the elderly. The database then enables interested customers to be informed about new offers after they have been researched. Careful statistical and other analyses of the database and marketing activities also give Saga exact knowledge of differential effectiveness.

In another example of community, Apple's passionate commitment to change the world through a user-friendly tool for education, life and work led to a distinctive community of Apple and Macintosh users.[2] IBM mainframe users, especially in the company's hey-day, constituted a community, which even had a colour! IBM users were distinctive with respect to, say, ICL or digital users. Both the user company and the people in the company were often detectably different, although to pin down the causes might be difficult. American Express card members, especially Gold Card members, form another group.

No user or customer fits the mould precisely. In any community or family there is always a spread.

The value of quality in marketing: a new model

In research giving results that shocked traditional ideas, the PIMS survey of 3000 strategic business units in 450 firms carried out by the Strategic Planning Institute in Cambridge, Massachusetts, in cooperation with the Harvard Business School over a period of 18 years, identified that *choosing to focus on quality is more effective than focusing on market share*. When customer perception of a business's quality ranked in the top fifth of those in its industry, the company achieved pre-tax returns on investment (ROI), on average, of about 32 per cent a year. When quality was perceived to be in the bottom 40 per cent, ROI averaged 14 per cent less. High profits correlated better with customer perceived quality than with market share or any other variable.[3]

As Tom Lloyd puts it in a fascinatingly argued book, *The Nice Company*:

> Market share strategies do well in the zero/negative sum positional economy but not in the positive sum material economy. And it is the material economy that matters in the end because material success is what matters.[4]

The value of quality is now accepted. It is much easier to sell a good product than a poor one. But, the concept of quality in marketing is much vaguer than for just products. There are ideas of legality, honesty, profitability and effectiveness, but whereas quality in the manufacturing arena has been extensively developed, rather less work has been done in marketing, and yet marketing quality is the final and crucial layer of added value, because marketing aims to weave together organization resources and customer requirements. It is not too much to say that marketing (including the whole sales and service process) has the most contribution to make in shifting a company from a competent commodity maker to a valued life or business partner.

A new model and set of goals for the role of marketing in developing quality is presented below, based on a rethinking of Maslow's classic hierarchy of values. In the process, this sets out a set of general goals for corporate culture and purpose which can galvanize people, processes and systems towards profitable and worthwhile endeavour.

Large organizations have so much to lose. Like the dinosaur, they exist, but constantly face extinction if they cannot find enough to eat, and this is terrifying. The bigger they are the more they need 'to consume'. There is no business so big that it cannot topple. (Small companies made more profit than the giant IBM in 1991/92!) To maintain their status therefore, companies develop tools to win 'business', fill capacity and keep the factories or service lines 'busy'. Hence our obsession with quantities: getting the numbers, now, this quarter, this year. Anyone or any thing forming an obstacle is the enemy. Unfortunately, the enemy is often the customer. We turn to 'aggressive marketing techniques' and 'strategies' (i.e. military campaigns) to 'win' customers and on the way we often lose them.

In other cases, as will be shown, marketers often educate customers into the behaviours that companies are trying to avoid: fickleness and inconsistency. Yet, the aim should surely be to create the means to satisfy needs, create jobs, develop vision and add value: to be an effective way to sustainable success, development and life.

In his seminal work,[5] the psychologist Abraham Maslow put survival as the first and basic human requirement. Focus on survival leads to a concentration on the immediate present and the need to oppose the enemy. If survival is the obsession of companies, then it is measured by the current balance sheet and profit and loss, not the needs of people tomorrow. This is surely the stage that many organizations have reached.

Maslow's 'hierarchy of needs' is widely used in internal management issues around personnel motivation. It has even been used by the Welsh rugby team to improve team performance and well-being. Surely it can also be used to describe the operational motivations of the whole organization? It is certainly interesting to do so. (See Table 1.1 for an edited arrangement designed to do some justice to a rich concept, and Figure 1.3 for a description of the key features and competences to be developed.)

For those not familiar with Maslow's work, it is one of the more influential contributions to twentieth century psychology. He argued that humans were driven progressively by an ascending set of needs. His typology, or hierarchical breakdown, begins with the basic physiological drives, especially survival, and ascends to self-transcendence (not included in the derived model). People need to have their most basic needs met first, and only then can they ascend to higher needs. The lower levels never cease to be important, but, as they are satisfied, the need to evolve becomes ever more urgent. Ascendence represents development to a more successful existence.

The proposal is that exactly the same kind of motivation can be described

Table 1.1   The organization quality hierarchy. A hierarchy of quality values based on Abraham Maslow's hierarchy of needs

Maslow's hierarchy of needs: people	*Related organization state*
Self-actualization	*Service mastery*
Achieving inner mastery, doing and being creative in what he or she is individually fitted for, integration, self-knowledge, joy in and the capacity to give.	Integration of personal, corporate and community aims in an effective, dynamic, innovative, lively organization, knowing and achieving its mission and potential in harmony with suppliers and customers. Joint problem solving, I to I (I∞I) marketing.
Self-esteem	*Treasuring our reputation: loyalty to customers*
Achieved through doing something felt to be worth while.	Community value directed. The desire to know that products and services change the world or add to it in a valued way. Authentic service laden and design value. Gain–gain.
Belonging	*Seeking loyalty*
Being welcomed into a meaningful relationship with others.	Relationship quality or value directed. Avoiding customer defections. TQM, zero defects, loyalty programmes, relationship marketing, win–win.
Safety and comfort	*Avoiding pain*
Effectiveness; taming the world, surviving tomorrow.	Product quality assurance, directed at avoiding trouble and defects; hassle-free production. ISO 9000 and BS 5750. Brand management. Price led marketing; discount loyalty cards. Win–lose.
Basic physiological needs	*Surviving by sales*
Security and survival; surviving now.	Profit quantity directed; survival. Price and sale driven marketing. Live–Lose.

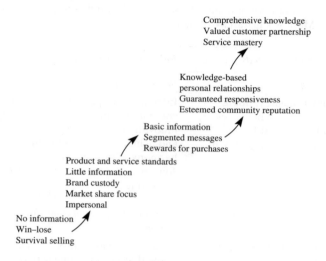

Comprehensive knowledge
Valued customer partnership
Service mastery

Knowledge-based
personal relationships
Guaranteed responsiveness
Esteemed community reputation

Basic information
Segmented messages
Rewards for purchases

Product and service standards
Little information
Brand custody
Market share focus
Impersonal

No information
Win–lose
Survival selling

Figure 1.3   The evolution of relationship quality

for organizations, who are after all full of people and operate in a human society. It then becomes a hierarchy of quality and quality values.

A quantity-obsessed business, *surviving by sales*, is probably focusing on maintenance and survival: basic physiological needs. One of the tests of a struggling company is that the monthly financial figures dominate attention.

Organizations then obviously progress by figuring out that the route to success involves using resources to improve product quality, beginning with an emphasis on reducing rejects: *avoiding the pain*. This is a decisive shift, but not yet a final goal. QA-based quality is now recognized as only a first and primitive step towards real quality, particularly since the challenge of Japan. Nevertheless, it makes a difference, as shown by the PIMS results above. Developing product quality is a prerequisite of relationship quality.

To progress beyond this requires concentration on improving the effectiveness of customer relationship and delivered value: *seeking loyalty*. Total quality management (TQM) focuses more on the customer's definition of quality and leads naturally to a customer-focused organization as the step to relationship quality. Many of the techniques in use in developing quality practice can also be applied to change the organization towards relationship quality. At this stage, many organizations also begin to think about loyalty programmes because of the value of loyalty. The debate about the cost of quality has been resolved, i.e. (i) quality saves money (by reducing waste), (ii) even if it did not, there is no choice: no quality, no business. The value of loyalty is also becoming one of the few certainties in an uncertain world.

Becoming community value directed increasingly means developing a mutuality of value: loyalty *to* customers creates loyalty *from* customers. *Treasuring our reputation* within the customer community is the first step towards creating the value stream that sustains the company into the future and has carried such British companies as Marks & Spencer to nearly £1 billion profit. At this stage, companies are very concerned about perceptions and how they are viewed. Therefore, PR, sponsorship, cultivating industry influencers, carelines and customer research all coexist with genuine guarantees and activities designed to generate real feedback for product and service development. Companies begin to take some pain to identify why customers are lost, looking for the root causes of defections.

Service mastery is then the blue riband goal. It is achieved when organizational and relationship effectiveness come together in product, process, information, goals and mutual loyalty: the needs of community and responsive company become increasingly self-supporting. As the purpose of the business is found from outside itself, rather than driven from inside, its future actually becomes more assured because it is the customer community that seeks its survival and continuation. The company (and its customers) know that it is making a difference, whether in the 'mundane' world of garbage removal and milk delivery or the high tech world of medicine and robotics.

This model of organization development benefits from giving direction to quality development goals; and by ensuring that they match our individual needs as managers, leaders, employees and customers, it increases the possibility of achievement, or at least positive movement. It replaces the goal of *quality as product specification* with *quality as customer partnership*. Perhaps the first toolmakers said, 'You hunt, you're good at it; I'll make your flints', but the reality is that no product finds its way to the customer without an uncommon amount of cooperative activity. This is what really drives economic development. Is it naive? Is it wishful thinking? Perhaps the question should be asked: 'Can any company be really successful, change the world in even a small and local way, become an icon of the times or even stand out positively in the crowd, unless it already somehow plugs into this factor?'

The need to talk with customers

The system cannot work unless you listen to customers and imagine yourself in their position. Everything starts there.

The commitment to changing the world and delivering a better future for society is what drove the Apple Corporation to its world-class status. Macintosh was originally conceived as 'Everyman's Computer': internal passion connected to an ongoing conversation with customers. Apple technologists, beginning with its founders, Steve Jobs and Steve Wozniak, were passionately committed to their own dreams and ideas.

However, customers rarely do the actual designing of products, especially when the very frontiers of their experience are being changed. What they can tell you is how they feel about current offerings – from you and from others. Apple's development began with listening to the ideas and desires of a small group of 'early adapters', the members of the computer clubs of the early 1970s. From these came the first ideas and the first product, intended for hobbyists. Later, the genesis of the best personal computer on the market, the Macintosh, was developed through feedback on Apple II, with information from journalists and users of the less successful Lisa and from first users and buyers of the Macintosh. From the company's involvement with thousands of dealers, customers and industry commentators came data to refine and develop the product until it had 80 per cent of the personal computer market.

Since then, customers have been returning to Apple again and again, and telling their friends.

The tragedy of junk marketing

Direct marketing and database marketing have nevertheless a problem: they are sometimes connected with the seedy end of marketing! It is a connection the industry leaders have disowned and transformed. For example, Jerry Pickholz, chairman emeritus of the world's largest direct agency network, Ogilvy & Mather Direct, and the US Direct Marketing Association's 1992 Direct Marketer of the Year, acknowledged in his acceptance address both the failures and the enormous past successes of direct marketing before describing the new vision. The historic problem was: 'As direct marketers we're used to thinking and succeeding in the short term.'

The result of thinking short term is a culture which manipulates the mailing to optimize response and not the business to optimize value.

There is a widespread view that direct means junk mail, tactical mailshots and, maybe, loyalty cards and newsletters. Chapter 6 describes this problem in some detail and shows both the barriers and opportunities for a more healthy cultivation of the discipline. In a 1994 workshop with direct marketing practitioners, the suggestion was made that direct marketing is often seen as the poor second cousin, its manager responsible only for short-term promotions while reporting, through a couple of levels perhaps, to the 'real marketing people'. 'So good?' was their reply.

If this is the image, then it is partly deserved, most significantly when direct professionals are happy to continue promoting and taking money for an image that falls far short of the real opportunity and potential of the discipline. When IBM first decided to go 'direct', it meant setting up a minor channel to sell personal computers (PCs) and supplies, or a function to generate leads. In the current, new strategy, IBM going 'direct' means 'the company', connecting the network of people to the community of customers through an information network, to optimize every encounter, every selling opportunity, every service moment, and to empower IMBers with the right information at point of need to be able to demonstrate and achieve personalized care. Why? Because every 1 per cent increase in customer satisfaction is worth $500 million to the company. This is some of the potential.

Jerry Pickholz then argued for new techniques, that are

- more conscious of the environment
- more honest and forthright
- more involving
- more useful to the consumer
- and even more successful

These are also challenges to be developed in Valuing Your Customers. Even if it was possible to be successful in the past with short-term thinking because the very power of direct marketing permitted such poverty of thinking, that time is over. The new era belongs to vision.

Scratch the surface of almost any well-known or active direct or database marketer and you will find someone who desperately wants to be committed to a long-term, value-added process of building loyalty, great relationships and brands, and thereby very profitable businesses. Marketers are frequently chronically cynical about their marketing and business leadership's capacity to commit to such an effective vision. Yet they know how these disciplines could really work to competitive advantage.

Let us first say something about 'competitive advantage'. Until the eighteenth century, 'competitive' only had the sense of 'competence'. In fact, it meant 'working together to achieve excellence'. This is the basis of true competitive advantage.

For example, companies in the retail sector are tired of brands that continuously focus on me-too promotions, contesting market share and thereby damaging all brands. These promotions aim to switch purchases between brands without adding to the total market. It is therefore zero-sum thinking of the worst kind. The consumer may seem to benefit from the reduced prices and margins that accompany this warfare, but these short-term tactical promotions prevent investment in genuine, long-term customer service. The retailer may gain little or nothing. Leading retailers are therefore looking for the 'category leaders': the companies with the vision to build new markets and not just steal share points; those who can move from win–lose towards gain–gain behaviour, and beyond.

If direct marketing has a problem, it is because businesses have a problem: short termism and survival mentality lead to unacceptable practices. Poor culture prevents optimum differentiation and competitive edge. Fortunately a consensus is emerging on new paradigms and business methods that are set to revolutionize this thinking, at least among a significant number of leading firms. 'We're trying to kill off junk mail – junk mail defined as "anything I didn't ask for and wouldn't be interested in" ' said American Express's vice president, Barrington I. Hill.[6]

The limits of the old style mass marketing

In fact, the reasons why companies first turned to direct disciplines derive from marketing's problem: the old mass marketing methods do not work well enough in the new world. The six issues that are mentioned below will be developed later:

1. Noise: there are so many messages out there, they get lost among each other.
2. The cost increases arising from fragmentation of the media: Where once it was possible to speak to everyone through a few key media at reasonable costs, there is now a proliferation of niche carriers and costs have risen ahead of inflation (of course, there is a corresponding targeting opportunity).
3. Impersonal, monolithic, one-way mass marketing no longer meets the needs of the era of the individual.
4. The structure of mass marketing is antagonistic to relationships; it is built on a win/lose mentality which is no longer applicable, if it ever was.
5. A failure to update the marketing mix paradigm from the old simplicities of the 4 Ps (product, price, place and promotion) means that marketers develop weaker differentiation.
6. Information-scarce strategies hamper the learning cycle, slowing improvement.

Why single-track selling in a noisy world is degrading

For decades, organizations acted single mindedly to develop the skills and strategies in brand building and communication which persuaded customers to buy the products the company wanted to sell. The skills were valuable, but their deployment was one way, single track, outbound, monolithic communication to the masses. This process shaped planning, product development, manufacturing, sales and marketing. It belonged to an era when mass manufacturing, mass distribution and mass marketing conditioned the industrial paradigm and was structure focused on optimizing the length of production runs, not customer relationships. Size equalled economy of scale and power. Companies relished power as the capacity to dominate the marketplace. The jobs of sales, marketing and advertising were simply to shift the tin the factories turned out. Any colour as long as it is black. Never mind the quality, feel the width.

Don Peppers and Martha Rogers (in *The One to One Future*) describe this as a slash and burn mentality, which might work while there is plenty of jungle left, but is very wasteful and degrading in the long term. The future belongs to those who cultivate their resources.

In consequence of the pressure to sell, the quantity and quality of the arts of persuasion developed to new heights, some of which perhaps exceeded the bounds of reasonableness and morality. For example, the timeshare industry nearly wrecked itself and Vance Packard's book, *The Hidden Persuaders*, revealed past techniques of subliminal advertising that have rightly been made illegal.

Avon Cosmetics has won thousands of trusting and eager Brazilian Indian women as customers for their cosmetics, including *Renew*, a skin improving treatment that burns off top layers of skin and which, once started, should not be discontinued. Using advertising techniques which Avon's own advertising manager admitted were not truthful,[7] Renew, which costs $30 a jar, was being actively sold, via the 'Avon lady', into families who had an average daily income of $3. Is this the shadow side of marketing?

In more sophisticated markets, the problem is that the level of marketing noise is steadily eroding value. The emperor of advertising may feel glossy and all dressed up for the ball, but more and more people are noticing the lack of substance. Relationship marketing consultant, Regis McKenna,[8] argues: What you do *for* a customer is more important than what you do *to* a customer. Few large companies have preserved the service values that belonged to earlier ages; those that remain are often 'one-man bands', survivors of a passing age. He sees obsessional quantitative measurements as the culprit, leading to barely justifiable selling practices, and challenges the effectiveness of this culture, concluding that those who continue to see marketing as a bag of tricks will lose to those that 'stress substance and real performance.... Advertising simply misses the fundamental points of marketing – adaptability, flexibility and responsiveness. The new marketing requires a feedback loop; it is this element that is missing from the monologue.'[9]

The fact that US consumers are confronted with over 3000 marketing messages a day, and 22 000 TV commercials a year,[10] while European consumers are being steadily chased in the same direction, means that the noise level tends more and more to dilute broadcast messages. An Eveready advert for its batteries, featuring a mechanical rabbit that just keeps on going, was named in the US as one of the top 1990 commercials for Duracell, its major rival! Forty per cent of those selecting it as outstanding gave the credit to the competitor. In the UK, adverts by some companies for direct insurance products regularly produce business for others. In fact, the main strategy of one company is to feature in the *Yellow Pages*, collecting calls stimulated by the advertising spend of others doing the hard work.

As a result people are listening less: top buyers watch 50 per cent less TV than they did a decade ago, and everyone seems to channel surf more than they did. Watchers are more sophisticated; they enjoy artistic images, but they less often naively convert this into compulsive buying. It is not that brand advertising does not work (although there may be times later when it sounds almost as if this is the case), but that its effectiveness is a relatively declining commodity. The quaint advertisements of the nineteenth century and into the 1930s, 1940s and 1950s testify to a time when the cost of creating interest and awareness was slight. Those days have gone.

Listening to customers, not fighting them

We have all been in those conversations where someone dominates the group with his or her point of view. As a person, how do we feel in a conversation that becomes a one-way monologue: at us? Do we enjoy talking to people who neither listen nor respond? How long do we listen to and value the comments of those we feel are exploiting us, taking us for a ride, on an ego trip of power?

On the other hand, when we find people with whom we can regularly share meaningful experiences we sometimes marry them, or at least make them our friends.

The mass-marketing method is essentially adversarial: it aims to dominate markets, customers, tastes and styles. Campaigns, strategies and targets shape the contest, and the contest is often with the customer. In a market share world, thinking is zero-sum. In a contest on price, the customer fights the supplier. As later chapters develop, the model that drives marketing has been teaching customers the very tricks we do not want them to have in a contest we can win in the short term but must lose eventually.

Pushing a stone uphill is hard work. So is paddling a canoe against the river. If the aim of marketing is to make products sell themselves, doing that needs a profound form of conversation: profound listening, followed by profound internal action to digest the message, then profound communication. The arts and processes of communication have always been invaluable to the structure of society. They depend on cultural skills that go back at least as far as the classic art of rhetoric, once felt to be one of the noblest attributes of the leaders of civilization. Good communication is a service.

If the structural reality remains that, despite the moves towards mass customization, most companies are formed to deliver a limited range of products and services on an ongoing basis, then the need to get customers to buy these items, and return for more, becomes even more paramount. All the more reason to shift from acquisition mentality to customer ownership, a long-term loyalty to customers which ensures their ongoing supply of demand to match the ongoing supply of products.

After all, there are a limited range of things you can do with customers: you can acquire the customers, sell them the product or service again (repeat sell), sell them a higher value version (up-sell), and sell them other products (cross-sell). Or you can acquire and then lose the customers. From that point of view, the mathematics of keeping customers seems quite simple and obvious for most businesses. (This will be fully developed in Chapter 5.)

So the arguments against the old, aggressive paradigm have also been developing on a pragmatic front: the need to survive as a successful business in a changing world. In consequence, the methods deployed must become less superficial, and more appropriate to a complex marketplace. The truth is very simple: attacking the inner feelings, objectives and needs of customers to convert them to your brand by persuasive force delivered in 30-second bursts is akin to learning to paddle a canoe upstream: hard work (but fun for macho types). There are easier and more effective ways.

Image advertising if it is any good, does work and it therefore still has a useful role, but if your brand depends on it the cost is high, and getting higher, while effects are reducing.

Inadequacies of the marketing mix concept

A growing group of academics and practitioners are also casting doubt on traditional marketing theory – about the marketing mix and concept of exchange when applied to international, industrial and services marketing companies. According to a Cranfield University study, these were 'developed using assumptions derived from ... the US market for consumer goods. This transactional focus is inappropriate. The study of retailing shows that, even if it is appropriate for fmcg products, it is not appropriate for the retailers that stock them.'[11] An expansion from 4 to 7 Ps is one example of the new thinking, to take into account the expanding importance of service and service delivery (see Chapter 8).

The new concept described below develops a much richer model for corporate differentiation. It aims to identify, for example, a total picture of the product, including the service and communication delivery process, human interest and targeting in order to measure alternative strategies and their effectiveness. In this way, the concept of quality widens from a mechanistic or assurance-based thinking into a useful way of discriminating effectiveness in securing customer loyalty and acquisition, with the database as the tool. Marketing becomes part of quality, or quality becomes part of marketing; i.e. the product as part of the managed relationship, or the relationship as part of managed product quality, become alternate ways of looking at the same reality.

Take an elementary example: two list brokers handle the same lists. One sends a fax 10 minutes after enquiry with a clear and reasoned recommendation, prices and quality of five best lists for a promotion. The other sends a long standard selection three days later. Are these the same products, and in whom would you invest?

Differentiating also on process and relationship can be much more effective than simply trying to produce easily reproducible product functions. The traditional supermarket has a big customer stewardship problem. One family spent £40 000 at a local branch of UK chain, Waitrose, over the course of 10 years. (This may seem to be a lot, but the average weekly spend in the UK is over £80. Many customers are therefore spending £100 or even more every week.) Yet, the same member of the family went most weeks without ever becoming known personally. Is it really competent that, having spent £40 000 over 10 years, the customer is still an unrecognized transaction? How long will it be before vigilante individuals start to question this and ask for the service values of yesteryear with the convenience of today?

The result is that the supermarket is limited in its provision of personalized service. For example, when new half-strength caffeine ground coffee was trialled on offer, one customer spent two months getting used to it, only to find one day that it was not on the shelf. No one knew why. 'Perhaps the buyer stopped buying it?' was the answer to the question. An offer was made to find out and inform the customer. Name and telephone details were taken, but nothing happened! On enquiry, the carefully recorded details had been lost! The name and telephone procedure was followed again. Again, nothing happened. After further persistence, there was still no call, but an apology in the shop. 'Sorry about the delay, we couldn't get anyone in Buying to tell us what the problem is.' After further delay, came the answer: 'We think it's not being ordered any more.'

This is not a problem of customer service training. This is an infrastructural problem, a system problem. When it was decided to stop stocking the product, the company did not know who would be affected, so action was almost impossible. The rest of the story follows this policy of ignoring the identities of individual customers. 'Shop early to avoid disappointment' is a marketing speak for, 'Be at *our* service'.

In the UK in 1992/93, the typical reaction to this story was: 'Do you expect anything different?' By 1994 this was changing. In Canada, Food City developed a programme with Air Miles to give their customers a personal card which is recorded at each shopping transaction and awards the customer free Air Miles (a promotion concept developed in the UK, literally offering free air miles that can be converted into flights) and also ensures that the customer is individually known.[12] As a result, information about the customer's shopping patterns can be built up in as much detail as required. A differential approach can also be made in the premium awards given to customers based on their value and loyalty. Technology and individual customer care are therefore in partnership, the former in service to the latter.

From mass marketing to individualized marketing: I to I

It is time to begin thinking less about the share of market you hold and more about the share of wallet among your individual customers. Whereas the 4Ps model was developed to support a relatively impersonal, transaction-based business economy, today's customer wants authentic, personalized service. When Henry Ford offered the iconic black Model T, the reaction was enthusiastic. Just let Ford try it today! Even toothbrushes are varied for age, the latest TV fashions, tooth and gum condition, smokers and more. What is happening? Tom Peters felt it was self-evident that we are living in 'Crazy Times'. Rapid change is the dominant feature of most social characterizations. There are two leading trends: both have been with us for some time; both are currently hurtling towards the end of the century and beyond.

One is the development of technologies and current scientific understanding. In the course of a few months in 1989, the bandwidth, or capacity, for telecommunications between the whole of Europe and North America increased from 40 000 concurrent sessions to 200 000. A few satellites and two fibre optic cables, each of which had a bandwidth of about 40 000, transformed the copper wire-based capacity that had been used since the beginning of the century. At the same time, British Telecom, the newly privatized UK telephone business, was laying the same fibre optic cable into private homes and businesses, creating a domestic capacity that had previously only existed between the continents of Europe and North America.

The second trend can be called psycho-social. While the consciousness of being an individual has clearly been developing for thousands of years, most analysts place the beginning of the modern sense of self *as recently as some time between the sixteenth and eighteenth centuries*. If so much change can happen in what is an instant of geological time, how much more can we expect? In fact, the pace of change appears to be accelerating: individualism has grown, particularly since the 1960s. The importance and roots of this trend are developed in Chapter 4. The outcome for the modern marketer is that there is no longer a mass market in the old sense of the word, as the spawning of the phrase 'one-to-one' testifies.

It is a test easily done. Ask yourself which 'segment' you feel you belong to. You will probably not like the idea. Although we may recognize or desire certain characteristics in common with others (who may not share other characteristics), such as becoming a Gold Card member, environmentalist or Armani client, each of us feels ourselves to be an individual first and foremost.

Hence, there are new challenges for the marketer, whose job must surely be to sense these realities and movements at work in the psyche of society (or a relevant part of it) and to react accordingly. Today's task demands individualized marketing, tailored to groups.

Even the words 'one to one', which strongly characterize the widespread recognition of these new times, have an impersonal feel. 'One' is what my grandfather said when he was being formal and impersonal about himself. Selling one by one is the essence of this new market. Gaining share of the market one by one – i.e. share of each individual's portfolio, not share of the anonymous market – is what it is all about. But to achieve this, marketing has to become I to I, person to person. For reasons that will become clearer, and to express the sense of dialogue, this is shown as I∞I.

While old skills are still needed, they must be enriched by new ones designed to tailor, personalize and target communications and services for relationship building. The new approach has real ability to enrich the organization at all levels. As we shall be exploring, profits can soar with the right techniques and policies.

For generations, marketing departments have been split into product or brand managers whose job is to fight for market share and push a product into the marketplace. The new age will focus on account stewardship. It makes more sense: Here are my customers. What will they want that I can sell them? How do I make sure they are my customers tomorrow and next year? Not just push, but responding to pull through. One survey showed that a single product could lead to 50 per cent annual customer defection. With three products, it became possible to keep the customer for life.

Brand management clearly needs to respond to a new challenge because persuasion can be expensive and inefficient: try persuading your children to eat their greens.

Brand management has always valued a long-term approach to brand stewardship. It takes a lot of money and time to develop a brand, and creating and sustaining a relationship between the customer and the brand also requires long-term investment. The brand must be adapted to suit the customer and the customer must be enticed to accept the brand.

Conclusion: the current and future roles of database marketing

Direct techniques and philosophy may have become tactical tools because they are the most effective means in many markets and channels to make real difference to sales effectiveness, as will be developed in later chapters. It is very effective to be able to select the customer and the message, to be able to do it in a matter of days, and to be able to test alternatives while doing so. But this misses the point.

Overmuch emphasis on tactical marketing (of any kind or whatever it is called) destroys brands and relationships and misses out on the real potential, which is community or customer relationship building. (There is an enormous difference between 'honing tactics' and 'tactical marketing': one means 'going forward' and the other means 'trying to survive'). *Nearly all great businesses are surely built on repeatable business: never sell to a customer once if you can do it again.*

The real database marketing opportunity in the 'caring, sharing '90s', the age of quality and customer focus, is therefore to take the organizational high ground. One hundred and fifty years of customer focus and communications, since the first days of mail order and fundraising, allied to more recent information technology skills development and an approach that is TQM biased at its core, form the pedigree for this new and still unrealized status. It is an idea whose time has come.

Database marketing is much more than just a tool to execute short-term, profitable promotions. It is a contemporary and fundamental method of working towards more profitable and satisfying relationships with customers through the power of relevant communication and information management.

Writing to its customers helped the Next group to stay alive during a financial crisis, helped a Spanish football club to continue when legislation threatened to close its grounds, kept Austin Rover selling in the dark days of the early 1980s when its quality reputation was poor and then helped it to capitalize when its new cars came on stream.

Years ago, Peter Drucker argued: 'The aim of marketing is to make selling superfluous. The aim is to know and understand the customer so well that the product or service sells itself.'[13] This is an aim that may remain for many an ideal, but for some it has become reality. Knowledge of the customer and the capacity to convert this into relationships will undoubtedly become as significant a core competence of many businesses in the future as skills such as electronics to a computer company or engineering to a car company.

In 1953, Irwin Bross made the case for getting closer to the customer through systematic focus: 'The purpose of studies in consumer preference is to adjust the product to the public, rather than, as in advertising, to adjust the public to the product.'[14] The Focus group, taking small groups – typically under 15 people – to discuss products and marketing, is one such method. Market research based on questionnaires to larger groups, either on the street, by telephone or by mail, have also been used extensively and effectively.

They are neither enough, nor are they practised enough. In fact, when one world-class IT business tried to run European level Focus groups with customers in order to find out what their needs and interests were for a planned new product division, local subsidiaries blocked the plans. Top management were afraid that unpleasant things would be said about their operations, and, although this was not the intention, fear prevented the initiative. Fear of hearing the truth from customers is one of the best and most frequently practised recipes to maintain mediocre products and services.

By contrast, systematically collecting customer information does two things:

1. It changes the organization enabling it to become closer to, and therefore more effective in dealing with, consumers.
2. It improves the company's capacity to communicate its new capability.

If direct marketers are to take the step into the centre of the organization to bring skills that are sorely needed, they may have to add some new motives and new skills, like organization and quality development; a greater emphasis on long-term thinking; service, loyalty and customer care skills and the ability to talk to and become top managers. If direct marketers do not take this step, any other marketer or manager with initiative and vision can begin to acquire and use the skills and resources built up in the industry to achieve the same end. The book is aimed at both groups.

Notes and references

1. Robinson, J.F., *Total Quality Marketing*, Kogan Page, 1991.
2. Sculley, J., *Odyssey: From Pepsi to Apple*, Fontana, 1989.
3. Buzzell, R.D. and Gale, B.T., *The PIMS Principles*, The Free Press, New York, 1989, pp. 107ff.
4. Lloyd, T., *The Nice Company: Why Nice Companies make More Profits*, Bloomsbury, 1990, p. 220.
5. Maslow, A., *Towards a Psychology of Being*, 1968.
6. *Business Week* (5 Sept 1994), p. 36.
7. Valjda, V., TV Nation, BBC2, 5 August 1994.
8. McKenna, R., *Relationship Marketing*, Addison Wesley, 1992.
9. McKenna (1992), *op. cit.*
10. Mander, J., 'The tyranny of television', *Resurgence* (No. 165; July/Aug. 1994).
11. Christopher, M., Payne, A., and Ballantyne, D., *Relationship Marketing*, Butterworth-Heinemann, 1993.
12. The Air Miles promotion is intended to be replaced by a customized loyalty scheme. Information from O&M Direct, Canada.
13. Drucker, P., *Management*, Pan Books, 1980.
14. Bross, I., *Design for Decision*, Macmillan, 1953.

2
The fundamental database marketing disciplines in 10 cases

Summary   This chapter will describe the essentials of a database (and direct) marketing through a number of best practice examples. It should help those who are new to the discipline, but will also, hopefully, structure the description of the power of database marketing in a way that will be interesting and informative even to the practised professional. Key points to develop will be:

- the basics of acquisition and retention, and the direct marketing cycle
- key elements in developing and executing a campaign
- how data is used to focus communication and messages
- the key applications in business-to-business and consumer marketing
- how database marketing works as an action learning discipline and a means to continuous improvement through the feedback loop
- the benefits of integration across the communications mix
- how long-term thinking is not only of practical value but has power in tactical situations.

You can observe a lot by watching.   (Berra's Law)

Where it begins: acquisition and retention

Direct marketing began as a highly successful and profitable way of implementing new customer and lead generation, and cross-up and up-selling to existing customers.

The authenticity and effectiveness of the acquisition and service strategies in meeting customer requirements creates corporate value (Figure 2.1). When Empty Toner Cartridge Ltd, a new company in a new market, wanted quick results, it used direct marketing.

Launched by management buyout entrepreneurs to provide a toner recycling service, it identified that 400 000 UK businesses had laser printers.

Getting started with customers

Lifetime
value
result

Keeping them. Changing   Increasing retained value.
the downward spiral   Moving with them

Figure 2.1 The three components of wealth

First, it carried out a pilot survey using selected business lists to confirm best characteristics; using this information it rolled out nationwide, getting a 10 per cent response to its targeted mailings. Within four weeks of the launch it had captured 2 per cent of the market.

AT&T Global won a 1993 Echo award with the help of Ogilvy & Mather Direct with a cross-sell mailing for business. AT&T's Merlin combined the functions of copier, fax and multi-line business phone in a piece of equipment about the size of a telephone. AT&T wanted to test launch in the Pacific Northwest using a house list of 1000 small business decision makers who already had Merlin equipment.

Because the Pacific Northwest was more than usually price sensitive as a result of defence industry cut-backs and the faltering lumber industry, the product – although better but more expensive than others – needed a quality mailing to establish credibility. The investment of $8.47 per piece included pre-production, production and postage.

Over 40 per cent of those mailed responded and 45 per cent of those converted to a sale, which was better than all projections and earned $49 for each $1 spent. Subsequently, with adjustments, it was rolled out across the USA.

These examples demonstrate some basic principles:

- Research lists/groups and proposition
- Test and review
- Roll out to successful groups
- Invest in success corresponding to need
- Adjust economics according to customer segment and activity.

Having identified the customer profile, the secret is to find others of the same type. If your customers are readers of *The Sun, The Times* or *The Washington Post*, then new customers are more likely to be readers of the same paper. Five per cent of Hertz's customers produce 52 per cent of their revenue. So Hertz naturally wanted to find more of the same kind of customer, and were prepared to invest significantly. This is an important secret. If you want to switch to loyal customers you need to offer something worth while. It may need a real premium to attract attention, not just a gimmick. (Hertz sent a top-quality remote control car to potential customers. To receive the control unit the customers had to ask a salesperson to call.) The total promotional expense, including the salesperson's time, was recouped within a few months.

Upgrading or developing customers through a premium service may also be a way of preventing attrition while developing value; for example, if, during a restaurant meal, the wine bottle is empty, we like to be asked if we want another. When American Express launched its Gold Card in the UK in 1981, it did not look for its new customers primarily among Visa and Mastercard holders, but sought to upgrade its Personal Green Card holders, selecting those most likely to switch. Gold Card holders now produce twice their share of revenue.

The money that organizations spend to acquire new customers could much more effectively be used to research and develop upgraded services for their existing customers. The secret lies in conducting the courtship to encourage both immediate consummation and an affirmation of the relationship through cross-selling.

A means of testing new ideas, including loyalty builders

Selecting key groups based on data and testing away from the blare of media publicity means that effectiveness can be ascertained, adjustments made, and any logistics resolved before going public. BT, the privatized UK telephone leader, secretly tested a loyalty scheme, Talking Points, in parts of London and south-east England, aiming to fend off its new rival, Mercury while it was learning.

Their method of promotion also illustrates how database marketing can be used to target key customers and deliver a long-term relationship builder. BT offered top residential customers – those spending more than £100 per quarter – points on all telephone time spent. These could be converted to the leading UK cooperative loyalty scheme, Air Miles, at a rate of one mile per £10 spent, or could be used in the Talking Points catalogue.

Holding on to existing customers creates one of the most effective barriers to entry of a new player, adding another differential layer to be overcome.

Four ways to succeed with database marketing

The first step is to identify the key differential advantages that database marketing can give to the marketer, throughout the sales cycle. There are four ways[1] in which database marketing can be used to cultivate strategic advantage, one or more of which may be appropriate for any responsive company:

1. *Strategic brand building*, with 'personality dependent' product.
2. *Trust forming and informing*, to generate trust for a platform or philosophy or to support a service relationship.
3. *Service provision*, through database marketing.
4. *Leveraging expensive sales channels*, particularly in the salesforce dominated company.

Success may involve an interdependent approach.

Strategic brand building

When a product depends on its brand personality for differentiation, traditional advertising is the norm. Communication is aimed at creating a sustainable, independent 'personality' for the brand. Customers invest the brand with attractive qualities (if all goes well): Heinz Tomato Ketchup is not just a bottle of sauce; Marlboro is linked to rugged independence; American Express has status and style. The customer may rely on the brand. Perhaps he or she gains by association with it.

While the broadcast monologues which typify brand building were criticized earlier, they are most successful when

– the message cannot be imitated;
– there is a sustained commitment to consistent brand building, as a significant investment;
– the brand is early into the field;
– confusing sales promotion messages are avoided (such as selling on price not personality and quality);
– the message is focused and consistent;
– a *large* amount of money has been spent.

Increasingly, however, database marketing is recognized as a major brand builder, or destroyer. In 1992 the International Direct Marketing Network (IDMN) initiated a survey of 221 big consumer goods companies across Europe and found that as many as 84 per cent of those companies were using some form of direct marketing, mainly for loyalty. Heinz UK now uses a database for all its product brands. The major benefits of image advertising over broadcast methods are focused spend and message. Personalized communication to individuals can meet several of the above criteria particularly well, such as non-imitable and focused messages.

In the US tobacco industry, there is a strong correlation between spend and market share. Marlboro, the market leader, outperformed the rest through powerful use of these methods. Between 1967 and 1989 its advertising investment was one-third more than its nearest rival, resulting in a market share, by 1989, of over double this rival.

Yet, Marlboro (Philip Morris) is now one of the most committed of database marketers. In the tobacco industry they drove the initial change. However, one of the big benefits they found was that they could target users of rival brands without switching their own brand loyal customers. A 1987 blind test with two million smokers provided responders to a questionnaire with two free packs of a new product, Merit. The campaign, with its follow-up mailings, switched half a million smokers who were not already loyal to a Philip Morris brand – something broadcast advertising cannot do. In fact, portfolio brand companies often encourage fickleness through intragroup competitive advertising.

What database marketing can do over image advertising is extend the manufacturer's or service company's *relationship* with the customer. 'Brand loyalty is a kind of continuity program', says Lester Wunderman. 'Good general advertising can shape a brand's personality, but only direct marketing can build ongoing, durable relationships … and that's where the profit is.' Ninety per cent of the profit of most brands derives from repeat purchases. Attracting and keeping brand loyalty depends on a bond based on dialogue and an authentic experience of quality, personal care and satisfaction. Loyalty is also trust and trust does not grow on tinsel promises. Private or 'own label' brands already represent nearly 14 per cent of all US grocery volume, and around 20 per cent of UK volume. One reason must be that the old allegiances cannot be sustained so easily by image advertising alone. After all, this is the era of icon toppling described by Faith Popcorn (see Chapter 4).

Case study 2.1   Huggies

One of the classic examples of such relationship building is Kimberly Clark's Huggies brand. In the early 1980s, Huggies, a disposable nappy, was trailing the market leader. In an attempt to transform this, in one of the first and longest running FMCG direct marketing campaigns, Kimberly Clark (the Kleenex company) invested $10 million dollars a year in a programme jointly developed with Ogilvy & Mather Direct which was an enormous success leading, for several years, to a 40 per cent compound annual growth in sales and a rapid 10 per cent increase in market share, becoming East Coast Number 1 brand.

Of fundamental importance to the campaign was an enormous mental switch, a paradigm shift from thinking of the sale as a transaction, a bag of nappies, to thinking of the child who needs to be clothed for several years; from one week's supply to 100 weeks' supply, from a profit of a few dollars to hundreds of dollars. This shift not only empowers the decision to invest in customer acquisition, but also directs the whole approach.

The campaign also recognizes a very basic fact: it is not the *whole* of the USA, the

UK, Germany or France that is the target audience. It is not even all the mothers. It is only the mothers who have babies of a certain age, and those who can reasonably be expected to use disposables and might need Huggies. Resources were now focused on locating these mothers: to establish the potential customer community. The names of three million expectant and new mothers were acquired yearly from nursing and medical establishments across the country. They were aggregated, put on a list file, and sent a communication called *The Beginning Years* binding together in what we would now call a magalog.

- a cover letter explaining the benefits of Huggies and the concept
- a promotion coupon, which could be redeemed from the first purchase
- a beautifully produced booklet on how to bring up your child
- a sample nappy pack.

The coupon was not so much a price promotion as a means of obtaining feedback on what was effective, making it possible to test and examine a variety of different creative and offer ideas and demographics. In later promotions it provided the means to track long-term success.

When the programme started it was stretching technology to allow each individual's coupon to be coded and matched to the mailing list, but even then, great effort was made to test coupon values, different magazine formats, letters, samples, timings and customer profiles for effectiveness. This so-called accountability, or measurability, is an essential feature of direct marketing. Focus groups can be used in the development of the offer and creative ideas, especially where significant investment is involved, but proposals can then be tested on real samples before roll out, and then further refined over the months and years.

Rather than spend money on short-term promotions that try to shift this week's transaction among customers whose patterns of spending have already been formed, the intention was to establish a loyal pattern from the outset. To retain and ensure continuing loyalty, Kimberly Clark then mailed a series of up to 14 *Beginning Years* booklets of exceptional quality. They included songs and finger games, articles on controlling TV watching, taming tantrums, or encouraging independence (in 'Your Baby at 21 months'), or on swaddling, choosing a doctor or soothing ('New-born' edition).

Each was timed not only to preserve the relationship but also to upgrade and develop the purchase through successively larger nappies to avoid the problems of 'leakage': when the nappy gets too small, things go wrong! This is a moment when a customer could choose to review the market, another kind of 'leakage'. In order to make sure they did not, Kimberly Clark encouraged size switch at the right time in the same way that a Rank Xerox salesperson may approach a customer renting a photocopying machine before the rental agreement has even expired in order to replace it with a better machine to pre-empt consideration of a switch in brand.

Furthermore, Huggies then developed a new product including *Pull Ups*, training pants which replace nappies, and extended the brand usage life for another few months.

More investment went into refreshing the list to keep track of movers. The quality of address correction to adjust for goneaways (or nixies) was phenomenal, an important economy given the cost of the mailings.

At the end of each relationship cycle, they say 'I'm sorry to say good-bye to a friend' – a respectful courtesy that may win goodwill among the network of mothers, or may retain the mother's custom for the next child.

Five key points emerge from the Huggies' case above:

– Long-term thinking, based on lifetime value
– Service intense communication and information to create goodwill and brand values, while cementing sales
– A feedback loop for action learning
– A very simple system was initially needed: by today's standards no fancy database is required for the basics of this programme. It could be executable with a good quality mailing list merging the multiple data sources. (Of course, all good things get more complex, the first law of systems. So, the system evolved, especially with the time-tied mailing series.)
– Investment in accurate data, in the information to power the ideas.

Chapter 7 further develops the nature of loyalty and brand loyalty and methods to increase it. However, the next way that database marketing can help develops the same theme.

Trust forming and informing

The second key application is in idea, opinion and trust forming. Whereas brand building usually depends on image and personality, it is often necessary to develop more complex and sophisticated messages, to build a platform of trust, confidence, knowledge and understanding about everything – from what you stand for to how you operate. It may be necessary to involve head as well as heart in encouraging action. Direct mail, in particular, benefits from the ability to speak personally to many recipients at once, with plenty of space and in a format appropriate to the objective, quickly and relatively inexpensively. Sometimes it is used to shape a decisive perception, sometimes to move people towards an interest and follow-up, such as becoming willing to see a salesperson. Establishing your credentials takes sophisticated communication, not always best achieved by advertisements, and even advertisements or on-pack information can benefit from a follow-up opportunity, through a careline, for example.

When Britain's Prince of Wales decided he needed to change his image, he turned to direct marketing to write to the 3000 people most influential in British society to set out his case. Direct mail was chosen because it could be precisely targeted, there was space to make the case – no artificial limits on length and little extra cost – and the tone and manner could be geared for the audience.

A leading supplier to South Africa's mining industry, a few years ago, was suddenly confronted with a major rival who threatened to strip 20–30 per cent of its market share at the next annual contract renewal cycle, and decided it had to do something quickly. It listened to its customers and discovered to its amazement that it was considered dominant and high priced. Responding to this with the help of its agency Ogilvy & Mather Direct, it created a quality direct mail campaign to customer decision makers, using a chessboard theme to explain the complexity, completeness and forethought of its service, with the result that it lost not a single contract. A message that no salesperson might have been able to develop and communicate so ably got home, reshaping its credentials. Salesforce time and energy was in fact significantly reduced. Direct marketing was relatively quick, inexpensive, private and precise.

Direct mail was similarly used by Hewlett Packard in parts of Europe to reshape its image among senior executives and CEOs in large and medium-sized companies, moving from its 'calculators and instruments' image to establish computing credentials. Their campaign also illustrates the principle of ensuring that you have the right data: telemarketing was first used to get accurate contact.

The use of information to build confidence and trust as well as interest is such an obvious part of marketing that it is sometimes overlooked. Later, it will be argued that information forms part of the *content* of many products. Mail order companies like Innovations, for example, use the catalogue to tell a story about every product. The story replaces the showcase and tactile experience.

The discovery of direct mail, and later telemarketing, by *non-profit* and charity groups led them to become extensive users of direct marketing because the format enables targeted ideas to be communicated, and action by way of donation, membership and signature can follow immediately. The 'product' is intangible; call it well-being or feel-good, or say that it is just plain generosity, but in each case the interactive dialogue format of the direct industry is ideal. Dr Barnado was one of the first to use direct mail: examples of his work from the nineteenth century are on display in their London HQ. WWF pioneered the use of database marketing in Europe, and, possibly, the term 'relationship marketing'. Writing to millions of members each year has helped it to move community ideas on the environment and nature. Its green mail order catalogues in Germany and Switzerland encourage a new lifestyle, an example it is emulating elsewhere across Europe.

Idea forming is also important when dealing with *industry influencers*: journalists, major users and user groups. As the story of the Prince of Wales illustrates, direct marketing can be a powerful tool. Yet, few companies have developed a marketing database for the individuals in their industry. Frequently, PR activities are managed via a PR agency who may maintain lists, but infrequently a database. By contrast, such companies as Apple have focused on managing relationships with their industry influencers for years. An effective information system which holds

- personal details about key influencers
- interests
- potential for influence
- attitudinal history
- the company's communication history

is a potentially invaluable ally.

In certain industries, especially information technology, finance and other fast-moving complex product areas, industry watchers and influencers often play a decisive role in market success. One industry that has had considerable information management resource dedicated is medicine. Doctors or physicians are so influential, and legislation is so strict, that contact is routinely managed by computer systems that brief the salesperson, tracking past communications and determining the next key message to give each doctor.

Case study 2.2   The Danish Post Office

Most of the ingredients of successful database marketing are found in an award winning, long-term campaign by the Danish Post Office which helped to create a new market.[2] Their requirement was to increase the use of the post as a means of doing and generating business among their customer community. This needed ways of using their own internal resources most effectively and a way of converting corporate attitudes and understanding. There were seven stages.

Planning and review. Rather than leaping in, they thought through what they were going to do, and subsequently analysed performance at every step of the way. Research played a substantial part. The campaign is also designed to meet the needs and opportunities of different groups cost effectively.

A campaign built on customer research and knowledge of needs, not ego. Surveys and research of the market, including a survey of 50 000 businesses, identified the issues, such as the high cost of the salesforce in Denmark and prevailing attitudes. They discovered, for example, that their customers felt they needed education and help to use the post more successfully. Furthermore, the survey became itself the first step in a dialogue marketing process, being used to qualify prospects and increase interest. One of the axioms of direct marketing is getting involvement.

Database development to gather information and feed it back into the process was an essential preliminary action. The database drives the campaign.

Involvement of interested parties, e.g. the 125 people in their salesforce. Their own salespeople were an essential resource for servicing the biggest customers, but could not be used with smaller companies. Ensuring that the salesforce understood both the motives and plan, and were ready to play their part with total commitment, was (and usually is) important.

Re-engineering the product, in order to add customer value and at the same time turning it into a promotion tool. The post remains the post (although different discount and service structures for user profiles already varies the offer), but the service the DPO offered to industry became more than just delivery of mail, it became delivery of the means to business. This meant that more consultative services were provided. These were met in various ways: for example, a 200 page book on direct marketing, a series of four seminars on direct marketing, and follow-up booklets, newsletters and 'how-to' cards on key topics were commissioned and given to interested parties to develop a long-term information flow.

Integration of multiple channels. Their campaign used the survey initially to build information and prospects. Telephone follow-up further qualified prospects, some of whom had a sales call while others were managed only by mail/phone.

A long-term commitment to developing the relationship through dialogue and useful, service-laden information is shown above. In fact, this was only the second phase of a project that began with the advertising agencies!

Database marketing may also be used with advantage for *internal marketing*, for example British Airways used direct marketing to help convert its employees to its new service culture. The use of database marketing in this way in large organizations is probably underused. Although internal communications happen (although rarely enough), are they developed on a systematic basis and with effective personalization? Microsoft CEO, Bill Gates, is well known for the use he makes of the internal network to receive and give communication. UK entrepreneur, Richard Branson, is another good example. All employees have his home number.

Service provision

This is so important that a complete chapter (Chapter 8) explores the principles. What idea can be more important than to communicate to customers the desire to be of service? Furthermore, good database marketing is also an information *service*. AECI transformed perceptions by describing a service already provided, a shift in opinion that was also a shift in knowledge.

Direct marketing has three ways in which it can enhance service experience, ways which also increase both brand awareness and trust:

- by turning an anonymous experience into a more personal one
- by enabling senior management or founders to communicate direct to customers or members, breaking down the remoteness of the organization
- by providing *relevant* information and help.

Eurocamp, a leading UK direct marketer of camping holidays, starts by selling through a brochure (an information device), takes calls by phone (convenience) and follows up bookings with a welcome pack, which adds genuine value to the holiday. It sends customers a well thought out and friendly wallet with information about the holiday location, including maps, local guides with personal impressions from Eurocamp founders and local people, plus language and cultural guides – all part of product fulfilment. The information content is both part of the product and a way of communicating, to distant customers, a tangible token of Eurocamp's interest and desire to be of service. Finally, it serves as a promise of good times to come and something, after the holiday, to hold onto for the future, aiding the chances of future sales.

Even the satisfaction questionnaire shows customers that Eurocamp genuinely wants to serve, providing valuable information to enable this and letting customers express their good or bad feelings, thus increasing their involvement.

Taken to logical conclusion, the personal, interactive direct database route becomes a new channel or business, as witnessed by the new 'direct' industries such as insurance, banking, vehicle sourcing, computers and software, holidays, office equipment, electrical components, etc. Traditional mail order giants like Sears began this trend, serving remote, frontier customers. Today, the frontiers may be time and convenience on the one hand, and the globe on the other. The Information Superhighway offers a new marketplace, potentially without frontiers. New tools of communication – for example, the telephone and brochure at the basic end and interactive TV, multi-media catalogues and visual stores, where you might 'walk through' Marks & Spencer, at the high end – will suit many. An increase in telecommuters will probably also lead to more and more 'cottage industry' and remote working, but by people with a real interest in reaching quality merchandise and services.

But the basics are part of everyday business. Dell Computers built an outstanding reputation and profitability in a crowded, tough market: IBM compatible personal computers. They pioneered the shape the industry is now tending to take. Interestingly, they do not see themselves as a 'direct' company but as a computer company aspiring to service and quality. Selling direct was the *means* to achieve this.

Quality product, communication and computer supported on-line telephone services replaced commodity product, and retail and salesforce overheads. Compaq achieved its growth by selling through dealers, but did not know who its customers were. On the same day that a Compaq representative claimed that the company could not have succeeded *without* dealers, Dell's top management claimed that it could not have been so successful *with* them. But the world is not binary, both are possible, as Dell and Compaq are now proving (each now uses both means).

Dell's teleservice people have instant access to customer records, product information, including unique selling points and benefits, plus availability and pricing data. All their marketing is direct, so they know what works and what does not. New advertisements are tested and improved, and customers have supported the rapid growth of what is now a billion dollar company out of their respect for good reliable information, powerful, guaranteed product, keen prices from cost savings on marketing and sales commission, and an ongoing low-cost, low-hassle relationship.

Direct sales like these are a service. Instead of having to go to some retail centre, or wait for a sales representative to call and go through the coffee and commission routine, or try to get an ill-equipped outfit to help over the telephone, customers deal, at best, with organizations professionally geared to respond, act, provide instant information and deliver. Their computer systems ensure that special deals and agreed prices are honoured, with all support on hand.

First Direct transformed UK banking attitudes by the development of branchless 24-hour, telephone-based services. A sophisticated database system not only backs up the 'cashiers' but triggers customer communications based on management parameters and customer behaviour. Customers gained from a business designed to achieve three essentials of banking: (a) to be accessible, (b) to know the individual customer and (c) to communicate effectively.

One of the best ways to serve is to personalize information, making it more relevant and interesting to busy people. This is the reason there has been such a fragmentation of the media. *Farmers' Weekly* demonstrates this principle *par excellance*, spawning a new technology in conjunction with RR Donnelley's personalized print-binding. Consider the challenge of any specialist journal aiming to produce a weekly for the American farmer. The micro and macro climatic range from the torrid south-west to the lush north-east, wetlands in Florida, mountain ranges, open prairies and vineyards, pigs and sheep and turkeys. Some farms are thousands of acres, others are small-holdings for organic vegetables. Anything that had material of interest to everyone would also carry a lot of waste in uninteresting material.

The solution was a questionnaire leading to a personalized magazine. The farmer indicated farm conditions and interests and each paper was then individually compiled, personalized and printed each week, using RR Donnelley's 'Selectronic binding'. The new paper provided more interesting reading, better targeting for advertising and a superb list. It also created accurate demographic and needs analysis to develop the paper's profile and story lines. As personalized communication it is a superb service.

The targeted, personalized paper becomes both communication and product in community building: medium and message wrapped up and personally delivered, with information management as catalyst and carrier. So, a problem, which becomes a challenge, becomes an opportunity to create a superb, added value, personalized service, creating and earning loyalty.

- Information enables redesign of the total product concept.
- Execution is redesigned, using the technology which triggered the business possibility.
- The new 'product' is also personalized mail, a communication that says 'we care about serving you', but the message is intrinsic, wrapped up in the total service value of the product itself and responsive to a customer need (perceived) and request (actualized in the questionnaire).

The technique is transportable to holiday brochures, catalogues, veteran/ senior citizen papers, and, in due course, to ordinary newspapers no doubt. New possibilities for this will also arise with the new multi-media electronic communications technologies appearing over the next decade or so.

Using the telephone for service (and selling)

The telephone is one of the easiest and most accessible of modern service and information tools and a key to a quality database marketing. It can be used to obtain information, to make outbound sales and service calls and as a response medium, particularly linked to freephone numbers. With the development of the new integration capabilities between telephone and computer (see also later chapters on CTI) these capabilities have greatly increased both effectiveness and measurement and evaluation options.

Other ways of using the telephone include:

- careline call numbers (e.g. on consumer goods packaging, the use of which is described later)
- checkup calls, to see if the customer is satisfied
- sales qualification and lead generation
- taking orders or requests for service
- progressing action and projects
- conducting surveys
- responding to written complaints.

Telemarketing is worth an estimated $73 billion a year in the US alone. Securicor Omega Express uses the telephone as an extension of the product and relationship. It is the UK's largest overnight parcels carrier with a 15 per cent market share and a turnover of over £200 million, delivering over 1.5 million parcels a week using 100 local branches, 14 sorting terminals, 3000 vehicles and 7000 staff. Like the Danish Post Office example on p. 33, their development began with asking customers a question: 'What's your improvement priority for us?' The overwhelming response was, 'A more friendly and faster proof of delivery service.'

One way this was done was by the use of electronic voice response. Customers can telephone a designated number and touch tone the parcel code assigned at despatch. Parcels are tracked from point to point through the network and vans are linked electronically. The computer can therefore provide automatic status information using simulated voice techniques.

The efficiency of service personnel was also improved. Two call centres for service and sales were set up, each with its own automatic call distributor (ACD). These were linked so that they effectively operated as a single unit: if call volumes increased at one location they would automatically be switched to the other. Calling line identification (CLI) detects the incoming telephone number, enabling the computer to access the customer record and display it for the telephone agent by the time the call is transferred.

The telemarketing software has scripts (or interactive conversation and data capture guides) to maintain consistency and control of telephone conversations. They are provided to the service agent via a series of screens which are logically determined by the answers to previous questions. The systems give management full information both historically and in real time about what is happening, including call and queue lengths, time to answer, abandoned call rate (an important trend indicator) and individual performance. Training techniques were geared towards developing individual confidence, in Securicor's experience the key to an agent's success. The results were 20 per cent reduced manning while improving service in a controlled, measurable and effective manner.

Leveraging expensive sales channels

The opportunities for database marketing with the salesforce are based on managing the effectiveness of the salesperson, customer relationship and organization (see Figure 2.2). For years, salespeople have sent ad hoc 'mailshots' and crafted personal letters which then disappear from the system. The new aim is to improve both, but even more important, to enable them to be more effective by leveraging their time and knowledge: freeing them from unnecessary activities and ensuring that when they do meet a customer or prospect they are well briefed, supported and directed. The same applies to the effectiveness of dealers, brokers and agents, although the politics of the situation may require mutual agreement on activities.

Figure 2.2   Leveraging the sales force (*source*: Jenkinson/O&M Direct)

Case study 2.3   Land Rover

In the summer of 1991, agency Craik Jones helped Land Rover to more than achieve its objectives in a campaign that illustrates brand building, idea forming, service and channel support. Land Rover wanted to sell 300 new Range Rovers over the critical four months before Britain's new year August registrations, and rather than cut prices, like many others during the recession, they wanted to establish Range Rover as a premium product. The approach included five features:

– Careful research, listening to customers and adapting the approach accordingly
– Strong link to brand, with powerful creative values
– Excellent offer designed to pull response, and pull it now, with a significant value component which (a) generated action and (b) generated goodwill (often the offer as call to action is trivial and uncreative)
– Attention to detail in implementation and internal communication
– Involvement of all parties, ensuring preparedness and commitment.

First, the agency clearly defined the marque's positioning in cooperation with advertising agency, BSB Dorland (i.e. strong emotional values of individualism, authenticity, adventure, guts and supremacy). With its high price – over £30 000 – it was competing with Mercedes, BMW and Jaguar. A series of linked advertisements captured emotional values and communicated how the vehicle's unique height and driving position gave it advantages such as extra visibility and safety, a feeling of calmness and confidence and a high degree of status. Range Rover was positioned both figuratively and literally head and shoulders above other luxury cars.

The Range Rover customer community consists of typically wealthy individuals who already own more than one luxury car and tend to be owners of their own business, senior directors or landed gentry.

Qualitative research of dealers and customers discovered that:

– Dealers had poor impressions of direct marketing. They believed that DM produced poor quality leads and wasted their time on test drives by 'tyre kickers'. Better targeting was necessary.

– Customers often did not test drive until they were more or less committed. Often, prestige car buyers did not even bother to test drive a car, perceiving a test drive as an unpleasant 10 minute drive around the block with the dealer. Range Rover was not high in their selection order. However, *those who drove the car had a good experience.* So both parties had problems with the perception of test drives, yet this was a key opportunity.

CACI, a demographic profiling company and authors of ACORN®, had taken the extensive information Land Rover holds about customers and created a robust profile. This was a sophisticated audience which receives a lot of direct mail. The challenge was to influence the perception of such a group, turning the difference into serious advantage.

Lists of luxury car owners were compiled from selections such as Investors Register and Wealth Register, filtered through CACI's profile. A mailing file of 50 000 prospects was tested for quality by 200 telephone calls, which also confirmed the match to profile.

A database was set up to handle the programme and the dealer force was specially trained and prepared. The offer was a 'private viewing', not a test drive: 'Take the car for half a day, with a hamper provided free, and have a picnic in the beautiful British countryside. Afterwards, keep these limited editions prints we've commissioned for the occasion. Have them anyway, even if you can't test drive, by telling us about your interests.' Range Rover thereby acquired valuable names. The look and feel and tone of voice exuded quality. To encourage immediate action, buyers got a free opportunity to spend a day at Range Rover's own 'Jungle Track' learning 4-wheel drive techniques, a premium service difficult to buy even if you are wealthy.

The result was 700 sales (vs. 300). Interested buyers could phone in to a central number and book a private viewing – immediately a convenient service. The database kept track of every dealer's diary. Confirmation details were sent care of the dealer, who got a full briefing including any special advice.

Follow-up research by telephone to three control groups of 200 not only found out more about the results but about ways to improve still further. There was a 24 per cent uplift in willingness to short list among non-buyers (a key objective), a 39 per cent uplift in 'easy to drive' (an issue with the big, 4-wheel drive image), and a 20 per cent lift in 'luxury car', factors that would build future sales on better brand/trust values.

Over two years, Land Rover attributed sales of more than £40 million worth of vehicles to direct marketing.[3] One of their ideas was a direct marketing support system for dealers. A computer system enables the 126 dealers to link up and generate communications. A central marketing unit buys in prospect lists on a national basis and provides dealers with leads locally, as well as a range of branded mailing materials which can be personalized for customer and dealer.

The Land Rover case above might not seem to leave much to the salespeople. In practice they still have a crucial role in completing the sales process, handling questions and so on. However, the total campaign is designed to integrate people, resources (e.g. jungle track, dealer network) and offer to optimize sales. Other cases highlight how the direct marketing campaign finishes the research with a crafted sales call at one extreme (e.g. AT&T had a campaign where the salesperson promised to hand over a stopwatch if he or she didn't finish proving that the customer could save money before the 10 minute time limit was up) or simply to generate qualified leads.

Some advanced applications have even developed statistical techniques for qualifying prospects. Salespeople will testify that the process of qualification is sometimes very complex. To aid in replicating this, semi-expert systems based on a score card are used to weight responses to a series of questions and then to assess the probability for follow up. One company that has developed this expertise is O&M Dataconsult, working, for example, with American Express Corporate Card and AT&T Business Systems in the US and Canada.

Database marketing's key planks

Database marketing can therefore be used tactically very effectively to generate profitable business, but goes way beyond this by supporting the acquisition *and* retention process. Lifetime value becomes the key to both long- and short-term profitability in both consumer and business-to-business marketing.

Database marketing can provide time-and-person-tied communication, inbound and outbound, for fully fledged relationship management: a discipline supporting all levels and parts of the responsive business, through the life cycle. Strategic application of knowledge and of communications can alter products, transforming them into personalized and commodity-proof service brands. As Figure 2.3 shows, there are five steps – a cycle of activity which is also a cycle of knowledge:

1. Establishing knowledge of customers, partly through research techniques, but including essentially their names and addresses and other behavioural and lifestyle data.
2. Establishing relationship investment policy decisions to determine how much can be invested in recruitment and the best route to achieve this.
3. Designing detailed tactical methods of implementation, in particular a set of criteria for personalized communications with individual customers timed and selected according to relevancy and optimal effective designed to add service and relationship content to product.

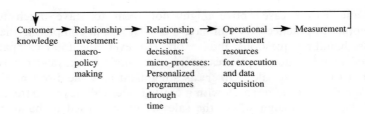

Figure 2.3   The cycle of knowledge: focusing of processes and activities through the power of knowledgeable thinking

4. Designing and implementing where necessary the operational resources for effective execution; this could include new resources such as a new business partner or call centre or the preparation of existing ones, e.g. by communication and training.
5. Measurement and evaluation of performance and consequent adaptation.

This process corresponds to the Plan–Do–Review archetype described in later chapters – as will also be, in greater detail, the above five steps. Database marketing, therefore, provides new techniques of market research by specifying individual customers and their precise behaviour and relationship patterns. Conventional market research, particularly qualitative methods, remains invaluable as a support.

Appropriately used, it can thereby enable a shift from 'brand management' to 'account stewardship'. Brand management becomes the servant of customer care and thereby the brand is truly preserved and nurtured. At the same time, the organization's resources can be developed and disposed to optimum effect through account focus: a conversation with customers that both:

– provides the information needed to develop products, business and marketing activity; and
– nurtures the relationship by focusing on the customer, not just the competition.

The attentive reader will note that there are not 10 cases in this chapter. There are either more than 10 or less than 10, depending on whether you include only major studies or also minor references, or where you decide the line should be drawn. This is a good indication of the nature of statistics and the problem of segmentation, to be discussed later.

Notes and references

1. I am indebted to ideas developed by Ogilvy & Mather Direct for the initial basis of this approach.

2. Wilhelmsen, L., '*The Danish Post*: The application of direct and dialogue marketing techniques to create a new market approach', *Journal of Targeting, Measurement and Analysis for Marketing*, **2** (No. 1).
3. *Precision Marketing* (31 May 1993).

3

New technologies: the rise of computer-aided sales and marketing systems

Summary Information systems are boosting marketing in four key areas which may be interlinked and which share a need for customer information:

- The *marketing database* as repository of customer data and tool for analysis and selected communication, particularly but not exclusively direct mail.
- *Telemarketing systems* which manage telephone traffic and provide operators with script and call management plus on-line support data.
- *Salesforce systems* to improve intra-team communication, forecasting and management information and to aid and direct the sales force in contact tracking and management.
- *Fulfilment* and order-processing systems which ensure that customers get great service and the company optimizes the order process for effect, value and information.

This chapter describes the basic features of these systems and their applications. Chapter 12 gives much more detailed system description, but focuses on the marketing database and telephone.

In five years, there will be two types of company – those who use the computer as a marketing tool and those who face bankruptcy.

(Warren McFarlan)

Together the four sets of systems shown in Figure 3.1 compose the computer-aided sales and marketing (CASM) systems marketplace with perhaps a thousand significant vendors world wide, of which perhaps a hundred, with their clients, are the market definers. The 'marketing database', which developed from a simple collection of mailing lists, is the

Figure 3.1 The growth of the CASM marketplace

key repository of customer information, linking and pooling data from other systems as well as integrating multi-channel selling and driving corporate direct mail and outbound communication. Telemarketing and sales management systems are operational front-ends (no less important for that) to handle deployment of organization resources. Administration and fulfilment systems are increasingly recognized as additional marketing tools to be integrated into a total customer-oriented set of systems.

The growth of the CASM marketplace is fuelled not only by business and cultural changes, but by technical changes in the information technology industry. The most significant driver for change has been the price/performance equation. Sales and marketing systems are demanding. They represent the latest, and perhaps last, major domain of business to be (successfully?) computerized. One reason for this delay is their complexity. The capability of RDBMS (relational database management system), and similar systems, has been a prerequisite for the easy implementation of functionally complex data systems and data access. Personal computing has also opened up possibilities for marketing professionals and the salesforce. The need to connect service, sales and marketing departments, especially to link field sales, has needed recent developments in wide area networks (WANs), general intersystem connectivity standards and distributed database management. Connecting the telephone to the computer is another new focus.

These systems are not control oriented with massive repetition of a few, basic, definable, transaction processes, like accounting applications. They are open-ended, value-generating, fluid, user-driven activities requiring more recent IT developments, such as:

- ease of use, e.g. graphical user interfaces (GUIs) such as Microsoft's Windows or the Apple Macintosh;
- ease of development and change through 4 GLs (fourth generation languages, i.e. computing languages which generate operational instructions in a common computing language such as COBOL from high-level user/analyst instructions) and CASE tools (computer-aided systems environment, a complete applications development toolkit for productivity);

- power in the hands of the user, personal computing tools;
- new software package design standards: most good sales and marketing systems feel like application specific 4 GLs, i.e. systems that design systems for specific applications, not like the kind of relatively fixed program function with which accountants are familiar.

Information systems now promise seven powerful aids to marketers:

1. *Long-term goal forming.* Aided by the power of knowledge and systems that can both continuously deliver and provide feedback, executives may gain the confidence to devise strategic goals for the development of customer loyalty.
2. *Policy focusing.* Information systems can focus and implement corporate policies for service and dialogue, rather than leave it to the whim of the operator.
3. *Planning power* arises from the ability to implement your plans effectively. The point of computing power is to enable human action on a bigger scale.
4. *Effective integration and balance* of programmes and priorities through communication of information to point of need, and the capacity to make the big decisions that come from an overview.
5. *Empowerment of staff*: marketers, sales and service people can be supported and aided in their work. Information is power; its denial may become one of the great rights infringements of the future.
6. *Dynamic responsiveness* (with the right systems). Information flow and system power together make it easy to understand and respond quickly.
7. *Performance appraisal.* Knowing what is going on: accountability and review, particularly when methods are used which intelligently convert masses of information into meaningful analysis, in partnership with qualitative research (see Chapters 15 and 16).

The vision provided by good technology is that, in creative, human hands, it can help to manage the relationship with customers, end to end, so that the value of customers steadily increases – a reward that can fund still better customer relationship management. Information of value flows from and to every part of the responsive business, each part enriching the other, improving productivity, performance and results. All systems share a need for information which is accurate and up-to-date about customers, and each interaction with the customer provides a means to ensure that this is so. Each part of the business should ideally take responsibility for the whole organization. There may be quite different producers and users of the information: e.g. a marketing user may need information whose source is order processing. Agreements for such support may need to be negotiated.

With reasonable implementation, this version is, in its crucial parts, realistic. Sales increases of 10–30 per cent are regularly achieved. Return on investment in 12–18 months (or better) is routine, provided the project is implemented reasonably effectively. Marketing and sales cost typically 15–35 per cent of total corporate costs and the right technology can either slash or more effectively redeploy these. As Moriarty and Swartz stated in one major research review,

> Creation of a marketing and sales productivity database is an investment in astute management. The database chronicles every one of a company's marketing and sales activities, from advertising that generates leads to direct mail and telephone qualification of the leads, to closing the first sale – all the way through the life of each account.[1]

However, the systems in the CASM marketplace tend to be sold to different management teams, usually by different companies and the proliferation of data in accounting systems of the 1970s and 1980s may be replaced by the proliferation of data in the sales and marketing systems. Furthermore, the system that drives company-wide implementation can be very significant. Very often, operational systems – for example, integrated client account handling systems – are driving the development of the new customer focus. This sometimes means delay in effective database marketing systems, which for many organizations is a most basic requirement.

The marketing database

The marketing database strength lies in the collection and management of a mass of information to produce 'information pictures' about the customer base and the company's marketing campaigns. It therefore assists the overall planning and execution of communication.

As a result, mail, telephone, sales, third party and other channels can be coordinated and strategically directed. For example, it is vital to ensure that salesforce activity with key accounts is complemented rather than under-mined by mail and telephone activity. It is equally important to ensure that an expensive resource is not used where a cheaper one can be equally effective. Each of the channels can source data, and each may need a comprehensive picture of the customer.

The marketing database represents the evolution of the mailing list into a new and sophisticated tool with powerful functions.

– Collecting and compiling data about customers. Merck & Co., the world's largest pharmaceutical company, purchased Medco Containment Services Inc., the country's largest mail order drug company, for $6 billion. Medco has data on the prescription use of 33 million people. Can you imagine

how powerful a direct selling opportunity this will provide for Merck! More conventionally, the system is 'fed' by the various systems in place across the departments and divisions and product lines of the organization, collating, assembling and sorting relevant data into a total picture of the customer; and customers' names and address processing and deduplication is typically the essential prerequisite; each company will have its own data structures but will probably conform to generic patterns.
- Selecting appropriate customers (in any quantity and sequence).
- Providing this to users and applications for mailing, telemarketing, sales, service support, customer loyalty programmes and other applications with whatever customer data is required.
- Providing for analysis of marketing activity to assess the short- and long-term effectiveness and enable improvement.

Case study 3.1   WH Smith

WH Smith, a leading UK high street newsagent and retailer selling books, stationery, music, gifts, sweets and tobacco, was looking for a complementary product line to balance its seasonal peaks and troughs, for example, before and after Christmas. It decided, during the halcyon days of the consumer boom in the mid-1980s, to go for travel and opened shops within shops, rapidly becoming one of the top UK travel agents by volume of outlets. By 1989, WH Smith Travel turned to direct marketing to try to counter the problems it was experiencing: consumers did not see that newsagent book shops made natural travel agents and the recession had ended the boom.

It launched a travel club (membership paid for 'free' travel insurance, guides, newsletter, offers and other benefits which together helped to increase their credibility) and began to collect information on enquirers and holidaymakers for systematic direct marketing, using interest and satisfaction questionnaires plus holiday bookings, creating a relational database of 450 000 people, 250 000 of whom were club members or their families, with the help of UK service bureau, The Computing Group. The use of a 'relational database' format enabled a structure which logically linked many different data elements, so that they could be accessed on-line and in a variety of formats. Booking and other data were grouped around households with contact and family names, e.g. who made the booking and who paid. WH Smith then refocused marketing expenditure, 85 per cent going to direct marketing.

This gave WH Smith and its branch managers answers to such questions as:

- for branch promotion planning: 'How many of my local Exeter clients have been on long haul holidays in the last two years?'
- for cross-sell analysis: 'What is the relationship between Caribbean and Ski holiday buyers?'
- for product and market planning: 'What is the most popular destination by customer type?'

as well as the capacity to select chosen groups for promotion, normally by mail.

The bureau looked after the database and all operational details, including data capture. WH Smith Travel's marketing management, who performed the campaign planning and management, were provided with on-line terminals for analysis and segmentation so that the location of the machine was an irrelevancy. When changes in the marketing team took place, the bureau provided valuable transition services.

In the circumstances, the club was a success, producing 60 per cent of all Travel's revenue, enabling WH Smith to hold turnover levels even in the downturn. Given the lack of synergy in the shops, however, WH Smith eventually sold out to Carlson Network, a US travel company.

What were they buying? The shops within shops were no use to them. The primary asset value was, of course, the database.

The database is a comprehensive source of marketing relevant data about customers. Structures to hold this need to be flexible to allow for the gradual, or even sudden evolution of data requirements as marketers think of new questions to ask customers and new information to collect. Data may be collected from many parts of the organization and from outside. This means that flexible facilities to import such data while standardizing it to the database format are needed.

Key to the effectiveness of the database is the quality of its name and address management, typically the means by which records can be matched and collated. Poor function and data here invalidates or damages the quality of database operations. By using the customer's name and relevant data about the status of the relationship (such as past purchases), communications can be made much more personalized. Obviously we shall be discussing this in much greater detail later. A good database will invest considerable software and other resources in ensuring that data is accurately collected and that duplicates are avoided. Marketing databases are frequently created, managed and operated by specialist service bureaux. One reason is that they developed expertise in name and address processing in the days of list management. Another is that companies can off-load the heavy seasonal processing load and cumbersome operational issues on specialists who also share resources around.

Because the database holds information about all customers, it becomes a valuable research aid, enabling marketers to find clusters of similar customers and to identify the reasons for this common behaviour. Tools for analysis are an important part of the system. These include facilities for cross-tabulation and segment counts (i.e. ways to slice up the database into meaningful groups and get count and breakdown analysis) as well as more advanced means of modelling the data, all of which are discussed in more detail later.

Communication programmes can then be developed to target audiences. These need to be personalized, but whereas telemarketing and salesforce systems tend to produce one-off letters based on an individual transaction (such as a telephone call or a sales call) the marketing database is typically used to generate a large volume of communication by letter, telephone or other means, to all the people to whom it is relevant. As techniques improve, this becomes increasingly focused and personalized.

The marketing database will usually hold a record of all communications to individual customers. This data can be used for two reasons; to measure effectiveness and as basis for the selection of future promotions (for example, mailing everyone who has not replied to a previous letter).

While a sales management or telemarketing system needs to be able to perform speedily, enabling an individual salesperson or telemarketing agent to work in a fast and uninterrupted way, the marketing database needs to be able to cope sometimes with very large volumes. They may contain hundreds of thousands or even millions of records. Users may want to find out about a single customer very quickly, or they may wish to process hundreds of thousands of records and produce a summary in a few moments. This is a challenge for both computer performance and design.

Sales management systems

The sales force has traditionally been high on 'flair'. The introduction of sales management systems need not reduce personal initiative, but it does change cultures and is frequently accompanied by considerable fear unless the salesforce is proactively involved.

Sales management systems aim to make one of the most expensive and potentially most powerful levers in the organization more effective. As such, most of these systems are implicitly focused on the organization's activities, rather than the customer's.

Their most potent impact is in enabling activity planning by establishing standard procedures (at the corporate or individual level); for example, in following up a lead. First, this ensures that the procedures are carried out; secondly, it reduces labour; thirdly, it enables measurement and improvement. Therefore, a company might decide that, after an exhibition, all contacts will receive letter A, to be followed up after three days by phone call B by telemarketing and then either letter C or an appointment for the salesperson. Lead and contract bids can be tracked and planned by carefully thought-through processes, without preventing innovation and ad hoc activities as needed.

Activity planning can also be implemented by agreeing actions with customers and prospects which the computer (relatively) infallibly remembers – for example, to call back on a particular day: a 'diary' system. The salesperson, or someone in telemarketing, will get a reminder on the day, even if personnel have changed.

Other areas include:

- the recording and reporting of activities, forecasts, expenses, customer information, etc., by criteria such as market, territory, product, customer type, price and channel
- the provision of technical and customer information to the salesperson during a sales call
- the use of some systems to capture orders, generate quotations or perform 'expert system' calculations, such as the best financial policy to offer
- planning and internal mail for communication to and from the field.

Salespeople demand ease of use. Good systems need to meet the work style of the salesforce and be so easy to learn that a time hungry, critical professional does not give up in frustration. Many salespeople have a natural affinity for interpersonal relationships but a low tolerance in talking to the computer.

Systems have two components: the 'content' element and the 'process' element. The content is the particular data structure: the type of data held, for example, about customers, salespeople or a call. The process element, as the name suggests, represents the operational process followed to execute a chosen task. Good sales systems are designed to enable considerable customization of the 'content', the particular data held, but usually around generic structures. There may be records for:

- company details and status
- contact details
- salesperson details
- territory details
- contact or call history
- notes
- actions
- diary
- business types, job titles and other useful codes
- orders
- forecasts
- internal letters

and others.

They will also provide a number of widely used *activity* processes. For example, there is surely no salesforce in which the salesperson neither makes contact with a prospect or customer nor records some follow-up action. Again, considerable flexibility is provided by the best systems in terms of options that will be specified and configured by each user company. No two companies follow up a lead in the same manner.

The involvement of the salesforce in the decision to implement will be crucial in winning their commitment. Typically, salesforce systems provide members with portable devices, or at least with access to their own, and it is essential that they are able and willing to use these devices. Equally, sales management must implement systems in a manner conducive to the development of an overall customer focus and account management.

The installation at Ciba Geigy Agrochemicals of a sales management system meant that the salesforce felt more empowered, and they spent less time filling in paper that gave them no benefit. Instead, they were armed with the information they needed, up-to-date and relevant.

Ciba Geigy sell chemical farming aids to farmers and agricultural distributors. In June 1991, they installed a software package called Ensure plus portable computers for the salesforce with databases on farmers, farms and the chemicals used, and also on distributors, products stocked and transaction details. This is updated daily by salespeople to head office, and by head office to salespeople. The link is by telephone line and modem to and from the company's central IBM AS/400 minicomputer. This also provides for electronic communication between salespeople and to and from the manager.

It helped them in very human ways (being able to make notes on such details as whether a farmer had a 'nasty' dog) and in business – for example, identifying prospects or being more professional in contact. Data on distributors included business name and address, contact details, account number, delivery details, products purchased, stocking levels, orders placed, delivered and outstanding and credit control information. Complaints are also recorded. The salesforce and management reported that they felt more supported by the company, particularly through better information and less paperwork. Requested data for a meeting, which might previously have arrived three or four days old, is now fresh.

Another valued benefit is the ability to interrogate for particular technical problems or complaints. Has anyone else had the same problem? They can then be contacted for help or information.

Sales management systems therefore offer gains in time management, productivity, continuity of knowledge and action, empowerment of salespeople, discipline and the direction of policy, and information for learning.

Telemarketing systems

The telephone has been a key sales and marketing tool since it was developed. In the US, telemarketing generates around $73 billion of annual expenditure, about a half each on inbound and outbound calls. UK growth is now faster than in the US, from a smaller base estimated by a Henley Centre report on telephone-based business generally, Teleculture 2000, at up to £10 billion, of which less than £1 billion is in inbound telemarketing. With the creation in the US in the late 1970s and 1980s of the first telemarketing bureaux – an operation that would perform or receive calls for clients – the need for systems to provide:

- fast track training through prompts
- testing and changing of scripts
- flexible data change
- validation of data
- action follow-up (usually mailing a brochure)

created the requirement for what became the telemarketing system.

Clients then realized that these systems could also be used internally, adding flexibility and responsiveness to service and sales, to standardize processes or to create new business opportunities, even internationally. Adobe Software, a specialist in fonts and other graphics software, has set up a telesales and service unit operated by agency, McQueen Direct, to encourage its users to upgrade to new versions of software and handle customer calls from across Europe. An international freephone number is provided to all customers with response in their own language.

Often telemarketing is linked to the use of 800/0800 and other freephone numbers for a fast, flexible, responsive and personal way to handle a wide range of needs (Send a brochure, what's my status? Do you have availability? I want to complain!). The telemarketer can also be used to 'qualify' a prospect (decide whether the person is suitable as a prospect) and if so to set appointments, saving sales time. Many service organizations use telemarketing as a method of handling service requests ('fix my drains'), and few (but increasing number) use it for

- outbound research into customer attitudes
- outbound enquiries into satisfaction (e.g. after equipment installation, holidays or other services – Manpower has for years telephoned every customer after a new person is placed on a contract).

The new technology has led to social changes, such as telephone banking. First Direct, the electronic/remote subsidiary of the UK's Midland Bank, uses telemarketing to handle and route all incoming calls, to provide access whenever needed to the customer database and to help in other applications. Scripted calls provide staff with guidelines to capture data and give prompt action. Because staff are also well trained, this is not intrusive. After each call, First Direct knows what happened, at what time, and the customer has been well and promptly served.

Inbound callers can be routed automatically to 'the most idle' staff member available. Other facilities are also available to manage inbound calls.

- Voice response and touch-tone prompting are available to route calls and 'switch on' particular computer applications or scripts. For example, Microsoft use this so that calls for help can be connected with experts in their application environment without delay; callers can even ask for information to be faxed automatically.
- The caller's telephone number can be detected and used to identify name and address details prior to connection (subject to legality).
- Queue length is managed, ensuring that callers are neither kept waiting too long nor turned away. This may include informing them of the length of the queue, inviting them to leave a message so they can be called back, switching the call automatically to another centre, perhaps in another city or at a service bureau, and advising management that queues are extending. All lost calls can be recorded for performance analysis.

Topic 3.1   Calling for caring: how the telephone aids customer care

With the emphasis that has existed in the marketplace on cost, much of the drift in phone use has been towards the automation of call handling. Some applications lend themselves fairly readily to this – for example, requests for product literature or even simple orders. Others need a more personal touch. Yamaha-Kemble Music (UK) is the British division of the world's largest musical instrument maker. They tried a voice-activated system for 18 months to capture names and addresses of people asking for brochures, but, according to sales and marketing director John Booth, 'Ours are niche products so there are unlikely ever to be more than 250 calls a week. But these could be about any one of 20–30 instruments appearing in current ad campaigns. A voice-activated system can't discuss products with people.'

The solution was to move the response handling to an outside agency with live operators who can respond flexibly to queries, supported by a database of answers and two experts as backup. The service answers questions and advises on the nearest stockist, passing on the lead to them where appropriate, e.g. for a demonstration.

But customer care is not just limited to inbound consumer calls. The Co-operative Bank faced unexpectedly heavy response to a campaign for its Gold Card. To avoid alienating applicants, while credit checking each application, the Co-op used a bureau to call people whose application had succeeded but who had yet to receive a card. The call welcomed the customers, verified name and address and confirmed that the card was on its way, surprising customers favourably: 'a graceful surprise'. Analysis showed that this approach also improved retention.[2]

Caring about customers can produce additional business. For example, US garden supplies company, Springhill Nurseries, calls its customers to confirm their order and then tells them of compatible special offers. Not only is this a thoughtful call, but 20 per cent of middle-sized to large customers are willing to buy one of the special offers. However, it is important to ensure that this does not become an irritating device.

According to the Henley Centre, only 22 per cent of middle-sized to large businesses are organized to deal effectively with customers and potential customers on the telephone, and just one bad experience can be enough to turn the customer away. Nevertheless, an estimated £10 billion per annum is spent on customer contact for sales, marketing and customer service functions in the UK, as well as 800 000 dedicated telephones.[3] We can reasonably expect that one of the big business growth areas of the next 10 years will be high added value customer service/support/care operations, often outsourced to specialists. These centres will bring together technology advances in telephony and computer integration, service process skills, human resource development and retention thinking to build and save customer relationships. As a US baby care firm told researchers, the commercial value of a careline service is its ability to hang on to a customer, even one who is complaining: 'At least we know who they are and can address the problem.'[4]

Telemarketing systems are built around *scripting*, a user language to define dialogues, i.e. navigation paths through service or sales calls. User managers specify the questions to be asked and data to be captured, including options and validation procedures. They may allow exit routines into other applications like order processing, insurance underwriting or technical help. Depending on the answer to any question, the system either specifies the next action or question (based on the predefined script) or provides options. New scripts can be set up from scratch, or based on an existing one. Scripts can be tested. Five or ten versions can be used and evolved in a morning, or long-term loyalty trials can be conducted. Scripts can be labelled and performance measured by the marketing database.

Other facilities allow sales and marketing to generate automatic outbound calls. United Artists Cablesystems Corp. used predictive dialling systems to increase the efficiency of their outbound calling by 60 per cent. UACC owns and services over 80 cable systems across the USA. Phone marketers are used to recruit new customers and to upgrade existing ones because much higher response rates are obtained by this system than by mail. Upgrade conversion rates, for example, have been reported as around 10 per cent. UACC's callers make more than 1.5 million contacts a year and increased call rate productivity through uner power dialling from 3000 a day to 5000. The predictive dialler, from EIS Inc., calls numbers on the list, filters out unanswered and busy calls and switches answered calls to an agent who is freed from the hassle of dialling, contributing to reduced staff turnover. Unsuccessful calls are automatically rescheduled. Call timing is based on factors like average length of call and the current ratio of engaged/ unanswered calls. It is obviously crucially important not to overdo calls. There are widespread complaints from consumers about being called by computers! (See Chapter 6.)

A great benefit is that all activity is measured yielding masses of data about calls, especially when integrated with computing systems. Optimum use of this information will be discussed later. Increasingly, the telephone and computer system will be fully integrated. So-called Telephony Systems Architectures, which provide for this, are available from companies like IBM (Callpath) and Digital (CTI). These are discussed in Chapter 12.

Administration is marketing too!

As businesses move towards direct sales and marketing, the need to think through the service from end to end increases. Success requires an holistic view: there is little point in acquiring good prospects or sales through an intensive focus on marketing effectiveness at the front end if customer relations are to be damaged by the administrative functions in the back office.

More and more companies are therefore looking at the entire range of 'moments of truth', the moments of interaction with the company, to see how direct marketing skills (from telemarketing to direct mail) can help and how information can be captured to improve customer profile knowledge. This is explored in more detail, in Chapter 8.

The new tools may be of great assistance to the traditional order-processing functions. Telemarketing systems are increasingly used in fulfilment, order processing and customer service. Salespeople may take orders on their lap top computer. The marketing database can be used to confirm orders, or to generate them. More and more companies are seeing the benefit of moving from a variety of separate service line computer applications to a central client-based focus. For example, financial services companies are implementing client information systems (CIS) which link all the different policy-processing systems to a single customer. Policy quotations, order confirmations or service enquiry handling are increasingly being seen as part of database marketing. The edges of traditional and modern applications are becoming blurred. The aim is to improve total quality of customer information and customer service focus.

However, it would probably be a mistake to think that the operation system can duplicate as the database marketing system in the medium term.

– Administration must be more conservative in its deduplication policy. This means there is a tendency to 'underkill', or leave many duplicate records on the database leading to additional mailing costs and inaccurate analysis. (One option is to hold multiple views of duplicates, e.g. the operational and marketing 'duplicates'. While this may help some service applications, it is another complexity.)
– Administration processing is transaction biased, and the operating environment designed to support detailed examination of individual customers or simple batch runs (e.g. statements) may not 'like' the batch

intensive database marketing environment needed to build the big picture and create personalized communication in volume.

- The probability is that purely operational applications like interest calculation and credit scoring and statements will take precedence over so-called marketing 'nice to haves', leading to considerable delay in delivery. So many complex operational systems may have to be finished before the operational CIS system meets the needs of the marketing department that their hair may have turned white.

Many companies have experienced the force of this problem. Unfortunately, observing common policy, many more will succumb to that experience before light dawns!

Technical change

Many new changes could impact direct marketing, such as the pen/writing interface to hand-held computers in the hands of sales and service personnel and customers, Neural networks promising automated analysis of vast quantities of data to identify patterns, and wide area communications linking people and departments – especially on the Information Superhighway.

Multi-media computing and electronic mail create CD, cable and phone communication potential: personalized (voice and print) messages can be linked to moving images (e.g. in digital catalogues of video images). For example, Freemans plc, a traditional British cataloguer, has been experimenting with a multi-media catalogue, partly to learn the art. Other interested companies, many of whom are working in collaborative partnerships, include Speigel, Catalog 1, Time Warner and Stargazer. As the 1990s unfold, these possibilities will emerge. Estimates suggest that electronic shopping will be worth $12 billion plus by 2003, but whether it will be implemented in a manner that consumers and businesses find acceptable and helpful remains to be seen (see Chapter 18).

In the meantime, good information systems can help to recognize individual customers, their past behaviour and changes in their circumstances in order to

- recognize more effectively when these moments arrive, including easily overlooked occasions such as anniversaries;
- ensure a more effective operation;
- look for patterns from the past that can help to predict or improve performance in the future.

Together, these systems, summarized in Table 3.1, are indispensable aids for future productivity for many, if not all, companies. Any company needing an accounting system probably needs a sales and marketing system. For example, any chief executive should be able to write easily and quickly to all his or her customers of a selected type, and set up for response.

Table 3.1   Characteristics of CASM systems

Database marketing systems	Telemarketing systems	Sales management systems
Used to manage overall relationships	Used in teleservice and telesales	Uses by salesforce and management
Key requirements of marketing databases:	Used to guide a telephone dialogue:	Aims at automating salesforce activity management by:
– Flexible data structures – Data import – Name and address management – Research profiling and compiling facilities – Mass mailing – Campaign and promotion recording – Personalization – Volume performance – Decision support, event triggering	– Call lists (outbound) – Call scripts – Data capture – Link to ACD/PABX (Automatic Call Distribution/PABX telephone switchboard) to generate or route calls – Statistics on call activity – Telephony integration, voice response as new developments – Flexible script and data capture set up and editing – Links to other software – Fast response	– Prompting follow up – Diarizing activities – Standard (modifiable) letters – Sales activity reporting – Forecasting and territory planning – Lead tracking – POS information – Internal electronic mail

Notes and references

1. Moriarty, R.T. and Swartz, G.S., 'Automation to boost sales and marketing', *Harvard Business Review* (Jan./Feb. 1989).
2. *Precision Marketing*, 26 April 1993.
3. Reported in *Direct Marketing International* (July 1994).
4. 'Read between the lines', *Marketing Services* (20 May 1993).

4
New people, new business

Summary Three great trends leading to massive changes, particularly in the last 40 or so years, are described: changes in technology; in the interior experience of people, their urge to express themselves as individuals; and a new global market, global consciousness, global quality. As a result, businesses are becoming more flexible, more transnational, but also need to be more personal, more one-to-one or I∞I focused.

The self is such a piece of ready currency in the 20th century that it is hard to believe that the whole concept of the self ... only began to appear ... around the early part of the 18th century. Before that people had souls rather than selves, and very different they were. Souls were more or less alike, they did not make endless individual distinctions; souls were God-given and in the hands of God, to whom they would return.... A question such as 'Who are you?' would be answered in terms of generalities – one was a Catholic or a Protestant, a farmer or a trader. But introspection did not exist; descriptions of people, if they appeared at all in chronicles of history, were similarly formulaic.... Then, quite suddenly, individuals – selves – began to appear in literature.
(Dr Nina Coltart, *Sunday Times* Lecture, 13 November 1994)

That the world is changing would be a cliché if it were not so real and significant. The world is always changing, but not always as now. Between crawling and walking, or between a leaf and a flower comes development, transformation. Walking is not a better crawling. It is something new. Is there a similar transformation taking place in society or is it just more of the same?

Early this century, Mercedes-Benz researched the market for cars and decided that the Europe-wide volume opportunity was 1000 vehicles. The constraint, they thought, was not buyers but the number of people who would be willing to be chauffeurs! This story tells us much about

- changes in attitudes to technology, class and interpersonal relationships
- personal and social mobility, and mental attitudes or paradigms over the century
- the way reality confronts expectations.

Two deep-seated changes have already been highlighted, changes that are both separate and interrelated. The first was a technological change. The steam, electric and combustion engines began a process by which humanity was both freed from nature and chained to technology. Information technology continues that process. While older engine technologies increased physical mobility through the transformation and exhaustion of matter, information technology increases the mobility of change itself through the management and transformation of the insubstantial and intangible: raw data.

Information technology may not be the only technology in rapid evolution, but it is the enabler of most technologies and is the paradigmatic technology for our half of the century – despite the fact that, in 1943, IBM's chairman thought the world market for computers totalled only six!

The *amazing* recent growth in individualization

Increase in individualization is another widely noted change. Trend observer Popcorn[1] describes consumer longing for individual recognition and for ways to express themselves as 'Egonomics', an economics driven by individuals, while Naisbitt and Aburdene note:

> The great unifying theme of the 20th century is the triumph of the individual.... The 1990s are characterised by a new respect for the individual as the foundation of society and the basic unit of change. 'Mass' movements are a misnomer.[2]

Dr Heinz Dallmer, president of German mail order giant, Bertelsmann, spoke on this theme at the 1992 Montreux Symposium: 'Over the last few years we have seen a dramatic trend towards individualization. Namely, the consumer is ever less prepared to respond in an undifferentiated way to mass messages' and Lester Wunderman, doyen of direct marketing, in a speech in Toronto, put it plainly: 'The post-war baby boom generation rebelled against massification. They were and are the "I am me" generation, which demanded attention to their unique differences rather than their similarities.'

Surprising as it may seem, just as thousands of years of technology change accelerated in recent centuries so dramatically that we can reasonably say a transformation happened in the last few centuries, so also did a transformation happen in personal awareness.[3] If the growth of individualization so widely noted was a local and temporary matter, then perhaps we could be excused for not taking much notice. If, in fact, people had been the same for thousands of years, then what would be new for the marketer? But if something new and dramatic is happening, and has exploded onto the world stage, is it not essential to pay attention and figure out what might be happening, and what the consequences might be?

In fact, among a great many anthropologists and cultural historians it is considered almost a truism that a new interior, personal consciousness has arisen in humans.[4]

Although, in the opening quotation to this chapter, Dr Coltart notes the change from the eighteenth century, others locate it slightly earlier, in the fifteenth century. It was then that really individualistic art, biography, diaries, portrait painting and characterization in literature began to develop in Europe, all signs of the new awareness, at least among the most educated and leading figures. While, to the layperson, it seems extraordinary to think that our way of looking at the world is not universal, this is the case. In fact, the sense of a personal interior space, the 'individuality' as we know it, is a very recent, Western-derived phenomenon. The evidence of literature and the arts as well as social and religious expression all indicate this (*see Topic 4.1, p. 62*). Yet now the new mode is sweeping round the Earth. Even the Japanese are less likely to chant company songs in the morning (did you know IBM workers sang company songs as late as the early 1960s?). Less than a century ago, almost no women had the vote. Today, almost everyone in the world is theoretically enfranchised (although in 'older' and tyrant cultures this may still not be very meaningful there are signs that this will change).

From slavery to demanding customers in just one century is a much greater social change than reaching the moon or creating the computer (see, for example, Table 4.1).

Table 4.1 Egyptian formalism and current 'Crazy Times'

Ancient Egypt	Late twentieth-century west
Pharaoh as god	Watergate *et al.* (Icon toppling)
Slavery	Political correctness
Rigid hieratic classes	Mobility of the individual
Natural order	Social reinvention by humans
3000+ years' duration	That was yesterday's product

Until relatively recently (and still in some cultures) women had their marriages arranged for them, and that was accepted. They certainly did not leave a marriage because it was inconvenient or unsatisfactory. It is not difficult to imagine that, in a society that expected and allowed such behaviour, it might also be reasonable to expect brands to assert marriages that were convenient to them, and find conveniently loyal customers. Are these changes not related? Consciousness shapes social order. If a ruler seems to be divine, then a certain society and way of ruling seems appropriate. Change that and democracy begins to flower. Much the same happens in every branch of social and economic life. Until comparatively recently, churches and religions ruled economic life (for example, cathedrals and temples were places of trade).

Today, we, that means customers, feel and assert individuality (not always socially) *and expect this to be recognized.* The Henley Centre, a leading UK research group, describe the *cellular household*, in which members operate in individual ways. Each person may have his or her own brands and interests. Communal family activities progressively decline, as do family brands. Yet as late as the 1950s, marketers still held on to a monolithic view of society with an hierarchical top-down control by a few aristocratic brands ruling their subservient domains – a direct continuation of an older social and psychological order. Resistance, it was thought, could be overcome by powerful persuasion, but little was needed because people naturally wanted to fit into social mores. This outlook may not hold much longer. The rise of individualism is a fact that will not go away. Marketers will need to continue to adjust.

Topic 4.1   How people have changed!

Literature before the fifteenth century includes idealization, archetypes, allegory, icons, personification, myth, legend, fairy tales, but no real characterization as we now know it. The change is much more than just technique. It is because, until then, the experience of oneself as an individual was either not really present or unimportant. Socrates' statement that the sum of wisdom is *gnothi seauton* – to know oneself – is at the root of Western culture, yet this does not mean an *individual* but a *universal* self.

In Chaucer's *Canterbury Tales*, at the close of the fourteenth century, we find a first thrusting into character, but even so, many of the stories and descriptions are allegorical and, in the charming pilgrims, there is not the depth of characterization that we find in Shakespeare, Dostoevsky or Bellow. The Wife of Bath has a gap in her tooth and this *symbolizes* her lascivious nature. Beowulf and Parzival are great literature as archetypal initiation sagas but not as individual character drama. Michelangelo's great statue David is of an ideal figure, yet shortly after, Holbein begins to create real portraits. What is special about the rediscovery of perspective in the sixteenth century is that it portrays the world from an individual viewpoint. An icon belongs to no one; it expresses a universal perspective.

By the seventeenth century individual awareness begins to flower and reach philosophy, in Descartes, for example. The waning of the Middle Ages ends an epoch, and an outlook, at least in the West.[5] Until then, people rarely believed that they could have their own *personal* thoughts and opinions. Kings were appointed by God ('the divine right of kings') and humanity belonged to a ladder linking nature through ranks of angels to God. Fifteen hundred years earlier, the king *was* a god, or god inspired, like the Pharaoh. Thoughts, ideas, culture, were given by God, gods, angels, to inspired personalities like Gilgamesh, Hercules, Moses, Socrates, Mohammed, Krishna, Confucius. This is the source of the word 'charismatic', which means having a god within. A genius is 'The tutelary god or attendant spirit *allotted to every person at his birth*',[6] and a 'genius' was therefore inspired by this spirit. Gods direct the fate of men and women, intervening matter of factly in personal and social affairs. What makes individual heroes special is not their own qualities but that the gods direct them.

We cannot conceive building the pyramids or megaliths today, at least not as it was done. In Homer's *Iliad*, consciousness is so different that the sea is not blue or grey, but *'wine-dark'*: so people even *saw* differently. There are no words in ancient Greek to correspond with our sense of 'mind' or even soul.[7]

So, we take for granted what was not obvious to our ancestors or other cultures, just because it is so totally obvious to us and we find it hard to imagine another way of knowing the world or ourselves. Yet, in earlier centuries and times, people felt tied to – a part of – custom, tribe, ruler, priest, tradition and ancestors, all of which was spiritually ordained and gave them identity. The individual person is given by something outside him or her. One of the greatest punishments in older civilizations was exile; it meant cutting people off from their identities – and then they often died. The witch doctor, nganga, is still a power in Zululand. Some reports even suggest that it was possible in older cultures, even the Maories, to access the memories of ancestors. Jean Auel uses this in her bestseller, *Clan of the Cave Bear*.

Clifford Geertz reports from Java how the local tribe have no effective sense of an individual internal self. They have awareness of an observably personal outer set of actions, but only of a common inner self.[8] When Voltaire defended the right of someone to their *own* opinion it was therefore a real paradigm shift. Tribal blood groups and castes have been replaced by a personal life. Descartes rejected all except his *own* experience: *I* think therefore *I am*.

The confessional autobiography, or narrative in self-knowledge, whether in a book, a meeting with the 'shrink' or conversation with a new contact or friend – 'Tell me about yourself' – exemplifies the modern world view, or *zeitgeist*. Through describing experiences – including sexual – the individual lays bare his or her soul. Perhaps the earliest of these is St Augustine's *Confessions* in which he relates his spiritual history, i.e. a description of his discovery of God's providential plan for him. The old and new worlds meet here in the narrative of his *own* life. By contrast, Rousseau's autobiography has been called the invention of 'Rousseau' and in turn of modern man who thinks that truth is not just something that is 'out there' – by an order of the universe, or in God's plan – but 'subjectively, in the unique experience and history of each individual'.[9]

After the First World War, verities of social class, the agrarian society, Church, male dominance, romantic wars for God, King and country, and a thousand years of the old order started to turn topsy turvy, to be shattered in the Depression and the Second World War. Then the 1960s rushed a new wave of individual assertiveness. The patterns given to us by the past were widely rejected. Today, we feel and assert individuality, (not always socially) *and expect this to be recognized.*

Today, culture makes an individual, but cannot be imposed from the outside.

Each of us makes it our own. Traditions, says Casey, an Oxford historian on the subject, 'have to meet the test: can they be authentic for me? Can I make them into part of myself?' So, too, with products. The brands we choose define our lifestyle. Is it time to update Voltaire: 'I defend your right to assert your individual life, not just your thoughts'?

Interaction with companies is changing!

There is not longer a mass market in any old sense. Nor can markets always be *segmented*, for there may be no preceding unity. Today, we may *group* individuals together based on feelings in common to form a market, but only by first recognizing their essential individuality.

Popcorn describes several important trends which reflect aspects of this process:

1. *Cocooning* leads to the desire for a safe, familiar environment. This has obvious implications for the company: Are you providing a safe, familiar environment or simply undependable and out for yourself? Is there relationship; or intrusion?
2. An increase in *Vigilante* consumers: critical customers who protest vigorously when unhappy. Two unemployed radicals in Britain challenged the economic might of the $24 billion a year McDonalds Corporation. When McDonalds sued the two individuals for slander in 1994, the reaction from population and press seemed to side with the little fellows, irrespective of the issues.
3. *Egonomics*: consumers crave recognition and ways to express themselves.
4. *Cashing out*: consumers are looking for personal and career satisfaction, in goals which express a better way of life. Suppliers need to reflect higher Maslow values.
5. *Icon toppling*: pillars of society, including organizations, are questioned and often rejected. People are tired of being mugged by life and giant companies that believe, like the dinosaur, that they are too big to be concerned about the little consumer. The little consumer has, like the lowly mammal, a powerful, invisible weapon called flexibility. Giant companies might need the same.

They all apply to employees, too.

In the movement from a mass world to an individual world, from socioeconomic groups to people, database marketing responds precisely as a corporate tool which enables *personalized* sales, service and communication to a large audience.

Global thinking, local acting

Database marketing is also a tool to respond to another trend which only seems to run counter to individualization. Any organization bigger than the corner store, and perhaps it too, needs to develop global thinking. Our economy is no longer local, and anyone who thinks so is at least 100 years out of date. So are ideas and social aspirations. Especially since the 1960s, brands and commodities, lifestyles, architecture, books, music, cuisines and culture have all dispersed globally. Ordinary people travel or live abroad. Several billion people speak English. The competition for the local store may come from a Swedish chain next week. The interaction of demand, currencies, markets, services and materials around the world is the physical corollary of the change in outlook of the individual. As the individual becomes empowered, the world as well as the neighbourhood increasingly belongs to him or her (and the sense of responsibility for both trends to grow too).

From mass manufacturing to flexible manufacturing

These changes are paralleled in manufacturing. Modern industry, in the aftermath of Taylor and Ford, adopted the mass production model. This focused on long, continuous production runs of identical product, with the worker as servant to the machine, an idea caricatured in Chaplin's *Modern Times*. This was discredited by Japanese production methods, as well as a number of European experiments.[10] It is wasteful, expensive and produces low quality. Marketing thinking will complete the reframing of business.

Best practice today focuses on dignity, empowerment and leadership on the shop floor, and process value and flexibility of tools and people. In a survey of manufacturing practice and trends, INSEAD identified important changes taking place in the factories of the world. Table 4.2 shows the priorities of manufacturers in Europe, Japan, and the USA.

Table 4.2   Priorities for manufacturing

Europe	Japan	USA
Conformance quality	Reliable products	Conformance quality
Dependable delivery	Dependable delivery	Dependable delivery
Reliable products	Rapid design changes	Reliable products
High performance	Conformance quality	High performance
Fast delivery	Product customization	Price competition

Source: Factories of the Future, INSEAD, 1991.

While priorities vary, there is a consensus on flexibility, service and quality. The study noted that quality had a lower emphasis in Japan because executives believed that quality improvement processes had been achieved. Lean manufacturing and just-in-time techniques focus on eliminating waste and idle inventory from processes. Manufacturing pursues the goal of becoming more service driven. (See also Chapter 8.)

Not only is the manufacturing process becoming more flexible, but the range of merchandise is becoming more varied. There are toothbrushes in different colours, different textures and materials, different shapes and different handles; toothbrushes for sensitive gums, for different age groups; disposable, battery and electric powered toothbrushes, or you can get your teeth cleaned at the dentist or use floss dispensed in various formats. The Japanese National Bicycle Industrial Company will assemble in a few days the bicycle you want from over 10 million options and exactly to size for almost the same price as a standard bicycle.

When the customer designs the product or service, the customer is also loyal to it. (Any consultant or agency knows that when clients start to describe what *they* want, the chances of winning the project increase.)

Channel explosion

Distribution channels were similarly limited and aimed to achieve mass effect. Now there are a plethora of complementary channels.

The company store went soon after slavery. Where once there would have been either one street of specialist retailers belonging to a guild, or one major provider, now there are three, four, five or 50 options. The telephone, the car, television, the computer, affluence, and lifestyle differentiation have all affected the change, as well as good, old-fashioned opportunistic entrepreneurism.

The last 30 years especially has seen the widespread development of

- hypermarkets, often out of town
- shopping malls, often out of city centres
- specialist retailers and boutiques
- franchises
- mail order
- catalogue retailers
- interactive shopping through TV
- home demonstration parties
- contract salesforces
- direct sales using telephone service
- affinity marketing
- sourcing specialists
- licensed manufacturers.

Charities and arts institutions have become important mail order and retail centres. Thousands of children distribute catalogues and product for WWF in Sweden. Successful concepts such as Ikea, Benetton, McDonalds, Marks & Spencer, Body Shop go global, often with franchise help. Despite forecasts to the contrary, the corner and convenience stores still survive. In fact, the US Wal-Mart chain is a fantastic success story in a niche that everyone thought was vanishing. Sales representatives, dealers, brokers, distributors, agents, value-added-resellers are all more important in both the business-to-business and consumer distribution chains. IBM shifted its small and middle-range computer sales effort in the early 1980s to software companies and dealers. Leasing companies often sell mainframes and they can also be purchased through catalogues. Some supermarkets, e.g. Tesco, sell computers. Companies use existing customers in member-get-member programmes. Customers themselves travel further and use specialist publications to look around. More and more organizations are turning to strategic alliances to distribute product. Consumers, therefore, have a greater choice than ever before.

Let us look at the purchase of a new car. Is it for company or private use? Will it be purchased through a finance company or financed by a bank, building society, credit agency, or the manufacturer or dealer's special facilities? Finance can be long-term rent, leases, hire purchase with variable deposits and terms, different residual values at the end of the term and the option to pay or not pay the residual. Maintenance and insurance can sometimes be included, as well as insurance on the payment. The car itself can be bought from the local dealer, or by telephone across the continent. Across Europe, you can take advantage of differential pricing in the various natural markets, and then import. There are sourcing agents who will find you the best deal and various specialist publications giving options, including used cars. Managing the used car market is now almost as important to manufacturers as new car sales. Whereas manufacturers like Ford once used a carrot and stick approach with dealers, working at arm's length, now they increasingly prefer a partnership.

The car itself will increasingly come with various service value-addeds. Mercedes-Benz and BMW use third-party Mondiale Assistance to provide emergency services in Europe. Ford has been testing an all-inclusive insurance cover. Motor insurance can be bought from a major insurer, through a local dealer or a chain, from a specialist, through motoring organizations such as the Automobile Association in the UK, or through direct insurance companies by phone and mail.

Implications for marketing: from monolithic to personal

These changes demand a communication and information response. Until the twentieth century, advertising was primitive or discrete. It was also remarkably personal, since communities were more static and smaller. Hawkers might shout their wares in the street, or call door to door. Retailers and craft shops relied on windows and displays. Word of mouth was important. Josiah Wedgwood's success in the eighteenth century was as much influenced by his innovative communication and marketing techniques as by his new product designs. These techniques included discrete direct mail to leading personalities and endorsements from them.

Mass manufacturing generated a need for mass communication to achieve the push to stimulate and focus demand. In a relatively simple world this worked. Today's communication must become more flexible, more personal (but not intrusive). This means relevant, knowledge derived communication which optimizes use of the various channels to create, preserve and develop a relationship, moving from a monolithic, impersonal world of advertising to a useful and flexible dialogue (Figure 4.1).

The changes in personal outlook, manufacturing method and marketplace are interrelated and lead to the new model for commercial activity (see Table 4.3). Technology development, particularly information technology, has been both a driver and servant and remains so.

Products are becoming more complex, and need service values to prevent them becoming commodities. Speed and responsiveness need to increase. Individuals can no longer be taken for granted, nor do they conveniently fit sociological labels or historic parameters (such as 'blue collar' or 'working class'). Hence, more attention will be given to creating and maintaining relationships of value: to loyalty generation through genuine service, attention and quality. Win–lose thinking becomes lose–lose results. Quality conscious companies are turning from dominant postures with their suppliers to arrangements which support joint problem solving. In the same way, as we move from survival thinking towards higher relationship values, a cooperative outlook becomes more important. If 'partnering' is the current trend with suppliers, what else should it be with customers?

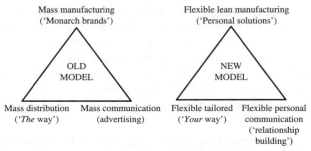

Figure 4.1   From mass to flexible methods

Table 4.3   The new marketing

From	Products	to	Systems
From	Commodities	to	Services
From	Transactions	to	Relationships
From	Short term	to	Long term
From	Slow	to	Quick
From	Reactive	to	Proactive
From	Hype	to	Information
From	Brand share	to	Loyalty growth
From	Win–Lose	to	Gain–Gain

In this new world, customers become individuals and are treated personally: I∞I.

Just as consciousness and technology have powered 'the problem', so they will power 'the solution', but both together. The computer is not by itself 'the answer'. But in the right hands, technology will be an invaluable aid in personal marketing and relationship building as we learn to adjust in the decades to come.

Notes and references

1. Popcorn, F., *The Popcorn Report*, Arrow, 1992.
2. Naisbitt, J. and Aburdene, P., *Megatrends 2000*, Sidgwick & Jackson, 1990.
3. For further information, Jaynes, J., *The Dawn of Consciousness and the Breakdown of the Bicameral Mind*, Pelican, is a fascinating account. If the causes suggested by Jaynes may be open to discussion, his historical account of the phenomena is illuminating.
4. Taylor, C., *Sources of the Self: The Making of the Modern Identity*, Cambridge University Press, 1989, p. 111.
5. For further information, the interested reader is referred to the Dutch historian Huizinga's seminal book, *The Waning of the Middle Ages*, and to C.S. Lewis's *The Medieval World Picture*, which gives a particularly clear account of the ideas current until the late Middle Ages.
6. Oxford English Dictionary.
7. Snell, B., *The Discovery of the Mind*, Harvard University Press, Chapter 1.
8. From the native point of view, in *Interpretive Social Science*, ed. P. Rainbow and W.M. Sullivan, University of California Press, 1979.
9. Casey, J., 'The culture essay', Editorial in *The Sunday Times* (13 March 1994).
10. Womack, J.P., Jones, D.T. and Roos, D., *The Machine that Changed the World* (published by Rawson Assoc.) is an extremely readable account of a $5 million MIT comparative study of the automobile industry.

5
The economics of loyalty

Summary While companies focus on transaction effectiveness, profit almost invariably comes from the loyal customer. How and why? The key findings of research are given. Lifetime value is described as the business driver. The consequence of this is that organizations must move from acquisition thinking to reconfigure around long-term retention management, i.e. the concept of guarantee management, solving problems, tracking and handling customers 'for better for worse'.

He who wishes to be rich in a day, will be hanged in a year.

(Leonardo da Vinci)

The average US company will lose 10–20 per cent of its customers each year, mostly through bad service.[1] Yet, companies can boost profits by 20–100 per cent by keeping five per cent more customers each year. One study showed a 25 per cent profit improvement in credit insurance and 85 per cent in bank branch deposits.[2]

MBNA, the American credit card company, transformed its industry ranking from 38 to 4 while profits increased sixteen-fold in eight years as a result of getting its customer defection rate down to just 5 per cent – half the average rate for the rest of the industry.

One US retail bank grew twice as fast as its competition, opening no more branches and with no better prices. Another grew substantially faster with less advantageous rates. The secret was better loyalty.

Another bank found that a 3 per cent improvement in retention led to a 7 per cent growth in deposits.[3]

And the changes were silent: there were no marketing or pricing signals to competitors. Furthermore, a customer who is lost through dissatisfaction with the service provider may be gained by a rival or lost to the market for ever, and will probably spread a ripple of attrition through bad publicity on the greatest communication medium of all: word of mouth. Defections are costing British companies £100 billion per annum in sales and a further £100 billion in recovering new customers to replace those lost.[4]

Yet we have paid lip service to loyalty. There has been limited emphasis on customer retention in marketing literature or practice until the 1990s,[5] and very few companies have measured their performance. Researchers and business people have focused much more on how to attract customers to products and services, than on how to retain them.[6] In his 1989 edition of the classic *Marketing Plans*, Malcolm H. McDonald, a leading British academic and professor of marketing, makes no mention in the index of loyalty, relationship, retention or lifetime value (although he has subsequently become a significant contributor to the field). In 1993, 80 per cent of UK managers considered they were spending too much money and time on marketing efforts to obtain new customers and too little on keeping customers.[7] Why are ideas changing?

The development of the concept of relationship marketing[8] has acted as a catalyst to customer retention, thereby popularizing a key direct marketing concept that had, unfortunately, got lost in the welter of junk and tactical mail. The term may have been first used in the direct marketing industry, e.g. by WWF. Early academic work focused on industrial markets[9] and service markets.[10] However, this literature did not examine customer retention economics and its pay-off.

The fact is, customer retention helps to predict the profitability of the company. Studies by Boston Consulting Group, Bain & Co., Ogilvy & Mather Direct, Profit Research Group, Oliver, Wyman & Co., First Manhattan Consulting Group and others[11] show that customer loyalty results in above-average profits and superior growth, agreeing that 'one of the key elements of business success and profitability is customer satisfaction, the more satisfied the customer, the more durable the relationship. The longer this lasts, the more money the company stands to make.'[12] Bain & Co.'s research showed that reducing defections by 5 per cent boosts profits by between 25 and 85 per cent, depending on industry[13] (see Table 5.1).

Do you know what percentage of your customers defect:

— by profit category of customer?
— by customer profile?
— by line of business?

If so, you are probably rare.

Table 5.1   Effects on profitability of reduced defections

30%	Auto service chain
85%	Branch deposits
75%	Credit card
25%	Credit insurance
50%	Insurance brokerage
45%	Industrial distribution
45%	Industrial laundry
40%	Office building management
35%	Software

Source: Bain & Co.

How does this work? The value of retention is a function of

- the initial acquisition cost
- the increase in revenue from existing customers
- and/or improved costs of getting that revenue
- the value of referrals
- size of the initial base.

Established customers tend to buy more, are predictable and usually cost less to service than new customers. They tend to be less price sensitive and may provide free word-of-mouth referrals and advertising. Acquiring a new customer costs more than retaining an existing one. The longer the relationship, the lower the cost of acquisition. Also, retaining customers makes it difficult for competitors to increase their market share. Consequently, companies earning greater loyalty can typically:

- Charge more money.[14] Once customers are happy with you and want to keep buying from you their disinclination to move can be reflected in a price premium or at least the capacity to avoid discounts.
- Expect greater share of wallet. Loyal UK shoppers allocate between two and four times as much of their monthly budget to their 'first choice' store as promiscuous shoppers and are, in general, twice as significant spenders as promiscuous shoppers.[15]
- Reduce administration costs – by 18 per cent in one study of the insurance industry.[16] In the US retail chain store environments, a 2 per cent retention improvement leads typically to a 10 per cent reduction.[17] Imagine what the effect would be in your company if every customer transaction was from a new customer who needed to have all details explained.
- Reduce marketing expense, since existing customers are more willing to buy from you, often by a factor of 5–8 times.[18]

- Reduce fixed costs as a percentage of sales (through greater success).
- Expect more referrals. The experience of customers filters into the marketplace by a wonderful or painful osmosis. The value of member-get-member programmes and spontaneous referral is well known. Between 20 and 40 per cent of new bank customers in the US arise from referrals.[19] The leading UK direct insurance writer, Direct Line Insurance, also has highest referral rates.
- Grow faster. Since it is common for a business to lose 15–20 per cent or more of its customers each year, simply cutting defections in half will more than double the average company's growth rate. In one exercise, improving retention from 80 to 90 per cent had the same effect in building the customer base as increasing customer acquisition rates by 50 per cent. In another, it took a 92 per cent increase in customer acquisition rates to produce the same discounted profits as a 5 per cent improvement in retention rate.

Improved customer retention provides two further subtle advantages:[20]

1. Increased employee retention, which feeds back into greater customer longevity – an aspect to be explored in fuller detail in Chapter 9.
2. Improved merger and acquisition decision making. The retention rate is a simple and powerful indicator of the future.

In many retail and brand markets, retention means keeping or improving the percentage of the customer's buying portfolio that you secure: the share of wallet. Improving retention might mean increasing share of purchase from 30 to 70 per cent. Other than this mechanical aspect, it makes no difference to the economics, although it will impact marketing and communication programmes. A simple spreadsheet matrix, breaking customers down by portfolio percentage and average order value, segments the market powerfully.

The two dynamics that determine company worth

As Figure 5.1 shows, there are two dynamics which determine profitability: first, the ability to acquire and keep customers, which depends strongly on service, including service led selling. Second, customer profit will increase as a result of the opportunity to increase their portfolio of purchases from you or to upgrade them: i.e. up-selling and cross-selling.

Most sales and marketing training and culture emphasize the second at the expense of the first. In fact, too aggressive a sales approach can damage retention. A survey by JD Powers & Associates found that only 35 per cent of US car buyers felt well treated by their dealers in 1993. 'People feel beaten up by the process' commented one dealer chain owner. 'You think you got a

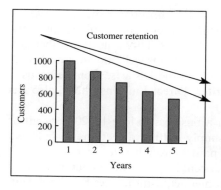 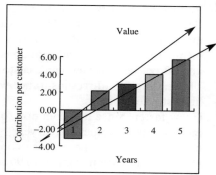

Figure 5.1   The two dynamics of the marketplace

good deal until you walk out of the door. The salesmen are inside doing high fives and the customer is lying in the street.'[21]

The corporate or brand value of a company is effectively determined by combining the retention rate of customers required and their annual contribution value. This is also the customer lifetime value (LTV), a key measure in database marketing.

The impact of the lifetime customer

Lifestyle marketing helped Honda's US owner-repurchase rate to over 50 per cent higher than the industry average of under 40 per cent. US firm Home Depot analysed its business and found that although typical shoppers spend only $38 per visit, they do so 30 times a year, year after year, and end up spending $25 000 each.[22] In two US banks, the retention leaders managed to gain a 10 basis points advantage in pricing over competitors.[23]

Domino's Pizza stores in Montgomery County, Maryland, calculated that although each order was worth only $15, a regular customer spent more than $5000 over the life of a 20-year franchise contract, thereby changing the attitude to customers. Each pizza order was now part of a £5000 dollar continuity programme.[16]

The Computing Group, a UK computer bureau providing services to the direct marketing industry, decided it could look at clients as providing monthly payments of £2000, £5000, or £10 000, or it could think of them as worth £120 000 or £300 000, or £600 000 over five years. This had a wonderful effect on attitudes. Production, account management and finance were involved in problem solving, leading to an excellent retention rate, for example no defections in two years, and The Computing Group became market leader in its field with steadily improving financial results.

One of the most powerful examples of the power of service to deliver long-term value in Britain is the delivery of the 'daily pinta'. Each delivery is worth very little, but the net present value from a household over 40 years can be around £8000. That is the value of acquiring a single new loyal household today.

To calculate a customer's real worth a company must take projected profit streams into account. A study of the US credit card industry by Bain shows that if the credit card customer leaves after the first year, the average business takes a $21 loss. If it can keep the customer for four years, his or her net present value to the company rises to about $100.

If the credit card company cuts its defection rate from 20 to 10 per cent, the average life span relationship with a customer doubles from 5 to 10 years, and the value more than doubles – jumping from $134 to $300. As the defection rate drops another 5 per cent the average life span of a customer relationship doubles again and profits rise 75 per cent – from $300 to $525. MBNA found that a 5 per cent improvement in defection rates increased average customer value by more than 125 per cent.

Murray Raphel tells a story from his shopping mall. Gordon's Alley Deli in Atlantic City, New Jersey, had an idea. When one new business moved into the local neighbourhood, owner Norman Gordon contacted the company in order to offer the employees a free breakfast during their first week. He obtained a list of their names and addresses from the management. Who could object to such an offer? Gordon then wrote a letter to his new neighbours telling them that in their first week he was offering a free breakfast and two more offers: a free lunch and a 'buy one, get one free': 21 of the 26 new employees came to the welcome breakfast with the opportunity to eat as much as they wished; 25 of the 26 employees used their free gift certificate; and 23 had a buy one get one free lunch. (The only free gift certificate not redeemed was the executive director who felt that so much was being offered to his company that he was duty bound to pay for at least his lunch.)

In due course the Deli found that it was averaging 15 steady new customers, worth $22 500 a year, as the result of one phone call, 26 letters and an invitation to breakfast and lunch. The Alley Deli takes this parable to its conclusion, sending out a weekly fax to around 30 companies in the immediate area with chatty news and information about the specials for the week.

Stu Leonard, owner of America's largest dairy supermarket in Norwalk, Connecticut, claims that, in a lifetime, the average person spends $246 000 in his supermarket. Did Waitrose, in the example cited in Chapter 1, realize it was dealing with £40 000 down and £100 000 to come, and if it did, following the BA example above, would it have behaved differently? Perhaps! Because one year on, in a mystery shopping test, it took only three days to answer a similar query correctly, and the group is now investing in a database.

Loyalty targeted activities must obviously be aimed at generating profitable business. One client was in despair at the realization that his representative had sold 10 million more plastic bottles at half a penny loss per bottle. In the same way, different customers have different profit profiles. It makes no sense to acquire a loyal but unprofitable relationship. However, before we stipulate an obsessive emphasis on profit, four points are worth checking:

1. The contribution to fixed costs of reduced customers.
2. Damage to reputation, e.g. relatives of forced out customers. Many US banks suffered bankruptcies in the 1980s as a result of attempts to get rid of unprofitable customers.
3. Unprofitable customers tend to leave anyway if your business is well focused.
4. Is there a way to make it profitable? For example, it often takes a motor insurance company 10 years to break even on the high costs of certain young drivers who are a drag on profits. On the other hand, Direct Line's founder Peter Wood has now set up a new company targeting such groups because others do not or cannot. Careful structuring or restructuring can turn a problem into an opportunity.

Improving the product set

One contribution to retaining customers is to improve the product set. Benchmarking and improving products is discussed in a later chapter, but research suggests that having the right product set can be crucial to retention. For example, research by Liswood Institute suggests a correlation in financial services between the number of products or services and the retention level (Table 5.2).

It may be equally important to have the optimum number of relationships. Customers do not have an unlimited supply of money, so more products, especially in financial services, may only dilute spend and

Table 5.2 Product mix to retention rate

Number of products of services in the relationship	Retention rate after five years (%)
1	15
2	45
3	80

Source: Liswood Institute.

squeeze margins. Thomas Petro of Profit Research Group found that between 1980 and 1992 the optimum bank cross-sell ratio was between 3.0 and 4.0, although this may now be increasing.[24]

The learning opportunity

Defection rates do not only indicate where profits are headed, they also direct attention to the processes that are causing customers to leave. By soliciting feedback from defecting customers, companies can discover the weaknesses that really matter and strengthen them before profits start to dwindle.

Businesses commonly do not hear from 96 per cent of their dissatisfied customers. For every complaint received, another 26 customers have problems, six of them serious. Customers with bad experiences are often twice as likely to tell others as those with a positive story. British Airways believes that every 1 per cent increase in *customer comments* equals up to £400 000 revenue won back from potential defectors and points out that Pam Am had one of the lowest rates of complaint among trans-Atlantic carriers just before going bust.[25] In consequence, they switched their emphasis from 'right first time' exhortation to investigating the problem areas. The 30 per cent who experience problems prove 'An enormous potential for learning', according to Charles Weiser, BA's head of customer relations. IBM has found that a 1 per cent improvement in customer satisfaction translates into $500 million dollars in increased sales over five years.[26] But, to improve satisfaction, the causes of dissatisfaction must be understood.

The cost of problems

Only 84 per cent of British consumers are satisfied with the goods and services they purchase by direct mail. Although only 8 per cent are actively dissatisfied, and satisfaction rose 2 per cent between 1991 and 1993,[27] as this is a £12 billion industry, that 8 per cent could be worth £5 billion to £10 billion over five years.

If you lose one customer for every five who have a problem, a common statistic, then each problem costs 20 per cent of the lifetime value of a customer. It makes their scrupulous study worth while.

Customers who do not complain are the least loyal to the company, according to the US office of Consumer Affairs, and common experience. Furthermore, customers who have had a problem and experienced a professional and responsive resolution are often up to a *third* more loyal than customers who have not experienced a problem.[28] Both the British Airways research and common experience shows that the refusal to recognize responsibility is frequently far more alienating than the original fault. The implication is that fielding and dealing with problems openly is a key element of success and one database marketing is well equipped to support, empowering service staff with information and driving the process. But making it work may require a culture change: the fear of hearing complaints is only too common.

Topic 5.1   Good and bad ways to handle a complaint

My father, who was born in the town that produces Marmite, and grew up with it as a daily fare, tells the story of how he lost his appetite after 70 years. One day he returned a jar of Marmite in a plastic bag because it 'smelt funny'. The letter he received in reply implied that there was nothing wrong with the Marmite (implying he was wrong) but gave a 30 pence (50 cents) voucher. He was not looking for recompense, he was just being a loyal customer, but this defensive and cheap approach actually turned him off the taste of Marmite!

By comparison, when took back a loaf of bread, which curiously contained a metal nut, to M&S, the local management came to apologize, head office wrote and sent a £15 voucher, and even the baker wrote to apologize, thanking him for pointing out the problem and saying that they had subsequently done an overhaul on their processes.

If you compare the level of loyalty of dissatisfied clients who do not or cannot complain, or are not well treated, with those who complain 'successfully', each incremental complaint handled may increase revenue by 50 per cent of the lifetime value of a customer, creating a new route for response generation and fulfilment. In service intensive industries where problems are a norm, the process of dealing with them may be the real acid test. For example, an insurance claim costs the insurer money, but is also the key to loyalty.

There are therefore four key tasks or goals for retention management (see Figure 5.2):

Task 1   To increase the overall value of customers who stay by improved up-selling, cross-selling and better margins.

Task 2   To get customers to voice their complaints in order to be able to answer them positively and learn; aiming to turn unvoiced attrition into resolved problems by talking about it (just like any marriage).

Task 3   To ensure that customer dissatisfaction is at least muted: a damage limitation objective to reduce the incidence of bad PR, so-called member-lose-member (M-L-M) to distinguish from member-get-member (M-G-M).

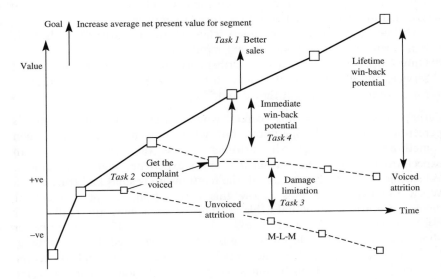

Figure 5.2   The opportunities

Task 4   By best practice, to convert the customer to a continuing or increased level of satisfaction and loyalty. The aim is to take advantage of the lifetime win-back potential, the gap between the value of a retained customer and a lost one. This is the ultimate value to be protected.

Perhaps problem Hotlines need *better* resourcing than for sales! Every customer who is converted from walking away, perhaps complaining to the world, is a customer whose lifetime value has been protected, and often increased. Those manning the service centres will meet complaints and dissatisfaction, and they need special temperament and training, but they *could* generate a better 'conversion rate', typically at around 50 per cent, than is managed by most salespeople.

What is the cost of unresolved problems? What is the trend of defection rates? How do they compare with leading competitors? What effect these will have on profitability and market share in five years? What effect will an improvement in loyalty among key targeted customer segments have on your profitability and customer base? What are the true causes of defection? *Why* are your customers leaving you? *Why* are they leaving competitors? Considerable experience shows that companies do not know the answers to these questions; nor do typical market research and surveys help.[29]

- Between 65 and 85 per cent of customers who defect say they were satisfied or very satisfied with their former supplier.
- Sixty per cent of US consumers claimed to be satisfied with their American car, but only 40 per cent repurchased.[16]
- Only 4 per cent of Comcast subscribers give the operator low marks for service, but 30–40 per cent, nearly 10 times more, said they would leave for a competing service if they could.[30]

Perhaps BA's discovery was correct: what matters is not the customer's perception of smooth operation, but what happens in a crisis, when something goes wrong! All customers assess the service against an expectations level which is trained by past experience and temperament. When this is matched or exceeded, the relationship is solid and trust exists. When the experience falls below this expectation, disappointment or disturbance arises. Sometimes this is triggered by a new, alternative offer raising expectations. More often it is an internal failure. If there is no better alternative, the relationship will be unstable, discontented, but continuing. In a stable relationship, customers (like personal partners) tend to become less and less 'fussy'. Habit becomes acceptance, until jolted. The syndrome 'Old cobwebs don't get noticed' applies. This is useful for present profits, but vulnerable to a competitor pointing out the cobwebs. The people to ask are therefore those who have defected, or who nearly defected. They can see the cobwebs. New customers are another useful group.

The answer is to build a learning culture, service process and knowledge resource that really focuses on quality service and relationships. How effectively can this be done when you are not aware of who your customers are? As Staffen Elinder, a Scandinavian direct marketer, puts it: 'The loyalty scheme buys you knowledge not loyalty, because loyalty can't be bought.'

Guarantee management

The answer seems to be encapsulated in the concept of 'guarantee management'. This will be developed further in Chapter 8, but the idea is very simple and very powerful and is exactly what is required to attain and go beyond a *treasured reputation*. A guarantee is a 'direct' device, it makes a marketing statement, promises a product offer, and invites response. A business can successfully develop on exactly this principle:

1. Establish what you want to promise (from knowledge of customers).
2. Establish how to deliver it.
3. Make the offer.
4. Invite response, making it easy if anything goes wrong.

A firm which is really committed to this idea will be very successful: it concentrates the mind, links product to marketing, creates the conditions for employees and managers to develop commitment to 'treasuring reputation/loyalty to customers' as outlined in Chapter 1, and in the process is also likely to win their commitment and goodwill, which any good CEO knows to be the pre-requisites for *service mastery*.

Empowering the organization

In fact, research shows a powerful correlation between customer satisfaction and employee satisfaction, the consequence of which will be developed in Chapter 9. When customers experience poor service, employees get demotivated, and vice versa. In a study of 23 branches of a commercial bank,[31] it was identified that employee and customer attitudes were powerfully correlated. Employees acknowledge customer experiences, and when they feel good about service, so do customers. When employees become demotivated, the standard of work further declines, leading to a vicious cycle. The good news is that most employees enjoy doing a good job. Resolve one issue and you resolve both.

When things go wrong there is a cost in putting them right, and in recovering customer attitudes. Everyone knows you can lose customer loyalty much more quickly than you can gain it. Not only is there relationship rework but there may be costs involved in meeting guaranteed service levels, or correcting mistakes. Explanations have to be made to management, or excuses have to be found (or the whole situation has to be hidden). This all takes energy. Getting it right first time makes sense.

A winning team also finds others wanting to join in. A losing team loses its supporters. Most organizations depend on suppliers and business partners, including retailers, dealers, agents and service component producers. Their motivation and commitment may decline.

Poor relationship management is typically a symptom of poor knowledge of customers. If customers count as quarterly sales figures, then the organization's resources are unlikely to be focused in the most effective ways. For example, employees may not be well informed about the people with whom they are dealing. Consider the difference in experience between two customers who phone a service company: in one case the organization quickly knows who is calling, has a full individual service history and access to prompt, helpful information. The other customer finds an organization that does not know who is calling and has no relationship history.

Other resources are likely to be ineffectively used and distributed too. Unless the organization knows about its customers in some detail, including the profit contribution made by individual groups, how is it able to deploy its resources in the most effective way? Very often organizations are suffering at the most basic levels.

A leading UK photo-processing company converted 9 million rolls of film each year to prints, using a pre-written name and address label to return them. Because of the cost, it did not capture the names and addresses. As the newly appointed direct marketing manager commented: 'We don't know if we have one customer sending nine million films, or nine million customers each sending us one film! Whichever it is doesn't matter. If we have one customer, the strategy is easy! Find a second. If we have nine million customers, it's equally easy: get them to send two films.'

To compete on loyalty, a responsive company must understand the relationships between customer retention, the quality of the business and profits. Database marketing is primarily a loyalty discipline because we can collect much more information about customers than we can about prospects.

It is time to turn the obsession with new customers, as evidenced by DMA awards given over the last five years, to a better cause. Database marketing is good for acquisition, but it is even better at retention marketing.

Conclusion: 3 simple aims and 4 profound competences

The aware organization will therefore have three simple aims on the path to a treasured reputation and service mastery:

1. To acquire new customers successfully.
2. To retain customers at a rate at least equal to the best in the industry.
3. To profitably optimize the business relationship through cross-sell and up-sell, thus maximizing profitability per retained customer from an optimum mix of products and services.

The fundamental goal or aim of the business must be to increase the real lifetime value of customers. This can be achieved by the interaction and weaving together of four core competences, to be expanded in later chapters:

1. Effective creation of knowledge, particularly about customers and products through information management, increasingly the key raw material for added value transformation.
2. Process skills with a focus on enabling continuous improvement, in all areas. This includes the need for flexible systems.
3. Machine and other resource deployment, particularly use of the telephone and computer.
4. Relationship development, i.e. architecting the organization to effect and sustain viable partnerships with internal and external customers (and suppliers).

A model that fits perfectly (see Figure 5.3) has been developed by Bernard Lievegoed, the late European consultant who was one of the pioneers of

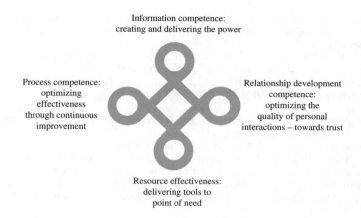

Information competence:
creating and delivering the power

Process competence:
optimizing
effectiveness
through continuous
improvement

Relationship development
competence:
optimizing the
quality of personal
interactions – towards trust

Resource effectiveness:
delivering tools to
point of need

Figure 5.3   The four core competences based on a model by Lievegoed

European organization development. This model will be developed later (Chapters 8 and 9) to provide an original link between the organization, individuals, products and service encounters. The model not only identified these four competences as the key to business effectiveness but indicates their weaving interrelatedness, and, as will be described later, how management most effectively centres itself within the business.

Notes and references

1. Timm, P.R., 'Use the profit power of customer service', *Executive Excellence*, Reichheld, F.F. and Sasser, W.E. Jr, 'Zero defections: quality comes to services', *Harvard Business Review*, (Sept./Oct. 1990); see also TARP studies for The White House Office of Consumer Affairs.
2. *Long Range Planning*, **26** (April 1993).
3. Reichheld, F.F. and Kenny, D.W., 'The hidden advantages of customer retention', *Journal of Retail Banking*, **XII**. (No. 4; Winter 1990/1).
4. Price Waterhouse survey (1994).
5. Clark, M. and Payne, A., 'Customer retention: does employee retention hold a key to success?', Cranfield School of Management Paper, 1993; Payne, A.F.T. and Ricard, J.A., 'Relationship marketing, customer retention and service firm profitability', 7th Annual British Academy of Management Conference, 1993.
6. Schneider, B., 'The service organization: climate is crucial', *Organizational Dynamics* (Autumn 1980), pp. 52–65.
7. Research by Cranfield School of Management on 100 managers in major firms.
8. See McKenna, R., *Relationship Marketing* Addison Wesley, 1991; Payne, A.F.T. and Ricard, J.A., 'Relationship marketing, customer retention and service firm profitability', 7th Annual British Academy of Management Conference, 1993.
9. Levitt, T., and Jackson, B., *The Marketing Imagination*, The Free Press 1983, and 1986.

10. Berry, L.L., 'Relationship Marketing' in Berry, L.L., Lynn, G., Shostack and Upah G.D., *Emerging perspectives on services marketing*, American Marketing Association, 1983.
11. E.g. Reichheld, F.F. and Sasser, W.E. Jr, 'Zero defections quality comes to services', *Harvard Business Review* (Sep./Oct. 1990).
12. Buchanan, R.W.T. and Gillies, C.S., 'Value managed relationships: the key to customer retention and profitability', *European Management Journal*, **8** (No. 4), p. 523.
13. Reichheld, F.F. and Sasser, W.E., Jr, 'Zero defections: quality comes to services', *Harvard Business Review* (Sept./Oct. 1990).
14. Rosenberg, L.J. and Czepiel, J.A., 'A marketing approach for customer retention', *Journal of Consumer Marketing*, 1984; Buchanan, R.W.T. and Gillies, C.S., 'Value managed relationships: the key to customer retention and profitability', *European Management Journal*, **8** (No. 4), p. 523; and Reichheld, F.F., 'The truth of customer retention', *Journal of Retail Banking*, **XIII** (No. 4; Winter 1991/2).
15. Dennison, T. and Knox, S., 'Pocketing the change from loyal shoppers', Cranfield School of Management Paper.
16. Reichheld, F.F., 'Loyalty based management', *Harvard Business Review* (March/April 1993).
17. Gilman, A.L., Smart Compensation and Smart Selling, (*Chain Store Age Executive*, **68** (No. 9; Sept. 1992).
18. Reichheld, F.F., 'The truth of customer retention', *Journal of Retail Banking*, **XIII** (No. 4; Winter 1991/92).
19. Reichheld, F.F., 'The truth of customer retention', *Journal of Retail Banking*, **XIII** (No. 4; Winter 1991/92).
20. Reichheld, F.F. and Kenny, D.W., 'The hidden advantages of customer retention', *Journal of Retail Banking*, **XII** (No. 4; Winter 1990/1), p. 19–23.
21. Quoted by Fierman, J., 'The death and rebirth of the salesman', *Fortune* (25 July 1994), p. 82.
22. Sellers, P., 'Companies that serve you best', *Fortune*, **127** (No. 11; 31 May 1993).
23. Reichheld, F.F., 'The truth of customer retention', *Journal of Retail Banking*, **XIII** (No. 4; Winter 1991/2).
24. Quoted in EDS client briefing.
25. 'First Direct customer first awards 1994', *The Daily Telegraph* (29 July 1994), p. 28.
26. Fierman, J., 'The death and rebirth of the salesman', *Fortune* (25 July 1994), p. 82.
27. Direct Mail Information Service (The Letterbox Factfile, 1994).
28. TARP studies for White House Office of Consumer Affairs.
29. Reichheld, F.F. and Dawkins, P.M., 'Customer retention as a competitive weapon', *Directors and Boards* (Summer 1990).
30. Brown, R., 'Keeping the cable customer satisfied' *Broadcasting and Cable*, **123** (No. 10; 8 March 1993), p. 10.
31. Schneider, B., 'The service organization: climate is crucial', *Organizational Dynamics* (Autumn 1980).

6
Health warnings

Summary Four challenges will be described in this chapter. They are:

1. The backlash of the aggrieved customer: the problems with poor quality direct marketing/direct mail and how to overcome them.
2. The need for a new organizational vision: moving towards a long-term quality vision.
3. The 'structural culture' which inhibits right change, i.e. how organizations become fixed into old and ineffective ways.
4. The immaturity of the supply industry: a new industry means that suppliers are still trying to keep up with customer demands.

Making databases of sensitive, individual consumer information available to marketers interested only in next quarter's sales results is like providing chain saws to a tribe of slash-and-burn farmers.

(Don Peppers and Martha Rogers, *The One to One Future*)

Beware the angry customer

Marshall McLuhan made the following prediction: 'One of the future aspects of advertising is the custom-made, the tailor-made. Instead of peddling mass-produced commodities, advertising is going to become a personal service to each individual.' This implies that the customer should be seen as a partner or associate, not a target enemy whose resistance must be overcome. 'You won't generate trust and promote a long-term relationship with a customer or prospective customer when you use detailed, personal information to make a one time sale to a stranger,' say Pepper and Rogers in an extension of the point quoted above.[1]

There have been many protests over the years about manipulative styles of marketing. JK Galbraith commented, 'Consumer wants can have bizarre, frivolous, or even immoral origins, and an admirable case can still be made for a society that seeks to satisfy them. But the case cannot stand if it is the process of satisfying wants that creates the wants.'[2] Mary McCarthy objected: 'The consumer today is the victim of the manufacturer who launches on him a regiment of products for which he must make room in his soul,'[3] while Erich Fromm felt the customer was often 'an object to be manipulated, not a concrete person whose aims the business person is interested to satisfy'.[4]

While there will always be a tension between those whose aims and values are driven solely by the desire to generate business – on the real basis that businesses need business to survive – and those who stand for a moral or environmental lobby, both these positions must be seen against reality. While many are very happy to have sweepstakes, discounts and lurid promises of a better life, many others are increasingly cynical and disenchanted, a trend that is increasing. Consumers (business or private) will always want value, but when they come to believe that the promises of companies cannot be trusted or that their activities are crossing boundaries of privacy, good taste or ethics, then the result is trouble: legal claims, lost sales, bad PR.

It is much easier and quicker to lose trust than to build it.

Schlackmans, a London, England agency, conducted research in 1987 which showed the public already becoming increasingly cynical of formula approaches, prize draws and insensitive personalization, (just as there was a 1993 backlash against Hollywood sex and violence). Customers do not like to be treated as tools, or fools.

The rising tide of objections

In 1993, consumers in The Netherlands who did not wish to receive unaddressed mail or free newspapers became able to register their objection through an industry self-regulation scheme pasting stickers to their letterboxes. It was estimated that 8 per cent would object to general letters and less than 3 per cent to newspapers. In fact at least 40 per cent of households said 'No'! Sticker production temporarily failed to meet demand.

The Swiss market is the busiest in Europe for direct mail. The result is that more and more Swiss people are complaining. Twelve per cent of Swiss households put a STOP sticker on their mailbox. The Swiss Direct Marketing Federation's campaign to convince consumers that direct mail volumes are reasonable and to counter environmentalist concerns – Switzerland is the most environmentally concerned country in Europe – with an argument that mail order saves petrol and is therefore eco-friendly, was seen as weak and defensive.

A survey of men and women aged between 20 and 64 and from the ABC1 socio-economic groups in Britain,[5] i.e. from the section of the population who receive most direct mail, identified that if the respondents could picture an image of the direct marketing industry at all it was either a remote, manipulative company using computers in a big-brother manner, or a cottage industry with isolated housewives stuffing envelopes, with no sophistication in either targeting or creative approach. 'What's direct mail?'

they said, in effect: 'We know of junk mail and post. If it's relevant, it's OK: it's post. If it's not relevant then it's junk mail.' The implication is that measurement of sales success must be not from 0 per cent up but from 100 per cent down. Those who feel they are getting irrelevant mail may think they are receiving junk mail. It may not be enough to think, 'We made a profit from 2 per cent'. The issue is, what did the 98 per cent think?

Bad practices in telemarketing which annoy consumers (and are capturing the attention of lawmakers) include simple misdemeanours such as being called at inconvenient times and inadequate targeting leading to irrelevant calls: blanket telephone campaigns by UK double-glazing companies is a prime example. (A stark illustration of bad practice and insensitivity is the US telemarketer who used automatic dialling equipment to play recorded sales pitches to prospects, and managed to feed calls to patients in private hospital wards via their direct-line telephones.) Over half of the 1255 US householders interviewed in a Harris Equifax consumer privacy survey regarded telemarketing calls as a nuisance, while 27 per cent saw them as *an invasion of privacy*.

Poor practice is bad enough. Unfortunately, telemarketing and direct marketing are particularly exposed to fraud because the seller is remote and not reproachable. Annual public loss through telemarketing fraud in the US is estimated to be as high as $15 billion, but what does it really cost in lost trust? Corrupt telemarketing practices moving from the USA to Europe range from premium rate services where consumers spend a fortune before they get to the point of a recorded message to overt scams, such as persuading callers to buy what eventually proves to be over-priced products enticed by free entry into sweepstakes with valuable prizes that no one ever receives.

Topic 6.1 Survey: What do consumers think of direct mail?

The overwhelming majority of customers, according to Direct Mail Information Service and the Henley Centre for Forecasting Studies, expect to be sent information *by companies to which they had given their name and address*, but only 50 per cent consider it acceptable to pass information on to other companies. Eighty-five per cent agree that they sift mail received and read what was of interest. In fact, 64 per cent agree that they had enjoyed receiving things in the post.

But there is an issue of control: consumers feel vulnerable. While 81 per cent are happy to receive information by post, since they could always throw away what was not of interest, only 50 per cent really feel in control of the information they are sent. Where is this going to go in the decades ahead? Surely this depends on our policies and practices. Nearly half had found direct mail an intrusion!

Gimmicks are increasingly out of favour. The use of a first name as a means of address is frowned on. Most consumers use a number of 'identifiers' to place items into the category of 'Junk Mail', most important of which is the cherished practice of overprinting. Sixty-four per cent regard this as a critical indicator and over 50 per cent think the word 'urgent' is another strong hint of unsolicited material. Other factors which influence their perception of a company include a misspelt name or address (40 per cent) and inaccuracy in addressing (69 per cent).

Television may be a mass medium with message overload, but at least it is seen as credible (see Table 6.1). Consumers seem to trust what they see on television because they are aware that authorities exist to control advertising. Direct mail is not perceived, on the whole, as a credible medium. It is felt that anybody with a few pennies to scrape together can send out junk mail.

Jerry Pickholz – who was quoted in Chapter 1 as saying, of the US industry, that its short-term outlook represented failure – proposed the need for better recycling technologies, better targeting, more consumer privacy, and more honest, forthright and involving sales messages that were useful to the consumer, rather than being intrusive, over-familiar and poorly targeted. He said of the US industry:

> People don't just think we're Big Brother. They think we're Big Rude Brother. . . .
> We're faced with a problem that is ironic, considering our job is to help our clients communicate with the public and look good while doing it. We look bad. In an age of increasingly entertaining advertising, our devotion to selling and salesmanship techniques has helped to tarnish our image.

Direct mail is active and cannot be ignored; and that is its strength in the right hands, and weakness in the wrong hands. Consumers often object to over-familiarity and find mailings very boring, complaining of the 'hard sell' image, while aspiring to brand values in television advertisements which they frequently find well made and sometimes funny (see Table 6.1). Direct mail must pass the brand quality test.

There are many people who respond to prize draws and sweepstakes: 9.5 per cent on average in UK surveys.[6] They therefore create millions of contacts and relationships, and can be a successful device. The issue is relevancy and style. James Rosenfield, an expert commentator on creative direct marketing, compares many sweepstakes to 'the fascination of abomination' described in Conrad's *Heart of Darkness*. Sweepstakes are the 'apogee of direct mail legerdemain, the most masterfully manipulative of all commercial efforts anywhere'.[7] He gives 10 out of 10 to nine different aspects of creative work in one sample mailing, and only 1 out of 10 for honesty/integrity/believability.

Prize draws and competitions particularly appeal to a certain type of individual, the community frequently targeted in the older days of direct mail as it built from its traditional base, e.g. the classic *Reader's Digest* reader on whom half the industry seemed to cut its teeth. Other recipients

Table 6.1 Common British consumer perceptions of media

Direct mail	Television
Specifically targeted	Untargeted
Irrelevance matters	Irrelevance matters less
Often rational	More often emotional, aspirational
Work	Entertainment
Boring	Interesting
Unrewarding (expect for prize addicts)	Rewarding
Visually dull	Visually stimulating
Personally familiar	Unreal
Selling	Story telling
Oh dear!	Oh yeah?

Based on various research sources, including the Henley Centre, Direct Mail Information Service and Private.

are not engaged by these devices, and they are often the new, better educated, more affluent groups with whom direct marketing increasingly communicates. For such audiences, 'reward' need not be purely material, but can be an enjoyable or entertaining mailing piece and other aspects of service, just as many TV advertisements are appreciated, as noted above.

Timeshare represents all that consumers find disreputable about junk mail. Research (see Topic 6.1) indicates a widespread feeling that if timeshare companies dupe people openly without fearing the consequences, there is no hope with the 'local businessman who claims he is a plumber and ruins all your pipe work'.

An independent survey by the prestigious UK Henley Centre for Forecasting,[8] in conjunction with Ogilvy & Mather Direct, therefore concluded that direct mail was potentially reaching a watershed. There *is*, they conclude, widespread acceptance of the medium, with the very term 'junk mail' an accepted part of social life. On the other hand, there is an active and vociferous group of sometimes influential critics strengthening distrust, such as this example in an article by the influential British columnist, Bernard Levin, in *The Times* of 13 August 1993. Mr Levin, generally a notably sane, liberal humanist, had first written an article in 1989 complaining that a mailing he had received from a publisher of *Business Week International*, was crass, stupidly couched, and offensive because he was invited to subscribe 'solely because of his or her (sic) level of participation and record of achievement in international business.' Mr Levin did not consider that he had such a record, and even if he did, why would he be seriously interested in a 'few lousy quid off' the publication? Four years later, he received a second mailing which offered even larger discounts, so he decided to 'bash these clowns' even harder and therefore asked for a volunteer to go and 'trash' the proprietor's offices and inject him with a considerable variety of noxious diseases 'to settle his hash'. Leaving aside the tongue in cheek, it is a powerful article which indicates both depth of feeling and the potential to arouse wider dissatisfaction.

It explains why customers reject everything that fails to show real respect. *Junk mail junks people.* Treating people superficially invites superficial responses, not loyal ones. A company without ideals is a company bereft of vision. It throws away reputation, honour and wealth. There was a time when people would die for their reputation. No longer, and for some good reasons; but a good reputation still has pragmatic value, not to mention better sleep at night.

Furthermore, the more we target, the more data we seem to need and the more exposed we are to fears of becoming Big Brother. Database technology is still rapidly evolving, which means that the opportunities to collect and use data will become more and more technically effective. We know what happens to society when technical competence exceeds moral competence. There are three obvious threats that this could bring to the industry:

1. We could find ourselves in a society that we do not like. We are all citizens first and our hearts are as vulnerable as anyone else's.
2. We could find ourselves very severely regulated. Minnesota Supreme Court upheld a law in 1992 restricting the use of automatic dialling equipment for making calls, saying that telemarketing calls are 'uniquely intrusive' in that the 'shrill and imperious ring of the telephone demands immediate attention'. Germany has very strict rules on telemarketing. The EU has been working on data privacy for several years and constantly threatens further actions affecting performance and profit. Yet around one in three major UK companies operating databases and using telemarketing in a systematic way are not aware of how the current EU Directive could affect their business.[9]
3. We could find ourselves with the increasingly vigilante consumers identified above.

The Henley Centre report cited above concludes that clients, agencies and suppliers need to invest in improving the quality of direct mail activities: more effective research, higher quality creative executions and a new focus on the longer term impact of direct mail and other direct communications on brand building. For example, it notes that while television advertising improved its status over the years, poor quality direct mail led to the 'junk' image.

Yet, the US Postal Service found that three-quarters of the advertising mail was found by consumers to be 'useful or interesting'. Efforts by the British industry's self-regulation bodies, such as the Direct Marketing

Association, has led to a dramatic reduction in complaints by consumers, particularly about timeshare, although it will take time for the memories to die. Pirate mailings from abroad are being regulated and prevented. Creative execution can do much to create or dispel interest and entice examination. So, while the industry experts rightly emphasize the importance of writing to the right person, and therefore selecting data analysis techniques as the database driver, the long-term future depends on a marriage between right relevancy and ethical and creatively satisfying material.

Knowing the supplier is regarded as crucial to the level of trust. Database marketing can also be effective as a way of informing and creating trust and awareness, but this must be the first step to overcoming the barriers. However, this again shows the value of preserving contact with your own customer community before turning to pastures new. But, when direct mail really works, it is not seen as direct mail but as a letter from a business partner or associate. Does anyone object to receiving a bank statement, a reminder from the dentist, a phone call that the ordered book has arrived, or information on new function in the latest software release?

The Henley Centre report concludes that, with the right changes, there is a fertile ground for rapid transformation. Without sacrificing short-term results, the real benefits of the new style direct marketing will be gained by those companies who are prepared to, and can afford to, invest for the long term.

The solution: 'authentic marketing'

Marketers develop creative formats by comparing what works with what does not. Most of the devices in modern direct mail are there because they have been proved to generate more pull. Fundraisers personalize a series of tick boxes, inviting a donation according to the level of the previous donation: and multiple items in the pack, pull-off stickers and opening paragraphs are all determined like this. Consider the difference between long and short copy (i.e. how much text there is in an advertisement or letter). Research shows that good long copy outpulls response because it gives a better chance to explain and communicate detail and interesting information. Direct marketing offers unique ways to measure performance of copy and other alternatives.

But, the skills of writing successful sales messages that build loyalty are a world away from those of learning the best tricks to persuade an indifferent audience to respond to an indifferent product. The difference is both motive and art: gimmicky tacticians or relationship builders? A response of 2 or 3 per cent may be profitable, but how is the total brand message being accepted? How about the 97 per cent? If only the tactical things, i.e. the immediate result, are measured, how do we know what is happening strategically?

One of the world's leading copywriters, John Watson asked the question, What is the principle that drives successful direct mail? His answer was *focus*, an exemplary truth, but he went on to say that the copywriter should remember that he or she is writing exclusively for the responders. The aim should be to try to get a 20 per cent lift from the 3, 4, 5 or 8 per cent who are responding, not to convert the rest. You are only writing to some of the names, he argues; the rest can be ignored. Now, in the hands of a craftsman who automatically produces quality material, a hallmark of Watson's work, that may be fine, but the less careful generate much of the 'junk'. One answer is quality of targeting based on data selection. Trouble is, perfection is hard to achieve. The other is to ensure that what is produced not only sells but stands the test: does this reflect the brand image positively?

Who thanks mothers for their custom when the children get too old to need a product? There is no ROI on it, is there? Yet such gratuitous care could transform one's reputation. By contrast, in 1991, to celebrate 10 years of the Gold Card, Amex sent out a mailing thanking 'loyal and valued customers' for their custom. In gratitude they said they had put together something special, but it was simply an invitation to spend large amounts of money on various decidedly luxurious indulgences. Customers complained in large numbers, feeling that the privilege was on the side of Amex. 'Who are you kidding?' was the response.

This is not authentic marketing; nor is it the stuff of sustainable success, which requires a combination of honesty with a genuine connection with and commitment to customer expectations and needs. The legendary Stan Rapp asks: 'Is it really necessary to fool people in order to run a viable business?' He is not the only one. Authors Kenneth Roman (a former chairman of Ogilvy & Mather Worldwide) and Jane Maas have written a book on the new values needed:

> There are things we do in advertising because they are the law, and things we do because they are right. What is truthful is clearly determined by the law. What is right is a matter of corporate conscience.... While its purpose is to sell, [advertising] must also have a sense of social responsibility.... Consumers need to be able to choose, rather than having the choice made for them. Tell the truth, the whole truth, and nothing but the truth.[10]

Research shows that being recognized as a regular customer is insufficient to build loyalty unless it is accompanied by other service factors, such as speed of service, friendliness and cheerfulness, helpfulness, knowledge and experience, and respect. For that reason personalization, one of the most frequently cited devices on both the positive and negative sides, will not, by itself, take the organization very far.[11] Just writing someone's name, perhaps with no basis of knowledge and a laser-generated signature at the end of the letter, may marginally improve response in the short term, but in the long term it erodes and degrades the market, for the company and others. Instead, genuine quality is needed, including quality knowledge: hence the database.

In fact, American Express is a legendary database marketer, as other examples in the book show, who spoke effectively to its own customer community in the 1980s. Between 1987 and 1990, Amex Gold Card membership doubled using database techniques. The 15 per cent of members who had a Gold Card produced 33 per cent of revenue. Furthermore, Amex has learnt much from its 1991 mistake.

So, new disciplines and approaches which respond much more closely to customer attitudes, and not only to simple calculations of short-term ROI, are in development (see Table 6.2).

Qualitative research in 1991 by the Henley Centre, with Ogilvy & Mather

Table 6.2 Development of new disciplines and approaches

	'Traditional'	'New'
Volumes	Higher	Lower
Results required	Short term	Short term and long term
Evaluation used	Immediate results	Qualitative research; database analysis; customer loyalty
Media	Direct mail	Integrated DM media; inbound customer helplines
Techniques	Continuous testing of all variables; statistical analysis	Planning disciplines using market research plus database analysis of long-term behaviour
Creative approach	Tried and tested	Creative development research; brand values endorsed

Source: The Henley Centre, 1991.

Direct, into the reasons for consumers being willing to accept direct mail indicated four factors, which do not operate in a hierarchy:

1. Subject matter
2. Brand relationship
3. Personality type
4. Creative execution.

The fifth factor, which they do not explicitly note, is the importance of timing. Three conditions must be met if the recipient is to perceive it as a service:

- Targeting in regards to timing and subject must be excellent.
- There must be an ongoing reason for communication based on a good relationship.
- The direct mail must have arrived as a result of a customer-initiated action.

The implication is that direct marketing must consist of communications programmes generated by a real interaction between company and customer, triggered by the customer either explicitly, or as a proper and reasonable professional response by the company (see Figure 6.1). Typical triggers will include freephone and other numbers advertised on pack, in TV and other advertisements and in the *Yellow Pages*. Sales promotion exercises can also generate requests for further information. By enabling customers to indicate their areas of interest and to choose an appropriate level of contact, a more positive attitude is engendered. It argues that,

> While the cold mail shot (and in this we include mass mailing, in-house lists on topics not specifically requested by the recipient) may continue to prove cost effective in response terms ... we believe that such approaches will increasingly be counter productive.... Consumers will demand more from their communications ... the aim is ... genuine two-way dialogue ... as part of a long-term customer orientation. This implies a significant change from current reality.

In this way direct marketing becomes both a service medium by providing information or help, and a relationship manager by providing a contact point. (This is developed in Chapter 8.) Fred Williams, president of America's J.C. Penney Life Insurance Company – which runs a massive telemarketing operation – knows the potential of the telephone: 'People really do appreciate that the telephone is a very easy way of finding out if someone has got the products they want and to do business.' But he recognizes that, to make it work, there must be quality, which currently means regulation: 'We have to be a regulated business and if we lost any sleep over that we wouldn't sleep at all.'[12]

But, prior to thinking of the law, quality organizations will be interested

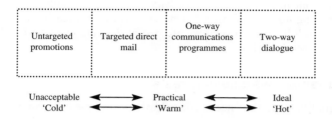

Figure 6.1   A spectrum of direct mail applications (*source*: Ogilvy & Mather Direct)

in excellent standards of customer satisfaction and skills. Making this work is partly an issue of culture, and partly one of training (although the two are linked). A survey for UK telemarketing bureau Merit Direct showed that around 20 per cent of British companies with in-house telemarketing operations do no training whatsoever. Part of the educational process should be to advise consumers of Telephone and Mail Preference Services, where they exist. By registering, consumers can opt not to receive unsolicited calls or mail. Although very few countries have such a service (particularly for the telephone), companies can nevertheless set up their own in-house suppression files of people who have no desire to receive marketing calls.

Get it right and something tremendous can happen. Get it wrong and the story is very different. The Breakthrough Centre is a workshop and resource centre in London for a group of small business and professional practice members interested in personal development and quality improvement. At the beginning of 1993, business was suffering, systems were inefficient, no database of members existed, records were manual. At times they felt they were badgering their members. The computer, they realized, could help them free up time for service. This was their comment:

> The money was not flowing. We were going nowhere. Then, somehow, we were able to make a massive paradigm shift and moved our energy out of anxiety and into service – what we believe is our core activity.
>
> Our energy on the ether and our voices on the phone now conveyed a new, exciting and compelling message of strength, clarity and support. People began to enjoy our phone calls; they even started to phone us again. We were definitely doing something very attractive as our membership has risen by 70 per cent in the last 12 months and our workshops are nearly always full with no effort on our part to fill them!
>
> We've learnt our lesson: from now on we're into service. I see this as the new competition of the 1990s; competition not formulated only on price but on quality of service, how much and how well we can do something for someone. The bitter and isolating experiences of the late 80s lead us naturally into a new way of doing business: substance in place of image, quality replacing quantity.

So our contentedly purring new toy with its clever little mouse will not be used for drumming up more members or packing 'em in at even bigger workshops. Instead, it will help us do what we are best at: looking after the Breakthrough Club. Click on, Claris!

Environmental awareness threats

One big quality issue that needs special mention is the environment. Direct mail is No. 1 public enemy to the environmental lobby, with both excellent and invalid reasons. The fact is that most direct mail uses sustainable woodland pulp. However, there is a lot that can be done, from the use of recycled material to better targeting and less wasteful production and design. Selectronic binding, for example, can reduce the amount of unread, unwanted material in larger brochures, magazines and catalogues. The US DMA is continually urging members to become more environmentally aware, providing them with literature and videos that show how this can be accomplished. It is urging businesses and the public to have a 'recycling culture' for catalogues – even a sharing of catalogues to reduce the number going out; and its Environmental Action Kit for marketers who wish to disassociate themselves from 'junk mail' is a 68-page handbook, available to companies wanting to become more environmentally friendly.

It has mounted a campaign for the use of environmentally acceptable vegetable-based inks and has produced its *Grassroots Advocacy Guide* to cover public policy issues such as solid waste management alternatives and to help marketers with their own public affairs programmes. Europe must follow suit. The European Union is finalizing proposals and directives that will hit the industry as hard as data protection. For example, those marketers producing excess packaging will be responsible for recycling it.[13]

In the area of eco-friendliness, it is time to be a leader and not a follower.

Vision: a way to lead

Earlier, it was pointed out how, in an age of short termism, the power of database marketing to deliver immediate benefits has swallowed up its potential to deliver even greater benefits as part of a long-term strategy of developing customer loyalty. Only long-term thinking can focus effectively on the real business goal, increasing customer lifetime value through loyalty. This is a great goal, genuinely beckoning, but never reached.

Short-term measures only produce short-term loyalty. Only policies with vision and commitment win loyalty. If you want customers to be loyal to you, you need to be loyal to them as part of the creation of a treasured reputation, or even service mastery. The problem with many short-term targets is that they conflict with standards of excellence and care. For example, one telemarketing company found that its decision to shorten telephone calls meant that customers felt less warm and receptive to it. In a bank study, it was found that the conflicts between the long-term values of customer care and the short-term targets of daily production were the main cause of both employee stress and customer distress.

Do marketing managers consider each piece of mail as part of a long-term process of gaining and keeping customers, or is the turnaround measured as a one-off transaction and immediate return on investment. Perhaps a 6 per cent response is profitable, but what is happening to the 94 per cent, and will the 6 per cent continue to buy?

Only the right kind of research answers this: research aimed at identifying not just numerical responses, but *why* customers defect or do not respond. As long as a 'survival by sales' mentality reigns, i.e. this mailing made money so why look further? – then nothing will change.

Sound, sustainable businesses serve customers. If that is lost, the legitimate needs of employees and shareholders will be unsupported, and unsupportable. Yet, in the large, fragmented world of the modern 'segmented' or 'differentiated' company – when the organization is divided vertically by different functions and tasks such as marketing, production and finance and subdepartments of these, with layer upon layer of management – it is easy for a group or an individual to lose sight of the ultimate purpose.

In the new way of thinking, companies serve and thereby create their own future alongside that of their customers. 'I've poured myself mentally and physically into the world of industrial competition,' says John Sculley, former vice-president of marketing at Pepsi and CEO of Apple, '... and discovered a new world where business has less to do with competition and more to do with building markets, where success is measured not by share points but by enlarging the playing field for everyone, thereby making the industry stronger.'[14] Sculley's secret of success is the continuous capacity to renew the organization behind a worthwhile vision, like Apple's 'to make a difference', rather than a retreat to the death of *stability*.

Developing organizations of substance needs more than two-dimensional, quantity-sifted, short-term thinking. Max DePree, CEO of the respected Hermann Miller organization, argued that, 'Managers who have no beliefs but only understand methodology and quantification are modern day eunuchs.'[15] Leaders must provide and encourage a kind of 'moral imagination': what DePree calls 'rationality', a sense of creative order and relationship based on a vision of service that respects people (employees, suppliers and customers) and creates authentic value now and for the future; a way that breaks free of numbers and targets as shackles, yet uses numeracy as an aid to understanding the real world.

It is an approach that values quality. Quality is a common word in today's corporation, but it will for ever stand for an uncommon reality. The quality built into the fabric, design and processes of nature in all its abundance never becomes common: it is simply wonderfully reliable. The quality of a Bach cantata does not diminish, nor is it harmed by the quality of Beethoven. Quality is not abstract. It does not exist in specification, but when an essential need is fulfilled. It cannot be achieved in one area in isolation from others. Quality means doing things without waste; providing solutions that are not excessive but more than meet expectations; building systems that are durable and can evolve, making people feel good. Quality requires the seamless integration of many components, both human and technical, each of a very high standard. It is said that it takes 12 pluses to cancel out one minus. Quality may involve cancelling 12 minuses to achieve one plus. Quality involves total attention to detail and the absolute cooperation of all.

Imagine a world in which 'quality' as a concept had no reality. Is it not a world in which there is no reason to make any decisions at all? Why choose one thing rather than another?

Information and numeracy

One of the single most effective ways to destroy quality is to stick a wet finger in the air and set short-term, arbitrary, numeric targets 'to get people working'. The gap between this and the renewing, ordering imagination based on intimate and profound knowledge of customers and craft is as wide as Ginnungagap, the void between worlds in Norse mythology. This is a numericism that wants to impose itself on the world. If you ignore the realities of the marketplace or the system and try to impose your own order onto it, is it so surprising that you should find yourself obsessed with survival, never getting off the bottom rung of development?

That is why W. Edwards Deming – arguably the greatest ever statistician serving the interests of business and organizations, a quality thought leader revered in Japan – argues against the dangers of misapplication of numbers. One of his '7 deadly diseases' is 'running a company on visible figures alone,[16] pointing out that there is no (obvious) way to measure the effect on sales of a happy customer. Among his 14 points for industry, is the need to eliminate numerical quotas, a system which drives performance not upwards but downwards, creating unhappy workers and customers (see Topic 6.2).

A truly customer driven organization is never run on quotas, although it will have guiding predictions and forecasts. Given the choice – and they will be – no reasonable customer would want to deal with a salesperson driven by quantity objectives.

Topic 6.2 Deming's recipe for industry

Deming's 7 *Deadly Diseases* (or 5 for Europe) and his *14 points for industry* are the bedrock of his management theory.

The full 14 points are:

1. Create constancy of purpose for continual improvement of products and service.
2. Adopt the new philosophy. We are in a new economic age.
3. Eliminate the need for mass inspection as a way to achieve quality.
4. End the practice of awarding business solely on the basis of price tag.
5. Improve constantly, and permanently, every process for planning, production and service.
6. Institute modern methods of training on the job.
7. Adopt and institute leadership aimed at helping people to do a better job.
8. Encourage effective two-way communication and other means to drive out fear throughout the organization.
9. Break down barriers between departments and staff areas.
10. Eliminate the use of slogans, posters and exhortations.
11. Eliminate work standards that prescribe numerical quotas for the workforce and numerical goals for people in management.
12. Remove the barriers that rob people of their right to pride of workmanship.
13. Institute a vigorous programme of education, and encourage self-improvement for everyone.
14. Clearly define top management's permanent commitment to ever-improving quality and productivity.

He also describes 5 Deadly Diseases:

1. Lack of constancy of purpose.
2. Emphasis on short-term profits.
3. Evaluation of performance, merit rating, or annual review of performance.
4. Mobility of management.
5. Running a company on visible figures alone.

For the USA, he adds excessive medical costs and the costs of warranty, fuelled by the legal system.

Numericism can distort reality, becoming a hammer to drive business operations. The result is that the customer ends up under the hammer, being reshaped and moulded. Numeracy, on the other hand, tells us what is going on, revealing the real health of the company, operation or process. This will be developed further in Chapter 15.

Numericism is the tool of the demon of the cold, survival-oriented, fear ridden, immovable and rigid business. It can lead to the vice of manipulation, such as, at worst, the banned subliminal advertising. When, however, does persuasion become intrusive, unethical and unwarranted? Fortunately, customers usually end up telling us in time, by voting with their feet. Numeracy and knowledge, by contrast, are tools of the architect of great, living businesses: showing how looking after your customers makes commercial sense, as well as being fun.

The strategic competitors are ourselves

'Strategy' is an interesting word. It means all kinds of things to all kinds of people, from pattern recognition of emerging opportunities to logical, rational goal setting. Some emphasize the process, some the goal. The word is often chosen when 'tactics' is more accurate and needed, but devalued. Just as the Eskimos have many words for snow, perhaps we should use many words for what we mean by 'strategy' according to context, including ways, goals, process, method, aims, direction, policy, control, purpose and guiding principles?

The source is obviously military; in Greek it is the art of generalship, deriving from 'control', i.e. controlling limited resources to overcome an opponent. When we are in the business of serving customers, this use is uncomfortable. Who is the real opponent? Customers certainly do not want to see any army advancing towards them over the hill, although that may be what they have often experienced. Surely, the real opponents are our own weaknesses, not our opponents' strengths: our inertia, apathy, dullness, lack of enthusiasm and care, ignorance, greed, lack of teamwork and purpose, and so on. Strategies are formed to make us fit players in the world market.

Whether they like it or not, organizations institute a 'structural culture' which may be a barrier to effectiveness or the greatest asset a company possesses. This was true of IBM, whose culture until the early 1980s carried it to pre-eminence. However, in a series of key moves, principally shifting focus from customer service and retention through valued people to low-cost production and 'box-shifting', these values were tampered with in the early 1980s. The old values were still given lip service, but they were no longer alive, nor were their practices renewed in action. Hence they become increasingly rigid obstructions, not energy generators.

The presence of this structural culture may prevent us from creating an imaginative design for new systems, which is also rooted in realism. Ideas are either dull or unworkable because our original thinking is in a rut. The old paradigm creates a block to vision, as demonstrated in the well-known gestalt experiments looking at shapes that can represent two figures according to how they are viewed (old woman or young girl is a well-known example). Forces of habit thereby mire change: e.g.

- The new system provides information about lifetime value. Will the organization change continue to focus on the short-term promotion?
- Will the new system be used effectively? A campaign management system

enables the organization to analyse campaign effectiveness in detail, and progressively improve. Will people take advantage? One financial services company had a campaign management system that had not been populated with data at any time in the previous two years.

Four damaging organization paradigms are described below: cost saving not value generation; focus on acquisition not retention; management through functional silos not value streams; control not responsiveness.

Cost saving not value generation

A teleservices department is given a target to reduce the average length of calls to seven minutes. The ACD system gives excellent information on who is failing to achieve this, and how long calls are taking. Scripts are progressively pruned in order to reduce time. But does anyone measure the optimum relationship between call length and style, on the one hand, and renewal rates a year later?

Focus on acquisition not retention

The continuous argument of this book is that the greater power of database marketing is in keeping, not acquiring, customers. But, even if the idea is accepted, culture change will still be needed. A survey of large British companies rated the importance of 18 marketing activities according to both general and marketing management.[17] The average position of those items that have a strong relevance to one-to-one marketing (e.g. customer care, telemarketing, customer direct marketing) is only 13 out of 18 to the marketing function and 15 out of 18 to the general management. That at least shows a trend: those closer to the issue are more aware. (Sales force management tops general management. Clearly, IT can have a big role here too.)

We also have an interesting vicious circle. If paying attention to your competitors (No. 1 importance to marketing) is more important than customer care (No. 10), then paying attention to competitors is certainly going to continue to be quite important! Changing such an ingrained mind set will not be immediate and will need champions.

Another vicious cycle is the Silly Spiral (Figure 6.2) which an acquisition culture institutionalizes.

Since organizations are losing customers and want to grow, they focus their scarce resources and some of their best resources – including many of the best salespeople – on the process of acquiring new business, mainly from the competition. Of course, the competition is doing the same thing. This effectively takes the organization's eye off the existing customer base, and is

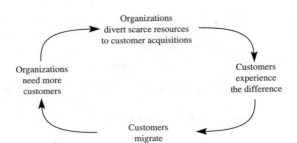

Figure 6.2   The Silly Spiral

experienced by customers as either a reduction in service or a failure to meet service aspiration levels, leading to defections. Furthermore, instead of focusing on what constitutes the unique and particular reasons why certain customers would be interested in a relationship with the company, it focuses on why customers might have an interest in having a relationship with another organization. One result is our me-too world. It is difficult to establish loyalty when there is no difference and no focus.

Migrating customers then generate renewed need for new customers. Fifty per cent of one financial services company's customer base had never bought twice. In another company, the figure was 70 per cent while, by contrast, Direct Line Insurance, the leader in UK Direct insurance, has been quoted as obtaining 50 per cent of its new business from customer referrals.

And so the silly spiral goes on. .... When marketers think short term, they saw off the branch they are sitting on and fall into the trap of following 'marketing driven' as opposed to 'market driven' approaches.

Management through functional silos not value streams

The third old paradigm is the traditional hierarchical structure developed by Taylor and Ford but rooted in French government bureaux of the eighteenth and nineteenth centuries and the thinking of Henri Fayol. This was, in turn, rooted in the Roman Catholic Church and the Roman Empire's management structures. Dividing the business into functional areas, each reporting to a different board member, creates a neat control system, but not necessarily a neat process flow. The company divides into functional and information islands rather than managing the total process flow and interaction with customers: creating a free-flowing satisfaction-delivery process – a value stream.

A business actually runs on processes, not functions; and most effort should be centred around the key transformation processes in serving customers, most significant of which is typically 'managing the customer relationship', or call it loyalty development. But if, as was pointed out in Chapter 1, database marketing reports to Below the Line Communications – a function within marketing which, in turn, reports to the sales and marketing director on the main board – and Service is another functional line, then there might be a little problem.

Every business tends to turn into cold spaghetti sooner or later. Encrustations of old ideas and practices, quick fixes and habits congeal around ever more tortuous procedures. The need to renew around fundamental value, to rekindle vision or the guiding light of the business, and purify the processes of achieving it should be a regular rhythm, like the pattern of the seasons. Our body changes its cells every seven years. This is not, however, the same as re-engineering, which throws out the past. Rather it is a renewal based on preserving certain underlying core competences, community and values into a new era and a new order. Changes are easiest when there is a continuing foundation on which you can depend.

Nor is it neurotic change. Mintzberg describes how advocates of strategic planning urge managers to go for perpetual instability,[18] an obsession which becomes dysfunctional. 'Organizations that re-assess their strategies continuously are like individuals who re-assess their jobs or their marriages continuously – in both cases they can drive themselves crazy,' he observes.

Often, core processes are simple and basic, at least at the top level; in one company, for example, they were as follows (slightly adapted for confidentiality):

1. Handling and routeing customer/prospect contacts to a contact (telephone handling, etc).
2. Satisfying the caller 'first time'.
3. Service follow up.
4. Relationship development planning, aiming to maximize lifetime value across customer groups.
5. Product development, dependent on usable information, and aiming to develop benchmarked best product.
6. Contact management, based on individual customers.
1. ...

The six core processes form a loop or circle, the first process being generated by the last. Together they define the horizontal flow of the business. (Additional support processes such as treasury would, of course, also be required.)

Control, not responsiveness

This mighty restrictive paradigm is dealt with in more detail in Chapter 16. A control-oriented culture and attitude tends to rigidity: fear of change, disruption and uncertainty all damage creativity, quality and responsive-ness, as Case study 6.1 illustrates. The aim must be to build the organization towards the ideals outlined in Chapter 1 – towards service mastery – and this is never enabled by fear. How this can be done is briefly developed in Chapter 9.

It is valid to think 'control' when implementing a guarantee management system, aiming to *ensure* satisfaction rather than impose it. Turn the issue on its head: instead of trying to architect what must happen in the physical world, try to architect what will happen in the experience world, ensuring that each customer is satisfied, to create both beautifully robust and flexible systems. The heart, a miracle of organic engineering does not guarantee an even pace, even under no-effort conditions. If it did, you would die. One of the first tell-tale symptoms of heart failure is when the pattern of heartbeat turns rigid and constant, for this is unstable. There is a story in Greek mythology of Procrustes, the origin of the procrustean bed. Procrustes was a giant who kept an inn at the top of a hill. He would put his guests in a special bed: if they were too short he would stretch them, and if too tall he would cut off their feet. It is an early picture of totalitarianism. Would it not be easier to design a flexible bed?

Case study 6.1   How a control-oriented culture damages creativity and responsive-ness

1. A financial services company had a promotional pack, offering insurance on loans, which was used with only one change for 10 years. If there had been numerous tests of alternative packs, and if the control had won each time, this would be a testament to design. At it was, there were no tests at all during the period. Even the one change that took place happened for arbitrary reasons.

The problems ran deep into the organization. For example, it was not untypical that when a new idea was put, a senior manager would first object to it until it was

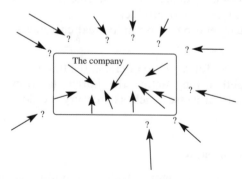

Figure 6.3   Blindness to customer concerns and opportunities

clear that the tide was running with the idea, at which point by a neat side-step, protests would arise that the new idea was already being done and that they had nothing to learn (Figure 6.3). There was a deep and widespread denial and fear of failure, and this was paralleled by competition for power.

Therefore, ideas were not looked at in terms of the opportunity to learn, but as potential threats to the hegemony of the functional barons. This led to a severe poverty in ideas rooted in an unwillingness to look at the problems as they really occurred.

If it is unacceptable and dangerous to acknowledge that something is wrong, then how can the organization ever learn?

2. The politics of power and pressure dominated a high street retailer. It turned out to be notorious for the way it dealt with suppliers. The culture of the organization was to impose unreal deadlines with threats if they were not achieved. This certainly produced frantic activity, but did not lead to considered progress. Activity was aimed at proving that activity was being done.

This extended to contracts with suppliers, including agencies, bureaux and other service businesses. Onerous contracts negotiated on a win–lose paradigm, and linked to price saving pressures, generated neither good will, nor the resource in the supplier to sit back and think, nor the most creative and effective solutions.

The environment led to lack of management continuity. In some cases, management would get out of trouble by moving on before the trouble arrived. In other cases there were casualties, either stress or exits. Short-term targets led to fire fighting which, in turn, meant that individuals were switched about at great speed.

Lack of management continuity meant that projects were not followed through, and managers and employees did not understand the reasons for actions. Commitments were not met. For example, a project to build a marketing database was intended to have three phases. The first was only a prototype, but this was converted into a functioning database in order to satisfy top management. The result was a poor quality, expensive and unconvincing solution.

Changes in tempo, management, priority and the sudden emergence of problems all led to an ongoing stream of changes in the requirements for the database and for the marketing programmes. This was expensive, frustrating to everyone, and damaged the credibility of each instruction. Retail management were cut off from reality by their policy of threats if their instructions were not met on time.

The politics of fear even led one major agency to resign the account.

3. The owner of a hotel chain, having been convinced in a seminar that guarantees are a good thing, decided that his chain would have one. The new guarantee promised to do 'everything possible' to remedy a customer problem. Everything possible is an interesting wording. It sounds like a lot but it can easily turn into a little.

The guarantee stated that if the company could not resolve the problem, the customer stayed free. A good offer. However, it was accompanied by a statement to the hotel managers that *if they were doing their jobs right, then there would be no need to pay out.* If the owner had to pay, managers were not doing their jobs and it was time to get rid of them.

Not surprisingly, the hotel chain was able to brag that they only paid out on two rooms per hotel per year![19]

Threats and weaknesses in the CASM marketplace

Given that the telemarketing, sales management and database marketing solutions largely come from different systems, there is a lack of cross-application function, systems may not communicate well or lack common 'look and feel' characteristics. Awareness of this is growing; vendors are trying to add functions to existing products or are buying up and consolidating products, especially as larger companies enter the pioneering field. A new generation of integrated systems is arriving. On the other hand, the fact that the systems are often bought by different functional barons perpetuates the problem.

The industry is still supplied by many small companies. Most of the 400 or so UK vendors are tiny (< £500 000 annual sales) affecting R&D and resources. The recession of 1989–93 has also affected development. While the US is better served absolutely and relatively, it has not yet reached anything like an ideal status. Yet an immense amount has been achieved since the mid-1980s when the time could be foreseen that every company with an accounting system would have a customer marketing database, and this is an industry that does not take long to mature. Already, perhaps 70–80 per cent of companies in matured markets have at least some kind of system.

Industry weakness is still matched by internal lack of expertise among users and IT staff. IT skills shortage was noted by the British Post Office as a barrier to the development of database marketing in 1989. The skill base is changing, many mistakes, some astonishing, have helped to shape a wiser industry. 'To err is human, but to cock it up completely needs a computer,' is an old and salutary saying. Many first-generation systems will be replaced or already have been replaced. They may have paid for themselves, but they no longer please.

Conclusion

Development is learning. The direct industry has earned itself an unenviable reputation as tacky, but it is a reputation it is seeking to overcome. Its extraordinary success in driving short-term, tactical marketing should not disguise its credentials as the creator and maintainer of long-term value streams. The truth is, it is the culture of the buyers of the services that often needs to be changed. Too many companies are mired in internal feuding, short-term targets and bureaucratic hierarchies. Fortunately, all this is steadily changing and will continue to change in the decades ahead. The challenge now is to learn how to develop an organization culture with long-term vision and a business that is flexible, responsive and directing its energies through the core processes to create and keep long-term value streams from and to our customers. Doing this needs quality information systems and the technologies and skills are now becoming available. The challenge will then be the cultivation of loyalty, which is the subject of the next chapter.

Notes and references

1. Pepper, D. and Rogers, M., *The One to One Future*, Piatkus, 1993.
2. Galbraith, J.K. in *The Affluent Society*, Penguin, 1991.
3. McCarthy, M., *On the Contrary*, Heinemann, 1962.
4. Fromm, E., *Escape from Freedom*, Routledge, 1991.
5. Direct Mail Information Service.
6. Direct Mail Information Service with *Precision Marketing* (19 Oct. 1992).
7. Rosenfield, J.R., 'In the Mail', *Direct Marketing* (March 1994), p. 28.
8. *Positive Response: The Prospects for Direct Mail in the 1990s*, The Henley Centre in association with Ogilvy & Mather Direct, 1991.
9. Merit Direct survey.
10. Roman, K. and Maas, J., *The New How to Advertise*, St Martin's Press, New York, 1992.
11. PSC Survey 1989. Quoted in *Positive Response: The Prospects for Direct Mail in the 1990s*, The Henley Centre, in association with Ogilvy & Mather Direct, 1991.
12. *Direct Marketing International* (May 1993).
13. *Precision Marketing* (7 June 1993).
14. Sculley, J., *Odyssey: Pepsi to Apple*, Fontana, 1989.
15. DePree, M., *Leadership is an Art*, Dell Trade Publishing, New York, 1989.
16. Deming, W.E., *Out of the Crisis*, Cambridge University Press, 1992.
17. 'Computers in marketing' survey by DunnHumby, 1992/3.
18. Mintzberg, H., *Mintzberg on Management*, The Free Press, 1989.
19. This story is quoted by Hart, C.W.L., 'The power of unconditional service guarantees', *Harvard Business Review*, July/Aug. 1988.

7
The nature of loyalty and relationship

Summary   It seems that the main reason we lose the loyalty of customers is that we don't care enough about the relationship. There is not much research on the subject, but what there is confirms this reasonable intuition. One way of retaining loyalty is through reward programmes, and here database marketing is an ideal tool. However, it turns out that there are hidden costs in this strategy and there may be other ways that are at least as effective either as alternatives or as complementary methods. This chapter looks at the psychology of loyalty, which is also at an early stage of development, and explores the nature of brand and the methods of retaining customers.

In a bonus programme, the bonus is the price for the information which I got. I buy knowledge through it, not loyalty, because loyalty is not purchasable.

(Staffen Elinder)

When the great entrepreneur, Marshall Field, was walking one day through his Chicago store he came upon a shop assistant who was arguing with a customer.

'What are you doing?' he asked.

'I'm settling a complaint with this customer,' said the clerk.

'No, you're not. Give the lady what she wants.'

In this way Field coined the phrase that became his company's motto. What customers want is, first, good product, second, an experience that goes with it, some of which comes from price but other parts from personal service, and, third, the means to regain satisfaction when things go wrong. The customer will then be an asset that will appreciate not only as fast as inflation but probably ahead of it.

Why do we lose customers?

Research into the general causes of customer loss is more limited than it should be, although individual companies have research from their own

Table 7.1 Why companies lose customers

	Reason	Percentage
(a)	Death	1
	Customer moves to another town	3
	Competitor wins customer over	5
	Lower prices elsewhere	9
	Unsatisfactory handling of complaints	14
	Lack of interest on the part of the supplier	68
(b)	Move away or die	4
	Personal relationship	5
	Competitor activity	9
	Product dissatisfaction	15
	No contact, indifference, poor attitude	67
(c)	Better product	15
	Cheaper product	15
	Too little contact and individual attention	20
	Quality of attention and service poor	49

Sources:
(a) Swedish Post Office, 1990: *Satsa på kunden (Focus on the Customer)*, Stockholm.
(b) McGraw-Hill Research.
(c) Forum Research, based on 14 major companies.[2]

customers. What there is seems to confirm that customers are up to 'five times more likely to switch vendors because of perceived service problems than for price concerns or product quality issues'[1] (see Table 7.1). Despite this fact, organizations pour enormous energy into countering competitor activity, while maintaining that loyalty programmes cost too much.

Product dissatisfaction accounts for up to 66 per cent of cases of customer migration, hence the worldwide focus on product quality. *Yet around four times more important than product dissatisfaction is the experience of customers of having little or no contact from the supplier, a general feeling of the supplier's indifference or poor attitude, or of poor quality when the effort is made.*

Other research by Cranfield University for Air Miles shows that large spenders, who can be assumed to have higher incomes, seem to be less loyal in supermarkets. Is this natural or is it just that retailers are failing to provide services that meet the higher expectations of this group?

'The sale merely consummates the courtship. Then the marriage beings. How good the marriage is depends on how well the relationship is managed by the seller.'[3] Ted Levitt's classic point is that it is just after a romance is consummated that the danger arises that one party, perhaps the man, feels less need to lavish attention. At precisely the same time, the partner is looking for reassurance. Yet evidence suggest that there is room for improvement. Should we be trying to celebrate more 'feminine' values in our marketing culture?

The ladder to loyalty is frequently shown as a series of steps beginning with awareness and interest until the sale, and then suddenly loyalty is achieved! Actually, considering loyalty to be the next step after selling is at the heart of the flaw in our management of customer relationships, it is no more true to say that courtship is a series of steps leading to marriage, then happiness ever after. The steps to the development of loyalty represent an evolution of mutual commitment (see Figure 7.1) that needs to be developed continuously. These steps can be described as follows and represent, it is proposed, a typical process:

1. An occasional buyer by convenience.
2. A habit buyer: someone/a company who regularly buys by habit and inertia, or absence of choice.
3. An active willingness to seek a company's products, convinced of its superiority in some dimension.
4. A willingness to give feedback in the form of useful complaints.
5. A willingness to recommend the product to someone else.
6. Someone who plans a lifestyle around supplier assumptions.
7. Someone who will be willing to help in product/service design and planning, e.g. WWF have a customer panel in Germany which gives feedback on their mail order trading, and many software companies have user groups.
8. Becoming linked associates: recognizing formal and mutual participation in success – as in many Japanese alliances, or the decision of Apple and IBM to build products together.

Figure 7.1 The ladder to loyalty

The grocer's 24-carrot loyalty knack

Grocers who want to create and sustain lasting relationships with their customers use a number of time-honoured techniques, whose principles cross boundaries. The good community grocer greets his or her customer with a smile and by name: 'Hello Mrs Horobitz, and how are we today?' There may even be a family question: 'And how's your son after his operation?' Produce is good and is laid out openly for display, and in the process of picking the customer's order the grocer would publicly reject anything considered unsuitable and ostentatiously but naturally throw it in the reject bin, in a gesture that says 'I care'. There would be an extra carrot added to the pile after the scale dipped and the right weight had been reached, an open display of natural added value. There might be an occasional treat such as an apricot for a child or a bunch of flowers at Christmas. The grocer would talk cheerfully but not pushily about products: 'I've got a nice lot of new potatoes just in. Would you like to try them?'

The above example demonstrates a number of key principles:

– Acknowledging the person, both as an individual and as a valued customer.
– Having a dialogue that enables warmth and knowledge to be developed.
– Being able to anticipate a reliable relationship, with few problems, which are promptly and courteously dealt with.
– Regular added value as a natural extension of the basic transaction.
– Special attention during relationship development.
– Graceful surprises.

Case study 7.1   How the Vermont Teddy Bear Company adds value and brand personality to its products

The Vermont Teddy Bear Company provides teddy bears of high quality. They offer a guarantee as follows:

> 100% guarantee. What does guaranteed for the life of the bear, mean? As teddy bear makers, we like teddy bears and we love the bears we make.
>
> If you are not happy with the bear for any reason we will refund your money or exchange the bear with no question asked.
>
> If your bear gets hurt in any way, we will fix the bear free of charge.
>
> That means, if your bear gets run over by a truck or the neighbours' kids have a tug of war with it, while sharing a bottle of beaujolais with your bear, he happens to spill some on his chest ..., we will fix him up free of charge for the lifetime of the bear. Since we expect our bears to live a very long time (like for as long as you will live) this is a pretty good guarantee.

The guarantee commentary is matched by other attention to detail in an attempt to personalize and enfriend the relationship. For example, in the company newsletter they explain how you order:

> Once you have picked the appropriate bear category, consider the best size and colour options. Then call us (we pay for the call), send us (you pay for the stamp), or fax us your order (the fax is a confusing machine so we are not sure who pays for what!?).
>
> Now here's what we do. We will get your bear and prepare it for your friend. Next we carefully wrap your bear in tissue and place it in a gift bag along with a card with your special message hand written by our calligraphers Marie and Trecia.
>
> All this is placed in our nifty shipping carton – complete with air hole so your bear can breathe. The last part is making the appropriate travel arrangements to get your bear to its destination on time! It's easy and a lot of fun.

This is not just good copy because it is light, amusing and relaxed. It makes tangible the service they provide. Not only do they give you a special message, but it will be hand written. Not just hand written but hand written by *calligraphers* who are not anonymous but called Marie and Trecia!

They treat the product with serious fun: the bear gets an air hole to breathe, establishing the mood which makes ordering fun. They are putting themselves in the mind of the consumer, who may well be a child (or the child in the adult). To a child's imagination it is not at all surprising that the bear gets an air hole. That kind of empathy is 'touching'.

A gazette or newsletter helps 'to keep in touch' with customers: '*The Teddy Bear News And Information Paper About Interesting Bears And Stuff Around Them That We Think Earth Shaking.*' Not only does it give information about the company and bears, but it is packed with general information, like the fact that it takes 40 years to grow a tree big enough to produce maple syrup (for the bear)!

In the newsletter are the results of the thousands of letters and articles they receive each year from customers, each one a story in itself. Customer letters are printed to provide interesting reading for other customers and continue the dialogue loop. The gazette is carefully timed to take advantage of as many moments of truth as possible, for example Valentine, Thanksgiving or Christmas, or personalized customer information. Direct response radio, with a toll free number has proved successful in generating business and, of course, adds to their accessible image. PR is another obvious and important communication medium and member-get-member. Thousands of thank-you stories testify to trust.

Brand loyalty

One of the most common ways to add value is to differentiate in the mind of the customer. The brand is an imagination, accessing an available personality and projecting it into the world, in the same way that a face does. It then becomes recognizable as an independent personality. One of the earliest to recognize this was Coco Chanel who asked a friend, after creating the classic perfume, 'Is No. 5 a person?'

Brand power can be defined as the ability of the brand personality to positively alter a customer's experience and perception of a product relative to those that he or she would have if the brand source was not known. For example, in a typical study, 51 per cent of customers preferred Pepsi over Coke in blind tasting, while only 23 per cent preferred Pepsi in open tests (i.e. knowing what they were tasting).

A customer's imagination alters the perception of his or her own experience, or, to put it another way, it actually changes his or her experience through the power of creative imagination. Gestalt experiments that we have all done demonstrate this principle: if we expect a form to become a bird, or a cube, then it usually does. In the instant of seeing anything, we slap our concept on the raw experience, the percept. Just as we perceive the outer world, we also perceive our inside world, inner things like feelings or thoughts or memories, and expectations shapes these experiences too.

Brand advertising seeks to build a familiar and favourable image to which we can relate and aspire and against which we measure other products and services. Repeated customer experience then inserts the product inside the customer's world, partly shaping his or her vision and sense of identity, depending on the significance of the product or service. 'Who am I? I am a person who buys Ford' (or Givency or Body Shop). Hence, the nationalistic loyalty to 'our products'. Buy French! is existential. When national product quality lets us down, as the British and Americans have experienced, pride in country and self-esteem is shaken. The status of the things we buy and wear changes our imagined estimation of ourselves, not to mention the estimation of others who project their own similar or different values.

The power of advertising to have this effect is its strength, its magic, its threat to social freedom, its opportunity.

Price led promotions devalue brands and customers

If adding value is the answer to differentiation, then one option is to achieve it by reducing the price. Unfortunately, reducing the price is easier than doing so successfully. Since the acquisition process is the initiator and not an end in itself, the way customers are acquired makes a difference not only to the immediate results but to long-term relationships. Customers who first buy because they like the price deals are customers who will be continually looking for price deals

That is perhaps fine if your company positions itself as an everyday price beater, but as DN Dunlop, founder of what is now the World Energy Council and an initiator of the Confederation of British Industry (CBI), pointed out in 1916:

> The old-established houses are those that have a reputation for trading in reliable goods. Concerns which cater for cheap trade are always more or less ephemeral, for the simple reason that the buyers of cheap commodities are seldom well-established and their existence is precarious. There is always, it is true, a large demand by short-sighted people for inferior goods, but this is a custom that must be constantly sought for it is fickle and uncertain.[4]

Many strong brands have been reduced into commodities by devaluing their image through price cutting. Suncrush, Kia Ora and Jaffa juice all suffered from a switch in the 1960s away from 'pure' juice values. Contrast this with Perrier's growth in brand value through careful husbandry.[5]

The *process* of acquiring new customers should therefore be geared to the pattern of the subsequent relationship, Furthermore, it should be focused on finding customers similar to those who form your natural customer community.

One might think that it is among at least irregular customers that the best chance to upgrade to loyalty occurs. This is often not so, for *irregularity* is then the pattern that needs to change (see Figure 7.2). Research by Ogilvy & Mather Direct[6] found that converting customers whose behaviour is fickle to loyalty may be harder than to switch *loyal* purchasers of another's brand to a new trustworthy partner. (This *does* mean that your brand or service should be superior, or at least perceived superior.) Competitor Loyals were significantly more likely to become regular buyers than Repertoire Purchasers. Furthermore, whereas there was *no* significant change in attitudes among the repertoire purchasers, an effective communication could generate significant attitudinal changes among regular buyers of a competitive brand.

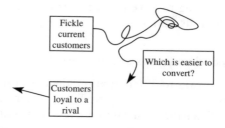

Figure 7.2   What is the best conversion option?

Loyal customers may be hard to win over, but once you do, they are worth the investment.

Of course, it is this opportunity that leads to the silly spiral described in the previous chapter, when organizations divert scare resources to wasteful customer acquisition. There is nothing inherently wrong with acquiring new customers – in fact I have spent much of my career helping my company or clients to do it.

The problem arises when the emphasis on acquisition leads to neglect of the current customers. And the money that many companies spend currently to acquire new customers could be used much more effectively researching and developing upgraded services for their existing customers, as in the American Express Gold Card launch.

Tens of billions of dollars of promotional activity spent on luring new customers is actually wasted. In a major international research project,[7] the effects of large-scale price promotions on the acquisition and retention of new customers *were found to be effectively zero.*

According to the study by Ehrenberg *et al.* of 175 sales promotion peaks across 25 leading grocery products in four countries (US, UK, western Germany, Japan), the average 'before to after' repeat level was virtually identical. Basically the effect was as if the promotion had not occurred.

In another study, Abraham and Lodish also found that new customers due to a promotion were small or non-existent for most situations.[8] According to the Ehrenberg research, customers may be attracted by a bargain but only if they are already familiar with the brand. Some customers watch for the opportunity to choose a promoted brand from among a portfolio of brands that they are willing to buy, or irregular customers will buy at promotion time. Generally speaking, customers do not switch loyalty to a brand just because it is on promotion. There may be a short-term lift in sales among customers who already buy the product, but no long-term effects. It seems that extra sales generated by large price cuts do not recover the full costs. If the intention is to reward regular buyers through price reduction, then it would seem that there should be a more effective way of giving value.

Familiarity is the key to willingness to purchase: the essence of branding, as Ehrenberg points out. This is a justification for advertising, and even stronger support for the cultivation of *repeat buying as a loyalty device.*

Why are private or own label brands gaining over the manufacturers of national brands? The reason is partly because supermarkets are building up their own tradable brand reputation, supported by regular custom, and partly because national brands have traded down, often giving the supermarket any real kudos that goes with the discount. After all, was it not the supermarket that gained this for the customer?

The secret of profitable customer acquisition is not to find new bargain-sensitive customers, but to seek and reward loyal ones. However, even this is wasteful unless your operating method encourages loyalty. The solution is simple: raise customer expectations, and meet them. Then periodically do it again.

The consumer's loyalty (business or private) is simply not for sale. It can not be bought for ever by coupons or deals. Real brand loyalty results from an emotional bond created by trust, dialogue, frequency, ease of use and a sense of value and added satisfaction. Loyalty is the reflection of a consumer's subconscious emotional and psychological need to find a *constant* source of value, satisfaction and identity.

In a world of change, we all need to find stillness.

How to generate loyalty

There are many ways to retention and loyalty. (Below, a discussion on the psychology of loyalty and the contrast between loyalty and retention is indicated.) Beginning with good products and services, loyalty can be developed by habit, by a simple contract such as a subscription, built by affinities or affiliations such as membership, developed by gaining commitments that are legal or moral pledges to purchase an agreed-upon minimum number of products, or it can be won from the consumer's ongoing expectation of satisfaction from excellent products or services backed by a pledge of quality and supported by superior reputation.

Cross-selling another product keeps contact and awareness foremost in your mind. Having a good range of products reduces the need to go elsewhere. Convenience helps. When a supermarket leaves out just one specialist, slow-selling brand they strip away another special reason to shop there, leaving only the ordinary and mundane. Range can be service. That's one reason why businesses can succeed with catalogues, as they enable huge ranges to be offered, which is especially useful in business-to-business marketing. Nationwide Value Added Distributors, described in the next chapter, have a catalogue of 25 000 office items!

Communication is essential. The use of customer magazines or newsletters is increasing for consumers and business to business; for example, it grew 152 per cent in the UK over the five years to 1991 – the newsletter cited in Case study 7.1 is one example. Thousands of retailers, travel companies, high tech businesses, financial service companies and industrial businesses make use of the idea. In the Netherlands, customer magazines represent 10.3 per cent of total marketing spend according to the Association of Publishing Agencies, the trade body. This, therefore, represents the possible potential in a mature market.

Communication can also be critical at particular times in the relationship: when there is a major new entrant into the market, at times of life change, or around critical moments in the relationship. Huggies communicated by sending a new nappy when there was a danger of leakage developing from too small a size. The South African mining company's defence was cited earlier. In a similar vein, Glaxovet developed a powerful marketing campaign when its 25-year near monopoly with its product Dictol, a preventative treatment for lungworm in cattle, was threatened. Farmers bought Dictol via injections by vets, and a direct mail campaign was targeted to new and existing users – the former receiving an offer of a video tape showing the effect of lungworm on the lungs and a mailing with a generally more emotionally charged tone. Existing users were reminded of their participation and the benefits, appealing to their rational good sense. Both groups were incentivized to fill in a form which then generated a complete specification of requirements/order to be taken to their local vet. At the same time, the information was added to the existing bank of knowledge and provided to the salesforce, enabling them to visit and brief the vets in detail, thus adding to their professionalism. Only 8 per cent of the market was lost, which was a fraction of the possible damage.

Loyalty programmes are mushrooming and aim to improve contact and communication while communicating thanks in rewards. Some, however, are quite dull. For example, most airlines send a mountain of complex information to frequent fliers, but a busy executive (anyone who qualifies as a frequent flier is likely to be a busy executive) is almost certain to feel hassled at having to read so much material before discovering what the benefits actually are, although they are usually appreciated. The British Midland programme manual is 40 pages long, including a total of 10 pages of technical and legal material. Many of these pages consist of a repetition of the same data, for example listing virtually identical offers from Hilton International and SAS International hotels, but each is allocated its own page, in full detail. There are small differences, but you need to *search* for them. Even if it is decided that each partner company needs its own page to preserve its own discrete brand image, it would make sense to at least provide some kind of simple summary. Updates continue the problem with no attempt to personalize new information according to usage patterns. British Airways provides various services, including emergency help, chauffeur to airport and others. Why do they not put just one number on the executive card? All the other numbers get lost in the mass of material.

Simplicity is itself a service.

Root cause analysis: *why* do we lose customers?

The starting point, therefore, must be to look carefully to find the holes down which the customer base is leaking, as well as what customers value. Organizations can only get to the bottom of their problems, and therefore on top of relationship management, by finding the root cause of problems. Why do things really happen? *Why are we losing our customers?* The problem is that it requires a rather uncomfortable view of the business.

Really effective root cause analysis depends on what Argylis calls double-loop learning: understanding not only what appears to be the direct cause of the problem, but also *the cause of the cause* – the real substrate problem, not the apparent one. The first layer tells us what is not liked. The second tells us how it got there and how to get rid of it. TGI Friday's big step forward came when they realized that when management blamed competition or the local economy for sales problems, the real secret was to take a hard look inside, as CEO Daniel Scoggin put it. By the time they had fixed the checklist of problems they identified, the problems with sales had usually disappeared.[9] Toyota sales staff in the Corolla division meet together for one day each month, and instead of puffing up their egos by celebrating supposed success, they spend the day doing root cause analysis to overcome problems.

Unfortunately, to achieve this we have to overcome our inherent defensiveness and fear of failure, one reason Deming insists that driving out fear is one of the key tasks for a successful organization (see Topic 6.2 in Chapter 6). Paradoxically perhaps, the more we want to find the truth, the less can we afford to be punitive. (This is developed in Chapter 9.) Quality tools that are helpful in developing root cause analysis include techniques such as force field analysis, cause and effect diagrams, the 5 Why's, and more, are described in Chapter 15.

Let your customers tell you what to do and what to measure.

Anticipating and solving problems through dialogue

TARP discovered that in two of every three cases in which the customer had a complaint about a product, the problem was not related to the product but was caused by the user not understanding how to use it.[10] Here is precisely an example of how database marketing can serve, overcome problems, and possibly build opportunities for further sales. Why not call to check, or at least make it easy for customers to call you?

It can also help to identify the real needs of customers. We expect the supplier to be an expert in his or her products and to be able to bring that expertise to bear to anticipate and remove problems in advance. But, many organizations labour under assumptions about what is critical to customers, which prove to be quite wrong. An Austrian shirt manufacturer discovered that its retail customers' priorities were finish, delivery and image, not full order fulfilment, flexibility and meeting the specification, as it thought.[11] Some hospitals in Britain's National Health Service have been accused of failing to take the customer seriously. Doctors thought that the clinical quality of their work was all that mattered while patients worried about delays, beds, comfort, food and privacy.

Database marketing lends itself to the dialogue of learning. A customer panel or association (a way of working proposed by Rudolf Steiner just after the First World War), such as WWF's cited above, is just one way to work on issues of service and performance and can provide the means for valued feedback. Group 1 Software, a Washington company that is the world's leader in deduplication software, meets with its customer panel twice each year, as well as having regular dialogue.

Knowing who you service is the beginning: who they are, what they buy and when (and when they do not). This is the basis for the responsive company getting to know its most valuable market: its business community. Researching your own customers intensively is more important than finding out about the customers of others. Trying to serve too many customers with conflicting needs can cause a situation in which no customers are served well.

Topic 7.1   Diagnosing values in the product

In Chapter 1, Maslow's hierarchy of needs was used to develop organization quality. It may also be used to identify the nature of customer expectations and the corresponding product profile (see Figure 7.3). Customer expectations of a service will orient more towards 'lower' security and survival requirements, such as distress purchases, problem solving, remedial work, essential and routine needs, or more towards 'higher' values of esteem and self-expression. These could include fun, enjoyment, learning, feel-good, exploring and sharing experiences. We buy an antique for a different reason or set of reasons to a utility chair. A Big Mac has a different profile to a meal in London's Langan's Brasserie. Context, however, is also important. A young couple may buy used furniture but be involved in asserting a new paired independence and self-expression.

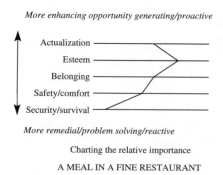

More enhancing opportunity generating/proactive

Actualization
Esteem
Belonging
Safety/comfort
Security/survival

More remedial/problem solving/reactive

Charting the relative importance

A MEAL IN A FINE RESTAURANT

Figure 7.3   Maslow's hierarchy applied to service

Amex Gold Card offered a product with lots of esteem and some belonging. Ten years later new notions of esteem, after the boom-time 1980s, seem to apply. The product adapts appropriately.

As a rule of thumb, communications need to match the value levels of the customer and product, suggesting an opportunity to rise up the scale while reassuring that lower needs will still be securely met.

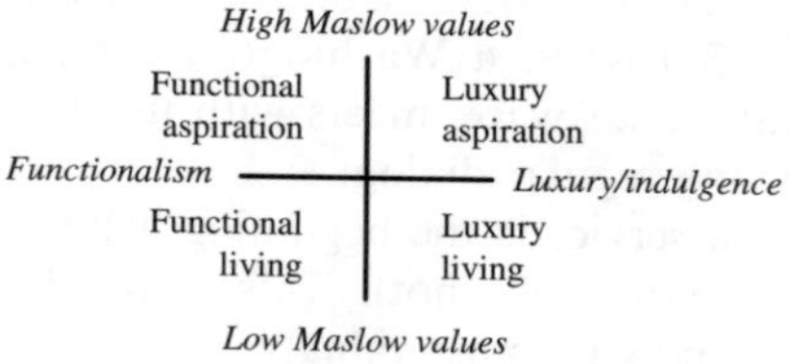

High Maslow values

Functional aspiration	Luxury aspiration
Functionalism ———	——— *Luxury/indulgence*
Functional living	Luxury living

Low Maslow values

Figure 7.4   Product values map

We may also identify a basic dichotomy between functional products – i.e. they do the job without any fancy, unnecessary extras – and discretionary, luxury, indulgent, celebratory products.

Combining the two polarities – the Maslow chart with functional/indulgence – gives a product values map (Figure 7.4), a typology of quality which divides products into four broad sets, for example:

– Functional aspiration: e.g. Mercedes, theatre, Open University course, cultural holiday, Marks & Spencer.
– Functional living: e.g. utilities, TV rental, supermarkets.
– Luxury living, e.g. Escort turbo, the cinema, stress workshop, security system, home help.
– Luxury or discretionary aspiration: e.g. BMW, charities, Niemann Marcus, Harrods.

Communities and clubs

As discussed earlier, any organization has its own natural customer community. This seems to be a more useful concept than a customer base (which is rather anaemic) or a market (which is rather anonymous). One potentially useful test is, to what extent can the customer base be recognized as a community and how far does it feel this community quality? Of course, an organization may serve more than one community, and it may well decide to appeal to a new one (although it is of critical importance that it does not do so at the expense of its core group).

When the United States Postal Service wanted to broaden its base of stamp collectors by appealing to a new, younger and more casual saver segment, they turned to the Elvis Community of Supporters. *First,* they designed and produce Elvis-related products, especially stamps. *Then* they mailed 700 000 people who had already either purchased an Elvis stamp or registered an interest in doing so: developing, not initiating relationship. The programme was designed to promote additional Elvis-related commemoratives and stamps in the Elvis series and *to enhance the value of saving Elvis stamps.* It received a 22.65 per cent response rate at a cost of $1.84

each. More than 3.6 million take-ones were placed in lobbies and gained a 3 per cent response, and a further 3.13 per cent response was obtained from the 25 000 information request forms used. In total the revenue generated was 25 times the promotion costs.

Clubs are an attempt to build this loyalty factor. Britain's International Royal Mail launched Business Portfolio club in 1989 aimed at 200 000 small company users of international mail with a welcome pack and quarterly newspaper, getting a 25 per cent response to offers, 15 per cent response to recruitment and around 79 per cent awareness in the community. Their aim was to position the Royal Mail as a full service to the business community and not just as a commodity carrier.

Efferm launched a club for cat and dog owners, building a multi-million customer pan-European database. The Whiskas magazine tries to cultivate a relationship, and for their higher value Sheba products, beautiful, sentimental, images aim to develop relationship based on shared attitudes. Direct mail was cheaper than advertising in reach per owner.

Most major chains now offer some sort of frequent stay programme. In general, members appear to be willing to pay more per night for a hotel room than non-members.[12]

Customer satisfaction is the worldwide No. 1 goal of Toyota! To demonstrate exclusivity to owners, Lexus provides special exclusive purchase offers such as a balloon trip and overnight stay, with gourmet five-course meal and champagne. A massive 54 per cent of owners called for information. They gave a personalized bottle of Beaujolais Primeur on the first day of the season, a watch with the correct time set at the winter–summer switch, saying 'We are ahead of time, and you are too'. When zip codes changed, they sent stickers with new codes before the date change.

The Huggies and Saga magazines also built a club. Portland Holidays has an informal club for a very special group of mature customers who rush to a particular hotel in Spain each year where the sense of camaraderie and friendship of staff re-enforces loyalty. To reinforce this, Portland now fly the manager, chef and some waiters to Britain each year, open on a Sunday and write to their regulars to invite them to come, book, and enjoy a champagne breakfast and morning get together. So keen were their customers to be 'first' that some were queuing *from 3 a.m.: mature* citizens! So now, they open even earlier. In the afternoon, the club holds a tea-dance in a local hotel.

Within the current customer base there are probably people or organizations who are not really part of your natural community but who were attracted at some point as a result of activities that induced them to buy. They may not be loyal; they may not be profitable; they may even have been acquired through some business acquisition. It may be that a part of the business or one or more of the brands can be positioned to meet their needs and to establish a fruitful relationship. But in the absence of such repositioning, the crucial step is to identify the regular buyers, cultivate them and seek more of the same.

The role and challenge of intermediaries

Intermediaries exist in many markets, e.g.

- retailers for FMCG
- brokers for insurance
- agents for holidays
- dealers for loans.

Do companies try to bypass them or work with them, or both? This depends on the opportunities, the nature of the openness in the relationship and the relative power of database and customer relationship values. It also depends on the degree of trust or mistrust in the culture of management.

Intermediaries can certainly disrupt the level of intimacy and direct connection between the provider and user. They can get rich by doing very little. On the other hand, they may own the opportunity to develop intimate relationships and may be an important gearing in service delivery. Many companies outsource specialist processes. Is this not the task of the intermediary? In that case, how can the manufacturer support this and make it a more effective and trusting partnership? Some examples were given in Chapter 2.

Many direct companies want to shift customer relationships from personal contact with a salesperson, broker or agency to a relatively impersonal direct sales business using the telephone and letter. That is a double-edged sword. It means an increase in human contact and/or dependability in the new channel. Direct human contact adds to the subjective element: both the risk of complaint and potential for loyalty. A club is one way that companies try to establish the 'neighbourliness' that direct contact with intermediaries *might* give.

How loyalty development goes beyond win–lose thinking

A community is a group of people who share something in common and this cannot be founded directly on competitiveness (although individuals who compete in a spirit of mutual emulation and development do gain great respect for each other). Traditional buyer–seller relationships were frequently adversarial or combative. The new paradigm emphasizes the value of partnership. Most of the emphasis for this is coming from customers looking for a new way of working with their suppliers, but many sellers are gradually accepting the same idea. The trend in business-to-

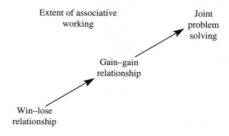

Figure 7.5   The developing buyer–supplier relationship[12]

business is towards the creation of 'Joint Problem Solving' where customer/supplier work together to achieve objectives. This is a high-value service relationship and achieves greater loyalty (see Figures 7.1 and 7.5).

Although the idea that a seller might want to achieve a partner relationship seems obvious, the fact is that it is not the dominant ideology and many sales and marketing people have been weaned on a culture of win–lose thinking which can only be overcome slowly and carefully: but it works. Highland Appliance, a US retail group, has turned away from the dominant perception of salespeople as commissioned pugilists by advertising itself as a place where customers will get unbiased information from non-commissioned salespeople, thereby trying to win the customer's trust.

The Co-operative Movement is an excellent example of a company founded in association with its own customers out of a shared social situation and need, solving problems together, rewarding customers for their shopping loyalty and meeting an aspirational need, to break free from the bonds of the company store and build worker independence. Even today, Britain's Co-operative Bank, although in a niche position, is one of only two banks to earn top marks from customers for satisfaction and referral rate and is, like First Direct (the other bank), a major database and telemarketing user.

Psychology of loyalty, rewards and the *archetypal moment*

What is loyalty? We recognize it when we feel it, but it is not easy to clarify what it is. Loyalty can be described as the 'willingness to retain and feel commitment to another because of duty or trust'.

There is an argument that businesses need only concern themselves with retention, or even that retention is in some respects more advanced than loyalty. It is true that for financial and many practical purposes retention is most important and is also most easily measurable. This, however, does not mean that loyalty as a force should be ignored. Clarks Shoes is a British institution. For generations children have been shod by Clarks, parents valuing the care that goes into good fittings for growing feet. But, when the children become young men and women and begin to make their own decisions, they move away from a brand associated with parental choice (at least for a few years). Interestingly, however, this same group, as parents, return to get shoes for their own children. Research suggests a deep and residual loyalty, and trust is carried forward. The essence of loyalty is beyond mere retention because now there is an active commitment and even a willingness to forgive, or, in the spirit of Figure 7.5, to give advice and feedback, to become a partner.

A proposal is therefore given for a model of loyalty and retention (see Figure 7.6 on page 127).

In the next chapter, methods of achieving loyalty are developed. Models of the assessment of service quality are also relevant here (see *Quality of Service, Making it Really Work* in this series by Bo Edvardsson, Bertil Thomasson and John Øvretveit, pages 75–111). What follows are a few key points.

Loyalty is influenced by what people *think, feel* and *do*. We are most conscious of what we think (perceive, imagine) and least conscious in our doing or willing. What eventually determines our loyalty, or the lack of it, is the 'archetypal moment,' or moments that we would call to mind about a company, the inner mental picture of the company, or its products and services, *and how we feel about this*. It may be determined by a particular powerful memory (if there is no particular archetypal moment, or no picture al all, loyalty will be weak). The archetypal moment may be:

- Do not know them
- An advertising/brand image
- A good or bad experience, typically a deed that was done by someone in the company, and the feeling it engenders
- A picture of a regular routine experience, simply part of the fabric of life, giving comfort (or beginning to bore).

We may picture a company's resources or products, the way the company works, i.e. the process of using or buying, the interpersonal, human side or its image and values, what it stands for, its identity. As a result, we may feel trusting, comfortable, or angry and disappointed. We feel known and acknowledged, or anonymous as part of a machine. We may feel we owe a debt after some act of grace, or effort, or after a series of rewards, or that we are owed a debt after a disappointment. We may assess the product well, but be unhappy about some aspect of the service or situation. Out of such material is loyalty created or destroyed.

The fact that satisfaction scores are weakly correlated with loyalty has already been mentioned. Why is this so? First, it has been found that positive and negative feelings (affects) can and do co-exist. Positive and negative feelings are not a bipolar continuum but two unipolar conditions.[14] So a consumer may feel good about a company but also dislike one aspect of the service. Feelings (or affects) are states of being and we can imagine a multi-dimensional psychological space in which attention can move from one place to another, so becoming aware of different feelings. These are not weighed against each other or totted up on a ledger: they co-exist.

So a satisfied customer in one realm can also be unhappy, and a dissatisfied customer can still buy.

Furthermore, if we look at a taxonomy of feelings (affects) we can identify those which are positive, those which are negative and one which is neural. (Table 7.2 indicates a taxonomy which has proved effective, although 'joy' is used as rather a rich concept which includes affects which are arguably independent, such as 'trust'.)

Among the negative feelings are those directed at the *situation* (like distress and fear) and those which are *self-directed*. For example, the feeling of guilt is directed at oneself: e.g. 'It's my fault, I didn't look after it properly.' Only certain feelings that are directed immediately at the causal agent, i.e. the company, its products or services. Only these would be included in a rational assessment of satisfaction. However, other negative emotions can and will be displaced and projected into future decisions to buy and can lead to defection. It is not the restaurant's fault that your partner chose to tell you over dinner one day that he was leaving you, but now you never want to eat there again!

Studies of satisfaction show that, 'Satisfaction is not the pleasurableness of the [consumption] experience ... it is the evaluation rendered that the experience was at least as good as it was supposed to be.'[15] Satisfaction is an evaluated condition which arises during a two stage process. It is summarized in the study by Westbrook (1987)[14] as: *consumption outcome → affect → satisfaction*. This study also showed that feelings, which may be less conscious (and which are described by one researcher as primitive and naive[16]) are more powerful drivers of word of mouth recommendations and future buying decisions than satisfaction, perhaps because of those very conditions. In fact, recent scientific studies are only now recognizing[17] what is obvious to many: the important role of feeling and emotion in judgement and decision forming.

In Figure 7.6, beliefs about the product lead to use and actual experience realized. These are compared with what the consumer expected as an outcome and converted into a satisfaction rating. However, satisfaction does not lead directly to future decisions to buy. These arise again out of feelings, shaped by beliefs about the product and memory as well as conditions prevailing at the time (Am I hungry? Is there a convenient store? What's my bank balance like?). In fact, feelings may influence which

Table 7.2 Taxonomy of feeling (affective) experience

Fundamental affect/feeling	Nature of subjective experience	Valence
Interest	Engaged, attentive, caught-up, curious, fascinated; when intense, a feeling of excitement and animation	Positive
Joy	Sense of confidence and significance; feeling loved and lovable; a good relationship to the object of joy	Positive
Agent/company directed		
Anger	Hostility, desire to attack the source of anger, physical power, impulsiveness	Negative
Disgust	Feelings of revulsion; impulses to escape from or remove the object of disgust from proximity to oneself	Negative
Contempt	Superiority to other people, groups, or things; hostility (mild); prejudice; coldness and distance	Negative
Situation directed		
Distress	Sadness; discouragement, downheartedness; loneliness and isolation; feeling miserable; sense of loss	Negative
Fear	Apprehension to terror, depending on intensity; sense of imminent danger; feeling unsafe; slowed thought; tension	Negative
Self directed		
Shame	Suddenly heightened self-consciousness, self-awareness; feelings of incompetence, indignity, defeat; in mild form, shyness	Negative
Guilt	Gnawing feelings of being in the wrong, 'not right' with others or self	Negative
Surprise	Fleeting sense of interruption of ongoing thought; brief uncertainty; amazement and startle	Neutral

Source: Izard, C.E., *Human Emotion*, Plenum Press, New York, 1977.

memories occur.[18] In other words, when we are angry, we are more likely to remember other negative things about the product or company.

Of course, some decisions are made with considerable rational input. This is particularly true in business-to-business marketing where the decision process tends to be more formalized and involves multiple individuals and

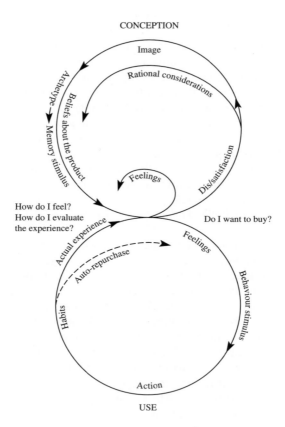

CONCEPTION

Image

Rational considerations

Archetype

Memory stimulus

Beliefs about the product

Feelings

Dis/satisfaction

How do I feel?
How do I evaluate
the experience?

Do I want to buy?

Actual experience

Feelings

Auto-repurchase

Habits

Behaviour stimulus

Action

USE

Figure 7.6 Loyalty process model

organizational specifications. Even here though, feelings of confidence, warmth, fear, etc., often influence decisions. Even in the most intellectual process, there is a final judgement: does it feel right? Einstein would judge a theorem on feelings, for example by its beauty. The 'feel good' factor is now a recognized force in political processes and the economy.

At the other pole, many buying 'decisions' are made with little or no real conscious involvement. The classic example is the direct debit donation or gas bill. Enumerable purchases are made out of habit and many companies rely on these for retention. Just as we may make a conscious decision to buy something, or we can react according to a sudden mood or feeling and go out and buy, we can also respond at a level which is largely impulse. Habits are patterns of support in our lives which remove the need to think. Familiarity is essentially a construct of habit. Image advertising tries to generate this through repeated exposure of images and the corresponding mental activity.

The mental picture which leads to a purchase decision may also be shaped by the effort involved. Convenience is a powerhouse of choice and action as every mail order marketer knows. Buying decisions may therefore be made which are *pre-conscious* (we buy out of impulse before we are really aware) or *post-conscious* (they have become habit).

Active loyalty involves the customer being *willing to seek* out a particular service location (e.g. a shop) and/or brand. For example, a customer may choose a shop because it sells a particular product, or may give up a product in order to shop in a particular store. By contrast, passive loyalty tends to be more motivated by impulse, convenience and habit. If *the conditions are right, then the customer will buy the product*. Therefore, making it easy makes sense, as in the case of Bell's *Yellow Page Directory*, or AT&T World Plus (Case study 7.2).

Bell wanted to keep more customer advertising in their directory. One problem they found was the hassle that small businesses experienced in compiling an advertisement that they liked, so they sent customers samples to inspect. A computer program produced a fully personalized directory page accurate in size, type and style with a personalized cover letter from the salesperson. There were 98 variables that could change with each letter or directory page. Bell printed five different variations of the customer's potential advertisement using different style, size and copy features to show alternatives and make it easy to choose and order. Production was done automatically by laser printing, so the system provided a complete and convenient personalized process. The salespeople followed up as needed.

Database marketing can aid this ease of use/familiarity factor by generating time-tied communications, such as follow-ups on a seasonal or other basis, or simply by making relevant communication with and presenting information to the customer. The contact itself can reinforce the relationship.

With regularly repeated, similar transactions, habit comes to the fore; but explore opportunities to add personalized service, thus making each experience more distinctive and encouraging more conscious ego-to-ego bonding.

Case study 7.2   AT&T WorldPlus

Often the problem is getting started. When AT&T launched its WorldPlus service in Europe, an international/local set of telephone services for the traveller, billed to an account, it followed an exemplary route. First it found a partner that its typical members could trust: American Express. By using American Express it acquired a list of the right kind of customers to write to (of course, the letter came from Amex), and working with Amex made it easy to handle billing and payment: it just goes on the card. Then there was a telephone follow-up to confirm that the first year's service was free: nothing need be done but say, 'Yes please'. That dealt with the inertia factor. There was then a mailing to people who did not immediately use the new service, offering an incentive/reward simply for using the service in the weeks before Christmas. Those who did will then have found how easy it was with even a voice recognition service for the no-tone phone.

Only with a database do we know if a purchase is regularly repeated. Only then can we ask questions like, 'If not, why not? Is there really a low repeat factor or is this a lack of marketing follow through? What opportunities are there to upgrade or cross-sell?' Microsoft (and Lotus) developed huge reputations and business selling packages across many users. However, for a long time, there was limited effort to cultivate any real relationship. All the available energy went into product development. They did not talk to customers, and hardly recognized their existence. Microsoft has now announced its intention to appoint an outside agent across Europe for its relationship management services. It seems obvious that there will now be a growth in these specialist relationship service companies.

The more the product or service has become a feature of positive image, feeling and behaviour patterns, the more likely that we will be truly loyal. At this point the supermarket becomes 'my store', the salon, 'my hairdresser', the computer company 'our supplier': all of which are identified with the affect of *joy* in Table 7.2. In all cases, the customer begins to identify with the brand and feels a sense of ownership.

Topic 7.2   Are all motivations the same? A taxonomy of motivations

An extraordinary interesting account, in rather difficult language, of the seven choice-shaping processes in people was given by the philosopher–psychologist Rudolf Steiner. He described a seven-step series of motivational forces by which the will to particular decisions and actions is influenced, from the imposed instinct common to animals to the delicate choices we make at destiny cross-roads, like meeting people and falling in love (see Table 7.3).

Of these seven, people are generally only really *conscious* for everyday purposes of three – wishes, motives and desires – although all play a part. These are the three that are most influenced and influenceable in daily life and interaction. Impulses shape countless, more instinctual, transactions, some by habit, some by human nature. Habits can become quite subconscious, as in driving to work without remembering having done so.

Table 7.3 Choice shapers, after Steiner

Action decider	Quality
Resolutions	Destiny crossroad
Intentions	Lifeshaper
Wishes	Aspiration
Motives	Ego choices
Desires	Conscious pleasure searching
Impulses	Inner drive
Instincts	Stamped

Source: Steiner, R., *Study of Man*, RSP, 1981.

Desires are similar to the need for comfort in Maslow, and ego choices are decisions like who or what to associate with, based on strong personal identification, a conscious decision to connect and be loyal rather than merely passive behaviour.

How do benefits and *rewards* that are provided contribute to this? These could include frequent flyer points, free 10 per cent extra, priority check-in, etc. Rewards and function have some capacity to meet a customer's search for pleasure, satisfaction and a sense of reciprocated appreciation; they may contribute to a real or pseudo-rational judgement ('A gives me points and B doesn't') and future anticipation of good times.

Rewards have clearly had a very powerful effect and do, certainly, generate huge quantities of business. American Express lifted sales by 20 per cent or more in certain markets with its Membership Miles scheme and Air Miles has similar proven success with clients. The limits of their effectiveness are discussed below. The more powerful the rewards, the more powerfully it will affect the brand, for good or ill.

Branding, through the world of imagery and personality, creates a 'being' with which the customer can identify: it generates a mental picture which determines familiarity, beliefs and feelings about the brand. The power of the Pepsi advertising in the 1960s/early 1970s ('... the Pepsi Generation') was its link to the values of the new generation of youngsters. There *was* a real new generation. The very fact that Pepsi were not the big establishment brand actually helped them. Brand values generated by imagery are reinforced when demonstrated in action. A customer who admires the values of the organization or product is more likely to develop active loyalty than if simply responding to an attractive image.

Developing real 'loyalty', however, means developing in customers at least an ego-based choice, a conscious and chosen decision to connect, to identify with an aspect of the brand, linked to the individual's own aspirational or developmental urge. In this sense, 'loyalty' is not the same as repeated passive purchase, it will be more robust to price and other new awareness factors.

As an IBM salesforce at the end of the 1970s, early 1980s, our team talked about how 'people do business with people'. It was the social interaction that ultimately made the difference to loyalty. This ego-to-ego bonding shapes much loyalty and is the reason that companies must, in Faith Popcorn's words, 'wrap their products in their company's soul and ethics',[19] thereby coming alive as people and not just as faceless, bureaucratic machines. 'Loyalty' in this case is personal trust, the most powerful of feelings, and it is and should be a joyful experience (not a points generating grind).

Do rewards generate loyalty?

There has been very little research on the effect of reward mechanisms on customer loyalty. As noted, reward systems such as points towards miles or redeemable stamps have changed behaviours. Green Shield Stamps were a powerful pioneer programme and millions of households avidly collected them. So successful are points programmes, on one level, that tens of thousands of firms have turned to one or other variant. The marketing press has announcements weekly of new points schemes.

Bay 6, a specialist UK DIY chain, has a plastic loyalty card scheme. The card fits on a key ring and has a bar code which can be swiped by the EPOS till. The leading UK airport business, BAA, targets its frequent fliers with a points loyalty scheme designed to increase sales in the shops and duty free sites at its airports. Ansells pubs offered customers a plastic swipe card which they can use when buying food. They receive points on joining and each subsequent purchase gains further points.

Partnership or consortium loyalty schemes in the UK include Premier Points, operated by catalogue retailer Argos since 1988, an Air Miles Programme has been in operation since 1988, American Express Membership Miles since 1993, and soon to be launched, AT&T, targeting 8 million consumers. Air Miles have been collected by 15 per cent (3.75 million customers) of UK households and 500 000 people used Air Miles to travel free in 1993.

At the same time, we see schemes being abandoned or cancelled, which sometimes is not surprising. Do vouchers for odds and ends of household items not relevant to the base product enhance and add value to the brand or divert attention towards extrinsic factors? Customers will have to carry a briefcase for all the loyalty cards they need – which is one good reason for a consortium that can offer more power and simplicity. The strengths and weaknesses of loyalty schemes should be considered.

What is not at issue is anything that promises a commitment to real added value within the scope of the core product. All evidence shows that this adds sales. However, many schemes are simply grafting an incentive or enticement onto the core product. Rewards may be more *intrinsic* or more *extrinsic* to the product. Intrinsic benefits contribute more positively to the brand and image by reinforcing it. Extrinsic benefits are those that do not have a high affinity with the core product concept. They are, particularly, benefits that do not become naturally embedded within the core product configuration (see Chapter 8).

For example, the ability to obtain a china mug if you buy enough petrol is probably an extrinsic benefit, and the grocer's extra carrot an intrinsic one. Intrinsic benefits are those that are perceived, consciously or unconsciously, as a further extension or aspect of the base product or service. Free champagne on first-class travel becomes an intrinsic part of the product. Extra miles with a business class ticket could also be an intrinsic part of the product.

Case study 7.3   Intrinsic and extrinsic bonuses

Should NatWest Bank, Britain's largest retail bank, be concerned that the Air Miles it gives on credit cards will be perceived as an extrinsic benefit (which it is)? One route is research, but the results of the research may only tell you how well you are using the tool. A credit card is a convenient way of paying, and a means to the good times that people seek. If it conveniently gives you the bonus of a holiday, this is easily linked to a credit card and NatWest brand values.

NatWest's concern could imprison the programme as an extrinsic benefit. Instead, they could send a personal note saying, 'This is how many points you've had so far in total, hope you enjoyed them, that's what we're here for, and thanks for the custom.' In fact there is only a current balance, and even that is being moved, at the time of writing, onto a generic Air Miles statement.

The aim should be to internalize the benefit so that it becomes an intrinsic part of the product/brand. Then the claim can be: 'We're the people who brought you. . . . In that case, before choosing a reward, figure out if you are happy for it to become part of the product specification.'

The provision of extrinsic reward systems is an extension of the prevailing culture. Children, for example, both at school and in the home, are often induced to behaviours through various reward and punishment mechanisms, based on a populist behavioural model, as are salespeople. This paradigm is now being increasingly challenged.

The research that has been emerging, particularly over the last 20 years, indicates that rewards (punishments are not so relevant here!) can and do change behaviour, but only as long as they are sustained. In 1972, two believers set out to prove the principle that rewards such as privileges or treats could generate permanent change. Their conclusion, which was backed up by more detailed research 10 years later by one of the members, Alan Cazdin, showed that *removal of the rewards leads to a decline in desirable responses and a return to baseline levels of performance.*[20]

Furthermore, research has shown that rewards can even lead to a negative attitude. Little research has been done in an organizational context, although Professor Ehrenberg's results quoted above showed a null or negative effect from price promotions. In studies of children playing maths games, of individuals deciding to lose weight, to quit smoking, or to use seat belts, there has been confirmation each time that rewards can induce behavioural changes but these have no lasting duration. Lewin, who was the founder of modern psychology, considered that rewards and punishments are used to elicit 'a type of behaviour which the natural field forces of the moment will not produce'. In other words, if we translate this to the commercial environment, rewards can generate sales which the natural product would not generate, *but only for as long as the rewards are provided.*

The problem with reward systems is that they do not reach deep enough into the human being. They can affect behaviour, but how do you change attitude? Affecting behaviour can be useful: if that means more sales, then few organizations would have objections. The problem is that the generation of those sales carries a down side. There is no such thing as a free lunch. If you want to change not only what people do, but also how they feel about you and what they think about you – in other words, if you want to change the brand and identity values – then something different or extra is needed. The most recent major study on the subject by Alfie Kohn[21] suggests that rewards actually damage relationships.

The first problem with reward systems is that they prevent you asking the fundamental question: Why? Why are customers not buying from you? Why can the children not get to sleep at night? Only by identifying the root causes of the problem will you have the opportunity to have the fundamental changes that will affect attitudes and ideas. The reward mechanism can operate like the painkiller that disguises the athlete's growing injury until it is too late.

Furthermore, if the relationship is forged on the premise that you are providing a reward, then it presumes the concept of a reward giver and a reward receiver. The danger is that reward receivers can feel that they are being controlled and manipulated. Rewards, after all, are promoted as a controlling principle by the behaviourists. When large organizations adopt them, they risk, in the extreme, being seen as a power player that the small business should try to challenge or take advantage of. Of course, when the customer simply experiences 'good goods', as Hermann Miller describes value and quality, the opposite is experienced: the responsive company becomes a community server and the value is internalized into the product. What matters is the tool and the implementation. (Perhaps, the move from mainframe and dumb terminal to server and intelligent workstation is a fair metaphor of the shift.)

Staying with the extrinsic motivator, it seems that the act of rewarding may actually induce opposition. In a study of children rewarded for drinking Kefir, a fruit flavoured yoghurt, the children were divided into three groups:

1. Those who were simply given the drink.
2. Those who were praised for drinking it.
3. Those who were given a free movie ticket if they finished the glass.

Which produced the best results? Perhaps, not surprisingly, those who were rewarded with the free movie ticket were most likely to drink and finish the yoghurt. The movie tickets are a good reward for drinking a glass of yoghurt. *But, a week later, they were the least likely to drink it.*[22]

Two series of studies carried out by Deci[23] and Lepper[24] showed how rewards reduced intrinsic motivation. For example, Lepper discovered that the provision of rewards reduced children's interest in drawing with magic markers once the reward had been reduced, and Deci discovered that providing a reward reduced the intrinsic motivation of individuals to tackle a puzzle. It is the principle that a hobby becomes work at the point that you get paid for it.

Alfie Kohn tells me an old American joke. An old man was getting insulted by a group of 10-year-olds each day. They would tell him how stupid and ugly and old he was. Rather than shout at them he called them together and told them that any of them who shouted at him the next day would get a dollar. Excited and amazed they all came round hurled abuse, and collected their dollar. 'Do the same tomorrow', he said, 'and I'll give you a quarter for your trouble'. The children thought this was still pretty good, and turned out again to insult him and earn the reward. Then he apologized and told them that on the following day he could only afford to give them a penny. 'Forget it,' they said – and that was the end of his problem. NatWest offered one point per £10 spent, then one per £20, and next?

There are plenty of organizations that have started out to win the loyalty of customers by giving them a good incentive, with the hope that they could scale back at some time. The problem is, you can not. Furthermore, by the time you give up on your reward mechanism, people may have been turned off the core product you are offering. If not, the loss of reward is a source of dissatisfaction capable of shifting the buying habit.

Anything you do that is manifestly designed to induce certain behaviour in someone is likely to be treated negatively. It is the reverse of the principle that says: you are not allowed to eat your greens! If rewards are experienced as controlling, then we are likely to recoil from them.

The question is: How do we ensure that what we provide becomes an intrinsic part of the total package of our solution, and generates the loyalty that we are looking for?

In W. Edwards Deming's work transforming the quality of Japan Inc., his quality methodology included the principle that rewards and bonuses are counter-productive in generating the best work from employees.

Incentives appear to have a detrimental effect on personal performance if offered when the task itself is interesting enough for incentives to be superfluous, or when the solution is sufficiently open ended that the steps to it are not immediately obvious and therefore interesting.[25] Rewards appear to improve performance only when extremely simple or mindless tasks are being performed, and then they only improve quantitative performance. In commercial terms: we can damage a great product by giving an unnecessary reward. We can induce purchase but not loyalty to a commodity.

In conclusion: why not work for loyalty rather than just reward led retention?

- Rewarded retention is a junky habit: it costs ever more to sustain.
- Rewards are easy to copy.
- Rewards divert attention from the real product: both by the company and customers.
- Rewards can be perceived as manipulative.

Rewards can best contribute to loyalty when:

- the base product offer is already good and differentiated, and the reward is intrinsic, i.e. perceived as an extension of the product;
- the reward is genuinely valued and perceived as taking some effort or cost, by the company, to deliver;
- there is a strong personalization factor.

The six best ways to use rewards

Here are six practical research-based suggestions on using rewards:[26]

1. Reduce the prominence of the extrinsic motivator proportional to the intrinsic motivations.
2. Create personalized surprises, after the event (like Portland's, or Lexus in Chapter 2).
3. Eliminate rewards as contest. At least they should be available to everyone who meets a certain standard.
4. Make rewards as intrinsic to the base product as possible.

5. Give people as much choice as possible about how rewards are used. (Where do you want to fly? What do you want to choose?) This reduces the controlling effect of the reward. However, it is important to make sure that in the process you do not raise the profile of the rewards so high that the product itself disappears.
6. Keep reminding people that the reasons they like the product are to do with the product.

Preserving customers: can we *secure* loyalty?

It might seem to be an ideal to lock customers into a condition of loyalty. But let us look at it in more detail. IBM was notorious for retaining customers in the 1970s. They had customers for life. There is absolutely no doubt that there were many very good reasons for this. Reasons such as quality of service, and even, sometimes, equipment. However, there were other reasons too. For example, IBM had a proprietary technology from which it was difficult and expensive to escape. They also had many techniques to keep customers. For example, data-processing managers knew quite well that if a recommendation to leave IBM was made, IBM salespeople would sometimes act to cast doubt on their credibility. 'No one is ever sacked for buying IBM', is a testament to the security of an IBM decision and the scare factor in reverse. Eventually, this contributed to a backlash and the greatest financial loss in history. The time came when organizations and data-processing managers wanted freedom.

There is a lesson in this. The USSR imposed a brilliantly clever system of manipulation designed to secure and keep people in a loyal condition. It did not work. For several decades a powerful empire was created and maintained. But, eventually it broke down. And, when it broke down, the past was shrugged off by most people as an evil dream.

Today is an era of freedom. We can no longer sustain societies like the ancient Egyptians. The time of authority, whether it is the authority of a Pharaoh or a dictator or a manufacturer or an advertiser is over. Of course, people, including customers, still want standards and credibility. They still want to be able to rely on knowable, proved standards of excellence. They want a still point in a turning world, a place and supplier and service and product line that they can trust. But, to try to strait-jacket a customer is no longer morally acceptable or commercially possible.

Modern people need autonomy, and free choice. They need to feel good about what they are doing. A freely made decision is always more powerful. People resent being imposed on; they resent being controlled; and they resist being changed. They like to be part of the decision making.

The moral keys to loyalty

Kohn suggests that the keys to authentic motivation are based on collaboration, content and choice. Collaboration means that people enjoy relationships and working together. They would rather have a good relationship with you than a bad one. Cooperation and working together; the more associative the better as it increases loyalty.

'Content' means making sure that the product is genuinely good. Herzberg said that 'idleness, indifference, and irresponsibility are healthy responses to absurd work'. He went on to say: 'If you want people motivated to do a good job, give them a good job to do.' The same applies to products. The issue is: Do customers feel proud of the products they are buying? Do they feel proud of the company providing it, or do they feel embarrassed to admit that they shop with you or buy your goods?

So the only sustainable loyalty is that which is really given. To win it requires an important complementary action by the responsive company. Customers will only be loyal to the company if the company is loyal to the customers. Quite obviously, if you want customers to return, enthusiastically, and to tell their friends and neighbours, you will need to act out of a certain commitment to them.

And that brings us to the deep flaw at the heart of modern business. It is the flaw that has led to the erosion of loyalty across the Western world and, in turn, to spiralling marketing costs. It is the flaw that has educated a generation of consumers and business people to fickle shopping habits.

The presumption of modern business is that it is an amoral activity. The rule is that whatever is legal and profitable goes. The principle duty of the organization is to satisfy its shareholders. The business managers proclaim their mission to give shareholders value and return on investment.

This is not to say that shareholder values have no relevance, but there is an escapable logic in this obsession. If the purpose of business is to exploit opportunities with customers in order to produce value for shareholders, then customers will presume a corresponding duty to exploit the situation for their own value. Hence, in business-to-business circles we have the win–lose negotiating paradigm that dominated through the 1960s, 1970s and 1980s. Ford, as customer, trained its buyers in the 'Hard and tricky art of negotiation': cold shoulders, hard stares and flat demands. So did virtually all the other big companies, certainly in the automobile industry. The consumer on the street also looked for the best deal. Often, they were taught it at work. Even the win–lose trade union negotiation told employees how to behave as customers.

As the business schools taught that market share was the key to profitability, and that this week's equity ratio was the key to life, the techniques of price promotion began to dominate much of business. Yet, price promotion produces no loyalty, as the Ehrenberg research showed. Instead, it provides an education in the art of fickle favour.

An amoral business world is a value-free business world. And a value-free business community invites customers whose priority is their own gratification, and nothing else. So, we set up a business community and a customer base each seeking its own gratification, and the chasm between has to be crossed by the marketing message.

The new marketing seeks to establish an association through dialogue and through a set of values that are mutual and community creating: the higher levels of organization quality. Such values are essentially moral. They are based on a principle of sharing which becomes gain–gain. What wins real loyalty of customers is their free choice to do business with you. This arises when they appreciate and share the organization's values, when the organization or brand becomes an interesting personality and one worth while supporting. The organization's dedication to quality and service on behalf of the customer then leads to a reciprocal appreciation.

The extraordinary thing is that this, by any reasonable definition of the word, makes business a moral issue. Good business, as the word suggests, is moral business (the term 'good goods', which powered Hermann Miller's phenomenal product and profit quality, is an example. Interestingly, it is also a traditional term, current at the beginning of the century, for example, by Dunlop, cited earlier, at a time when 'my word is my bond' was still used. The very word 'goods' speaks volumes). IBM's founder, Tom Watson, was an extraordinary individual, many of whose sayings have the quality of a sage and are deeply moral, including 'respect for the individual' and 'the customer pays your salary' (both extraordinary in their time and the foundation stones of the company).

So, the ideas, the imagination and techniques of business will need to be more coloured by a moral, value laden outlook if they are going to be successful in winning and keeping customers in a loyal relationship. This, of course, does not mean a moralistic attitude. That would simply be talking down to customers. Companies which carve a great reputation for themselves, for their quality and dependability, are always associated implicitly at least with moral worth: with integrity, honest value, and a guarantee of worth.

Notes and references

1. Whiteley, R.C., *The Customer-Driven Company*, Addison Wesley, 1991.
2. Whiteley, R.C., *The Customer-Driven Company*, Addison Wesley, 1991.
3. Levitt, T., 'After the sale is over', *Harvard Business Review*, Sept./Oct. 1983.
4. Dunlop, D.N., *British Destiny*, The Path Publishing Co., 1916.
5. Christopher, M., Payne, A. and Ballantyne, D., *Relationship Marketing*, Butterworth-Heinemann, 1993.

6. Confidential cat food study by Ogilvy & Mather Direct using target audience from CMT national shoppers survey.
7. Ehrenberg, A.S.C., Hammond, K. and Goodhardt, G.J., 'The after effects of price related consumer promotions', *Journal of Targeting, Measurement and Analysis for Marketing* (1994).
8. Abraham, M.M. and Lodish, L.M., 'Getting the most out of advertising and promotion', *Harvard Business Review* (May/June 1990).
9. Scoggin, D.R., 'Customers go out the door when success goes to your head', *Wall Street Journal* (11 August 1986).
10. Goodman, J., Malech, A. and Adamson, C., 'Don't fix the product, fix the customer', *Quality Review* (Fall 1988), European edition, pp. 6–11.
11. Quinn, M. and Humble, J., 'Using service to gain a competitive edge—the PROMPT approach', *Long Range Planning*, **26** (April 1993).
12. McCleary, K.W., Weaver, P. and Cornell, A., *Hotel and Restaurant Administration Quarterly*, **32** (No. 2, Aug. 1991), pp. 38–45.
13. Carlisle, J.A. and Parker, R.C., *Beyond Negotiation: Redeeming Customer–Supplier Relationships*, Wiley, 1989.
14. Westbrook, R.A., 'Product/consumption-based affective responses and post-purchase processes', *Journal of Marketing Research*, **XXIV** (August 1987), pp. 258–70.
15. Hunt, H.K., *Conceptualisation and Measurement of Consumer Satisfaction and Dissatisfaction*, Cambridge, Marketing Science Institute, 1977, pp. 455–88.
16. Zajonc, R.B., 'Feeling and thinking, preferences need no influences', *American Psychologist*, **35**, pp. 151–75.
17. Damasio, A., *Descartes' Error, Emotion, Reason and the Human Brain*, Picador, 1995.
18. Isen, A.M., 'Towards understanding the role of affect in cognition', in *Handbook of Social Cognition*, (eds) R. Wyer and T. Snill, Lawrence Erlbaum Assocs., pp. 179–236.
19. Popcorn, F., Speech at Montreux Symposium, 1990.
20. Cazdin, A.E., and Bootzin, R.R., 'The token economy: an evaluative review', *Journal of Applied Behaviour Analysis*, **5** (1972), pp. 343–72; also Cazdin, A.E., *Journal of Applied Behaviour Analysis*, **15** (1982), pp. 431–5.
21. Kohn, A., *Punished by Rewards*, Houghton Mifflin, 1993.
22. Birch, Lipps, Marlin, Rotter, *Child Development*, **55** (1984), pp. 431–9.
23. Deci, E.L., 'Effects of externally mediated rewards on intrinsic motivation', *Journal of Personality and Social Psychology*, **18** (1971), pp. 105–15; also a number of other research projects through the 1970s and 1980s.
24. Lepper, M.R., 'Dissonance, self-perception, and honesty in children', *Journal of Personality and Social Psychology*, **25** (1973), pp. 65–74; and a number of other research projects during the 1970s and 1980s.
25. McGraw, K.O., 'The detrimental effects of reward on performance: a literature review and a prediction model', in *The Hidden Costs of Rewards: New Perspectives on the Psychology of Human Motivation*, ed. M.R. Lepper and D. Greene, 1978.
26. Kohn, A., *Punished by Rewards*, Houghton Mifflin, 1993.

8
The power of service in sales

Summary The value of service, and the contribution of database marketing to service quality, through the capacity to personalize, transform and analyse the product, are developed in this chapter. A new model of the service product is a central tool for planning and analysis. A number of key concepts, including moments of truth, archetypal moments and guarantee management, are developed further.

Successful businesses are about relationships – making them good makes them last. To be good is to give wisely.

(Webster Munroe)

The marriage of service and sales

Database marketing is a *service*. The mail order cataloguer or any direct marketer selects and displays like any retailer. Selection, presentation, information, simplification, convenience and problem resolution are characteristics of service and of database marketing. Deliveries, guarantees and keen prices are others. Leveraging service to attract and retain customers is at the heart of database marketing. Marketing itself becomes service and the boundaries of product and marketing become blurred.

Quality selling is a service. Consider this scenario: a prospect rings up and asks:

'I am interested in buying your products. Please can a salesperson come and demonstrate them to me.'
'No. I am sorry we don't have any salespeople.'
'Well do you have a brochure that you can send about your products?'
'No. We don't have any brochures.'
'Well, do you have some samples that you can send me?'
'Sorry, we don't send out samples.'
'Helpful, aren't you?'

When the Huthwaite Research Group studied effective sales methods in the 1970s and 1980s, methodically testing on 35 000 calls, they found that the most successful behaviours were collaborative, problem solving, empathetic *and in conflict with all that salespeople were being taught*. Not 'close early and often' but 'identify problems and seek agreement on needs' would be a simple summary.[1] The sales process becomes *useful* to the customer.

While good-quality selling is essentially a service, paradoxically, service can be considered as a sales activity. Service is *the creation of relationship value through acts of care that satisfy customer needs*. Service creates the company's future: ensuring that customers wish to return to the same source for future purchases. Service creates tomorrow's sales; it is selling through a long-term window. The promise of future service, if credible, also produces today's sales. Take this scenario:

'Where shall we buy our next computer from?'

'Well Bob's Computers were very helpful when we had that problem with the printer.'

'And they offer to swap or upgrade the machine if you are not happy within 30 days with no penalty.'

'OK get it from Bob.'

Or this:

'I was just thinking I needed to hire a car for my holiday. And here's a letter from the company I hired a car from two years ago. They remembered that I hire a car at this time of year. How convenient, that saves me the trouble of looking around.'

The old controversy of above and below the 'line' (i.e. image and brand advertising versus direct response and sales promotion), which is now increasingly resolved into 'through the line' marketing, is therefore less important now than the vertical line between sales and service: '*Across the line*' is the new paradigm, representing the marriage of sales and service (Figure 8.1).

Service companies want both to sell and to continue to enhance service.

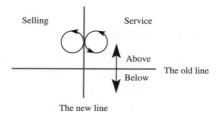

Figure 8.1 Across the line marketing

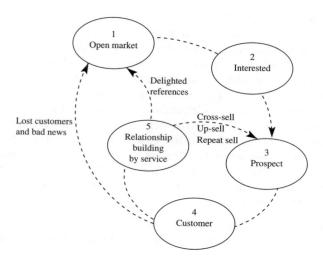

Figure 8.2   The sales cycle

Sales driven companies need to add the service for which database marketing is admirably equipped. Huggies booklets for mothers, Rank Xerox's *Best of Business* magazine for its leading customers and Ericsson's technology trend studies and magazines, mailed to customers and consultants in over 20 countries, are all examples. Figure 8.2 is based on a model developed by Ogilvy & Mather Direct and shows how service acts in the sales cycle to retain customers.

Marketers develop loyal customers by development from a broad and 'faceless' market. Here, brand and image advertising is most likely to be significant. Database marketing aids at all stages, but particularly from stage 2 (Interested), after individuals show an interest. As Ted Levitt argued,[2] and as the previous chapter argued, the 'after the sale' phase is when loyalty is created or impaired. Customers appreciate care and become ripe for more products and service, spreading their delight by word of mouth, or they become disappointed, drop out and share the bad news.

Can big business be personal?

At one time businesses were small and personal and they knew most of their customers. Traders looking for business in the higher ends of the market would usually approach with a letter of referral. Service was typically very personal, and each craftsperson knew his or her customers intimately, including their special interests. The shoemaker would even keep copies of the lasts for the shoes of individual customers.

As one commentator put it:

> A grocer used to be very fussy about his cheese. Cheddar was made and sold by hundreds of little factories. Representatives of the factories had particular customers and cheese was prepared by hand to suit the grocers, who knew precisely what their patrons wanted in rat cheese, pie cheese, American and other cheeses. Some liked them sharper; some liked them yellower; some liked anise seeds in cheese, or caraway.[3]

We aspire to this personal touch even in the world of big business. The need for reliability, which seems to triumph over all other service demands, arises from anxiety through decades in which product quality deteriorated and confidence slowly dissipated. Sometimes we mistake reliability for sameness. In a world where things are unreliable, it is always good to be able to rely on a Coke. But even more money is paid for the distinctiveness of a fine wine, from a select vineyard, in a good year.

If you phone Thames Water, the largest water utility in the UK serving some 12 million people over 6000 square miles of Greater London, the customer agent who answers knows everything there is to know about their relationship with you – every request, product, service complaint. An information system enables transformed customer service and a very large company can acquire a more friendly personality, provided culture and training empowers the teleservice agent.

Service starts by thinking from the customer's shoes. One interesting way to do this is to act it, sometimes with the help of drama therapy type techniques. Get physically and imaginatively into the role of customer and see what it is like. Being a mystery shopper is another. Sometimes this can make a big difference to the approach, like this off-beat response by a British and international human rights organization, Charter 88, whose supporters are often among the busiest, most high-profile people.

Thinking about this problem, Charter 88 sent a mailing pointing out the problems of frequent 'Junk Mail' and gave a cast iron guarantee: 'We think you want to support us, but don't want to be constantly hounded. Give us £25 now and, if you prefer, we won't ask you for money again for a year.' They got an 11 per cent response and 63 per cent of responders took up their no contact offer. The impact of personal involvement showed through too. Hand-signing letters doubled the response to 21 per cent. For an £850 investment, they generated £20 000 (a 22 : 1 ratio).

Service is therefore an active commitment to thinking from another's point of view, and it takes more than lip service; it takes passion and commitment. *Androcles and the Lion* is a play by George Bernard Shaw and tells a story which dates from the Romans. One day, a Christian slave called Androcles escaped and was fleeing through the woods when he came across a lion with a wounded paw. Bravely, Androcles ventured close and eventually won sufficient trust to be able to pull a thorn from the lion's paw. Some time later, Androcles was recaptured and brought to the amphitheatre for the crowd's pleasure, to be fed to the lions! Of course, the lion who was introduced into the arena to savage and kill him was the same lion that Androcles had rescued, who now returned the favour by treating him gently, to the crowd's amazement, leading to Androcles' eventual release.

Six important points in this tale are relevant to the service company:

1. Androcles did not know in advance that his service would be needed: he had to respond in the moment.
2. The service deed was a unilateral act of giving. A generous deed, putting the 'customer' first.
3. It took some risk.
4. In the longer term, Androcles gained a lifesaving reward through 'customer' appreciation.
5. The lion, as customer, was the judge of quality ...
6. ... and was intimately involved in the process.

Topic 8.1   The recovery of service commitment

Resurrecting service attitudes is likely to be increasingly important to both commercial success and quality of life. There have been many negative connotations to the concept of 'service', especially in Western and English-speaking countries. It has been a 'bad' word. The root is the Latin 'servus' meaning 'a slave'. To be 'in service' in Victorian England meant working as a servant, one of the lower classes.

An older ideal of service held it as a gift to the gods or tribe, and personal sacrifice and duty were highly rated, as in the stories of Job, Theseus, the Pandava brothers in the Mahabharata, the great Indian epic, or the culture of the Plains Indians. Serving 'God and Country' was an important deal until devalued by First World War butchery, late colonialism and modern individualism. The Sanskrit word 'seva' meaning 'service' carried the sense, 'to cherish, honour, and worship', with a feeling of joy and connection with the divine. (Since the ancient ruler was considered a divine or semi-divine being, service was a higher calling.) Even the word 'Slave' is thought to arise from a corruption of 'Slav' meaning 'glory' after the Romans took many Slavs as slaves.[4]

Christ washing the feet of the disciples has powerful iconic value in Western culture. The 'washing of the feet' is the first stage in spiritual preparation on the Christian mystical path. Knights in chivalry, including kings and lords, took vows to serve those in need. The legend of St George, the maiden he helps and the dragon he kills symbolize the overcoming of the lower self (dragon) and attainment of higher self (the maiden) through courageous service. In the same way, successful service demands that we overcome lower values (like inertia, lack of care and low creativity) and institute positive values.

A new transformation of service is now taking place. Today it is neither a divine honour nor an imposition. It is neither the gods nor the ruler nor ancient duty nor the boss that produces great service (although the right boss is a great help). Today's service motivation is increasingly part of our own development as professionals and human beings. New thinking is turning the manager, business and front line into servers (not servants) aiming to overcome the enemy within: inertia, lack of imagination and lack of care in meeting needs. The Body Shop, 3M, and Stew Leonard's Dairy Store are well publicized representatives, or take the Vermont Teddy Bear guarantee or the Alley Deli welcome. After awarding a large project to Digital Equipment Co., UK, British Telecom commented: 'Digital were prepared to *put themselves out and help us …*' It is this quality that makes the difference, and more and more people are finding that it makes a difference to life too: it becomes more joyful, more meaningful, more worth while.

Discretionary effort is the difference between what you have to do to keep your job and achieving 100 per cent of your current potential. It is this that most people really do want to achieve and companies maximize. Modern businesspeople know that fear is no longer able to sustain this motivation. 'Unless I meet these standards my business/job will go' *does* produce results, but also produces an increasing number of people who keep their heads down, avoid trouble and give about 10 per cent of their real creativity and enthusiasm.

A rational understanding of the economic benefits is more effective but not yet inspired. '*I* want to be served well and therefore I realize that others do too,' works, but is rarely passionate.

The next chapter gives some indications of how to create the conditions for such exceptional service.

So important is service, that even manufacturing is increasingly dominated by service factors, as noted by the joint European, Japanese and US survey cited in Chapter 4. According to the American National Association of Accountants, manufacturers' service activities account *for 75 to 85 per cent of all value added.*[5] The Japanese are increasingly confident about production quality and are now focusing on service-related issues. When American office supplies service leader Inmac started up in Japan, they found their service proposition (next day deliver) only a 'me too'. The question asked was, 'What do you do different?'

In many companies the service department once consisted of second-class citizens who repaired malfunctions, maybe … (see Figure 8.3). Today, service is a key differentiator and service functions are increasingly taking leading roles. In best practice, every part of the business is recognized as having a service function. The product is wrapped in the service values of the business.

In Chapter 1 it was pointed out that to the four basic Ps of marketing, we may add another three: people, processes and physical context (Figure 8.4). These particularly represent the added value of the service business.

For example (at an estate agent):

- People: How friendly, skilled, *knowledgeable* and helpful was the individual? How human and *personalized* was all contact?

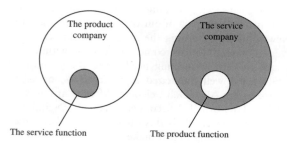

The service function   The product function

Figure 8.3   The service company transformation

Figure 8.4   The 7 Ps of service

- Process: Do they send details only of *relevant* properties, in a timely way? How do their systems help this?
- Physical context: How is the store furnished? What is the ambience? What tangible elements of service are there, such as the information sheets, and of what quality are they? Do I need to go in or can I make my request in my home *by phone*?

Database marketing has something to offer in all seven parts of the marketing mix, for example:

- It adds to, changes and helps analyse the product, as will be developed.
- It facilitates in making channel decisions through customer knowledge.
- It enables offer price testing.
- It enables promotion testing, as well as offering an alternative method.

Process differentiation, supported by excellent IT, is an increasingly powerful way to competitive advantage, and the reason for the develop-ment of so many 'direct' businesses. Another example to add to the many others given neatly demonstrates the particular capacity of information technology to add value in a direct business. The $1 billion US company, Nationwide Value Added Distribution, harnesses robotics, computing power and advanced distribution logistics with personalized, customer-oriented service to retain its relationship with the dealers who are its customers. It carries 25 000 office items and can service orders down to a single pencil by 9 a.m. the next day, as long as it gets the order by 6 p.m. the previous day. Also, the order can be delivered already customized to the individual dealer ready to pass on to the customer. Packages are made up with the dealer's logo already on board and ready for shipment.

Seventy per cent of orders are placed direct by the dealer, who has access to a sophisticated system with full availability information and specification. That involves the dealer, builds loyalty and aids Nationwide. Going one step further, it is putting terminals on its customers' desks, working with the trade, not against. The dealer's larger customers get a terminal as if it had come from the dealer, but all servicing is done centrally. Now *that* is sophisticated database marketing.

The service process involves two levels of customer and collects data about both, including contact names. The service system binds all three parties into a loyal and trusting relationship. Database marketing is adept at involving the customer and designing information and service rich mutual dialogue through the process of service delivery.

Commodity transformation

Service transforms the commodity in personalized interaction with the customer. It generates relationship values through a series of interactions at the service front line. These are the threshold moments of truth when clients and customers test our development. To what extent will the quality of our processes, resources, people, information, etc., come together? To what extent can we put the customer's genuine needs and preferences first, not as slaves, but as partners? Then, good service transforms commodities.

Let us explode one myth. Service is an *extension of*, and not an alternative to, the production process for the service marketer (for other service businesses, see later). It is the most sophisticated, transformed and value added of all commodity production processes, and is most effective in a personalized relationship, which is itself a service. McDonald is the world's most widely distributed manufacturing plant: a distributed network of thousands of small factories.

A commodity is defined as 'any item of nature which has been transformed and brought to a suitable place for consumption'.[6] In that sense, every service marketer provides a commodity, although the process of transformation and delivery may be extended over time and space, as in ongoing support of systems, or long-term use of equipment. Service, as we have seen, is the process of adding extra value.

As discussed, commodities may be converted into brands, but within the brand the emphasis on consistency makes one production unit identical to all the rest. Service goes beyond this, *to make the individual can of Pepsi differ from every other can* (see Figure 8.5). There are millions of identical cans of coke. When in a café you ask for one and it arrives, seconds later, in a tall glass with ice; the can has become unique, the experience personal, and worth perhaps three or more times the 'standard' price. The commodity has been brought to the place with style.

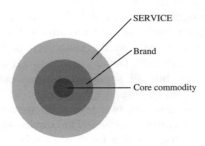

Figure 8.5 Service differentiates brands

Customer responsiveness

A few years ago, my wife arranged for us to have an evening out and booked theatre tickets. After a thoroughly enjoyable performance, we went on to dinner. As we were returning to our car, a few minutes before midnight, my wife asked me if there was anything special about the day. I thought about this. It had been a lovely evening, but this was not what she meant. Then she reminded me that it was our wedding anniversary. I had forgotten it!

From such situations, marriages have crumbled and relationships divorced. Ours was (eventually) saved by my wife's sense of humour in the face of my incompetence. Many business relationships are saved by the same good humour, but not all.

The future will be marked by an intensification and deepening of business relationships. The model in Figure 8.6 is of this dynamic threshold with customers: a two-way dialogue and relationship that needs to adjust to individual customers and customer groups, and their changing needs over time, as well as the organization's changing needs and capabilities.

The interaction includes all communications, including product and service delivery, customer complaints and requests, telephone contacts, both inbound and outbound, promotional and service mailings, educational and promotional events, e.g. seminars and previews, and face-to-face meetings or encounters.

It therefore includes all moments of truth, potential and actual, and of

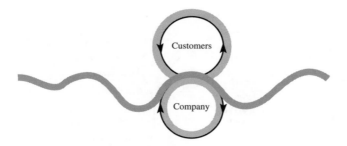

Figure 8.6 The dynamic organization threshold

course all databased marketing activity. 'The moment of truth' is a concept developed by the consultant Normann and popularized by Jan Carlzon, chief executive of SAS (Scandinavian Airlines). A moment of truth is each and every moment when the customer experiences the organization and is therefore able to form some judgement of it. Examples are checking into a hotel room, receiving a parcel in the post, looking for a user manual, calling up for help or to place an order, and so on.

These develop during the cycle of the relationship and through life stages (see Figure 8.7). (Of course, there is a corresponding cycle for business-to-business marketers, tailored for each industry.) Huggies disposable pants for the child getting potty trained and the timed series of mailings over the first two years illustrates the principle.

One of the key steps for any organization is to model the moments of truth. In the first instance this means identifying all the points in the relationship where customers and company meet. It can then identify:

– the opportunities available to collect data;
– the customers' required and likely experience;
– the personal or impersonal aspects of the experience;
– the follow-up required or expected from the organization and/or customer;
– the next event.

Laura Ashley found that customers who bought fitted curtains spent typically £3000–4000 over the next year in new wallpaper, carpets and sofas. However, customers lacked confidence in young Saturday temporary staff, so they brought in more mature women and trained them, increasing sales by 120 per cent.

It is also essential to understand the moments of truth that are being missed. These are the implicit points in the relationship which the organization is overlooking and therefore failing to initiate relationship action, like the missed anniversary. Christ spoke of the sins of commission,

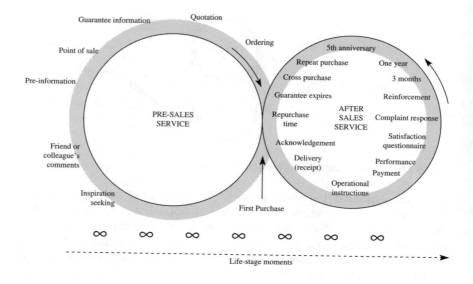

Figure 8.7   The moments of truth cycle: representative moments

what we do but should not, and the sins of omission, what we fail to do, the sins that drive away two-thirds of business. One credit card company found that its retail customers received only two contacts, a welcome and a procedures guide, after they agreed to accept the card, before receiving a potential stream of unwelcome letters from a 2 inch thick manual of standard payment disallowal letters. An automatic computer update of the bank account also helped to remove any reason for warm contact. The relationship scales were heavily and adversely tipped for the card company.

Moments of truth analysis also enables companies to identify data collection opportunities, as well as communication and service points. The methodology is discussed further in Chapter 11 on Data. By doing an exhaustive analysis, development needs and opportunities become plain.

In a fully realized database marketing environment, most moments of truth would yield an information content for both parties which, at the same time, raised the warmth and value of the relationship. It would involve a raised consciousness, at least by the organization, in the preparation, execution and review of each and every encounter. To be really successful, the encounter would become more vivid, actual, pleasing and memorable to customers.

This could involve all aspects of the business. In fact, one has to call into question the real value of any part of the business that has no relationship with customers:

- IBM brings customers into, for example, its Rochester lab for intensive sessions reviewing and planning the needs for new computer systems.
- Toyota works extensively with customers in designing new models, with a custom leisure centre to help.
- A major consumer leisure company realized its finance department was a key customer relationship manager, while a financial services company realized its administration department could sell loans during address changes.
- General Electric has installed a call centre in the United States, equipped with a library of 750 000 commonly asked questions to aid customers with their queries. The value to GE is 4–6 times the cost.

In many companies, communication and relationship management systems are inadequate and fail to honour the integrity of the relationships they wish to create.

By contrast, First Direct are in the top quartile of British banks in a Boston matrix measuring 'customer satisfaction' and 'willingness to refer', and are one of only two banks in this quartile. In addition to being the first British bank serious about remote banking, they achieved technical leadership with implementation of an event management or event trigger system. This enabled them to predefine a series of possible customer events and to programme a desired response, an idea first promoted by the author in 1988. Marketing management define 'rules' and customers are subsequently selected by the database system for communication, promotion or service, based on their event or behaviour history.

This concept, an *event trigger*, links three ideas:

1. The recency/frequency/value behaviour thinking that has driven mail order for decades: *Who*?
2. The moment of truth concept: *When*?
3. Contact management techniques developed for salesforce management systems and telemarketing scripting, with emphasis on process management: *What*?

An event trigger can be defined as 'the configuration of a system to recognize particular customers and their relationship at a moment of truth and thereby stimulate an appropriate action according to a predetermined and evolving policy'. KLM's European Customer Support Centre in Amsterdam provides Europe-wide 24-hour telephone service cover. Telephone systems are linked to the computer to capture performance data and improve service. Every type of call is coded and according to the call a personalized response is triggered. This response can be built out of a menu of text components with personalized insertions. Further calls may also be triggered.

American Express, using the monthly statement cycle, respond to each individual customer's profile over the last month and generate, using their relationship billing facility, a unique statement with a range of offers. The offers are provided jointly with their service establishment base and target individuals based on types of activity, location, usage of card in specific establishments and desired changes.

The system enables a sales representative to agree with a restaurant an offer to be made to selected customers. The criteria for the offer are agreed and submitted as a programme which then goes into a library. The system automatically selects suitable card holders based on their precise spending profile: type, location, value, establishments.

All sophisticated continuity mail order companies have developed sophisticated, statistically driven systems to drive a programme of communications to customers designed to maximize retention. Time Life developed a scoring and system to drive this for its worldwide operations. Of course, driving communications like this is only half the equation.

In one leading holiday company, analysis of the moments of truth generated significant creative potential to change: capturing prospect details that had been lost before, sending apologies for lack of availability, doing additional mailed and telephone research, setting up priority booking facilities, mail order sales, custom brochures and so on. Previously, management had focused on speeding each transaction. The new thinking focused on the relationship to be managed.

See Chapter 12 for the system implications of event trigger/event management.

The archetypal moment

The most important moments of truth are the archetypal moments, a concept introduced in the previous chapter and described as the most significant key to the presence or absence of loyalty. It is the picture and feeling of the event experienced by a customer that best sums up his or her loyalty or disinterest in a company or its products. It may be simply an ad image, or an experience: a problem resolved, an act of confidence or faith in the customer, a lack of care and attention, a friend or friendly service, a superb delivery or design, a constantly reliable service, a succession of failures, and so on, but always self-actualized by the customer.

A company will be more successful the more it succeeds in creating positive archetypal moments and overcoming or preventing negative ones. Achieving this depends on two elements: the product/system components created by the processes, resources and so on of the company, and the creative response of the individual in the moment, which are developed in the rest of this chapter and the next.

A service product model which extends benchmarking capability

The accountability of database marketing extends to its capacity to help us assess the parameters of the product offer. To do this, however, requires a knowledge of what is being analysed, which is not easy with the service product. What is a taxi ride, meal or holiday? A simplistic description is easy, but a real definition involves a configuration from a set of potential parameters.

The service product, therefore, introduces us to vagueness, complexity and imbiguity. The greater the service content, the more likely it is that the product consists of the capacity of systems of people, processes and equipment that can be tested, exported and franchised but, in a sense, comes into being only in memory, imagination and experience (see Figure 8.8). Such a product cannot be *seen*, but exists only in the moment by moment of life and service delivery: as the crystal suddenly appears in the super-saturated solution.

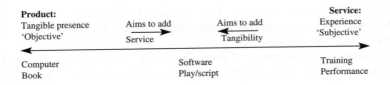

Figure 8.8 The product existence continuum

The selection, configuration or weaving together of attributes which make up a particular customer's actual service product may be

- optional
- configuration choice
- menu choice
- components of the process of service consumption or access
- added value extras
- product enhancements
- bonuses
- pricing or payment benefits

and some service product examples are:

- *Holiday*: Booking process, tickets, information pack, flights, type of holiday, season, type of accommodation, particular centre (hotel), room, meals, excursions, payment terms, problem resolution, etc.
- *Fast food*: Queue, Big Mac, chips, Coke, sauce, table, packaging.
- *Taxi*: Ordering, arrival time, Mercedes, from the office to the airport, with air conditioning, payment by account, friendly conversation or silence as needed, recognition.
- *Computer*: Configuration advice, free delivery, free software, system components, help line, on-site maintenance, guarantee, finance, etc.

All the more reason to find a useful model to analyse effectiveness. There have been many attempts. The following proposal is based on original research supplemented by an Ogilvy & Mather Direct study[7] and a proposal by Ted Levitt.[8]

Each and every product begins first with an idea (or concept). Take *the most tangible product you can think of*, and you *start* with the *idea* you are thinking. Even if you find a new product, Apple's Newton for example, and see it for the first time, the first question is 'What is it?'

So the core of a service product is a concept: a haircut, a flight to New York, a holiday in France, a personal computer. This is the core, generic, essential or commodity concept that can then be personalized in two ways (see Figure 8.9):

1. *Brand image*. Not 'a radio' but 'a Sony radio'; not 'fast food' but 'McDonald's', i.e. a brand image which makes the business or brand unique among commodities.
2. *Customer personalization*. Personally recognized, configured, cooked, delivered: service elements that made the service product unique for the customer. It is often more difficult for others to replicate customer unique aspects for they invariably include something of the personal relationship between buyer and seller. All true personalization of service and relationship does this. Of course, false, unwarranted or inaccurate personalization is simply a unique form of customer insult, not service.

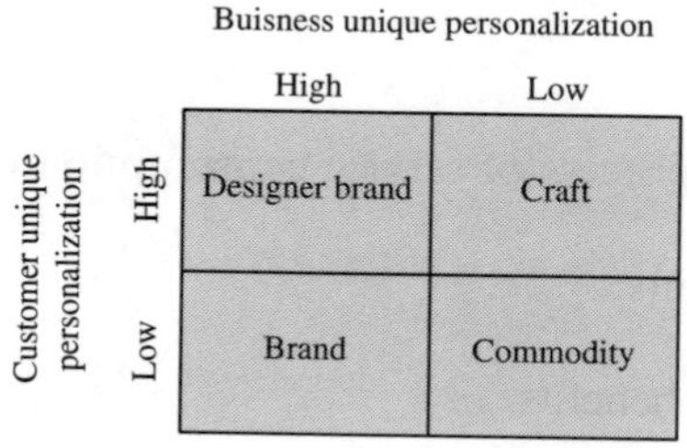

Buisness unique personalization

	High	Low
High	Designer brand	Craft
Low	Brand	Commodity

Customer unique personalization

Figure 8.9 Product personalization matrix

These two elements of brand and service were also identified in Figure 8.5 (page 148) as the elements that make the generic commodity unique as a brand, and the generic brand unique in customer service. The service brand is therefore built up out of three levels in the customer's mind: base or core product, brand image and personal delivery process/experience. Branding and service experience are interacting, interpenetrating components, like a lemniscate (i.e. a figure of 8), each part weaving into the other. Together they differentiate and provide distinction.

Brand expectations set up service expectations. At best, this means that the customers are favourably inclined to expect that they will receive and are receiving a good experience: 'Everybody says this is good so it must be. . . .' But it may also mean that expectations are set too high and are therefore easier to topple. Brand and service need to be congruent. If they are not, bad publicity is likely to increase. On the other hand, good service builds service reputation which turns into brand values, as for Marks & Spencer and The Body Shop, both of whom claim to have no marketing departments.

The clover leaf service product

The specific service product is therefore a *brand image* and a *service experience* which is woven in the moment of truth from its *delivery attributes* – which correspond to elements of the four core competencies of the business described at the end of Chapter 5.

1. Physical or tangible features; the essential or core item
2. Activity, movement or process elements
3. Relationship or personal features, the human touch
4. Information content, including data supporting or developing brand values.

A service product consists, therefore, of what we provide and what the customer experiences. These are united in an act of knowledge which is also the customer's judgement of what we provide. Image and reality meet. The customer perceives not only *what* we provide, the tangibles, but also the *way* we provide, the intangible values.

Perhaps the best way to represent this is by an illustration (see Figure 8.10), the magic of the clover leaf. The aim should be to craft and shape the service elements until they deliver the proverbial crock of gold. The brand both unites the four elements of the total service product and wraps them in its values and image. Customers experience tangible, process, information and relationship elements of the service.

One of the advantages of this model is that it has complete synergy with the organization model (which will be developed in the next chapter). This should not be surprising. The distinction between company and product is partly artificial and meets in the moment of truth.

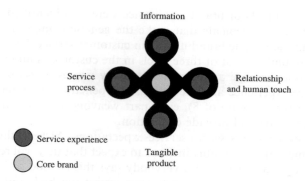

Figure 8.10 The four-leafed clover service cycles

Database marketing makes it possible to identify the unique product elements that made up a customer's individual service package (or many of them) and to assess the impact on satisfaction and profitability. By parametrizing attributes of the service and capturing their details for the customer in the marketing database – when, what, how, etc. – it is possible to analyse service impact and effectiveness. Statistical modelling can then be very effective in finding patterns of significance. Defining the product in this way can also help with benchmarking, see Table 8.1.

Table 8.1 Analysing the product

Product attributes	Process attributes	Information attributes	Relationship attributes
Customer rating of importance: – reliability – responsiveness – assurance – empathy – tangibles	Customer rating of importance: – reliability – responsiveness – assurance – empathy – tangibles	Customer rating of importance: – reliability – responsiveness – assurance – empathy – tangibles	Customer rating of importance: – reliability – responsiveness – assurance – empathy – tangibles
Customer rating of own product quality: . . .	Customer rating of own product quality: . . .	Customer rating of own product quality: . . .	Customer rating of own product quality: . . .
Customer rating of competitor product quality: . . .	Customer rating of competitor product quality: . . .	Customer rating of competitor product quality: . . .	Customer rating of competitor product quality: . . .

In a service product, intangibles become ever more important. A hi-fi is demonstrated, from stock carried, choice advised, installed, guaranteed, with guidance, and booklet on use. Each of these can be related to one or more of the above elements. The customer constantly judges, consciously or unconsciously, all four strands against expectations, needs, desires and competitive solutions.

The overall importance of the peripheral features of the product are well illustrated by Normann, who also originated the 'moments of truth' concept. The positive and negative service cycles shown in Figure 8.11[9] shows their effect on customer satisfaction and employee motivation.

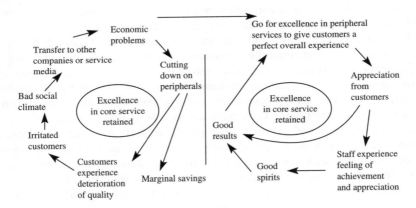

Figure 8.11   Positive and negative service cycles[9]

Going direct is already a *process* differentiator. It makes certain kinds of physical contact and tangible experience difficult. That is one reason why many direct products such as insurance have little tangible content. The product is then an idea, a feeling and a potential action, not a 'thing'. In this case there is less loss of reassurance or tangibility. In other products, the loss of direct product tangibility is overcome by strengthening the effectiveness of the other three elements. The catalogue, for example, is information, a tangible resource and a representation of what to expect; it is a personal document, a guarantee statement, and a convenient way to access product, information, etc. It also presents the brand values.

Research by Parasuraman and others[10] shows intangibles to be more important than tangibles in determining customer satisfaction. Their so-called SERVQUAL dimensions are now increasingly popularized as the five main service experiences:

– reliability
– responsiveness

- assurance
- empathy
- tangibles.

Others are: competence, access, courtesy, credibility, security, and understanding or knowing the customer. Process and relationship elements, particularly, are aspects of the service product's tendency to 'crystallize' in the moment. It is not surprising, therefore, that customers typically rate reliability as the most important service experience. What they are really looking for is something they can trust.

Loss of face-to-face contact can reduce relationship quality, but the telephone makes personal contact, albeit only verbal, almost instantaneous and easy – a process, relationship and information benefit.

Personalized communications can have the same effect. Ogilvy & Mather Direct research[11] confirmed the importance of the personal, human touch – e.g. courtesy, empathy, knowing the customer – in an age that often tries to turn service into a machine process. When UK company, Portland Holidays, began to phone customers who had expressed dissatisfaction in their holiday questionnaire, the customers were surprised and pleased to get such an immediate and personal response. They were even more surprised when asked what kind of compensation would be satisfactory. In many cases customers settled for lower compensation than the company would have offered without the discussion, and customers were happier too.

Service marketers are frequently urged to add tangibility. With database marketing, it is in fact possible to add 'touch' in three ways:

1. Keeping *in touch*, by maintaining vital contact, acknowledging the relationship through the moments of truth.
2. Making the relationship more *touching*, by using creative skills to add heart to the relationship message.
3. Making the service and communication more *tangible*, such as
   - a VIP tag on delivery
   - a yearly statement of what the customer spent
   - a certificate of attendance
   - a photograph.

With the safesforce it can:

- fill the gaps in the relationship – between visits (add *touch*);
- brief and remind the salesperson of actions, events, information about the customer, enhancing the care factor (more *touching*);
- turn the intangible meeting into a more *tangible event* – premiums to leave, follow up, guarantees, etc. – as well as a more relevant event (relevance is the nearest intangible to tangibility; it 'touches the situation').

The smart product

One of the most important developments over the next years will be the increasing 'intelligence' and information content in products. Information is not only a component of the product package in its own right, as in a railway timetable or library database, but will increasingly transform the process, relationship and hardware components of the product. More and more products, for example financial products, consist almost exclusively of information (or expertise) added value.

Case study 8.1 How companies are smartening their act by informing customers

One of the greatest strengths of database marketing is that it enables the company to give relevant information to customers. The Cryder Greek Catalogue is targeted at the home-based wood worker with a wide range of wood-working tools, supplies and woods. To attract attention it turned over the valuable top right-hand corner of every second page to displaying plans for the creation of interesting projects.

What were the results? First, products nearest the displays sold better, so the space can be used to highlight key products. Second, total sales increased and were extended longer, indicating better 'shelf life'. Similarly, Smithy Company sell machine tools to inexperienced and amateur customers by including in their catalogue extensive, easy to understand graphics and text on applications and methods. WWF uses its catalogue to educate, selling its message for a new earth and its products at the same time.

Audi UK have an in-house team of support operation managers. There are nine experienced technical support people who handle around 1200 telephone enquiries and complaints every week, satisfying most queries almost immediately.

One of the most effective pieces of information to give is a quality quotation. Viglen is one of the fastest growing PC direct companies in Britain and winner of a Customer First Award in 1994 because of its ability to handle even the most arcane questions competently and promptly and to be able to deliver a written specification and quotation by the next day. It has three information support teams, a pre-sales advice, one involved in direct customer care and a third which specializes in free technical support for the lifetime of the product.

Naturally there is a database on which every enquiry is logged. Every time a customer rings the entire history of his or her dealings with Viglen is available immediately on screen. Furthermore, corporate customers receive priority numbers.

In turn, process, relationship and hardware elements of the clover leaf may feed back information leading to a virtuous circle of continuous improvement of knowledge. Take these examples:

Smart hardware: IBM ships computers, such as the AS/400, with in-built problem detection and the capacity to auto-dial an expert computer system for further diagnosis and give full audit feedback; they also carry on-board question-and-answer databases for many 'common problems' with dial through to worldwide information centres. From hardware to firmware: Nitilin is a new wonder material which is used in bras. It 'remembers' the shape it should adopt and, as soon as it is warmed, readopts it.

Smart processes: Securicor's investment in being able to tell customers where their parcels are, including automatic, voice and sound-activated questioning, speeds solutions. The National Distribution Company, described later in this chapter, has invested in systems and processes that not only nourish their customers' business but serve their customers' customers.

Smart relationships: Huggies invested in turning a rank commodity into a caring partnership. 'My nappies taught me how to play with my child!'

Information: This is a service and is itself increasingly a product as well as an important component of products (see also Topic 8.1).

Massey Ferguson wrap it all up with a really smart system. It helps the farmer to improve the yield from every section of the farm. Their system links the farmer's tractor with a satellite-based Global Positioning System which records the latitude and longitude of the tractor's movements and captures the yield for each square yard automatically. The data is fed straight to the farmer's desktop computer and produces various yield maps showing variation against target.

The farmer can use this to do his or her own 'root' cause analysis on soil, seeds, fertilizer and so on. Soil sampling can be more effective. This binds Massey Ferguson and the client together, rendering information to both. It is not a tractor Massey Ferguson sells but a laboratory system. This is an extra carrot with a difference.

Product analysis

It is therefore crucially important that the computer database system is able to record the total service package, or at least all meaningful elements of it. For example, in making a decision about the effectiveness of a particular insurance product, it may be necessary to link the product not only to the marketing promotion, but also to the particular script that is used. Furthermore, if customers telephoning for an insurance quotation are kept waiting for a long time, this could affect take-up and loyalty. An insurance product that has had a claim is a different insurance product from one that has not, both to the customer and the company.

It should therefore be possible to configure the database to recognize the different elements or entities that are likely to be relevant to total service product mix. A technique such as regression analysis can then be used to link customer satisfaction and retention to key ingredients of the product. It is less important to adopt a particular model of the product than to recognize the needs to be able to link service components in an information system and measure productive effects. This is covered in more detail in Chapters 11 and 12.

Analysis can also be done to identify the customers' perception of the importance of various attributes in the service product, and by linking this to their own satisfaction, identify priorities for investment and improvement (see also Chapter 16). Database marketing is therefore more than just a marketing communication medium: it also aids service product design, e.g.:

- personalizing relationship, product or process
- ordering methods
- delivery methods
- payment methods
- information services, e.g. catalogues
- creating and delivering communications which create and sustain intangible service value, e.g. thank you letter, special offer, communication
- producing information-rich tangible elements, e.g. an information pack
- interactive communication, e.g. complaints handling.

Guarantee management

'Bugs' Burger Bug Killer (BBBK) is a Miami based pest-extermination company owned by S.C. Johnson & Co. which built its business around 100 per cent commitments to its hotel and restaurant customers. Most BBBK competitors claim to reduce pests to 'acceptable' levels; BBBK promises elimination!

> You don't owe a penny until all the pests on your premises have been eradicated. If you are ever dissatisfied with BBBK's service you will receive a refund for up to 12 months' services, plus fees for another exterminator of your choice for the next year. If a guest spots a pest on your premises, BBBK will pay for the guest's meal or room, send a letter of apology and pay for a future meal or stay. If your facility is closed due to pests, BBBK will pay any fines, as well as all lost profits, plus $5000.

It is worth reading twice.

Is this direct mail copy, a business philosophy and commitment to customers, product description, corporate strategy, operational goals or definitions for processes, or is it all of these? The BBBK guarantee emphasizes the process relationship (including client's customers) and brand values to overcome relative intangibility. Normally, BBBK would be most noticeable when something goes wrong, but such a guarantee builds trust and keeps the supplier in mind. It is a perfect illustration of the direct marketing philosophy, with the result that **BBBK** charges 100 per cent more than rivals, is closer to its community (it is a regional player) and has disproportionate market share. Even with end-to-end commitment and processes designed to match, it only has to pay out less than 0.4 per cent of turnover.

A powerful service guarantee works. It produces companies that stand out from the crowd, and, if taken seriously, forces commitment to quality. The result is a double impact:

– Better quality service.
– Contented customers willing to pay for assured quality.

'Guarantee management' is the end-to-end establishment of a market-moving commitment, a guarantee of delivery supported by systems, knowledge and processes. It is an idea that was developed earlier as a support for the development of *treasured reputation*. There were four components:

1. Establish what you want to promise (from knowledge of customers).
2. Establish how to deliver it.
3. Make the offer.
4. Invite response, making it easy if anything goes wrong.

It is quite obvious that a guarantee hits straight at the problem of reliability while providing great marketing leverage. And a *guarantee is essentially a direct marketing device*. It is targeted, it communicates and it invites response. Link it to a database and you have great analytical and targeting power, e.g. for follow up. When The Firework Company got its delivery wrong to one large customer, it called back the next year immediately after delivery to check whether everything was right (after having double checked anyway before delivery).

With the capacity of database marketing to deliver quality information about product components, it becomes possible to progressively architect a business around a customer commitment, to design and evolve a total service solution. Manpower grew from $400 million to $4 billion in 10 years. They call every customer when a new person is assigned and, if not satisfied, they do not pay. Not only is it welcomed by the customer but it lets Manpower know how both it and its temporary staff are relating. The worker is still paid but can be more effectively assigned in future. As a result, Manpower gets to know its business better too.

A real commitment to a guarantee conditions the company's attitude – as we saw with BBBK. When Manpower CEO Mitchell Fromstein considered dropping the guarantee, the *employees* reacted. They were proud of their standards. A service guarantee gets valuable customer feedback, provides the means to complain, sets standards (e.g. Federal Express, absolutely, positively by 10.30 a.m.) and produces great copy focused on relevant customer need, which may need research.

A good guarantee.

- promises what customers want: relevancy
- does not conceal conditions: it achieves simplicity and clarity
- makes tailored, meaningful offers, not mild or insulting ones
- does not make itself risk free, or a joke to everyone
- creates easy response methods – easy to invoke without guilt
- measures long-term effects: lifetime value.

These are, of course, disciplines of database marketing. But guarantee management is more than just a guarantee, it is a systematic development of service relationship.

Defections management, and complaint handling

One of the best ways to use a guarantee, as was noted with Manpower, is to find out about dissatisfaction, handle it effectively and improve retention. But a guarantee is more than a device, it is a way of thinking. It can be as simple as offering a careline and actually wanting to hear about problems and questions (sometimes it only becomes a problem when there is no answer to the question). The real test of a company's commitment to service quality is the way it responds when things go wrong. According to expert Vincent Mitchell, it is indicative of its philosophy[12] translating into how it reads the marketplace and therefore its chances of survival. The real aim of the guarantee and careline is to create a corporate *lifeline*.

Problems may even be an advantage, if they are properly dealt with. According to British Airways research, customers who have experienced their recovery system are 5–10 per cent more satisfied than those who have never had a problem with BA. The Royal Bank of Scotland found that customers whose grievances had been settled were considerably more likely to buy RBS products in the future than those who had never complained. Settling the problem openly, politely and speedily produced a more positive customer, even if the final decision had not gone in the account holder's favour.

Surveys by RBS showed that 40 per cent of dissatisfied and 60 per cent of satisfied customers would repurchase, while 80 per cent of those who had a resolved problem were prepared to buy again. The RBS policy, therefore, was to make it easy for customers to complain. They send customer service questionnaires to their 200 000 customers every six months. Initially, their survey of branches showed that the most effective were small local offices with a strong community relationship. They have been able to transfer some of these values to larger branches. Their next task is to be able to say to each of their branches how much an extra point on the customer services index is worth.

When problems arise, research shows that customers expect[13] to:

- receive a prompt, personal apology, with someone taking responsibility;
- be offered a fair solution: the customer must see an effort towards reinstatement;
- be shown that the company cares: empathy, compassion, demonstration of understanding;
- be offered some value-added, symbolic atonement: this is a token of sorrow, not a pound of flesh;
- have a follow-up check, especially if the customer felt victimized.

Case study 8.2   Guarantees and carelines that have worked

Neil's Yard is a London-based Personal Development Centre running a busy schedule of workshops, many by outside trainers. Their offer – for every completed feedback sheet you can claim your free entry voucher, worth £5.00, for one of the events organized – gives information on the quality of trainers, enables people to off-load their unhappiness and gives a reward which induces repeat business.

Toy manufacturer Little Tykes spends more money on customer service, such as care lines, than on advertising: 2.5–3 per cent of annual net sales. It receives up to 30 000 calls per year in the UK. This is used to track and resolve problems with products, and relationships, and can be used to target sales and special offers more effectively. About 25–30 per cent of callers have complaints. Is this a bad figure, or does it mean that Little Tykes has created an environment that welcomes communication?

Since Virgin Atlantic found that each of its customers with a bad experience *will tell 17 people*, and with a happy experience four, they have been further committed to solving problems. It provides all 3500 members of staff with chairman Richard Branson's home telephone number and they do call him direct. In 1993 Virgin received 18 000 customer communications, through a variety of channels, of which half were core complaints. Others were suggestions of improvements and congratulations. Branson and Virgin's managing director phone unhappy customers personally in many cases. According to Branson: 'If you take the trouble to call customers you can win them back and keep them for ever.'

In 1988, chairman Bill Marriott Jr of Marriott Hotels personally read 10 per cent of the 8000 letters and 2 per cent of the 750 000 guest questionnaires the company received *each month*.[14] The result: occupancy rates at Marriott have consistently averaged about 10 per cent above the industry norm.[15]

The Birmingham Midshires Building Society in the UK was a 1993 winner in the Customer First Awards. It is convinced that a focus on client satisfaction is the best route to corporate regeneration and actively committed itself to this path. One of its first acts after winning the 1993 award was to write to its 400 000 clients to ask them how services could be improved still further.

Questionnaires are used by Midshires as a vital tool in collecting information on customer needs and trends. Many tens of thousands are sent out each year with an average response rate of over 20 per cent. One of its good ideas is to provide expert counselling to borrowers in difficulties, which is a reason why its record on mortgage arrears and repossessions is better than the industry average.

When the author put the same idea to another leading finance house it died a death. They were busy researching techniques to squeeze the troubled borrower harder. By contrast, Midshires CEO Mike Jackson believes that recommendations from clients who are delighted with their treatment make them a powerful and free salesforce. A team advises customers whose money may be in old or uncompetitive accounts and newcomers to the company comment on the passion for excellence that permeates the organization.

Empowering effective treatment is recognized by Midshires as key. Good methods include awareness training, dramatization and improvisation, particularly for archetypal moments, scripting, information services about customers and products, and investing confidence in people.

But, if you are going to try to handle complaints, you better do it well, and listen. BT interviews 13 000 business customers each month and has now empowered relatively junior point of contact operators to offer goodwill gestures, including cash payments, in recompense for problems. Yet, when *The Sunday Times* sent a mystery shopper complaint to the chairman, it took seven weeks to be answered. In the rest of the test, only one company expressed shared concern, although both Texaco and the Body Shop offered personal meetings. A 1994 Henley Centre report, *Teleculture 2000*, found that 65 per cent of customers react to even one badly handled call, such as rudeness, delays, lack of efficiency, with a probable decision to take their business elsewhere.

Complaints may arise from simple annoyance, a minor shunt on the Maslow scale, or a severe, survival-threatening bump, generating a feeling of victimization: 'Why me?' It is not necessary for physical life to be threatened. I left an important notebook on an Air France plane, reported it three times in Paris and then in London, each time complaining that the only response I had received so far was, 'They probably threw it out with the trash', and I *still didn't receive a call or letter.*

British Airways concluded from their research (Figure 8.12) that it took good service *and* good product to create a relationship, but that customers were slightly more forgiving if the service was good but the product had suffered. Poor service generated complaints. In that case, complaint-handling procedure better be good or the feeling of poor service will simply be reinforced.

How the organization can change its culture, systems and processes to take advantage of quality database marketing will be discussed in Part Two.

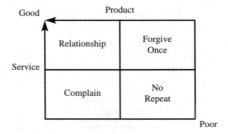

Figure 8.12 Effect of deficiencies in product and service

Topic 8.2 A taxonomy of service organizations

Service companies divide into three kinds,[16] whose difference is becoming increasingly important. Failure by governments to distinguish between them is damaging the quality of post-modern society. Someone may devise better names for them, but that is a secondary matter.

1. Those which provide something from the human, or of the human spirit, to the human: *service creators*.
2. Those which care for individual rights and well being: *service providers*.
3. Those which provide a commodity, enhanced by service: *service marketers*.

The first group, *service creators*, includes educational and religious institutions, artistic, sporting and other cultural activities. The name derives from their essentially free, creative function arising from the depths of human spirit and striving. They depend on the innate perceived quality of insight, talent, knowledge or performance. Few, if any, commodities change hands. The act of 'consumption' changes the consumer, as in the catharsis of *Hamlet* or the learning of golf skills.

The second group, *service providers*, includes legal, medical, governmental, fire, police, military (for defence purposes), aid and lobby groups and other NGOs. They are concerned with meeting and developing citizens' rights as defined from time to time. Essentially everyone has more or less equal rights under their regime, although there may sometimes be hard choices. Like the first group, they may have marketing activities, for example, in fundraising. Here, the act of consumption creates community value in maintaining the individual status.

The third group, *service marketers*, are an extension of the basic economic process. They are concerned with transforming nature and bringing it to a place of consumption but with an ever richer service laden content. Transforming commodities is a process of adding value through shared human skill and effort. This may include a personalized production process and delivery to the customer in a convenient, tailored way. The act of consumption is the last process in the value chain.

The difference might be clarified in these three archetypal examples:

- the university: service creator
- the hospital: service provider
- the hotel: service marketer.

Each provides accommodation, each caters for a human need, and each has its own dynamics. Of course, a private hospital may also offer hotel services (a better room, food, and so on); a hotel might offer a weekend programme in chamber music, flower arrangement or golf; and a university might offer pastoral care. Furthermore, any one sector will have aspects of the other two. Every business flourishes only by the mix of these elements: a manufacturing business has R&D and personnel policies, an advertising agency, creative excellence, pensions and job control.

Why is this distinction therefore important? Because, to develop the full potential, culture and policies need to vary. *Creators* work out of the individual initiative for self-expression which, when recognized, is funded by others: Shakespeare's essential work was not bought – how could it be? – but funded. Creators are never businesses in the normal sense of the word, although they do depend on financial support and often earn considerable sums. Information, knowledge, know-how, inspiration dominate this sector. Michelle Pfeiffer's relationship with her customers is managed through a fan club. Many arts and leisure organizations build supporter bases, each a kind of fan club, like the Friends of the English National Opera.

Providers operate out of a shared responsibility, duty and care; they 'command' our obligation to support (hence taxes) and relationships are often imposed by laws and community expectations. Processes and even-handed relationships are most critical in this sector.

Marketers are entrepreneurs whose special capacity is the ability to organize and unite endeavour for the fulfilment of opportunity and need. They have the most tangible services. The whole economic process, despite the fierce competitiveness that attracts the eye, is actually a field of enormous cooperation, from field to plate. *Marketers* unite energy, insight, materials and people to create new surplus to fund the health, well-being and growth of society. In many service businesses, the customer is a part and partner. Nowhere is this more true than in database marketing.

The customer's association or partnership in each case, although different, is the key to the cultivation of relationship value.

Notes and references

1. Rackham, N., *Making Major Sales*, Gower, 1987.
2. Levitt, T., 'After the sale is over', *Harvard Business Review* (Sept./Oct. 1983).
3. Wylie, P., 'Science has spoiled my supper', *Atlantic* (April 1954); quoted in W.E. Deming, *Out of the Crisis*, Cambridge University Press, 1992.
4. Gibbon, E. *Decline and Fall of the Roman Empire*, Penguin Books, 1987 (first published in full edition, 1781–1788 by Strahan and Cadell, London).
5. Quinn, J., Baruch, J. and Paquette, P., 'Technology in services', *Scientific American* (Dec. 1987), p.50.
6. Steiner, R., *World Economy*, Rudolf Steiner Press, 1972.

7. Ogilvy and Mather Direct, Internal European taskforce: *Service Driven Companies*, unpublished internal communication, 1993.
8. Levitt, T., *The Marketing Imagination*, The Free Press, 1983.
9. Normann, R., *Service Management, Strategy and Leadership in Service Businesses*, Wiley, 1986.
10. Parasuraman, A., Zeithaml, V.A. and Berry, L.L., 'SERVQUAL: a multiple-item scale for measuring consumer perceptions of service quality', *Journal of Retailing*, **64** (No. 1; Spring 1988).
11. Internal *Adopt a Country* programme.
12. 'Home News', *The Sunday Times* (3 Jan. 1993).
13. Zemke, R., 'Service recovery: a key to customer retention', *Franchising World*, **23** (No. 3; May/June 1991), pp. 32–4.
14. *Fortune* (10 Oct. 1988).
15. 'How master lodger Bill Marriott prophesized profit and prospered', *Fortune* (5 June 1989), pp.56–7.
16. Steiner, R., *Social Issues*, Anthroposophic Press, 1991.

PART TWO
RESOURCES AND CHANGE

Summing up Part One, the successful business in the new age will probably have many or all of the following characteristics:

1. Persistent visionary thinking focused on serving the customer community.
2. A 'people' business, through and through, valuing people, whether they are customers, suppliers or employees.
3. A committed learning strategy, based on customer experience and interaction, with the courage to innovate.
4. It will behave in the knowledge that loyalty, integrity and morality are reciprocated and congruous virtues: customers reward companies over time as companies reward customers.
5. It will nurture internal and external goodwill as the chief care of board to front line employees.
6. Knowledge processing is a core competency and empowering point-of-need tool of the business, and a primary raw material in the company's value-added transformation steps. (The information systems development process owner will probably be on the board, but will be marketing or marketing literate. The relationships development process owner will probably either be ex-IT or IT literate.)
7. It will use information not as an internal weapon but as a map, to judge where the company is relative to where it wants to be (and where it has come from).

Part Two explores how to make the change, focusing on enablers and practical issues: culture, database, software and system tools, data and its collection, name and address processing, and tools and ideas for change and project management.

9
Changing the culture

Summary Some companies seem to think that installing a marketing database automatically delivers loyal customers. It does not. This chapter considers some of the organization change issues, and in particular the culture and organization structure which is most effective. Using a wonderful old legend as a metaphor for service excellence, some of the conditions for treasured reputation and service mastery are described, followed by an introduction to change psychology.

The greatest martial arts are the gentlest. They allow an attacker the opportunity to fall down.

(John Heider)

The importance of company culture in employee attitudes and retention can be considered as another aspect of brand, to be developed and stewarded carefully. Success in this world of change depends on integrating three factors (Figure 9.1):

1. *Niche focus.* All business leaders recognize the need for focus, or as Tom Peters called it: stick to the knitting. Focus also means getting close to customers, and the ultimate focus is one-to-one marketing: the ability to be able to respond to the individual customer and his or her needs.
2. *Customer service* is the process of delivering the organization's focus. It arises in the moments of truth that build loyalty. Customer service is the human orientation of the business, the process of adding relationship value in each exchange in such a way as to delight customers.
3. If organizations are to achieve this, they will need *TQM disciplines and culture*. TQM is the logistic and process discipline, as well as the sense of teamwork that enables the other two elements to operate.

Only when these three are integrated, respecting the environment and the trends of the times, can the organization be truly effective in improving quality, reducing costs and delighting customers. Database marketing is a child of this age, a discipline which, at its best, is a niche focus, a service and a TQM discipline. It aims for measured improvement in long-term customer satisfaction at reduced costs. As we have seen, it is capable of improving

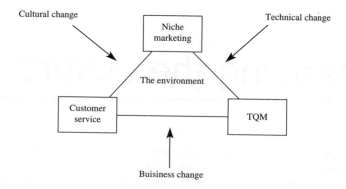

Figure 9.1   The triangle of quality

quality in the most simple of ways: personalizing (niche) a service (service) effectively (TQM) transforms it in the eyes of customers.

The customer as 'strategist'

Concentration on strategy setting as a formal discipline of goal setting obscures the commonplace reality: the customer is increasingly the organization driver. Mintzberg has always argued that it is not the cold logic of strategy but the emergent reality of what was called the customer threshold that drives organizations. For example, it was not a formal strategy that took Honda into the USA, as the business school described it, but Honda executives getting stopped and asked questions as they rode about on their bikes.[1] Such conversation is the essence of marketing advantage and database marketing.

One of the best techniques for 'vision' and 'strategy' building is to write a corporate brochure for your customers, setting out where you want to be, your planned guarantee, and then honour it. The brochure can help to make the promise vivid and win support and understanding. It is also a creative way to tackle a business plan. (This is an advantage of database marketing companies: they constantly write brochures called catalogues, and measure the response.) As CEO of an IT service company for marketers, it was the clients I talked to daily who shaped my thinking and hence the company. While all CEOs and marketers can take advantage of this opportunity, it becomes equally obvious that database marketing is an ideal discipline for this approach to strategy:

- it makes sense to use front line resources, and
- a systematic process helps, i.e. a development loop identifying customers,

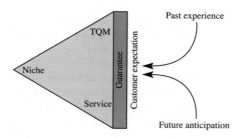

The aim is to keep moving expectations positively
... and delivering!

Figure 9.2   Guarantee management

obtaining information, analysing it, changing and re-offering the service to identified customers.

The aim is to use niche focus, service and TQM to create and sustain marketing advantage through an evolving and delivered guarantee which meets or exceeds customer expectations (Figure 9.2).

Topic 9.1   A service parable about champions

One of the most important legends of the Middle Ages in *Parzival*, or Percival in the English version. It is also a wonderful Wagner opera, a BBC radio play by Lindsay Clarke and helped to inspire a film. (One of the key characters, Anfortas 'the fisher king', is a symbol of decay in T.S. Eliot's poem, 'The Waste Land': 'I sat upon the shore fishing, with the arid plain behind me', a scene transposed to modern Manhatten in the film *The Fisher King*.) The story is told by several medieval authors, including Wolfram von Eschenbach,[2] and like all great legends it has something to tell us still.

Parzival, although he becomes an Arthurian Knight, is a lonely and therefore modern figure, 'a forerunner of our time' as one commentator put it.[3] He is brought up in the forest by his mother who wants to protect him from his father's fate – a hero who had come to an untimely end. Parzival delights in the wonder of the woods but one day sees some knights riding through the forest, their armour shining. He wants to be one too, runs after them and eventually joins Arthur's court, before setting off on adventures. His mother, wounded with grief, dies of sorrow.

Parzival is so naive that he causes offence, for example thoughtlessly following a rule his mother gave him, 'Always kiss any lady you meet'. Her own knight-partner, discovering what has happened, is so upset that he spurns her, leaving her in misery.

Parzival's horse carries him through the woods to a castle, to a very special group of knights and their king. This is the Grail Castle; its inhabitants are the protectors of the Holy Grail. The castle is magical and only those with the right credentials are able to find it. Unknown to Parzival, he is the one eagerly awaited. The king is sorely wounded from misuse of a holy spear, and the wound will not stop bleeding until a new king comes. Amazingly, there is only one thing that Parzival needs to do to be recognized as the new Grail King – to ask a very simple question: *'What ails thee?'*

Or, What is the problem? How can I help? Of course, to ask such a question requires openness, recognition and willingness.

Parzival fails. Trusting his mother that he should never ask a question of a stranger, he says nothing and in the morning awakes to an empty castle and mocking laughter. Parzival then becomes aware, with the help of others, of his failures, naivety and inadequacy and sets out, shamed, to change and put things right.

The legend continues through many adventures during which Parzival matures through trial and error, deep contemplation and commitment and a series of meetings with people who help him on his way. He acquires self-knowledge, sensitivity to others and the courage to act when necessary. He begins the innocent fool, full of potential but unskilled, thoughtless and therefore destructive in action. Maturity prepares him for the point when he can eventually find his way back to the castle, this time with his half brother, symbolically black and white, to 'ask the question' and thereby inherit his duty.

The Parzival legend above has much to do with running a business. From slogans and thoughtlessness to what Deming called 'profound knowledge' or what Oliver Wendall Holmes called 'the simplicity on the *other* side of complexity'. It is a story of self-development through trial and error to the capacity to care, to serve, to meet another's needs. Lindsay Clarke's play particularly captures Parzival's need to take personal responsibility – not just obey external authority. Parzival becomes the 'perfect knight' and a model for chivalry who gains the Grail. Is this not at the heart of quality development, of continuous improvement? Error and learning towards a goal of perfection. (Six sigma quality, although not always a wise goal, means 'perfection in natural standard'.)

Parzival had to grow and change. This process is sometimes lonely, often difficult, but ultimately rewarding. He is willing to look deeply into himself, symbolized for example by '40 days' of self-absorption (a symbolic period in Jewish/Christian tradition) wandering through 'the forests'. He eventually becomes a king by becoming a server of others. Root cause analysis may need a similar willingness to 'venture into the forest and see where it takes you'.

Accepting profound change takes what Argyris called double-loop learning: finding out not just what went wrong and why, but *why the cause was caused*! The root causes. This needs helpful organization conditions for greatest success.

If leaders want to get the best out of their company, they need to connect the psychology of the individual with the psychology and pattern of the company, key elements in Deming's Profound Knowledge. The Maslow hierarchy (indicated in Chapter 1) can be linked tentatively to culture and trust norms in evolving organization and delegation styles (see Table 9.1).

Table 9.1 Cultural evolution

Maslow value	Action driver in company	Delegation and trust norms
Survival	*Orders* Blind followers DEAD	Little trust yet; direct and detailed orders BOSS
Security and comfort	*Procedures* Naive followers ASLEEP	Can you make suggestions for my consideration? DECIDER
Belonging	*Culture* determines normative behaviour; war stories, doing it how it is done round here DREAMING	Keep me informed of what you are planning that is new, just in case REVIEWER
Esteem	*Champions* Individual initiative is welcomed, but people also want regular 'strokes' and recognition and initiative still needs checking; there may be fear of failure AWAKE	Tell me what you have done, afterwards COACH
Self-actualization	*Parzival condition* Champion as server, doing their best because that is what gives satisfaction; performance is its own reward; openness to learn; the individual gives to the team, works with the 'brother' INSPIRED	Tell me if you need me SERVICE MASTER

Western businesses modelled on the Taylor principles (used by Ford in setting up his Baton Rouge mass-manufacturing facility) are dominated by procedures and orders. By contrast, leading Japanese and Western firms have shaped a new paradigm: 'We are beyond the Taylor model: business . . . is now so complex and difficult, the survival of firms so hazardous in an environment increasingly unpredictable ... that *their continued existence depends on the day-to-day mobilisation of every ounce of intelligence,'* said Mr Konosuke Matsushita, of Matsushita.

Great companies around the world emulate this. At their best, they also create conditions in which champions flourish, but as part of a team. Apple teams often selected their own colleagues. IBM have traditionally had 'consultant salespeople', individuals of senior manager *status* who still sold but with legendary skill. Part of their job was to help less experienced people. In the West, our cultivation of champions often sets them against others, promoting the champion *or* you as winner. This can be self-defeating. In Japan, by contrast, it is difficult for a 'salary person' to become a champion, only the team. The challenge is to cultivate teams of champions, heroes and heroines in the struggle for excellence.

For this, orders must become shared, worth while, inspiring goals in which the champions have participated. These goals become a 'leading image' which draws people together in vision.

Procedures must become processes *on* which people work in continuous improvement, based on shared policies and values. A procedure is a rigid set of rules. A process is living, dynamic movement. A plant grows in processes and is dissected in procedures. A process is actually invisible except in enlivened memory. (It can only be observed in momentary snapshots.) Processes are carried out with skill, procedures with blind ignorance, like Parzival's blunders. Knowledge is an enabler of skill, and the marketing database a source of the information that leads to it.

Policies and values guide processes and enable individuals to act out of initiative in the situation. Procedures define action and kill creativity. A *policy* of customer satisfaction frees the individual team member to become an empowered creative champion resolving the situation, the problem of the moment, thereby transforming the service product in the moment of truth. For example, ServiceMaster Company, a fast-growing maintenance and food service firm in the US, treats its uneducated workforce with exceptional respect. However the CEO's attitude is 'before asking someone to do something, you have to help them to *be* something'.[4] The result is that ServiceMaster has been one of the most consistently profitable companies in the United States.

The powerful correlation between customer satisfaction and employee morale[5] means that a procedure driven company kills employee motivation, making them unfree and uncreative, and thereby kills customer satisfaction: service by machine procedure is not fun. Enthusiastic people sell their product by infection.

As a test, Rover put 120 production line employees to work selling cars over the phone. During the course of six weeks they spoke to 120 000 prospects and sold an additional 3000 cars. The original intention had been to give shopfloor workers a concrete experience of the importance of customer service, quality and reliability by talking direct to customers. The experiment proved so successful that Rover has continued the practice. Potential customers experience the real enthusiasm, commitment and knowledge of those who make the cars and this shines through. This is one of the problems of telemarketing bureaux divorced from the product or service. To be really effective, clients should ensure that tele-workers experience first hand the product they are trying to sell.

Case study 9.1   Barclays Bank complain about complaints

Barclays Bank, one of the top four British clearing banks, announced in August 1994 that they were switching their emphasis, signalling a tidal wave of change in which DBM skills and tools will be at the vanguard.

According to Barclays, top management are now as much on the line for customer satisfaction and service standards as profits. Upset by criticism of standards that focused on profits while customers complained and employees were laid off, they have appointed an internal watchdog and established a £2 million initiative to change the way complaints are handled, supported by a database that codes problems into 15 categories and 100 headings. Every branch manager is empowered to solve problems within 24 hours, with an internal marketing message to all staff, 'We're banking on you to keep customers'.

One reason for the change is that, previously, customers would not talk to them. Despite massive criticism to the press and surveys, *they* had received only 7000 complaints from 7 million customers. They hope a sincere apology, effective handling and a new approach will change attitudes, as it can. The aim is excellent, as are the technology initiatives, but how effective will their project be? If the top person is *'on the line'*, that spells commitment, but it *could* mean that service is driven by fear. That would be self-defeating, because it would not generate maximum commitment to satisfied customers, but maximum danger avoidance, in which customers become a problem.

Nearly three out of four banking customers cite teller courtesy as a prime consideration in choosing a financial institution.[6] If you want employees to behave with 'problem solving courtesy', then perhaps you should start by showing such an example to them. Business resources and systems should be deployed to serve those who serve customers.

Harnessing the value of employees

Some employees deal directly with customers day after day, building a powerful bond of trust and expectation, and when they leave the company the bond is disturbed. Toyota remains the dominant player in Japan because of its strong dealer salesforce. Because salespeople stay over 10 years on average they get to know customers well. This enduring bond gave them leadership over Honda. But in the USA – where car salespeople have a rapid turnover (60 to 100 per cent annually) and customers have no relationship with the salesforce – Honda's product advantage was enough to give it driving leadership, the relationship factor in the service product. (While the first step must be to retain employees, a database can at least help to retain information.)

Shared policies which value standards of care, excellence and quality become deeply motivating – customers buy and co-workers enjoy selling and service. A culture which values, respects, pays attention to and supports the individual within a team context enables individuals and the team to flourish. The individual comes to the aid of the group through carrying inward awareness and responsibility for it. The group supports the individual by recognizing the qualities he or she brings.[7] This has implications for pay and performance measurement.

Empowerment requires sharing the following five organizational ingredients with front-line people.

1. *Information about the organization's performance, goals and policies.* Mastercare shared its strategic goals and customer outreach plans with employees who responded enthusiastically, raising its customer retention rate by 25 per cent.
2. *Personal recognition, and shared reward* (financial and other) *based on organizational performance and customer feedback, not individual commission.* In its research, the Forum Corporation, identified that rewarding employees *financially* for being customer focused and having specific goals for improving quality *do not* have a strong correlation with favourable customer outcomes.

   Many retailers have found that commission packages designed to improve productivity and customer service have led to lower productivity, job dissatisfaction and a sales-by-intimidation erosion of customer loyalty and retention.[8] Corning's suggestion programme for its people, rewarding them not with cash but with awards, special dinners, local publicity, etc., generated about forty times as many suggestions. Metropolitan Life discovered that its people preferred personal recognition to cash awards. The wrong carrot takes away motivation, often transferring allegiance from pride in work to beating the rules.

   Of course, it only works if the base pay is felt to be fair, easing employees over survival and comfort levels. An increasing awareness of the destructive effects of commission systems based on numerical sales levels is also arising, but is beyond the scope of this book to detail.

   The issue is, what enables employees to want to make customer service vital? What really matters is the employee's experience of worth. The customer cannot be more important than the employee, or the employee becomes a slave-servant, and subsequent demotivation will damage customer relationships. The employee cannot become more important than the customer, or the reason and livelihood of the service marketer will be lost. The employee and the customer should be equally, but differently, important.

3. *Total process overview and system knowledge that enables employees to understand and contribute to organizational performance.* Rover, as a second phase in their experiment, took white-collar workers on a rota basis and gave them an experience on the product line. Information on results lets people learn and adjust.

4. *The power to make decisions that influence organizational direction and performance.* If you do not give people important decisions to make, they start to think that the small decisions they make are important, and then everything gets stuck.

5. *The necessary resources.* It makes no sense to ask people to do a job without also supplying the means to be really successful. If you really cannot afford it, then try discussing the problem together and find out how to make the resources affordable.

Case study 9.2   Enterprising culture in a social and cultural movement

One of the most remarkable examples of enterprising culture is the anthroposophic movement, taking its lead from Rudolf Steiner, a social, philosophical and scientific initiator who died in 1925. There are 50 000 people who are members of the worldwide anthroposophic societies (a non-religious personal development movement; 'anthroposophic' means 'wisdom of man'), *and no less than 10 000 institutions inspired by its members.* That means one institution for every five members!

For example, there is the world's largest independent schools movement: the 600 or so Steiner or Waldorf Schools, many hundreds of homes, workshops and communities for the handicapped – Camphill Communities and others – medical practices (anthroposophical medicine is an advanced homeopathic form and the third recognized medicine in the EU), therapy, toiletry and medical manufacturers like Weleda using pure, natural products, social banks, artists and artistic schools, research foundations, colleges and universities, consultants, 'biodynamic organic' farms, craft workshops, shops, traders and more. These are not economic powerhouses, but they have attracted thousands of coworkers, as well as tens of thousands of customers, who value the ideas and culture.

Everywhere, clients and customers testify to a quality, profound value at very reasonable prices. For example, independent studies of biodynamic farms shows their productivity per acre and the quality of products sold under the Demeter brand as higher than surrounding conventional farms, with soil conditions that improve year after year.

What makes this possible? Look at the rapidly growing Steiner schools, 'service creators' in the typology of the previous chapter, taking children from kindergarten to school leaving – and strongest in middle Europe. Most of the teachers are so committed that they are willing to work at salaries below state norms to help as many children as possible to attend: an expression of high Maslow scale values. They value an approach which recognizes the individual, both at the organizational and pedagogical levels. As Albert Schweitzer said, 'I don't know what your destiny may be, but one thing I know. The only ones among you who will be really happy, are those who have sought and found how to serve.'

Each school is independent and autonomous, while recognizing itself as part of a worldwide association. The schools actually have no head teachers, so teachers take responsibility together in a college with membership open to everyone with commitment. The output, so to speak, are young people with ideals, enterprise, maturity, balance, initiative, independence, intelligence and a wide sweep of cultural and scientific understanding. Universities and colleges are on record as valuing the independent thinking of these students. This is achieved through a curriculum and method first worked out by Rudolf Steiner which seems to bring a balance of artistic, scientific and active learning suited harmoniously to the child's age.

Not surprisingly, growth happens mainly by word of mouth, an ideal that many organizations are trying to meet. Each school nurtures its own lively community based on shared values and goals. Parents come together to learn about the education or enjoy fun festivals together with students and teachers. Regular newsletters commonly keep communication flowing, with parent and pupil input too. There is even a novel tele-service process: class groups divide into 'telephone trees', where the parents pass messages down chains, with the last people phoning back to confirm (wouldn't a bank love it if customers did that for them?).

Creating an enterprising culture

We noted in Chapter 6, citing the example of IBM, how organizations institute, whether they like it or not, a 'structural culture' which may become a barrier to effectiveness or the greatest asset a company possesses.

Culture is an intangible mood and flow of mission, psychological life and behaviour, becoming tangible or visible in the patterns, systems, workplace, processes and ideas of the company. Culture is a process by which the inner takes form in the outer. The total organism can be described as a 'structural culture', embracing:

- the inner, intangible, psychological: called the soul or spirit of the company by Tom Peters and Faith Popcorn;
- tangible and observable outer forms and activities: streams of activity processes, systems and physical environment;
- a tendency for both to become rigid and habitual, unless renewed.

The word 'company' derives from Latin 'breaking bread together'. Once built and shared, a culture is strong: it is difficult to overcome or change even when negative. Just as the lines on our faces are formed by the regular habits of movement, deriving in turn from psychological life, so habit lines are formed in the company. New policies, standards and directives are sometimes easy to make, but are real only when they actually become part of the new culture, the *done* policy not the *said* policy. Then they, in turn, tend towards rigidity.

All organizations are located somewhere along a continuum. At one end is the tendency towards pioneering enthusiasm, rapid change, warmth, excitement and fire fighting. Lots of lovely soul! The culture-led excitement Tom Peters encourages. At the other end of the continuum is a tendency towards a colder culture characterized by more firmly differentiated forms and procedures. Lots of safe control! *In extremis* these become, respectively, chaos and stasis. Another reason to integrate and balance.

Change itself must adjust to the prevailing culture. Pioneers like models and ideas. Formed, differentiated companies like plenty of 'what to do' processes.

Professor Sathe suggests[9] that the essence of corporate culture is in shared:

- sayings, e.g. our customer is the boss – i.e. shaping ideas;
- feelings, e.g. we care, the company respects me – i.e. relationship values;
- doings, e.g. managers talk with customers, celebrations – i.e. processes in action;
- things, e.g. shirt sleeves, open offices – i.e. resource sharing.

These four aspects of culture link to the four interacting realms of the organization (see Table 9.2) and the four key areas of organizational development, the clover-leaf model, which has already been outlined (Figure 9.3). The first two elements correspond to the more inner, intangible side of business; the latter two to the more outer, observable – the mind and body of the company! To stretch the analogy, the company is related to the human archetype.

Any activity, such as product design, production or team building will involve elements from all levels. A successful organization will integrate these in a way that is effective and congruent. The sequence is defined by the increasing 'substantiality' of the operating levels: a mission or goal is less 'tangible' than culture, which is harder to define than a process, which is less concrete than a physical resource. By these means, the organization's ideas incarnate into practice and into the service product.

A healthy and effective company knows itself and its purpose with a clear, integrated control vision and feedback (ego); it has an engaging, lively, curious and interesting personality capable of interacting positively with others; it has healthy bio-rhythms and processes – immune and other systems to transform and respond to the outside natural world and to deal with waste and foreign bodies – and a sound set of limbs, etc., built round a flexible and responsive bone, nervous, skin and organ architecture.

Table 9.2 Model for the four organization fields

The four organizational fields *What the company consists of and* *equivalence in the human being.*	The four development fields *Some corresponding focal points for* *organization development.*
Sayings The shaping world of mission, direction, form, identity, intentions, plans, arising from the relationship between the demands and opportunities of the environment and the shared intentions of the team or leader. EGO	Customer service mission, as the organization driver, including concepts of niche, retention, and relationship management, lifetime value, customer defined quality, service, moments of truth, the internal customer; buyer–supplier relationships.
Feelings The social world of shared attitudes and behaviours, including the ideas, stories, politics, relationships and morale. PERSONALITY	Corporate culture, in the narrower and normal sense, i.e. creating conditions for success through leadership, empowerment, teamwork, flatter organizations, missioning, innovation, brand and identity development, internal marketing, the learning company.
Doings The movement world of processes, skills and designs, which is observable only with the ability to think, watch and remember. LIFE PROCESSES	Lean management, including JIT, SPC (statistical process control), ISO 9001, continuous process improvement, outsourcing, root cause analysis, corporate re-engineering, logistics, activity-based costing.
Things The physical world of resources, computers, vans, meeting rooms, mailing packs; tangible and concrete. PHYSICAL STRUCTURE, SKELETON AND FLESH	Information management is perhaps the most important resource. Information architecture, networking, data/data centre management, right sizing, software re-use. Also, Treasury, and other resource and asset deployment systems, warehousing, office environment.

Information itself becomes the means to operate between and through these levels.

Lievegoed's clover leaf model of the organization,[10] which has already been introduced, has the great advantage that it exactly matches and provides continuity with the service product model in the previous chapter, supporting the validity of both models, and correlates with this model too. It has been used by consultants in at least five continents for nearly 40 years, but is not as well known as it deserves. One further advantage is that

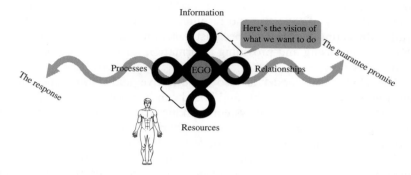

Figure 9.3 The clover leaf model of the organization (based on Lievegoed)

it works equally well at the individual, departmental and organizational levels, and provides flexible, open, total system thinking.

In Figure 9.3, an attempt has also been made to show the link to both moments of truth and the organization threshold described above, and also the more inner and outer aspects of the structural culture.

The figure shows the four core competences or faculties of the business, the more inner and the outer aspects characterized above as 'body' and 'mind', and the central source of direction and control, the 'ego' – both at individual and organizational levels. It also shows the main flow of activity in the business, changing from a hierarchical architecture to a process flow/ relationships architecture. This horizontal process flow or business stream also links directly to the dynamic organization threshold described above: the moments of truth represent an interchange of information and resources between company and customer, I∞I, as part of the relationship-building and service process activities.

1. Each individual is in the centre of his or her own clover leaf and has relationships to develop, works *on* and *in* processes, and needs resources and information, including corporate policies and other guidelines, as well as practical information. Being 'in the middle' means 'in charge, with responsibility for a given set of goals and processes, resolving challenges – with the means of so doing – being an individual but part of the team'.
2. A department or process group has similar characteristics. The manager is in the centre, with the department carrying out its tasks/processes.
3. A company operates in a similar manner, with the board 'in the middle' taking responsibility for providing the direction and necessary coordination for others.

In each case, leadership (personal or corporate) occupies a central role, as the brand personality did in the product clover leaf. The 'weaving' design recognizes the reality of the workplace and the need for flexibility and point-of-need delivery of expertise and resources: the service product moment of truth. Marketing becomes a specialist function/process owner in relationship creation, using and providing information, processes and resources in continuous flow.

The clover leaf model is also an effective audit tool, operationally synergistic. Individuals, teams and board can be reviewed for needs in each area as a coordinated set of system thinking. It can be flowcharted using a charting model designed to match (see Chapter 15). It can be linked to the product model and measurement of service product effectiveness.

The WWF example in Case study 9.3 also illustrates the importance of integrating specialist teams, e.g. advertising agencies. Partnership arrangements with agencies and other direct marketing industry suppliers will be a key determinant of success. The practice of working with a diverse range of agencies on a project basis has to be one of the most old-fashioned, wasteful and unproductive methods known. In 1994, Barclaycard, the leading UK Visa operator, discovered it was working with 50 agencies on a project basis – and Barclaycard is only one of Barclays brands. That form of association dissipates knowledge, commitment and relationship.

The need for partnerships with suppliers is now commonplace in manufacturing, but, in a situation that requires some of the most creative, service laden, just-in-time work that any organization can have, why is practice still so bedevilled by the old-fashioned win–lose, competitive mentality?

Case study 9.3   WWF's green catalogue in Germany

Panda Versandhandel GmbH is a service company dedicated to 'co-operating' WWF's green mail order business in Germany. It is a WWF core process, but is outsourced to a carefully constructed network of process specialists for effectiveness and then managed as a series of core processes, with leadership operating at the heart of the business. Over the course of seven years it has grown from virtually a zero base into a significant mail order operation with many hundreds of thousands of customers. This required considerable investment in acquisition.

Relationships: The acquisition is based on very careful analysis of customers in order to find more of the same type. Like any effective mail order business it knows the importance of customer loyalty. The WWF customer is a strong community crossing many socio-economic lines but typically better educated and, of course, concerned. They know exactly how much it costs to acquire each customer, and how much the customer is worth. In fact they not only know how much it costs to acquire one customer, but almost exactly what it costs to acquire and keep *each* customer. Extensive analysis of the individual customer's buying patterns therefore determines communication frequency, content and timing, varied across the base.

A commitment to service quality, remembering that these customers are also

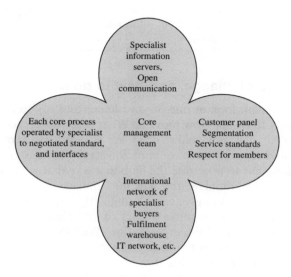

Figure 9.4   WWF's green catalogue business in Germany

donors and supporters of the WWF mission, permeates every part of the business. I∞I thinking is essential to WWF.

Process: If customers fail to buy, special catalogues are sent, which are designed to promote reconnection. A large customer panel gives feedback on ideas and practice to make sure that customers want to stay. Packaging and delivery processes are altered to meet customer expectations and feedback, e.g. a machine binding parcels with biodegradable string not plastic was installed by customer request. Telephone service standards, product ranges and catalogues are all put under the mill of customer response and satisfaction. The result has put millions of Deutsch Marks into WWF Germany's environmental programmes, and become another programme in its own right.

Resources: A network of specialist buyers who share in the success of their products, a long-running agency partnership, a dedicated scoring, analytical and planning team in a consultancy (all of which are in the same building), a partly owned fulfilment and service house, a strategic alliance with EDS (the IT network concern), and more, all contribute to a powerful team.

The mail order computer system provides front-line service people with instant access to information on customers, and that database does the same for the analysts. The task of management is to ease any problems.

Control: The management structure empowers different specialists to become responsible for core process activities. The CEO coordinates. Each is a process owner and is rewarded on the added value of that process contribution. For example, buyers benefit according to the success of the products. An open quality of communication and discussion among teams, a fear-free listening exchange, promotes learning. Activity and information 'flows' freely round the clover leaf. In the modern, empowered organization, information and clear common goals often replace order command structures.

The challenge of change, and how to do it

Try this experiment: look at one of your hands and say to it, 'Move!'

It is unlikely to do so. Now move it. What is the difference? *Telling* your hand to move, will not make it move; it requires a more intimate, penetrating and mysterious act of consciousness. (Try it.)

Our thinking has to penetrate the limb in a way that we cannot normally follow in order to stimulate the will into movement. In the same way, exhorting the business to move can be singularly unproductive. To actually change the organization requires an act of consciousness penetrating the staff – the 'limb forces' of the organization. We have to be in the midst of, and in intimate dialogue with, the co-workers of the business. Management by walking round the clover leaf flow.

Similarly, the people in the business seldom look at the words, but at the deeds – and so do good consultants. This does not mean that words are unimportant, they are vital because one thing must lead to another, but the importance lies in what eventually happens. Customers, employees and consultants all look at the 'done policy' not the 'said policy'. So can management. That is challenging because it leads to the need for personal change, the basis of the Parzival legend, as well as root cause analysis of the company.

Topic 9.2   Re-engineering or re-thinking companies?

Around 80 per cent of corporate re-engineering projects are said to fail. This is a very severe rate and suggests that there might be something wrong with re-engineering as currently practised.

One common problem is simply callousness. The aim is to get rid of 30 per cent of employees. They know it, hate it and resist it.

Re-engineering is characterized by two things: focus on processes and on starting with a clean sheet. The latter is a problem. If you really get a clean sheet, it is like corporate amnesia, and that is an illness. And if you ignore the structural culture it either bounces back or blasts the project.

The emphasis on processes is right but insufficient, because it ignores these cultural attitudes. Really radical thinking goes deeper than the clean sheet; it goes to the underlying thinking that forms the organization, the double-loop learning Argylis described. Form tends to follow consciousness, and how people feel and think will influence their behaviour. Pascal said that it is easier to change thinking from action than action from thinking, but that is just another idea. How do you change action? Impose action and you are also imposing an idea before people have had a chance to think it themselves. On the other hand, thinking about change does not always make a difference either: think of all those habits you have promised to end. Change happens when the inner desire exceeds the old habit, and it is most effective when it is voluntary ('with will') rather than constrained.

Culture or interior attitude institutionalizes itself into form. Therefore, unless the culture is changed, there will be a tendency for the same problems to re-emerge (known as a *leitmotif* in psychology). That is why so many organization development projects focus on culture change. But changing culture by itself will not be successful unless processes are also changed. The existence of the old processes will tend to drag the organization back into its old ways – behaviour shifts thinking, according to Pascal.

Plato said that things came from primal ideas, the Platonic forms that shape what happens: here is the model, now we do it. Aristotle preferred a more evolutionary way, working out under wise review: this works, so let us do it. Some people prefer one method, some the other, and the best is perhaps a little of both. Between the two are our feelings. Feelings mediate between thinking and action.

So successful change requires a focus on both thinking and behaviour via feelings and participation.

The outcome of change is often not known in advance. The most successful change occurs when the process of discovering the required change becomes itself the process of engineering the change. Managers searching for new values are challenged and, in the process, changed. If they then try to *force* these new values on others, why are they surprised that a rejection, as of a foreign body, takes place?

The problem, as Deming has been pointing out for many years, is that we impose new goals, or targets, or objectives, on those around us. Then we inevitably meet resistance. Sometimes, it is necessary to be firm, but it is helpful to appreciate what is involved.

Change is in fact a kind of death. Research shows that employees who go through change processes react in the same way as people suffering bereavement. In both cases, the Kubler Ross grieving model (Figure 9.5) applies. It shows changes in emotional and personal energy, rising to anger and falling into depression, before final acceptance. Developed in studies of bereavement grief, it has been shown to relate much more broadly. People feel that they are losing 'part of themselves' when a major change takes place: it is like cutting off a limb.

The reason is simple. Who we believe ourselves to be is tied up with what we do and who we know. Losing some of this may be like losing part of ourselves. Just as the lines on our faces are worn in by movement and become part of our 'self', so our everyday actions and responsibilities are worn into our 'self', and the more of a habit they are the stiffer they become,

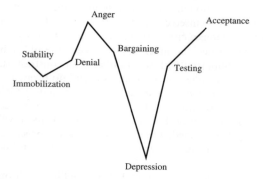

Figure 9.5 The grieving model (*source*: Kubler Ross)

and the more it feels like an amputation to lose part. People feel grief at losing a limb, or a job function, unless they are very inwardly flexible.

The question is: How do we encourage that flexibility of inner attitude through positive setting, such as how much better it will be afterwards, and creating over time a climate of trust? A Knight's courage and the Healer's care need to come together. Surgery is usually chosen voluntarily (i.e. with some courage and a conviction that things will be better after), done under anaesthetic (i.e. with care and skill for minimum pain) and given time to heal. Then everyone celebrates the new, dynamic person. It is quite a good model for organization change.

There is also an often ignored and fundamental principle in change processes: something must be constant; there must be a stable point around which the wheel turns. If change is a loss and a fear, reassurance about ongoing commitments is vital. The first question to answer, therefore, is: What shall we never change? or, What should not be changed at present?

Just as most people would find it easier to die if they *knew* they would still be around 'across the threshold', so will most employees more easily cross the threshold of change if certain fundamentals – e.g. a job, key values, same status and pay – have certainty.

If job security is genuinely not possible, many organizations have found the best way is to respect people, share this and negotiate a creative way forward. This action secures certain value constants even if job constants are impossible. The ability to do this is a litmus test of corporate flexibility and responsiveness.

The good way to do this is to set up a process by which the customer community – whether directly, through research, through stories shared from around the employees themselves or otherwise – gives the information that explains why change is necessary. Since the organization is serving the customers, their dissatisfactions with price, performance, function, feeling, etc., become an objective basis for management and co-workers to tackle the issues more creatively together. By making the data as lively and as real as possible – for example, through drama, story telling and real contact – the issue becomes alive and more shared.

However, the way some managers try to get commitment for change can delay the project before it gets started. For example, a typical scenario: consultants are invited to audit the company; a number of items of dissatisfaction are aired to them; these are fed back to commissioning management who are irritated and claim that the complaints are unfounded and incorrect. The aim must now be to 'change the attitudes of the employees until they conform to the *right* attitudes and outlook'. They forget that management really are the cause of many problems; they forget the importance of employee morale; they forget that the real knowledge of problems is buried among the employees.

The consultants are therefore asked to advise with interval marketing programmes that will help to achieve this. The employees profess commitment but passively resist, thus making progress painful for everyone.

The story of the Five Blind Indians is a useful metaphor. Each of the five felt an elephant, describing it progressively as like a banana leaf (the ear), a rope (the tail), a tree trunk (leg) and so on. Each was right, but not completely so. In the loss of the overall picture, they could at least give a very detailed and intimate description of what it felt like from their perspective.

First, it is necessary to understand why employees (or customers) are right before you can show them the overall concept. Doing it this way makes the process sweeter.

Managing change is therefore a four-step process:

1. Creating warmth, enthusiasm and goodwill to participate.
2. Creating light, understanding, sharing ideas, sparking.
3. Creating movement, flow, shifting the ideas around, creative tension, allowing for conflicts to emerge, adjusting towards consensus creatively, letting the differences resolve into better ways.
4. Creating form, defining the agreed solution and putting it into practice.

When things seem to be at a standstill, or stuck, to get them going you reverse the process.

1. Define what are, agree, recognize the obstructions.
2. Get some movement going, trigger some challenges, present things to shake the complacency (fear is one way only).
3. Create some light, some understanding for the need for change; brainstorm the problems.
4. Muster the warmth, commitment and goodwill to start.

It is similar to a breathing process. Given the obvious link to what older cultures called the four elements – warmth or *fire*; *air* or the realm of light; *water* or the realm of fluid flow and turbulence; and *earth* or the solid form of things – the model is called *Elementary Change*, but the idea is neither new or proprietary. The forming, storming, norming, performing model of team building is based on the same archetype and it is taken up in the project management discussion in Chapter 10.

Topic 9.3   Corporate audit

Here is a self-diagnostic of useful questions:

1. Does marketing (a) often, (b) sometimes, (c) never deal with suppliers to the production parts of the company?
2. Is the working relationship between IT and marketing (a) good, (b) patchy, (c) poor?
3. What percentage of all the interactions with customers (MOTs) are analysed by marketing: (a) >70 per cent, (b) 35–70 per cent, (c) <35 per cent?
4. How involved is marketing in corporate process design: (a) very, (b) fairly, (c) not very?
5. Is there a core, documented and owned process for customer relationship management: (a) yes, (b) in part(s), (c) not really?
6. Do you know the payback on your marketing database: (a) yes, (b) soon, (c) no? (Zero if you do not have one.)
7. Is marketing defined as: (a) a series of processes, (b) a set of skills, (c) a function?
8. Do you know the lifetime value of your key customer groups: (a) yes, (b) some, (c) no?
9. Do you (a) regularly, (b) sometimes, (c) never measure the effect on lifetime value (retention rates and values) of organization and process changes?
10. Which is more important in corporate measurements: (a) process improvement, (b) target or quota achievement, (c) cost savings?
11. Is it (a) easy, (b) possible, (c) difficult to get resources to invest in next year's opportunity?
12. Do you know the reasons why customers/prospects do not respond or buy from you: (a) mostly, (b) sometimes, (c) not really?
13. Do you know why customers stop buying from you: (a) weighted root causes, i.e. by importance, (b) some knowledge, (c) not really?
14. Do you (a) adapt to the answers, (b) make some changes, (c) persuade customers they misunderstand.

Give 3 points for the first option, 2 for the second and 1 for the third each time. 'Don't know' scores zero. Total less than 24 and you could be in severe trouble. Over 30 is a good platform for improvement.

Notes and references

1. Mintzberg, H., *Mintzberg on Management*, The Free Press, 1989.
2. von Eschenbach, W., *Parzival*, Penguin, 1980.
3. Hutchins, E., *Parzival, an Introduction*, Temple Lodge Press, 1979.
4. Heskett, J.L., 'Lessons in the service sector', *Harvard Business Review* (March/April 1988), p. 118.
5. Buchanan, R.W.T. and Gillies, C.S., 'Value managed relationships: the key to customer retention and profitability', *European Management Journal*, **8** (No. 4), p. 523.
   Reichheld, F.F. and Kenny, D.W., 'The hidden advantages of customer retention', *Journal of Retail Banking*, **XII** (No. 4; Winter 1990/1).
   Normann, R., *Service Management, Strategy and Leadership in Service Business*, Wiley, 1986.
   Schneider, B. 'The service organization: climate is crucial', *Organizational Dynamics* (Autumn 1980), pp. 52–65.
6. Leeds, B., ' "Mystery shopping" offers clues to quality service', *Bank Marketing*, **24** (No. 11; Nov. 1992), pp. 24–6.
7. Idea based on 'The motto of the social ethic' by Rudolf Steiner, in *Verses and Meditations*, 1979, p. 117.
8. Gilman, A.L., 'Smart compensation and smart selling', *Chain Store Age Executive*, **68** (No. 9; Sept. 1992), p. 134.
9. Sathe, V., 'Implications of corporate culture: a manager's guide to action', *Organizational Dynamics* (Autumn 1983), pp. 5–23.
10. Lievegoed, B., *Managing the Developing Organization*, Blackwell, 1991; see also Lessem, R., *Developmental Management*, Blackwell, 1990.

10

Creating the technology: getting the database project right

Summary One of the most important steps is creating a suitable database. Unfortunately project success is not guaranteed. This chapter describes the many barriers and methods to effective results.

On the proof of God
The fifth way [of proving the existence of God] is based on the guidedness of nature. Goal-directed behaviour is observed in all bodies obeying natural laws, even when they lack awareness. Their behaviour hardly ever varies and practically always turns out well, showing that they truly tend to goals and do not merely hit them by accident. But nothing lacking awareness can tend to a goal except it be directed by someone with awareness and understanding; the arrow, for example, requires an archer. Everything in nature, therefore, is directed to its goal by someone with understanding, and this we call God.

God's role
Management involves making a plan – providence – and implementing it. The planning of the world is done immediately by God, the implementation by means of others. For the best plan is the one which takes into account the particular circumstances in which actions take place, and God's plan must therefore extend down to the minutest details. But the best implementation is the one offering the greatest fulfilment to the beings being governed, sharing with them not only goodness but the causing of goodness; a good teacher doesn't only teach his students but makes them too into teachers.
(Thomas Aquinas, *Summa Theologia*)

The quotation above, from the greatest thinker of the Middle Ages, illustrates the task of project management. It is more exciting if less exact than this formal one from project management expert, Turner:

An endeavour in which human, material and financial resources are organised in a novel way, to undertake a unique scope of work of given specification, within constraints of cost and time, so as to achieve unitary, beneficial change, through the delivery of quantitative and qualitative objectives.

Another interesting model is presented below.

Topic 10.1   Having a baby

Pregnancy (the process) is the means by which the child (the goal) takes form and comes to independent life: giving birth to a new being. If this being is to be born healthy to welcoming parents, the process itself must be right. Every embryo actually recapitulates the whole of human evolutionary learning. Essential steps cannot be left out without damage. The process should not only prepare the new being, but the parents. The 'client sponsor father' who 'sparks' the process and the 'project mother' who nurtures it must be guardians and must/will evolve themselves. The 'mother' must commit herself to this project. The process includes uncomfortableness, pain and changes. There should be regular communication between 'mother' and 'father' as well as constant subtle 'exchange' between 'mother' and the developing 'embryo', with harmony and cooperation in purpose and process. The process must respect natural laws and the needs of the developing being. There are economic, psychological and energy costs, some unexpected. At the end, and in the process, there can be immense satisfaction. The result changes the world, hopefully for the better. We need to learn to live with the new born, for birth just brings a new phase of development.

As we have already noted, making change is not easy. Later, we shall be discussing tools and techniques for quality improvement. This chapter will focus on the database implementation project. Inevitably, this centres around the technology itself. However, the technology project will also be put squarely in the context of other aspects of organization change that need to take place.

The problem with projects

The technology system should match the organization needs as closely as one half of a walnut shell with the other. However, since both halves may be in growth, with movement and interaction, this may be difficult.

A major study of IT development in Britain sponsored by the government discovered that only 11 per cent of companies are successful at implementing IT, although 68 per cent *think* they are successful. This gap of complacency is itself a problem.[1] If this is true for IT projects in general, how much greater is it a problem in a new area of application? (See Figure 10.1.)

Implementing in a new area does have two advantages: there may be

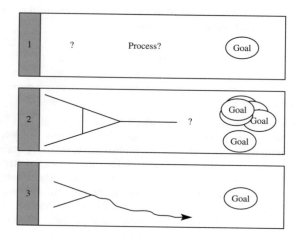

Figure 10.1 Common causes of failure
1 Clear goal, but how will we get there?
2 Project gets confused among changing goals.
3 Project runs out of fizz, resources, priority, etc.

fewer people saying, 'We've done it and it doesn't work' and there may be fewer bad habits. Unfortunately, there is also less experience of what can go wrong and of what is needed.

A UK research project found strong agreement with the proposition that companies wishing to establish marketing databases do not always know at the outset what is relevant and what is not. Furthermore, according to IT managers, marketing departments are a third less effective at communicating their needs than the finance department, and have a poorer understanding of the business benefits computer technology can offer. There is a similar lack of confidence by marketing in the IT staff's grasp of the marketing process. Between 50 and 72 per cent (different parts of the company have different ideas) of companies do not know how long it will take the marketing database to pay for itself.[2]

Implementation will be a pioneering enterprise. In a sense, every project is a pioneer: it takes the company somewhere new, bringing a new child to birth. If this were not the case, there would be no need for a project.

The problem with going somewhere new is that it is also pioneering, and *pioneering is risky* by definition. Pioneers fall over waterfalls and get drowned, they are attacked by wild animals and lost in deserts. Pioneers meet natives who object to newcomers arriving and changing the status quo. Pioneers run out of food, water and supplies. Pioneers make wonderful discoveries, but on their return to their home base they are not always believed.

Anyone with much experience of projects will know that these are not merely quaint descriptions. This is the real thing.

Company operations consist of processes, which are enduring activities, and projects, which are task oriented, aimed specifically at an end that should be achieved within limited resources and time. A project is intended to achieve goals that enable the organization to achieve a further set of goals. In doing so, however, it must contend with the weight of the past. History is a very real force in the future. Newton proposed a law stating that objects would continue in the same direction until another force was applied to them. This law tends to operate in the social realm as well.

In the process we must overcome inertia, habit, fear, failures in communication, impatience to have the solution immediately and all that is involved in transforming thought into deed. People know that projects mean change; they are a threat and an opportunity, and that means that responses are very varied – some wary, some exploitative, some manipulative, some showing denial and avoidance. A 'positive' process is shown in Figure 10.2.

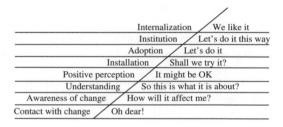

Figure 10.2 Project stages

The problems with technology projects rarely lie with the technology. There can be problems arising from incompetence, from inadequately developed techniques and from unskilled people. However, most problems are failures in vision, in attitude and in politics: i.e. 'people' problems. Virtually all commentators agree on the issue of the 'people' elements in technology projects. People do not participate in the commitment needed for success. It may be failure in imagination, at one pole, or the feeling that 'they' prevent us acting, at the other.

Typical problems are: users who are insufficiently involved to really think through what they want, changes of mind, fear that the project is being used to forward a private objective, political ends being tied into the project, lack of faith and therefore resources, changes in commitment, win/lose contracts with suppliers, impossible targets, unreal expectations, and many more.

Common processes which lead to lack of commitment are actions which generate the following:

- Fear leads to paralysis of will.
- Mistrust leads to conflict, criticism and scorn.
- Doubt/uncertainty leads to lack of confidence in information and promises.

The process of creating a successful project, therefore, means overcoming a whole series of barriers. It is rather like piloting an aeroplane:

- You need to know where you are starting from.
- You need to know where you are going.
- You need a course, a navigation specification.
- You need to update yourself regularly on where you are.
- You need to know the effect of outside and new forces, such as winds of change, and make adjustments.
- You need alternatives if your landing place becomes decommissioned, for example, under fog.
- You need to check and re-check your fuel to ensure that you can reach your destination.
- You need to start the journey with more fuel than you need, just in case.
- You need to keep your passengers regularly informed on progress.

In practice, this makes project management one of the most interesting jobs, and is illustrated in Figure 10.3, taking up the problems outlined in Figure 10.1.

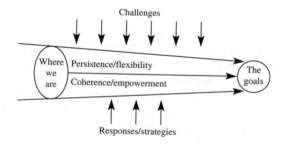

Figure 10.3 The nature of the task

Case study 10.1   How to wreck a project

A divisional sales director in a major financial services group felt that the database would lead to 'his customers' being sold to independently. He therefore gave every reason he could to kill the project.

The managing director of the direct marketing division considered it a criticism that top management should want to centralize. He therefore argued that it was not justified.

The marketing director of a third division was 'too busy' to become involved; perhaps he was afraid of looking stupid since he had little understanding of direct marketing.

A new top manager was recruited to provide expertise and central skills. He politicked to replace the managing director, and succeeded.

The official project sponsor 'filed' a report showing the need for an organization change project because it was contentious.

The chief executive was told that everything was fine. (When he entered a meeting, the room went frigid and conversation died.)

The user project manager was changed half way through just after starting to understand what was happening.

Supplier selection was expedient. The best candidate was excluded from tendering. Job change is rapid, so the new project manager was able to get himself transferred again before the project went live.

What happened?

Project stages and types

A project is likely to have three major phases:

1. The first is defining objectives and goals. In the process it will involve assessing the present and the changes that need to be made, as well as ensuring that resources will be available.
2. The second is the process of creating the new solution. This involves detailed specification, development and testing – a team process.
3. The third element is implementation. This is often overlooked by immature project managers, but is crucial to overall success. Many projects fail at this stage.

The project needs to be carried out with the minimum use of resources, and time with maximum reliability. It will operate under three constraints: cost (including internal resources), time and functional quality. One of the clichés of project management is that it is possible to have two of these but not all three.

Projects fall broadly into four types (Figure 10.4).

Many IT projects are 'bright': requirements are straightforward and a standard implementation process will work, perhaps using a package. Many

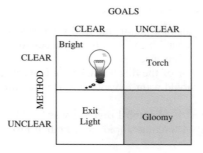

Figure 10.4 The four kinds of project

organization change processes are 'torches': a good facilitator can help a team to find the new set of goals required. Others have a clear destination but are uncertain how to get there. Marketing projects are often of this kind. However, given that even the goal may be as vague as 'lots of loyal customers please', marketing IT projects may well start 'gloomy'. Of course, a basic mailing database is a relatively easy, low-risk project, but it would probably count among the 68 per cent of failures noted above because it missed the real potential.

Software development phases

Classical or common stages of software development are indicated in Figure 10.5.

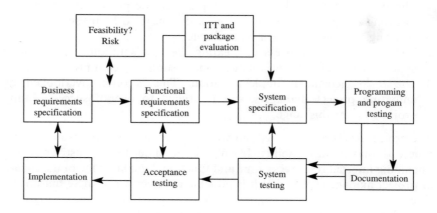

Figure 10.5 Classical software development

The *business requirements specification* (BRS) includes overall business objectives, description of the 'A point' or current status, and new requirements ('B' point). It is common to give a basic data model indicating the data architecture needed to support the system. How it will be done is of less concern but general feasibility, risk analysis and return on investment judgements are started.

Try to seal requirements as much as possible. Throughout the project, there will be changes, and a process of acknowledging, accepting, deferring or rejecting changes is necessary. Poor change management is a big issue (see Case study 10.1).

On approval, the high-level BRS is broken down into a *functional requirements specification* (FRS), detailed system functions to meet the specified business requirements. The two halves of the walnut shell should fit tightly. Both of these stages should be closely assessed by user management before final acceptance. However, the FRS will also need a very detailed IT evaluation in order to ensure that it is rigorous and consistent.

Although the FRS still says 'what', not 'how', one can begin to assess implementation options. These might include bureaux, standard packages, software tools and platforms. The FRS would normally specify policies for implementation, such as an operating system, system architecture, proprietary platforms and so on. The decision to implement by a bureau or in-house solution could be made at the outset of the project, if there are clear business reasons for doing so; but often this will not be decided until the FRS is complete.

Topic 10.2 Checking and making specifications a simple way

At some point in the systems development project, it is probable that a requirements analyst may come to you, the user, and ask whether the specification is satisfactory. There are two things you should do. First, read it carefully and thoughtfully, spending enough time to do justice to the document. This needs planning ahead, so enter it in the diary early. In the process, you may think of a number of questions which you should discuss with the analyst. This is business as usual (apart from giving it enough time, which is rare).

Second – which is a powerful technique – you should devise a set of 20 questions which define the things that you want to be able to do. Give these questions to the analyst and say, 'Will the system which you have specified do these things?' This can be iterative, sending the analyst back to modify the specification more than once.

But, if it is so powerful when reviewing the specification, is it not equally powerful up front? Imagine someone asking whether the proposed solution is satisfactory. What are the questions you would ask? Write them down now and ask them, right at the beginning.

The FRS, once approved, can be used as an invitation to tender to suppliers of software packages or custom development (or both, modifying a package). Once a supplier, whether outside or inside, has been selected it will be that person's responsibility to develop a *system specification*. This breaks down FRS into instructions to the programmer, usually in two parts: a logical specification and a physical specification. The logical specification indicates, independent of particular hardware and software conditions, the precise system operations that need to be achieved, while the physical specification translates these into a specific implementation environment. The aim of the system specification is to *specify how* the FRS is to be achieved. It involves a detailed data model, a full and comprehensive breakdown of the processes including input, control and output specifications for each program and the interfaces between programs, subsystems and systems.

If a decision has been made to implement the use of a package, the system specification will involve a description of all the changes, in detail, that need to be made.

The system specification is passed, progressively, to a programming team who will be responsible for developing or altering the system to meet these changes. Programs are written and tested by individuals and teams, and when completed are passed on for *system testing*.

At this stage, *documentation* also needs to be produced. Documentation is one of the most overlooked areas of system development. It is expensive, and where budgets are slim it can sometimes be ignored. It is sometimes possible to evade this, but that may also cause a disaster. Much documentation is poor, often helpful to neither technical people nor users, although standards are steadily improving. In one survey, 85 per cent of marketers indicated that they did not feel that marketing system documentation met their needs. Some system developers use a CASE toolkit which automatically produces quality documentation, but is often rather systems oriented. If it is a package, check the documentation to see how it will handle modifications. Assign significant budget/selection value to this area.

System testing should assess the match between the initial specification, the programs that have been delivered and the documentation. It should ensure that software systems and subsystems work harmoniously together. The most effective way of doing this is to specify during systems specification the test of quality.

System testing is carried out by IT personnel. Users should be aware that one of the effects of putting the development team under time pressure is that they will reduce the amount of time they spend testing. If so, it will be users who discover the problem or problems, and they may be finding them for years to come! It is common to design an *acceptance testing* phase for the user team. Is it as expected, and as wanted? There is a difference between 'expected' and 'wanted'; there is also a difference between both of these and the system specified. Systems are often delivered as specified but not as wanted, which is often only discovered when marketers start to use them. The problem lies in the difficulty of imagining what you do not have, and sharing it with someone else. This is one reason for the popularity of prototypes and packages.

Case study 10.2   Change management failure

Goals or objectives often change once the project has begun. A crucial part of successful project management is change management, the process of managing change within the project itself. Failure in change management is a major source of project failure. In one niche bank, the direct marketing manager, who was user project manager, approved a series of changes, often passed on from top management who were going through a strategic IT and business redevelopment process at the time. Otherwise, the changes came from the maturing knowledge of the direct marketing team.

For example, mid-way through the project, it changed from a batch system to hold data off-line to a critical data resource to be linked on-line into the branch network, with severe technical implications.

Each change was estimated individually by the software supplier, and approved. *However, no comprehensive manual was kept, nor was the overall effect assessed,* both of which are essential.

Over time, the project cost doubled. This became a problem only when it was realized that top management had not been briefed, nor had they changed the budget. Now life began to jump.

The user manager and the supplier should have taken time earlier to review what was happening, agree a strategy and present it clearly to the sponsors.

There is a clear tension between, on the one hand, battening down the hatches, preventing changes to keep control and prevent derailment, and, on the other, the problems of inflexibility and consequent risk of safely delivering a specification that is no longer valid, or is less effective than it might have been.

Software development methodologies and tools

There are many software development methodologies. For example, analysing business requirements may follow a strict procedure with a template of standard questions and defined content and style of output. Many software companies are implementing international quality standards like ISO 9000/BS 5750 and its British IT variant, TickIT. ISO 9000 certified suppliers guarantee that they have a formal and thorough process, but not necessarily the best.

There are also many proprietary methodologies, e.g. LBMS. Some are simply procedural and others are linked to the use of software toolkits, or CASE tools. All such methodologies tend to become bureaucratic. Their advantage is that they are reasonably assured, but most work on the assumption that the final requirement is known, and just needs defining: *bright* projects. The problem with a database marketing system is that it tends to get to 'those parts of the organization that other projects cannot reach'. As long as it is only a stand-alone, batch mailing tool that is required, simple methods work effectively. Some techniques, designed as they are to meet transaction processing requirements, may even be an overkill.

However, if the organization is genuinely involved in radical, long-term change, then a creative process of getting out the 'gloom' may be required.

Topic 10.3   Prototypes

Many projects have benefited from the use of prototypes. In fact, many software developers use prototyping tools as the method of developing the functional requirements specification and this must be the direction of the future. The advantage is that instead of writing everything into a document to which the user must respond with enough imagination to interpret correctly, the prototype is a moving, interactive tool which lets the user try out ideas, check functions and operations and specify changes. In that sense, it fulfils something of the role that a software package provides, giving the user something tangible to which he or she can react.

A danger is that the user will make presumptions that the 'real' system will fill in missing pieces. The prototype is unlikely to be complete, if it were it would not be a prototype.

Rapid application development

Rapid application development (RAD) is becoming attractive. It is partly a creative workshop process and partly an analytical method. The advantages are:

1. It is fast, as the name suggests.
2. It brings a number of people together, so they understand each other's point of view thereby improving the specification.
3. It is creative and enjoyable.
4. It is more likely to make people aware of, and to understand, the need for change, and to commit themselves to it.
5. Solutions are more radical.

RAD is most effective during the BRS phase, leading into the functional requirements specification, but it is frequently linked to prototyping (see

Topic 10.3). It involves a series of workshops designed to enable a fully representative group of executives to specify, understand and agree (all three are important).

- the mission, or purpose, and goals of the business and how this project affects them;
- the key result areas to be achieved by the project;
- the critical success factors involved, i.e. the priority areas that must be achieved in order to make the project successful;
- risks and value judgements;
- the new business processes required.

Critical success factors (CSFs) can be cascaded to multiple levels, and each critical success factor may have a number of critical success factors involved in achieving it.

It needs a facilitator whose job is to challenge the group positively to prevent complacency and habit; to progress the process; to manage and maintain the social dynamics including the resolution of conflict; to keep people focused on relevant issues; and to record decisions. Typically, the decisions and judgements are noted on flip charts and displayed around the room during each workshop. They are subsequently transferred into documents, tidied up and circulated for approval by all members.

RAD takes up more executive time, because the executives need to be present throughout the process, but it dramatically reduces the overall length of the project, and often improves its quality.

Case study 10.3   Specifying business requirements

A leading leisure company decided its existing database was no longer adequate. This had been installed for over three years, ran on a mini-computer and failed to meet four needs:

1. Name and address processing needed improvement
2. Analysis facilities were weak
3. Performance was inadequate, an analysis exercise could run for 12–20 hours
4. It was not properly linked to operational systems: valuable data was lost and no resource was supplied to telesales and service people.

The IT company that did most of their systems was asked to provide an analyst. However, after a basic feasibility study it was clear that the marketing team could not adequately specify state-of-the-art requirements and the business analyst did not understand the application, so an independent consultant was asked to lead the BRS phase. However, capital approval for £150 000 was secured. The consultant conducted a series of brief interviews to obtain background then led three group sessions:

- with the management team to confirm business mission and objectives, and critical success factors;

- with a cross-section of management and service people, from CEO to front-line supervisors to do root cause analysis of loyalty and satisfaction preventers, and then to develop ideas to improve service and retention;
- with a similar group to identify all existing moments of truth and to develop ideas for new contact management strategies.

Finally, a number of sessions were held with the direct marketing manager and team and managers of the front-line functions: sales, administration, etc., to confirm requirements and identify any further specifics. The process was experienced as educational, revealing and helpful. For the most part, all the knowledge of requirements existed, but had to be revealed, often when two functions shared perspectives or when junior and senior staff shared perspectives. Front-line had raw phenomena; top management, perspective.

These were then combined by the consultant who added specialist technical knowledge to produce, first, a BRS then an FRS. The latter was then converted by the IT company's analyst into an ITT and he managed the selection, change and install procedures.

Several other change requirements were also identified:

1. The database would need to link to the sales reservation system to ensure that loyal customers were recognized and to improve data and name and address capture. This meant re-negotiating plans for the ongoing development of this system.
2. Telesales people were rewarded on speed and bookings. New measurement criteria and policies were established with an ongoing evaluation of results.
3. It was realized that the telephone system was inadequate. Sales went through an ACD, and everything else went through a conventional PABX. Another project was undertaken to:
   (a) link reservation systems across two locations;
   (b) include all customer contacts, including all managers and CEO to the ACDs with telephony systems to handle switches and collect data.
4. The budget was recognized as quite inadequate for the opportunity. A presentation was made to representatives on the group board, led by the consultant.
5. Members of the group board realized that there could be group-wide opportunities, and a plan was put in place to use a version of the system as prototype to test opportunity.
6. A culture shift from tactical marketing to long-term relational marketing, already beginning, was reinforced.
7. Research began into new products and new personalized communication vehicles.

Getting agreements required negotiation and explanation, but a change in CEO created a six-month delay and the direct marketing manager left before implementation began. The consultant led a refresher session to renew understanding and commitment.

Marketing transformation: a process of marketing change

A database marketing targeted RAD process is shown in Figure 10.6. Marketing transformation is a way to develop and implement a successful marketing system. It links system and business change to better ensure the right solution for the right problem.

Figure 10.6 emphasizes technology-related change and definition. It is a workshop and analytical method designed to build teams and consensus for change across the company: figuring out the system needs, operational service changes and product opportunities, linking moment of truth, product analysis, root cause and other recommendations in this book.

As already noted, a successful database marketing project will probably break into several change projects, typically:

- MOT (moment of truth) development: changing the communication and contact policies and practices;
- technology or IS build project, designed to produce the needed information systems tool;
- service or service product development project, designed to update and change the 'clover leaf service product' to take advantage of the new technology;
- organizational change, designed to ensure that the new technology is optimized, e.g. in acquiring data and customers – this should embrace both processes and people/culture.

The illustrated marketing transformation process emphasizes the IS development project. Overall it integrates a number of compatible change models described elsewhere in this book, including Lievegoed's 'plan, do, review' and Deming's 'plan, do, check, act' (see Chapter 15). It also uses the elemental change model (previous chapter) and recognizes the classic team forming, norming, storming, performing process. In practice, it would be adapted to need.

The basic steps are simple:

1. Preparation, creating conditions to begin the project, or project investigation.
2. Planning, idea generation, requirements specification using a number of workshop and analytical tools.
3. A breakdown into a number of projects, typically technology build, organization change and product development.
4. The integration of these in rollout implementation.

Tools and methods are described below to give the flow, but more detail is generally given in Chapter 15.

After *preparation*, stage 2, *lighting the fire* (Figure 10.6), involves an

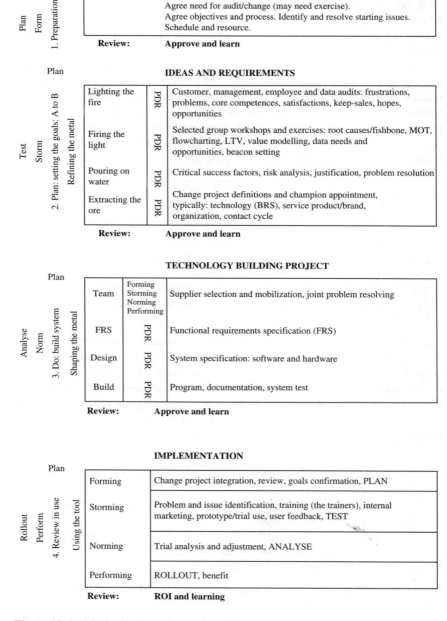

Figure 10.6   Marketing transformation

assessment of the current A point and the planned B point for the project. Fundamental analysis of the current status of the relationships with customers is the foundation. This can involve many activities, including:

- *Fishbone*, or cause and effect analysis, is a group brainstorming technique which usually takes place in two stages: evaluation of problems and then opportunities. Brainstorming around five to seven key topic areas, such as information, products and processes explodes issues like, 'What prevents and what enables loyalty?', 'What prevents and what enables customer satisfaction or service?' by breaking down causes and effects. It is best done in groups with a cross-section of roles and levels from across the company.
- *Surveys* of customer satisfaction are complementary to internal fishbone analysis. Wherever possible, existing satisfaction questionnaires would be used to save time and money. Questions are categorized and a Pareto analysis used to identify the most significant causes of satisfaction and dissatisfaction and defections. (Pareto was the Italian economist who discovered the 80:20 rule, i.e. that 80 per cent of almost anything you care to choose is caused by 20 per cent of the inputs; 80 per cent of all ice cream is eaten by 20 per cent of the population.) Satisfaction analysis is a useful input, but, as we have identified, it is important to discover the real reasons why customers defect. This may involve special surveys.
- Conventional *SWOT* analysis.
- *Employee satisfaction* and motivation surveys in open discussions using focus techniques like drawing, picturing, cartoon work, metaphors, drama and discussion lead to valuable insights, provided trust exists for openness.
- Discovering the '*keep safes*' is another useful input into any change project. These are the values, policies, practices, strategies, service modes, etc., which management, employees and/or customers want to retain and keep safe. Finding and logging these (a) reassures, (b) provides a platform for change, and (c) sometimes allows challenges of the prevailing assumptions. An associated activity is recognizing the *core competences* of the business.
- *Moment of truth* (MOT) analysis identifies the current and desirable MOT and the data is collected and potentially available at each with the right technology. It asks how the organization wants to model its relationship with customers as part of a guarantee management programme.
- Detailed *process mapping* reveals the 'done policies', including wasted and counter-productive energy, e.g. by deployment flowcharting. Mapping the process flow against the responsible parties or functions using a set of standard icons for decisions, actions, meetings and so on shows where things can go wrong and where responsibility may be divided, uncertain or even unknown.

– It is usually helpful to do a *core process* map to establish 'relationship management' ownership. This can be quite an insight, for it is typically fragmented and may have no champion.

The results of such analysis are shared and communicated among the executive team on an ongoing basis. *Beacon setting*[3] then establishes the future B point for the company: a goal or goals it wants to achieve. This is a creative imagineering process to develop the guiding principles (aims, policies and values, identity) of the company and the consequent business needs (functions, processes, resources). The tension between creative ideas and realities of life is reflected in the process.

Having completed beacon setting, the stages of warmth and light in the elementary change process have been completed. At each stage, it is appropriate to do a 'plan, do, review'.

Now comes the translation of the new intentions into reality. This is always a struggle and two key inputs are risk analysis and justification: *pouring cold water* over some of the ideals. *Critical success factor* (CSF) analysis prioritizes key tasks and is an input to *justification*. Each CSF is weighted according to its probability of success and value and a decision is made as to the extent to which the current project will have a realistic impact on the goal. Value, risk and impact can be converted into financial terms.

The *plan for change* will break down into interacting subprojects which can be identified by an analyst, but is best established through a project definition workshop. This involves all key executives and is a formal process of identifying the required change processes and forging a work agreement: *extracting the ore*.

Although we have identified technology, product, organization and MOT change as the four generic types, in practice five or more subprojects may be involved. These can range from education to improving data quality. Sometimes coaching top team change is important. The key mission or goal of each subproject should be to meet some aspect of the beacon-setting goals. Each has a satisfactory conclusion which becomes the driving goals for the subproject. For the IS project, another output at this stage is the business requirements statement (BRS).

Each project should have a user project manager, or champion, and a project facilitator who is a process specialist. One project facilitator can service a number of projects. If more than one facilitator is needed, and often it is helpful to have two, they should be a team. The project team must establish:

– actions that need to be performed
– desired goals or outcomes to be measured
– how they will be measured
– process review steps and methods
– critical success factors and risks.

Topic 10.4 Justifying the plan

Justifying a project is a difficult task. For one thing, it is necessary to try to guess a future. This is difficult; every manager knows how complicated it is to try to predict exactly what the benefit will be, especially as you might be held to account for it later. This justification process is a semi-scientific, fairly rigorous way of trying to get a group or individual to assess the probable project value. It must be tested by reasonableness and depends as much on intuition as on science. But it does force a certain rigour which is more likely to get both an approximately accurate answer and also one that is likely to be acceptable within the organization. There are seven steps:

1. First the critical success factors or 'do-wells' that the project is intended to address are identified. (This should have been done already.)
2. These are then ranked in expected order of importance. The ranking sequence is done simple as a check for the next step designed to assess reasonableness.
3. The value to the organization of successfully completing each of these critical success factors is determined. This will normally be determined as an annual value.
4. There must always be a risk that the success factor or 'do-well' is not achieved. Some people's critical success factors are really 'nice to haves'. When they meet the test of reality, people realize that the chances of fully achieving them may be quite limited. So, the question is, how much of this benefit are we really likely to see happen? This can be assessed as a percentage.
5. There may be a number of factors which contribute to the production of the benefit or the performance of the critical success factor. How much can really be put down to this project or system? Is it 50 per cent, or 70 per cent, or more?
6. A simple calculation can then be done to link these together. Seventy per cent of 80 per cent of £500 000 is £280 000. Over three years this is worth £840 000.
7. The final step is to do a discounted cash flow. This brings the future stream benefits back into present-day monetary value, and enables it to be compared with the costs. An ROI analysis can then be done.

Risk management

Ready! fire! ... then aim! Project management is very popular. After all, it produces activity and visibly gets things done. It is wiser to plan and continually assess the risks involved:

- when there is a basic specification of what is likely to be done and why, to identify whether the project can actually continue and the obstacles to overcome or be bypassed (forewarned is forearmed and the best way of ensuring problems will be solved)
- once the project is fully specified (effectively an update)
- regularly, throughout the project (is the airport still okay to land on, are we on track and is there any difference to the wind?)

Assessing risk effectively is a powerful behaviour at which we are very bad for the following reasons:

1. We do not like to admit that there might be a problem.
2. We want the project to go ahead, and therefore manufacture reasons why it will be successful and avoid discussing the problem.
3. Since frankness is uncommon, should you ever begin to be so it may be assumed that the problems are much worse than you admit (because that is usual), so to keep the project going you keep the statistics going by yet again denying the problem.
4. The partnership with your outside supplier lacks trust. Neither party shares the truth with the other. If you have just completed an arduous negotiation about delivery, function and cost, squeezed the last drop of juice out of your supplier, asked him or her to absolutely commit that the project will be successful before you sign the contract, what are the chances that they will then immediately give you their frank assessment of all the things that could go wrong? Would you want to be told that you are part of the problem?

However, if you can get all the relevant people together in a reasonable mood of frankness, risk assessment is an illuminating and powerful tool. One simple and effective method is by the use of meta-modelling. Everyone gets a number of post-it pads and writes down on each a problem they can foresee. This has the advantage of enabling everybody to give equal input, although some may think of more problems than others, and it is relatively anonymous. The post-it pads are all pasted on a wall or white board, then sorted into groups with shared points or outlooks. These are then summarized onto a flip chart and the group, especially any key people within the group, are then asked to assess these one by one. Is the *likelihood* of this happening high, medium or low? If it happens, will its impact be high, medium or low? Focus on risks that have a high impact and probability and try to find a solution for them.

In one project, a director of the company had been appointed sponsor/champion, a very important role in context. One of the risks was that the company might go on the acquisition trail. If this happened it would probably have a high impact on the availability of this sponsor. The question was asked, 'So how likely is it that you will acquire another company?' The answer was, 'Well, it's pretty certain. We are already negotiating contracts!' A new champion was found.

New techniques of risk analysis, including software supported mathematical techniques, have been developed but they are beyond the scope of this book. A positive, trust-generating attitude will go a long way.

Essential project management techniques

Never finally agree to a project until you have met and interviewed the project manager, if only for personal chemistry, but also to test gumption and self-confidence. Can this person say 'No' to you if necessary? Will he or she have worked positively and creatively with the problem first?

There are five key task areas for projects and project managers (see Figure 10.7):

– Clear, achievable goals
– Commercial competence
– Technical competence
– Process management
– People and relationship management.

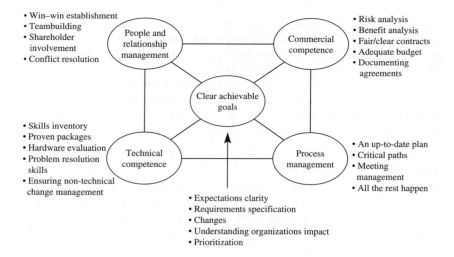

Figure 10.7   The five key project management tasks

Clear, achievable goals

It has already been pointed out that one of the difficulties with marketing projects, like those in organization development, is finding out what you want. Even when you think you have done that, it is not the end. Establishing clear, achievable goals translates into clarity of specifications and of user expectations. When there is a mismatch between expectations and specifications, as there often is, the result is almost certain disappointment. Frequent problems include:

- The assumption by the client or user that someone else knows what he or she wants, probably by clairvoyance.
- Inadequate marketing resource is available to respond to needs and review project activity.
- Goals do not stay still. A continuing muddle in requirements, with never-ending changes, can mean that clarity is never achieved. Imposed, and uncontrolled changes by the client user are a particular problem when commercial power is used to establish the whip hand over an outside supplier.
- Wanting too much, too early, for too little, with insufficient experience. It is a cliché among those who service clients that they take for ever to decide to do something, then want it yesterday. A good project manager has the courage and professional confidence to tell the client, as a service, when expectations really have no chance of being fulfilled.

Specification problems also occur when the client asks for an improved version of something that is obviously inappropriate: making progress in the wrong direction, a bad solution with go faster stripes. This happens when the old ways of doing things block the imagination.

Project managers must insist on clarity, test assumptions, ensure creative activity to open the imagination and be firm with woolliness. They do not have to do it all, but they must see that it is all done. These are Saturn and Mars qualities in the model given in Table 10.1 on page 219.

Case study 10.4   No clear goals

If the project is set up with no clear goals, it may wander vaguely. This typically occurs in situations where the project is run by junior, inexperienced or IT people with insufficient strategic input. Goals and objectives must be related to the fundamental purpose of the organization. When the project is set up with strong technology and weak business input it is effectively a wandering project.

One project in a financial services company was effectively taken over by its own IT department. They were fascinated by the potential as well as technical issues such as name and address processing. They researched a data model, developed a functional specification and eventually implemented a system under the approving gaze of the marketing department who had 'unfortunately' been too busy to specify their own requirements. To be fair to IT, it is more common that marketing has insufficient commitment, than that IT indulge themselves. But, perhaps, if you cannot get the input you need, it is best not to do it at all.

Commercial competence

When an outside vendor is servicing the project, the first step is to choose a reputable supplier (and the second is to make sure that the supplier is still among the leaders). Prioritizing on business benefits is another. Spend time identifying issues, tasks and responsibilities. Reduce risk by selecting a working package with as little change as possible. Take time to do risk analysis and develop contingency plans.

A contract should primarily be a sound record of agreement and a plan for commitment and partnership for mutual benefit, not a threat. It should establish and protect the interests of *both* parties. If not, it is unlikely to be a good solution. A good contract typically includes:

- a statement of general provisions, such as confidentiality, rights of ownership and communication
- a schedule of maintenance and service facilities specifying what will and will not be covered, with examples that make the issues concrete
- general terms and conditions for the specified project
- provision for the development of a specification which is then incorporated. (By designing the contract like this, mutual cover is provided at an early stage and people can get on with the job. The first phase of any project should be confirming its specification. This then becomes part of the contract.)
- provisions to resolve differences by negotiation and discussion, including the use of a facilitator before going to court or arbitration. (Ninety per cent of problems can be resolved by open discussion if the two parties learn to listen to each other.) In the same way that marriages break down because neither party is really hearing what the other says, so do project partnerships dissolve into conflict.

It is important to establish a safety net, i.e. that if the probable budget were to overrun by 60 per cent, the project would still be at least viable. Projects do overrun. As with any other activity, things can go wrong and variation will take place, particularly as the arts of estimation are by no means guaranteed, especially in an unclear world. If the project would not be profitable if it overran by 60 per cent, then you should probably not undertake it. (At the very least, there should be a contingency of around 30 per cent.) The budget should be clearly broken down and understandable among the parties.

Topic 10.5   Software project costs

As a guideline, on top of the costs of software packages, the costs of development may break down according to the following format:

- Software programming	up to	40 per cent of project cost.
- Project management		10 per cent plus
- Identifying changes and requirements		15 per cent plus
- Functional requirements specification		10 per cent plus

– Systems specification	10 per cent plus
– System design	5 per cent plus
– Testing, acceptance and QA functions	10 per cent plus
– Training	5 per cent plus
– Documentation	10 per cent plus

This is a very loose guide. For example, if many users are involved, training costs could greatly increase. In a project with Britain's rail network, the marketing services division laid on a series of training and development workshops for over 60 users. The four days of workshops included a general refresher on database marketing, practice in the use of the system, and computer-aided training, using the system to solve a number of simulated business problems. A hand-holding facility was then provided for individual users as they returned to work. This can be contrasted with another unmentionable company that installed the software and told the users it was available.

As a rule of thumb, the more you spend at the beginning the better the project. The less you spend at the beginning the more the total project costs.

Technical competence

The technical competence of the user project manager and team is either covered elsewhere or is a subject beyond the scope of this book. However, two observations are important. First: it has always been amazing to note that whereas it is unthinkable that a financial director would trust the development of an accounting system to a computer analyst who did not understand double entry book keeping, marketing and sales directors will happily commit to individuals who have no relevant experience. Use people who have already made their mistakes.

Second: name and address processing needs specialist skills (see Chapter 13).

Process management

A project manager needs do very little other than ensure that everyone else is doing the right thing at the right time.

Project planning, evaluation and review (plan, do, review) are therefore the steps in project management. The ability to think in terms of a complex set of interacting activities is one hallmark of a good project manager (Jupiter quality in Table 10.1 on page 219). Another is flexible process thinking, seeing work as flow, and finding, like water, new ways to flow around boulders (Mercury quality).

To assist this there are a number of software/planning techniques for project planning and as a user you may want a copy of the project plan on your own personal computer. Common tools are:

- GANTT charts. These break the project into a number of tasks, each of which is specified as a number of activities and resources with beginning and end dates. These are laid out on a calendar schedule, usually with activities down the left and dates across the page. It is therefore possible to see total scope and status at a glance. It is common to use the GANTT chart by setting up the plan lines and then showing progress to date by comparison.
- A PERT or critical path chart. This is more complex than a GANTT chart, but has the advantage that it shows the interaction between projects (see Figure 10.8) and prerequisites for each stage. Some subprojects can proceed in parallel without being affected, while others need prior input. Total lapsed time will depend on the end-to-end concatenation of all the critical parts. A PERT chart shows these relationships.

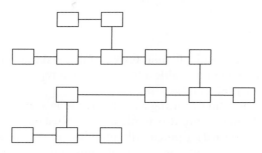

Figure 10.8 PERT chart format

The techniques are easily done on a piece of paper (perhaps easier). The real advantage of software is ease of update (so make sure it is used). Practise doing it on a flip chart or paper; it is a very useful general tool and even if you are not adept at first, the skill will improve because it is 95 per cent common sense and thoroughness.

One of the most useful steps in process control is the *weekly project status report*. You may find a reluctance to report so frequently, but unless the project is either proceeding at a very slow pace or is extremely short, a brief weekly update is very helpful. It should consist of no more than one page and is most helpful as a series of bullet point reviews under four headings:

- Actions this week
- Decisions this week
- Issues and proposals
- Milestones status.

The discipline of reviewing the project under these headings is itself helpful.

Ask your supplier to notify you quite objectively and briefly this way, saying that no responsibility will be accepted if the problem has not been identified. Regular documented meetings with a standard agenda to review progress and all aspects of the project and status should be held to look for problems, not to fix blame but to develop solutions. The 'Important but not yet urgent' activities (Figure 10.9) are the key to reduced stress.

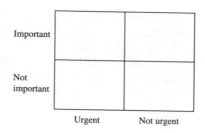

Figure 10.9   Urgency matrix

It is important to read all minutes carefully, asking questions where appropriate. Review the time table and budget on a regular basis, and invite open discussion of problems.

Plan acceptance testing thoroughly. This is the last chance to assess the quality of the solution before it is implemented. Rushed acceptance testing simply rushes you towards a potentially looming pit. In the same way that you expect your vendor partner to meet commitments, plan to provide enough time and resource to meet your own. Clients hold up more projects than suppliers.

People and relationship management

Project managers frequently find themselves having to set up a temporary team, with limited resources, to achieve challenging goals against opposition in a short period of time. This is a real challenge to people management skills and the manager's ability to get on well with people and get the best out of them.

There are two key 'people' areas and they both involve issues of trust: building teams and handling conflict and power plays. Any project involving several people is a microcosm of the world's problems and opportunities: success can only come about to the extent that a level of shared commitment to working together is achieved. The two most important qualities required by the project manager in this domain can be described as the Venus and Mars qualities (see Table 10.1):

- caring, nurturing and listening capabilities that are needed to build a team and deflect conflict; and
- firm capacity to intervene, to face up to and to resolve conflict and power.

Together they constitute the ability to say 'No!' and build 'Yes!' (Of course, there is absolutely no gender distinction behind the Venus/Mars label.)

The team-building process is generally reckoned to go through four stages (although aspects of all stages will be found at each one): *Forming, storming, norming, performing*. During 'forming' the team builds awareness of each other and the task. There may be norms of behaviour and fair performance, but they are built out of general social and professional skills and societal norms. By the time 'norming' comes, the team has begun to build its own unique norms, which means agreements, understandings, shared culture, aims, stories, and trust. The key to 'forming' is to spend time building a clear picture of the goal to be reached as benefits – as something that encourages participation – and also gradually introducing the social interchange: go for a beer or a meal or a walk; talk about personal things, and get to know each other.

However, 'performing' can only come about when the team has actually gone through the process of struggle, disagreement, etc., the 'storming' which constitutes sharing and later accepting the *differences*, in style, priority, skills, contribution, method, aims and ideas so that they can be bound into a greater whole. We never trust another until we know that he or she accepts something of our difference, even our flaws, and also recognizes our needs. This process can also build a far more robust and effective solution, if only because everyone has a reason to make it successful.

The danger, however, is that the project breaks down in conflict. Handling disagreements, getting them on the table, talking about them objectively, negotiating creative solutions out of them is a chief skill of project management.

Conflict and anger can take two forms: *hot* and *cold*. Hot anger/conflict explodes, is passionate, noisy, on the table. Cold anger/conflict lurks under the table waiting for the right moment to stiletto the other in the dark. Both are dangerous, even frightening. Hot anger tends to blow over more quickly and is easier to work with, just because it is openly visible.

With hot anger, a time-out to settle down may be helpful, plus space to speak the problem and really put it on the table, with each party not being allowed to speak until the other has completely finished. The aim is to move the conflict from the belly to the head, making the issues objective and allowing anger to surface and dissolve. Avoid blame and recrimination: turn the matter into a set of useful and objective issues to resolve. Angry people are often unaware of their own motives, like fear, jealousy or worry, and by bringing these to the surface, but expressing them in an objective way, i.e.

what the worry is about, the problem can be dealt with. One key problem with hot anger/irritation is that the individual may quickly get past it but others are still feeling the effects. Helping them to accept is one strategy; another is making sure that the 'angry one' realizes the effect and does something to 'make up'.

With cold anger, the individual tends to be cynical with respect to the effect on others. Cold anger is depressive, disempowering. With really deeply cold anger, it may be difficult to do very much other than walk away or block. If the anger can be 'warmed' by empathy until it comes to the surface, it may be possible to deal with it. Often the issue is finding the root cause. At a negotiation level, it will normally be very important to have very clear and agreed rules with a powerful and understood return to status quo in the case of contravention by either party until the situation changes.

Power is related to cold anger and conflict in that it often feels cold. People who use power ruthlessly are bound up in a long-running cold conflict, perhaps with everyone. Meeting this power is crucial. Power can also be constructive: 'Power is the ability to get things done', said Rosabeth Moss Kanter in *The Change Masters*, and R.J. Lovell described it as 'the medium through which conflicts of interest are settled'. The most common power issue with the client is the owner of the purse. The great danger is that the supplier's fear of losing it makes the messenger afraid to bring bad news. The most commonly used style by subordinates for upward influence is the rational presentation of ideas. It results in defeat (failure) twice as often as it is successful. A much more effective way is simply challenging,[4] but on the basis of the authority that belongs to someone delivering an important benefit, the critical function needed. This must be backed by inner authority, the mature self-confidence that comes from experience, and the support of subordinates or team. 'The power of managers may appear to flow from higher authorities, but true power is obtained by gaining the support of subordinates' was a finding of Barnard.[5]

Beyond these issues of anger, power and conflict is the general problem of trust. On the whole, trust is fairly uneasy; and the more competitive the environment, the more true this is. In studies by Carlisle and Parker,[6] Americans were nearly twice as likely as British negotiators to begin with a gesture of cooperation, but still represent only 27 per cent of the population. The two dangerous polarities are blind trust and mistrust: neither is real. In present social conditions, it makes sense to start in the middle, willing to build trust and therefore voluntary, unlegislated cooperation, but ready to step back towards some agreed rules.

What really must underpin the negotiation process, however, is conviction that win–win is more successful than win–lose. If that conviction is thoroughly accepted, then problems can be negotiated, perhaps quite legally, perhaps very trustingly, but in any case with much greater chance of success. Win–lose or zero-sum thinking is tied to negative power and cold anger, and it is self-defeating. The central fact of Machiavelli's life is that he was tortured and ejected from office for his last and potentially most creative years because he was not trusted.

So, at every stage, the successful project manager is aware of the win-needs of all the project participants. This builds the team.

Key qualities of the project manager

A model of the project manager and his or her tasks and qualities that has found acceptance among professionals is shown in Table 10.1. It is based on the archetypal qualities associated over thousands of years with gods in the myths.

Table 10.1 Project management for demi-gods

Archetypal God/champion	Tasks	Qualities
Saturn	Identifying the *goal* or *future*; specifying or capturing the *requirement* based on what needs to be different from the past	Holding the 'big picture'; taking responsibility for a distant outcome
Jupiter	Establishing *policies, agreements, contracts*, as well as styles and *methodologies*; understanding the *network* of activities; guarding the process in understanding *implications*	Ability to hold and attend to detail within the big picture; judgement
Mars	Detailed project *planning*, initiative taking and *interventions*; making things happen; countering opposition	Initiative and courage; forcefulness; positive use of power
Apollo/Sun	*Balancing, harmonizing, reconciling* other activities, processes, events; reducing tension and conflict	Maturity, energy and common sense; negotiation skills; morality: personal reputation as trustworthy
Venus	*Nurturing* relationships; *supporting* team members; taking *care* of a wide variety of ongoing activities and the people involved in them	Sensitivity, responsiveness, openness, listening ear, warmth, without softness

Table 10.1 *continued*

Archetypal God/champion	Tasks	Qualities
Mercury	Stimulating *change*, quickening, *innovating*, engendering *flexible responses*, finding *imaginative* action	Flexibility, imagination, problem-solving intelligence.
Diana/Moon	*Monitoring* and *checking* the pulse of activity; giving and receiving *feedback*; *recording* decisions; identifying progress and *status*; being *in touch*	Control; ability to prioritize; analytical capacity; punctiliousness – probing and methodical

Software packages or DIY?

The issues involved with selecting software routes are highlighted in Figure 10.10. The four sets of dangers are shown in the Boston matrix and the solutions outside. The vertical axis shows the solution method and the horizontal axis the project objective.

Choosing a software package is always the preferred solution for computers, but not always for businesses. A software package has already been designed and built, and is probably in use in a number of installations. That radically reduces the risk. Chapter 12 discusses software design considerations, including the marketing database as a 'toolkit' rather than a set of fixed functions. This increases flexibility and future-safe characteristics of the solution, but also costs more and therefore adds to the advantage of a software package, whose cost is amortized across many users.

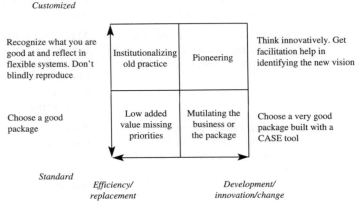

Figure 10.10 The lurking dangers in software selection ... and the solutions

Even if you should find yourself the very first user of a software package, at least, as with a prototype, there is something in front of you that you can experiment with to see how resilient and friendly it is. With a software development project, you are buying an unmade future. This does not mean that it never makes sense to have a system built for you, but it does mean that it is greatly preferable to modify an existing system or configure a tool to meet your needs.

When choosing a software package, it is helpful to develop an invitation to tender which becomes an objective reference. Potential software suppliers are asked to comment on the match of their system. Asking the software developer to confirm in writing the level of match with your specification provides some measure of legal protection and, if your specification is rigorous, increases the possibility of identifying shortfalls in the solution.

However, this is not enough. You must also meet them. It is vitally important that you try out the system, experience it and the people in use, and come to your own conclusions (do not remain content with a demonstration by the supplier). A system that technically seems to meet all your requirements may be hostile in use, or at least not adapted to your style of working, although you will need to learn; and if the system is so simple that you can master it straight away, it is probably much too simple. Systems may also have functions that you had not considered which become important once you are aware of them.

Examine documentation rigorously. This is an excellent signal of the maturity and quality of the system. If documentation exists, is easy to follow, comprehensive and professional, then that is a good indicator that the total system will be reliable and well supported. If documentation does yet not exist, it is probable that the system is still in flight, so to speak, and may not be robust. (The vendor may also not have the resources to invest in documentation.) Is it leading edge technology from a supplier dedicated to supporting you excellently as a test bed, or an unsupported and insubstantial offering?

Always discuss with current users not only the system but the level of support received. User comments can be one of the best guides to decision. Always ask for a complete list of installations and choose at least a couple at random, not just those recommended. If the supplier is unhappy at your contacting them, probe in detail to discover why. There may be excellent reasons, or there may be a skeleton in the cupboard. Early users may have had problems, but what is their current experience? Try to identify problems that users had and how these were dealt with. Finding problems is not uncommon; the real test is how they were serviced.

It is an excellent idea to have an Escrow agreement. This provides an updated copy of the source code of the software package to a lawyer, bank or other registered professional organization. The terms of the agreement state that if the supplier should become bankrupt or otherwise fail to support the system, you will be given access to the source code – the language in which the software was originally written – to enable you to maintain the system yourself. However, if the system is very complex, this may be impractical and your safest solution is to use a system with a future.

Finally, involve as many potential users as possible. They feel empowered, they can provide good insight and if they support their decision, their commitment to it is likely to be enhanced.

Notes and references

1. Kearney, A.T. *Barriers to Successful IT*, DTI, CIMA, 1990/91.
2. 'Computers in marketing' survey by DunnHumby Associates, 1992/3.
3. 'Beacon setting' is a development based on the 7 Beacons Model developed by NPI Consultancy of Zeist, The Netherlands.
4. Schilet and Locke, quoted in Lovell, R.J., 'Power and project manager', *International Journal of Project Management*, **11** (No. 2).
5. Barnard, quoted in Lovell, R.J., 'Power and the project manager', *International Journal of Project Management*, **11** (2), May 1993.
6. Carlisle, J. and Parker, R., *Beyond Negotiation*, Wiley, 1989, p. 50.

11
The starting point: data

Summary This chapter describes the nature and uses of data, the two main approaches to selecting it, how to decide what is needed and how to design for flexibility.

There is no substitute for information. The most powerful analysis methodologies cannot (in most situations) compensate for a lack of information. Before becoming deeply involved in a statistical analysis, managers should make sure that all available sources of information have been trapped.
(Richard J Courteoux, *Direct Marketing*, March 1987)

The most fundamental element of the database is data, the information raw material on which the entire structure is built. Research by the Institute of Direct Marketing shows that the decisions arising from data are typically at least 300 to over 600 per cent more effective than, for example, creative treatment or response mechanics (yet creative work may receive attention and money out of all proportion to effect).

Quite clearly, data is the most effective discriminator by which to identify profitable, responsive customers. This is no big surprise. Modest creative treatment to the right people is likely to be more effective than a lot of creative attention to the wrong people. This finding agrees with our general thesis about the importance of relevance, authenticity and swimming upstream. Data is the raw material that enables this, and if the quality of data is overlooked it will be difficult to achieve maximum effectiveness by any other means.

Surveying the data

There are four basic kinds of raw data:

1. *Performance* data obtained from actual customer activity, behaviour and relationship
2. *Primary research* data obtained direct from the customer, e.g. completing a satisfaction or profile questionnaire
3. *Secondary research* data from independent compilers such as NDL, the lifestyle data collectors (see below)

4. *Outside* lists, when matched back to our files, can provide us with other information about their behaviour and interests. Accessing such data from other companies depends on industry and legal restrictions – as well as good sense.

To ascertain what data should be contained within a database there are two classical techniques to adopt. The first looks at where we are now and the raw material to hand (the bottom-up approach); the second starts by asking, 'what do we *need* to implement our strategy' (the top-down approach). The latter leads inevitably to an evaluation of potential organization and marketing changes that may be needed to obtain the required data.

The bottom-up approach

Surveying the data is done by a data audit. This identifies all sources of data and attempts to assess its extent and reliability. It is often carried out as an IT systems exercise, using very strict procedures, cross-referencing each data item in existing systems. A marketing team can identify available information by locating all sources, spreading a wide net to identify and record all available data that may be useful. These sources will include: existing computerized systems, such as a sales ledger, order-processing and sales support systems; and hard copy data, which may have been collected from competitions, questionnaires or reader offers. British Rail Intercity had to send placement students around the ticket offices in order to collect information on season card holders from paper records. It can be quite astonishing what is found.

One of the most useful steps is to print data out and look at it in various sequences. Often the intelligent and experienced eye can see at a glance that something is wrong, or recognize a potential gold mine.

A data audit should indicate such factors as completeness and sufficiency of data, consistency with known data from other sources, validation processing and procedures followed during capture, and recency and frequency of update. Statistics can help us to check quality, for example, by looking for unusual values.

Source data should be identified and described, so that it is clear what it represents, its reliability and update frequency (or recency). This provides a basis for designing a data structure to hold the data and provide marketing functions based on a judgement of usefulness.

Advantages of this approach are (a) we do not overlook what is available and (b) it can give good ideas and expose poor practices. It is also frequently used when marketers or agencies need to get urgent action and results. It is also very realistic.

The top-down approach

Although we still need to audit data, a more strategic approach to data content can be achieved by asking; what do I need to support my marketing? It may be that all the data needed is already there and can be accessed. For example, it may be clear to a company selling office supplies that it will achieve most discrimination by recording 'customer', 'business sector', 'number of white-collar office employees', 'existing spend on office supplies by category', 'other office supplies suppliers' and 'customer purchasing plans'.

- Standard industrial codes (SICs) give 'business sector'
- Telemarketing research provides the 'number of white collar employees'
- Order history gives 'expenditure within a product category'
- Salesforce research provides 'alternative suppliers'

We can also envisage the data we need for

- order recency
- order frequency
- order value
- total value
- average order value.

by designing low level data fields to hold and compute this information.

Alternatively, it may be necessary to go through a data requirements exercise as described under 'Marketing transformation' on page 205. For example, one of the most powerful ways to identify needed data is to do a Moments of Truth analysis, looking at the *needed* data to perform effectively and the *available* and *missed* data that could be produced for another potential user. Often different parts of the company are producers and users and it may be important to negotiate support from one group, for whom collecting the data is only an overhead, on behalf of another (or yourself). 'Negotiating' support rather than demanding it makes sense: there is a cost, even if only hassle, and that needs somehow to be borne and resourced.

Very often a combination of top-down and bottom-up methods will be employed, using experience and intuition to assess the information that is most needed and an audit of available data in order (a) not to overlook valuable information and (b) to find the shortfall.

The role of the marketer is also to exploit new and currently unknown opportunities. Additional or different information will inevitably be required as we develop. Since it is difficult to recover data retrospectively, it is often better to retain data the *may* become useful. Falling costs of hardware and software helps the difficult choice of what to retain. It is sometimes more expensive to archive than to purchase additional capacity.

Finally, we may need a leap of imagination to see how the organization needs to change to collect the data it requires as described below. The aim will be to capture the appropriate data at the first attempt, with a minimum of effort.

Raw and transformed data

Data is the raw material from which information and knowledge are derived. In fact, data or information is a kind of ethereal substance. It can be transformed by added value processes in a manner similar to the transformation of raw materials in a production company. Quality is as relevant to data transformation as it is to materials.

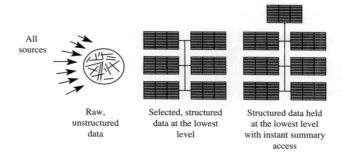

Figure 11.1   An evolution of data

One bank held a meeting for its top executives on data quality. This seemed a fairly unexciting topic to them: 'Data is boring', as the project manager put it. By the end of the meeting, their attitude was very different. Six sigma quality standards for data seemed as important a target for them as for silicon chip manufacturer, Motorola. After all, the primary raw material, perhaps the only real raw material, of a bank is data.

Data is nothing but potential until it becomes information, and worth little until it becomes knowledge; and knowledge is worthless until it changes practice; and practice is most valuable when double-loop learning takes place and becomes know-how.

The need for data

The extent of information required would be dependent on the type of business activity expected of the database. Business-to-business marketers will typically have considerably more complex data requirements than consumer marketers.

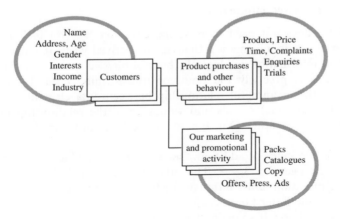

Figure 11.2   The key elements of a database

Other than technical or legal reasons, however, there are only three key reasons for holding data: (1) personalization, (2) to understand the customer community profile or profiles, and (3) to understand and improve the effectiveness of the company's marketing and service activities. (Figure 11.2.) All three explode into a complex set of possibilities. Understanding customers becomes fundamental input into organization development. Similarly, personalization means much more than adding the individual's name at the top of the letter. It is everything associated with the process of creating relevancy and, therefore, potentially includes product and service development, customization as well as long-term tailoring of relationship management programmes and offers. In one sense, personalization and marketing effectiveness data are only the inner and outer aspects of the same thing: getting close to customers.

Data may also need to be held for reasons that are not directly useful to the marketer. The two principal reasons are:

1. To meet data protection requirements. This may involve (e.g. in the UK) registering on the data record whether the customer's permission for use of data has been requested, and if so what the responses were.
2. For technical reasons associated with computer processing to maintain accuracy and validity. An example of this would be a history of when this record was last updated. There may also be fields to define linkages between data elements.

While the marketer may need to make IT people aware of legal requirements, software designers should take care of the technical requirements automatically.

Core data and derived information

The database does not need to hold the customer 'age on file' or 'order recency' since this is information that can be derived when required. Many such items of information will logically but not physically exist in a database.

In fact this is precisely the point of transforming data. Information derives from the meaningful relationship between data elements, in much the same way as tonal moods and values lie in the relationship between notes on the musical scale: D to F may have a different value, depending on the key.

There are two kinds of addition. One is arithmetic, which is a numerical, straightline change: $2 + 3 = 5$. The other is a chemical change, which is qualitative, quantum shift, intuitive: hydrogen + oxygen = water. Data addition is of the latter kind.

What do we know if someone has a $50 000 mortgage?

We may guess a few things based on average conditions, but add a second piece of data, such as a $45 000 or $200 000 house value insurance policy and you get wildly different information about the customer.

The benefits of a computer database begin to come into effect the more we derive information from basic data (see Table 11.1).

Table 11.1   Simple transformation of data

Data	Information provided
Current date plus First order date:	How long has this individual been a customer?
Current date plus Last order date:	How recently has this individual been a customer?

When a prospect upgrades to a customer this will be represented in the database by the presence of order records, from which changed customer status is derived (Figure 11.3). Frequency of orders can be derived from the sum of order transactions; annual frequency by the sum of order transactions divided by the age on file, in years.

The benefit of using a database is that complicated software programs do not have to be written and maintained to count the number of transactions or to check the existence of transactions. This is carried out by the (relational) database operating system. The information we need is calculated or computed at point of need; for example, when the customer is on the phone or in a mailing selection.

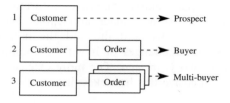

Figure 11.3   Changes in status convert to information

Some common consumer elements and business elements are listed in Tables 11.2 and 11.3.

Table 11.2   Common consumer elements

– Customer ID	– Acquisition date
– Name elements for personalization	– Telephone number
	– Response/purchase history including product, price, date, source
– Address: mailing delivery and geo-analysis/credit screening	
– Gender	– Mail/promotion history linked to campaign
– Date of birth (not age)	
– Income	– Lifestyle/demographic code
– Commitments	– Prediction/credit scores from model/card
– Original acquisition source	

Table 11.3   Common business data elements

– Company number	– Equity capital
– VAT number – classification	– Authorized capital
– Industry type	– Fixed assets
– SIC or internal codes	– Contact name(s)
– Parent company	– Contact title(s)
– Address – postcode	– Contact telephone(s)
– Telephone number	– Contact interests
– Telex	– Sales contact
– Fax number	– Financial year end
– Number of employees	– Credit limit
– Turnover	– Purchasing strategy

In deciding what data to retain, there are costs associated with additional data and these may need to be borne in mind. The costs of data are related to acquisition, retention and utilization.

Storing data is not particularly expensive. Information, however, will degrade and, over time, be no longer applicable. People move house, become married, change jobs, and die and the database needs to be maintained to reflect these changes or it will be communicating with an audience as it existed two years ago. The more extensive the scope of the database, the more expensive this housekeeping will be.

Designing databases for quality

The more information we retain, the more resources we shall need to devote, and therefore the more complicated the structure of the database becomes. The major cost of a computer system is normally its complexity, increasing exponentially. While it is vital to ensure that the database is adequate, comprehensive and sufficient for the job, unnecessary complexity and over-caution in insuring for the future may also seriously compromise effectiveness. Be realistic. Be pragmatic.

Once we have identified the data we need to retain in a database in order to provide us with our marketing information, database designers would normally take over the task of splitting up this data across the necessary database tables and would apply the disciplines of normalization (or simplifying the data into more basic structures, see below), to decide how to place them on the database tables.

Normalization is a technical term as basic to IT as direct mail is to marketing. Its explanation, therefore, is as simple or as complicated as the explanation of direct mail.

It is the process of deciding how much data redundancy is acceptable. (Data redundancy means holding a piece of data more than once.) An example would be holding the description of the product on each order record rather than on the product master record.

Ted Codd, an ex-IBM engineer, is credited with designing relational databases. He described three 'normal forms', each of which has an increasing rigour. So, for example, with the first normal form there would be no repeating data elements in a record. If a customer has bought several products, each product purchase would be a separate record. With the second normal form the descriptions of the products that have been purchased would be held on separate master records.

The third normal form is the most rigorous. Any data functionally dependent on a field other than the key will be held elsewhere in another file. These are explained in more detail in Topic 11.1.

The relational approach to analysing data can logically be applied to other database systems, although the physical way in which information is stored on the computer may be different. In relational databases these two are generally synonymous, and this is an advantage. We are now used to spreadsheets, and each database table can be thought of as a two-dimensional spreadsheet with one row for each record and columns corresponding to the fields or attributes.

The internal structure of the data must also be designed for satisfactory performance. One part of this is so-called normalization, splitting the data structure down to its lowest common denominators and assembling a design based on this in which no data is repeated unnecessarily. In practice there is often a benefit from compromising and backtracking from the rigorously normalized data structure, which maximizes flexibility and would be considered best practice in operational systems in order to provide processing efficiency. Remember that database marketing is often characterized by very intensive batch or sequential processing of large amounts of data, hundreds of thousands of customer records, and millions of transaction records may be searched to target the customers we want, which is very different to transaction-processing systems.

An example of the need for compromise is customer profiling. Rather than rebuild the customer's classification status or score each time from the base, low level, data, it may be assigned and stored periodically, saving workload.

Imposing order: categories and tables

The quality and design of category values or codes in the reference tables which drive data cleaning and classification can be a significant issue. For example, a motor insurer will have tables of all the vehicle models on the road. At input time, the table will be read for a match, and if one does not exist an error check will be given to the service representative enabling correction. The data can then be stored as a code. This both assists the quality of input, preventing 'things like Frod Capir tow liter' for a Ford Capri, and ensures a standard for analysis.

Creating the tables initially, and then maintaining them, are both significant and important tasks. Tables can be used to convert product codes from different eras, divisions or catalogues into common codes, or SKU level data can be summarized into product group codes. Postcodes can be read and assigned to salespeople or dealers, source codes can be looked up to identify valid promotions or catalogues and extensive use is made during name and address processing.

Requirements will be increased in complex communication cycles, such as business-to-business and telemarketing. Here a company may go through a very extended qualification and selling cycle from suspect identified, initial screening call made, decision maker identified, decision maker contacted, sales presentation booked, sales presentation made, contracts presented, contracts signed, to final sale. However, within the cycle there may be fluctuations in the temperature of the prospect. We may get a warm prospect in the qualification cycle which may then cool. Such basic data is often retained at the promotion history level, i.e. at transaction time, and at prospect level to indicate current and highest status reached.

It may be difficult to assign exclusive categories to customers sometimes. For example, it is common to classify customers according to the method of payment. A model may look at direct debit customers, credit card customers and cash/cheque customers and place individual customers into groups accordingly. Each order, however, may be paid for in a different way and, usually, the most recent or first method of payment is not the most useful way of classifying. So how do we assign the customer? Classification may be based on a hierarchical progression (if a person has ever paid by credit card he or she is classified as a credit card customer, otherwise he or she is a cash customer) or else many categories must be established to handle all permutations, or there may be a 'multi-method' code. If the raw data is held, of course, then decisions can be made at run time, but at the expense of further processing.

Fast count techniques

A management information summary of a database for fast counts and analysis is another useful way to get a total view of customers (see also Figure 11.1). Normally this will span the database tables of customer (or prospect), purchase and promotion. A summarized count of customers, at least for significant data, can be achieved by viewing the database as a two-dimensional table, in the form of a spreadsheet. Each customer is a row in the spreadsheet and each column represents a significant piece of marketing information – e.g. recency of last order, customer age on file, customer age band, frequency of order, frequency of communication, peak order value, total spend, average order value, payment type, product type – categorized in each case by a list of allowable values, so recency could be based on current date minus last order date and translated into bands of 0–30, 31–60, 61–90, 90 + days. The columns are clearly exclusive. Each customer would be classified once only into each column by the most significant category (or permutations).

The marketing information extract, in other words, fully classifies each customer according to our most common information requirements. This classification can be produced periodically to reflect the urgency of our needs and our requirements for up-to-date information. It gives useful insight and a condensed breakdown of the most useful information for marketing, planning and analysis.

In large databases of many thousands of customers this tabulation can produce a very big file, larger than the capacities of spreadsheets to handle data. In this case the *extract* can be summarized. Instead of one row per customer, there is one row per classification.

Typical marketing data requirements

1. *Campaign/programme* (e.g. summer season catalogue): this could hold a description, details of the user, product(s), objectives, overall results, costs per 1000, variable, fixed and total costs, cycle, average 'sale' value, average customer value increase; defaults for medium (e.g. magazine reference, linked to type, e.g. off the page), suppliers, 0800 number, score card model, segmentation model, personalization fields, scripts, etc.
2. *Promotion* (e.g. week 23 mailing): this could hold description, start date, mail/communication/insertion date, response curve, suppliers, quantity, costs per 1000 and variable, fixed and total costs, costs/'sale' value/profit per application, costs/'sale' value/profit per acceptance, acceptance rate, offer code, typical APR, actual APR, offer value range, source code, advertisement/creative/pack codes, total quantity (circulation), air time (broadcast), 0800 phone number, score card model, segmentation model, average customer value increase, personalization fields, script, etc.
3. *Promotion group or segment* (e.g. previous buyers): description, selection conditions, duplication index against house file on cold list, quantity ordered, quantity mailed, owner ID (to manage restrictions), cell code, response cost, average customer value increase, personalization fields, etc.
4. *Media details*, including description, circulation, cost per unit, script reference and average length.
5. *Partners/3rd parties*, with type, customer profile code(s), product set, owner, quantity of branches, name and address of contacts, relationship and relationship owner, data restriction class, policy rules on uses, etc.
6. *Fulfilment* details, including script, processes, effectiveness measures, returns, satisfaction, etc.
7. *Tables of classes* and internal data, e.g. for products, processes, moments of truth, salespeople, regions, etc.

Name and address data

This topic is so important that the whole of Chapter 13 is devoted to name and address processing.

Collecting quality information by organizational change

Often, one of the most effective and necessary steps in database building is thinking about how to collect customer data. *In fact, this may be the single most important discriminator in database marketing effectiveness.* The Huggies programme hinged on collecting information on expectant mothers from hospitals and nursing homes. Key methods include:

- changes in technology
- staff training and attitudes
- partnership with third parties
- loyalty cards and other relationship programmes
- new policies and processes.

The use of syndicated questionnaires, with other companies in partnership, worked for British Rail.

Asking people their names when they phone is one basic and good idea, even if you cannot sell at that time. Name and address software can also help with quick capture techniques. Portland Holidays changed their practice when they realized that customers phoning for a holiday they could not satisfy at that time were still a prime long-term opportunity – perhaps a relationship could be developed with an apology and an offer for the following year.

GKN Vending, UK leader in commercial vending machines, started collecting the names of existing users of jug coffee machines, instead of just looking for non-users, when they realized that contract renewal was an opportunity: 40 per cent of users would change their incumbent supplier, with the right approach, at the end of the one-year contract. By collecting data on the decision maker, the incumbent, contract dates and satisfaction levels, they could tailor a great programme to win friendship and allegiance. By the time the incumbent tried to renew the contract, GKN were more friendly with the company staff than the existing supplier. Furthermore, they collected invaluable information about the profile, strengths and weaknesses of other suppliers – valuable not just for selling but for acquisition, for example looking for those with best retention records.

Many organizations have changed their practices and procedures in order to collect information. For example, supermarkets with store cards, such as Food City or Tesco. There are also companies that collect data but do not use it: such as jewellers, with the name and address of a customer who brings in jewellery for repair; or hotels, with names and addresses of customers.

Marks & Spencer, the UK retailing leader, had 14 million transactions per week but no information about customers. Determined not to lose margin, control or disrupt selling operations it created its own store card. The base grew rapidly to two million customers and gives valuable information on customer activity and a base for further marketing. M&S developed financial and mail order products with great success.

A leading direct sales holiday company found that while it had installed software systems and telemarketing to handle its holiday bookings, there were no such facilities for the finance administration and customer service functions that dealt with tens of thousands of customers each year. By installing similar facilities in these back-office functions, they not only improved the quality of service to customers, but also gained invaluable information. The use of CTI to help with automating data capture is described further in the next chapter.

IBM put bar codes on customer and prospect seminar invitations which could quickly be swiped using an electronic pen when the customer checked in for the event. This updated their database.

Investment in data quality may mean changing attitudes and procedures. Some salespeople are said to be notorious for avoiding administration. However, research suggests that salespeople, but not their managers, are no less willing to use computers than any other group. The secret is to get them to realize the value, particularly to themselves.

By contrast, the bank described above found that it had acquired significant issues with the quality of its data as a result of casual and undisciplined procedures and attitudes among staff. A first suggestion was to bring the disciplinary manual into the situation and threaten staff with punishment if they failed to meet standards. On realizing that they were, like many manufacturing company, a producer, transforming data itself, they also realized that the same TQM techniques – measurement, continuous improvement, 6 sigma quality, communication, right first time, teamwork, encouraging responsibility for quality, working together on the system to achieve excellence, and so on – could be used for data quality standards. To do this they needed to create a culture which focused on data quality and this could not be done with a disciplinary manual, but only through skills and value education, involvement, and by recognizing staff for the greater quality achieved. Data quality moved from being an uninteresting subject (the reason why quality was poor) to a focus of the organization's total quality endeavours.

External data sources

There are numerous external data sources, including lists and data compilers. List compilers capture the names of shareholders and of the directors and senior officers of public companies from public records; they call to find decision makers for key product groups in larger companies; they produce specialist magazines, some free, and sell the list of subscribers; they send out millions of questionnaires about lifestyles; they collect warranty records for numerous companies and aggregate the data to get a broader picture; they go to the public records of voters, such as Britain's electoral roll; they analyse census records to find socio-demographic clusters, label them and assign post- or zipcodes; they collect data on bad debt from public records or by sharing data between credit providers; they then start to mix the data together to get ever richer combinations.

We have probably all had the experience of looking for a house or apartment and seeing some houses and streets where we could not imagine ourselves living, others where we would like to imagine ourselves living, and finally some that are right for us. This is informal geodemographic profiling from the personal point of view. CACI started geodemographic profiling with Acorn which clusters addresses according to census and electoral roll data. The census provides information on a small group of houses (individual data is private) and these groups are then clustered with others according to common characteristics. Any property in the cluster is assigned the relevant Acorn type. Mosaic is another such product with 58 postcode types built out of 54 variables (e.g. movers, average time of residence, household age, farm or flat addresses, occupation groups, financial data including credit judgements, housing standards and size) and further clustered into 10 lifestyle groupings: prosperous pensioners, older couples in leafy suburbs, families in inter-war semis, older communities, singles and flat dwellers, and so on.

NDL's BehaviourBank contains facts on 3 million direct mail responsive UK families (a similar, larger scale service is available in the USA and also in other countries). On average, there are nine BehaviourBank families in every street in Britain and 75 per cent have purchased via the mail in the past year. They also share the privilege of being people willing to fill in a questionnaire, the National Shoppers Survey, in exchange for a sweepstake entry. Data collected includes age, children's age, charge cards held, income, home and pet ownership, size of home, marital status, occupation, sex, size of family, appliances owned, betting interests, personal business interests, charitable and social concerns, cultural pursuits, entertainment interests, fashion consciousness and women's clothing size, financial, health, sport and hobby interests, newspapers read, holidays taken, allergies and other personal details.

Combining databases creates even more power. Census and credit data can be combined, or credit and lifestyle surveys. Equifax Europe, a leading credit profiler with information on more than 44 million consumers in approximately 22 million households, combined data with NDL International's lifestyle data to create a geo/lifestyle targeting system called Images. Hundreds of characteristics were used to develop Images.

Data protection laws and practices

There is an increasing move towards data protection laws, although the situation is very variable around the world, and even within the EU. The EU's data protection directive aims at standardization. Variations across US states makes keeping track of the rules complex, although, on the whole, restrictions are still less than in Europe. As well as laws, of course, there is also good practice, the industry recognizing that only by maintaining standards voluntarily is it possible to prevent possibly punitive legislation taking place.

To get an idea of how emotive the subject is, how would you feel if you applied for a credit card offered by a charity, with each purchase yielding a small donation for the charity, and were turned down because the previous tenant of your house had a bad debt?

Angry?

Yet it makes excellent statistical sense for the reasons above: demographics apply as much to credit risk as to purchasing habits. Yet to make a decision infringes our personal space and, not surprisingly, has recently been made illegal in Britain despite the objections of the credit profiling industry.

Here are some general principles that make good sense (many are laws in some countries):

— Never hold data about someone who does not want you to: give that person an opt out.
— Do not write to people who do not want to be written to; apart from anything else, it is a waste of money.
— Do not hold less data than you need to be effective, nor more than is acceptable: in particular, avoid sensitive areas such as racial and religious data.
— Make sure the data is accurate and up to date.
— Make very sure that your collection methods are honest and fair: it may and should be a crime in your country to collect data by false pretences, such as for a survey which 'helps us understand the market', but really means 'lets us mail you'.
— Allow customers to see their data at little or no charge.
— You are responsible for your own data: even if you rent it out, you should ensure that it is going 'to a good home'.
— You are responsible for the data you use: even if you rent it, make sure that it 'came from a good home'.
— Protect data while you hold it.
— Make sure your database records the customer's permission to use the data, and when it was given (or not).
— Use any national goneaway (or nixie) file to clean lists, and perhaps your database; it prevents a waste of time and money and prevents you looking stupid.
— Use any scheme, e.g. Britain's Mailing Preference Scheme and the corresponding Telephone Scheme, which allows consumers to indicate a wish for a blanket suppression of direct mail.

Topic 11.3 Normalization

The most widespread logical standard for database design is reflected by the relational database normalization standards. These are rules for the way data is divided up and interrelated, so as to provide a logical framework and rigorous design methodology. Just as bricks, timber, plasterboard and nails come together to make a modern living space through the guidelines of the architect, so data is connected through the database management system. But whereas the architect builds an imagined form out of the components, the database is more an architecture of decomposition. Data is broken down into automatic elements according to formal rules.

For most database design purposes there are three levels of rules that should be applied, and these were first laid down by Edward Codd who was an IBM engineer and is attributed with being the father of the relational database.

First normal form

This defines the basic unit of information, which is normally the file record or the entity in relational database terminology. To conform to the first normal form the record must have the following properties:

1. *A unique key* which identifies the record and ensures that a particular key value always means the same thing. This is known as the primary key.
2. *Atomic data elements*, i.e. no field or attribute for this record should be capable of meaningful division. An address, for example, should be split into its component lines, a premise number and postcode should also be separated from the main address lines.
3. *No repeating data elements*, so that if a customer has purchased several items then this data should be held in a series of records rather than a series of fields constituting an array within a record.

If we allow for array structures in data, then no matter how many slots we allow another slot will eventually be needed and meanwhile all those extra slots are wasting space.

Second normal form

Each data field must be functionally dependent on the primary key. If the primary key consists of several fields then each data field must be dependent on all the key fields. For example, a customer company may have several sites. The company name should not be held at this site level as each site would have the same company name, and we would have redundant data. The company name should be held in the customer master database table with the primary key of company number only.

The site name, telephone number and contact should be held at site level however.

Third normal form

All data fields that are functionally dependent on a field other than the primary key of the record should be removed and placed in another file. For example, the order record may contain a product id. to identify the product purchased, but should not contain the product description. The product description should be removed and put into the product table which has the primary key of product id. Again if we repeat product description at every order record we shall have massive duplication and redundancy of data.

Data models

It is customary for companies to develop a 'data model' of their organization, which becomes the information architecture that drives the business. This is sometimes called information engineering. Effectively it means understanding the key information building blocks, or *entities*, that drive the organization. This provides a model or map of the business, and is unique for each organization. Many companies value this very highly, and will even insure its privacy.

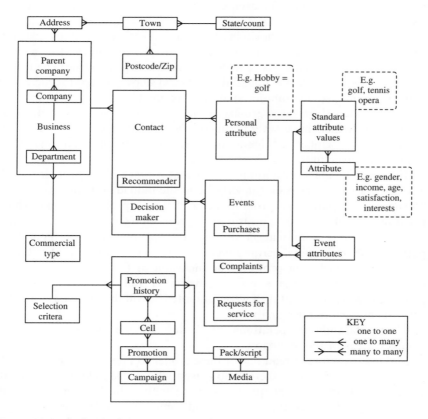

Figure 11.4 A simple data model

A simply entity or data model is shown in Figure 11.4. It is not necessary to understand exactly what everything means. However, most of the entities will be self-explanatory. An entity is simply an important, organizing unit of data, such as an address, contact or event. There may be many pieces of data, i.e. 'fields' or 'attributes' as they are often called, which belong or potentially belong to the entity according to normalization rules.

Entities may have a one-to-one, one-to-many or many-to-many relationship:

- one wife to one husband (Western convention)
- one mother to many children/many children share one mother
- many women attending many classes/many classes each with many women.

These are shown by the 'arrow' marks in the diagram. So, for example, there may be many companies for each commercial type, but not (perhaps) the reverse.

The attribute entity is a flexibility tip. The marketer can thereby add new data types about an event or individual; for example, for a new questionnaire about interests. The design becomes open ended. (The model only indicates the principle; not all the technical steps required for successful implementation, so a computer analyst is required.)

Some models show large groups or entity domains, such as contacts or events, which then have several subentities, e.g. influencers and decision makers, or an embedded hierarchy, e.g. the company and marketing programme structures.

There will be many promotions to a client contact. Each promotion will have used a particular pack (or script) and the individual mailing will have belonged to a particular promotional cell, i.e. a promotion unit whose performance will need to be measured. A promotion consists of several cells, usually testing a combination of 'list' (i.e. people) and 'method' (e.g. particular letters, offers, scripts, creative, etc., i.e. media types) within a campaign or marketing project. The inclusion of the customer will have been determined by the selection criteria. A full record of who was promoted, why, and what they were promoted to will therefore be stored for subsequent performance analysis.

Clearly data about operational marketing activities is one of the most complex areas of the database.

Making the effort to read one of these models is interesting and useful. If you are not an IT expert, there is no reason why you should be expected to understand it, so freely ask questions of the analyst. In the process you will get a very good feel for the flexibility and comprehensiveness of the design. A really excellent ploy is to ask dumb questions: 'But will it do this?'

The data library and quality maintenance

Creating a database is a considerable investment, not just in costs but in opportunity to succeed or disappoint. The resource should therefore be managed to provide the best possible service to all. A useful concept is the *library*. This seems a better name than 'warehouse', a term popularized by IBM. A library is a place where precious information is guarded and made available for interested parties to read and turn into knowledge; it is a community resource and is free; librarians are professionally trained to help to find required information; users are expected to maintain the quality and to 'return after use'.

A unit should ideally be mandated to manage the data resource, as librarians, on behalf of the whole company. It should ideally be a service unit, trusted as guardian and adviser for and on behalf of all, including the CEO or group, to whom the data ultimately belongs. Of course, this can simply be the function of the marketing department, or members of it, or a bureau function.

Their responsibility will vary, but typically will include data control and quality assurance, 'right first time' training and systems improvement, expertise in analysis and access, table and attribute maintenance support and data protection. However, it is important that users do not decide that the responsibility for quality belongs only to this group. It belongs everywhere. The librarians are simply resource and process experts facilitating all-round quality and having the time to check and help improvement.

The first step is to look at the processes of data capture to ensure that software and processes get quality right first time. Many producers are measured by standards of performance which do not include data quality. Their objectives of speed and multi-tasking may be barriers to collecting data or to quality checking. Good software can help: validating entries, speeding data entry, for example by entering postcode or zip plus premise number and reading the address off a national file (see Chapter 13). However, data quality requirements may also need to be persuasively explained.

Data control procedures, checking batch file processing, managing data that goes out to bureaux for keying, chasing monthly or other cycle updates can all be important tasks. When extensive data is rented it is normal to use a bureau to handle all this.

Seed lists must be included in all mailings and outgoing files. These are internal people (or contractors) who receive a copy of all mailings to check the end of the process. If names are rented out, the seed lists ensure that they have only been used as contracted, e.g. one time use. If data has gone to an outside laser printer or mailing house, seeds ensure proper use. Normally marketers will insert these lists automatically, but maintaining, checking and ensuring their right use is important.

Quality assurance of all incoming batch data and data processing is a painstaking task. Data should be dumped to print and sight checked for anomalies; standard test programs can also be run, looking for consistency and completeness. Deduplication reports should be carefully checked and all records rejected dealt with. One direct insurance company had a two-year-old stack of rejected name and address records. The insurance policies existed but the data was too poor for the database and no one had had the time to arrange it. The reject file had reached 2 per cent of the total database.

From time to time the database's integrity should be checked. One marketing company found that an error in processing had damaged the integrity of the database and records were not being correctly assigned to customers. By the time the discovery took place, over 10 per cent of the transaction records were incorrectly assigned.

Data tends naturally to decay. People move, die, stop buying. The company needs to invest in processes to deal with this: mailings to find out status, talking to customers on the phone, outside screening against files of deceased or goneaways, and checking against the national mailing preference schemes. Regular sample exercises to contact and check quality is important.

One good idea is to rank the most vital data, decide on its useful life and then automatically trigger prompts to service staff, or letters, to check the most vital data on contact.

This costs money, but all good things do.

12
Quality information tools

Summary   This chapter describes functions and criteria to set up an information systems resource to support customer marketing.

Knowhow is an asset. An organization which can accumulate and store information effectively will thereby increase the value of its knowhow in the balance sheet.
(Karl Erik Svieby and Tom Lloyd[1])

The direct marketing industry has been through two phases and is entering a third. First, it was used by a limited set of specialist companies, the mail order businesses, or consisted of a relatively ad hoc set of activities, often called 'mail-shotting'. Direct marketing meant direct mail. Technically, it was dominated by list-processing and list management techniques processed in batch, usually by specialist organizations. The first generation marketing database was a merge–purge system (see below).

Beginning in the mid-1980s, database marketing developed. An increasingly wide base of companies developed interest and expertise and many specialist units exploited the opportunities. Techniques developed including, relational systems, on-line access and increasingly sophisticated links to telemarketing, sales and administration systems. By the early 1990s there was an explosion in the CASM marketplace, as Chapter 4 described. This is continuing.

Companies very strongly agree that they will continue to see an increase in the use of computer technology for marketing over the next five years.[2] Yet, nearly one-third of UK companies still have no marketing database, and the figure is greater in other European centres.

Ahead of these laggards, a third phase in direct marketing development, representing the leading edge of marketing technology, is now developing. This is characterized by three features:

1. Systematic, automated, company-wide responsiveness to customer interaction with corresponding scored and targeted customer communications to develop sustainable relationships. This is called 'event trigger' or 'contact management', but 'event responsiveness' may be a better name.

2. Full integration of the telephone and the computer, with a database of customer information linked to business applications and EIS (executive information systems) services, often on a wide area network. This is a feature of intelligent networking.
3. Focus on the interaction of technology and people, with technology used as supporter of the front line, a dominant methodology of the balance of the 1990s.

Companies are using IT facilities, particularly client/server and telephony architectures, networking, object-oriented systems and integration of workbench tools.

Topic 12.1 The evolution of computing technology

List marketing began with direct mail, which meant mailing customers. Mailing lists were simple 'flat file' lists of customer records, each list compiled according to some interest, product purchase or other criterion *connecting* the customers.

List processing used merge–purge, the industry term for merging a number of different lists and detecting and deleting duplicates. Because customers were held on separate lists, and there could be a list of customers for each product that had been purchased, some way was needed to bring the lists together into a common format and overall picture, to identify multi-buyers and avoid duplicate mailing.

Merge–purge also supported cold list mailing (see Figure 12.1). In addition to mailing their own customers, direct marketers frequently rent lists from other direct marketers. These so-called 'cold lists' will be aggregated. As a customer may therefore appear on a number of lists, some way of purging duplicates is required. Until the end of the 1980s, merge–purge was the backbone of the direct marketing

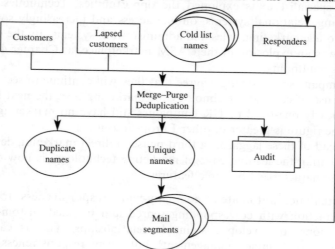

Figure 12.1 Merge–purge flow

industry. It was used for most of the so-called database marketing applications. Even today it is a very widespread and important application, particularly for the acquisition of new customers.

All lists are input, including any suppression files of customers or bad debtors. Lists are merged, sorted and deduplicated on names and addresses. Techniques of name and address matching became increasingly sophisticated and form the technical basis for database marketing (see Chapter 13). A clean file is produced for mailing and another file of the duplicates. Obviously full reports of duplicate matches by input file are given to management.

Tape base systems

Mailing lists were commonly stored on computer tapes, to save money. The use of computer tapes was first developed by IBM in the 1960s and became increasingly important until the late 1970s. Even during the 1980s they were frequently used for the processing of certain batch applications, such as payroll. When processing is intermittent or periodic, and simple lists are employed, tape storage is an adequate medium. However, tape storage works like the common cassette tape; you have to wind the tape to find the track you want.

What happens if a series of people phone to ask for information and each is requested to wait until the tape has been wound, or rewound, after use for the previous customer?

Disks

The first important development of computer disk technology was the so-called Winchester Disk invented in IBM's Winchester Laboratory at Hursley in the UK in the mid-1970s. Disk storage brings new possibilities. Many files can be stored on the same disk. Software can then be used to collect individual data that is needed for a particular enquiry. All the files that are necessary can be searched through quickly and virtually instantly.

The disk mechanism rapidly accesses and retrieves needed data. A disk is shaped like a vinyl record but stores data on a magnetic coating. It spins at high speed with an arm moving in and out from centre to periphery to read off each of the files as required, like being able to put a record needle or CD arm directly on the particular note or phrase of a song you want to hear. Databases can now be designed so that any piece of data is only held once – irrespective of its different applications or the number of users who want to access it – and is then retrieved and assembled to order.

There may be 10 000 order records for a product, but each order has a product reference and the product details are held once only in a master record. The key advantages are:

- Flexibility and accuracy.
- If you change the name of the product once you change it for everything.
- Instead of holding the description of a product 10 000 times it needed only be held once.

The key disadvantage is that if you are reading 10 000 product purchase records to select customers you may have to read 30 000 or 40 000 records to collect all the data you need.

Fundamentals of a marketing database system

A marketing database system is a repository of transactional and marketing information merged from several sources into a single, integrated database about customers and marketing programmes. It provides sophisticated selection and analysis capabilities on any of the data fields, hopefully suitable for use by marketing people. (The purpose of holding data is to make it accessible: mining through the mass to the ore.)

A database needs software subsystems designed to provide:

- database creation, data import and export
- maintenance and feedback from the response cycle, including all parts of the business
- campaign and marketing management
- selection and output, potentially including, automated event responsive functions
- management information and decision support
- database analysis: clustering, value modelling, prediction
- response analysis
- assistance to service and sales.

Whatever data you decide to collect, it will soon need to be updated and changed. Therefore, from the beginning, it is essential that the database designer thinks about how to make this possible. Software systems can be a barrier to change. Traditional software designs created maintenance problems even in the days of static business. What is needed is software tools, not software functions. These can then be used to serve an ongoing stream of business needs.

The database can serve many different applications from service to order processing to sales. Some possible applications may not yet exist. When Securicor set up its call centres it had not yet created a voice response service, and when Ciba-Geigy gave computers to the salesforce they did not at first take it with them into customer calls.

An application generator allowing design and maintenance of the core system is therefore preferable to third generation, hard programming. Such a generator should ideally be not simply a standard CASE tool, but be designed to meet the core needs of a marketing database.

Software design

In 1986, looking at the state of the art in software, The Computing Group, a leading UK bureau, realized that it needed to do something different. Most software packages performed relatively fixed functions to a relatively fixed data format. The *soft*ware was rather firm, yet, every marketing database, with or without telemarketing, fulfilment and other linked applications, was different. Its usage, data model and applications varied. However, there was a set of *core generic processes*.

A marketing database, it was realized, needed to be a set of tools. It should be:

- able to define for each client a unique and changing data model;
- an interface for new files or sources;
- able to give access in weird and wonderful ways;
- able to give the output of chosen data to a chosen program or application;
- a record of what was happening.

Telemarketing software companies such as Brock and Blue Sky were similarly creating tools to script a conversation with fluid data input and output. Later, sales control systems, e.g. Ensure, enabled contact *projects* to be defined.

This focus on core generic processes and tools to re-engineer predates the excitement of process re-engineering and signals the new industry. Design of 'functional tools' rather than 'functioning operations' is vital to several marketing system components. These include:

- name and address matching
- selection of customers (for analysis or communication)
- selecting and routeing of output and output data
- creation of personalized output text
- programming or scripting of call response
- designing and using event or contact strategies
- workflow management
- new customer, campaign or product level data attributes
- reporting and executive analysis
- campaign/promotion structures
- new file processing
- communication between systems, especially telephone and computer.

Data structures also benefit from flexibility to allow:

- new data attributes
- evolving data values (e.g. comparing price on relative price bands over five years, rather than absolute values)
- new event types with their own data fields.

In each case, there may be generalized principles, with implementation local, particular, and changing.

The marketing system, therefore, aims to be truly *soft*ware, a re-use tool for adaptation and adoption according to the changing needs, and learning. Software re-use techniques have subsequently matured, and it seems that they may revolutionize software, making it even more of a team culture. (Software re-use is an attitude of mind, design methodology and set of tools which construct systems out of interlocking pieces of software, or 'objects', in much the way that a car is assembled from standard components. By designing standard components using 'domain analysis' and 'object level programming' rather than operation specific function, there is greater flexibility to disassemble and reassemble systems.)

Topic 12.2 Basic marketing database activities

1. Data is imported, set up at database on an ongoing basis from other systems or outside sources, and reformatted to conform to the database. For example, product codes or customer group codes might be standardized.
2. Data – batch and on-line, including names and addresses – passes through software and human quality control before updating the database. This is as important for on-line users.
3. Address validation ensures that the address is correct and standardized in format.
4. Duplicate matching ensures that no customer is included twice while new transactions are added to an existing customer.
5. Data is added and its integrity checked.
6. A summary may be calculated, for example, the total orders and value by customer or marketing programme, and placed into summary records.
7. The database may be a resource for customer service, or simply an analysis and communication system.
8. It may generate prompts on request or through an automatic feature based on a diary, triggering the salesforce or marketing to follow up leads or generate mailings.
9. The marketing function sets up marketing programmes with focused communication to generate sales and service opportunities which, hopefully, produce responses, orders or follow up. These are new updates for the database. The selection of customers for inclusion requires access to all the data in the database and very sophisticated and friendly for choice and definition.
10. A record of all mailings or communications including time, pack, marketing programmes for each customer allows feedback of response data, linkage back to the promotion and consequent response analysis and statistics on the performance of marketing programmes, salesforce, service and customer orders to be calculated.
11. Marketing analyse data to produce customer profiles and performance models (described in more detail later).
12. There is often a need to export data on computer files, for example, to a laser printing company in order to print personalized letters. Or lists could be rented to other direct marketing users.
13. New data fields and files may be needed for a new file with new fields (e.g. for a questionnaire) or new fields on an existing file. Alternatively, new field values may need to be added, e.g. new models, to validation tables. So, maintenance of

the 'data dictionary' (allowing set-up of structure, content, and valid values in the database) is an important and ongoing task and needs a user friendly interface.

14. The 'data dictionary' will also be accessed during selection, reporting and other activities to reference available data. It is a core user tool.

15. Several parties may want to create mailing promotions during the same period to the same groups without duplicating mailings to an individual.

Bureau or in-house?

Of all the UK marketing databases, 94 per cent are managed in-house, according to one survey, but many of the most effective are implemented via a bureau, at least in the beginning.

When you invest in an in-house computer resource, it becomes a fixed cost and capacity. By contrast, although a bureau may charge some basic fixed price, costs after that are usually dependent on usage, and it will typically have excess resource for peaks. They will have specialized control and application systems and expertise: the core process and competence of the bureau is marketing database functions, whereas this is only one of the many processes in the typical organization.

These are good reasons to outsource to either a facilities management or full service operator, but crossing the organization boundary can create vulnerability. But, if a good service contract and a strong cooperative working relationship exist, then your management may be 'extended' in the best sense of the word.

The issue is control in a crisis. Usually it *seems* possible to have more control over internal resources. Internal communications *ought* to be good. In practice the politics of relationship and cooperation need to be assessed on a case by case basis.

In asking a third party to look after your database, you are delegating or mandating control to them. They usually have ways of doing things, and if you ask them to operate too far out of their norms, this can cause problems and a reduction in the in-depth support you have been looking for. You may therefore have to rely on their procedures.

You can set up a fully controlled environment internally that operates exactly as you wish it. The question is, how confident are you that you are establishing procedures that are as good as those that have stood the test of time in a successful bureau?

A good bureau will have a client-centred approach, committed to your needs. On the other hand, they have their own strategic needs and balance your requirements against those of many others, and profit objectives. It may be possible to create greater strategic support internally, but many organizations find that marketing systems come lower in the priority order than operational systems.

Deciding whether to use a bureau or to build and operate your marketing database in-house can be aided by the following rules of thumb:

1. Have you developed a marketing database before? If you have not then you are pioneering and the risk is greater, which is a good reason to go to an outside specialist.
2. Have you operated a database before? The same applies. Marketing databases can be resource greedy, have major peaks and are complex to operate.
3. What is your core business? How central to the business is your database? If you are a mail order company, or a direct insurance business, then your database of customers runs the company. This is a good reason to have it in-house. If your database is only for periodic promotions, use a bureau.
4. What management resources are available? Never have a resource that cannot be managed. The more valuable the resource, the better the management needs to be. Will there be enough to provide cover if someone is ill or on holiday? If some of your staff leave, will you still have continuity?
5. Do you have peaks and troughs in activity? If you resource for peaks, which are few and far between, then you will have a lot of idle resource, which is a good reason to use a bureau.
6. How stable is your management team and culture? When WH Smith Travel moved its marketing team, there was a short period when there was no one really responsible for the database operational control devolved to the bureau. Later the new team was briefed by them.
7. How will it integrate or interface with other systems? The more tightly coupled, the more need to run in-house, though, as computers, they can be connected over telephone lines.
8. What other commitments are there on IT? How do they feel about it? IT functions are often overstretched and delighted to see a third party carry out a project. This is particularly true if they see the project as a non-strategic or non-core process.
9. Have you proved the value of the marketing database already? It is a good idea to pilot or prototype any new process. Bureaux are a good way of setting up a system which delivers a substantial percentage of the requirement, relatively quickly and cheaply, with low commitment of resource and time to prove the concept.
10. Eventually the marketing database should be a significant corporate asset, especially if a real vision of the potential is developed. Therefore, it should either be in-house or in a tight partnership with the outsource specialist.

Centralized or decentralized?

Bringing data together adds value. Uniting two pieces of data creates new elements: chemical not arithmetic addition. Uniting and increasing the overall sources of data can improve its accuracy. Hence, in large companies with different divisions or businesses, the creation of a single system across the group will often provide maximum benefit to all. By pooling data, each unit has access to superior information, making superior business performance possible (although not guaranteed). A database resource can be centralized and its use decentralized.

The system should therefore typically be a common resource. A *common resource* helps the board to achieve perspective: to provide a *coordinated set* of goals and policies, to maximize group profit while supporting individual businesses.

Ideally, all units should retain a *common right of access*, any constraints determined by the customer's preference. The CEO has the responsibility to ensure that appropriate business units are established to focus on the overall development of the customer relationship, through its life cycle of opportunities.

For example, one consumer leisure group recognized that their customers went through a natural life-stage process: single, married, children, etc. By structuring different brands carefully, all groups could more effectively be managed. Instead of operating separately, the corporate database can now help to 'pass them on'.

The only good reasons not to build such a resource are when

- units have very different core businesses
- the culture and use of computing is very different
- overlap in customer communities is limited and a common resource step changes implementation costs or time.

Design/technology criteria

A 'relational database' is now recognized as the route of choice for a full functional database, but this does not strictly imply a relational database management system (RDBMS). Design criteria are conditioned by use: a batch tool to support mailings is very different from a database continuously accessed on-line, in real time, by a wide variety of users. One of the most successful mainframe database systems is Marketpulse which uses the Model 204 database simulating much of the function of an RDBMS, but optimizing performance.

Client/server architecture is increasingly preferred. If the database is to serve both marketers and sales/service people, it needs to support transaction intensive front office applications and computer intensive

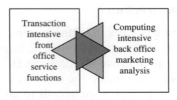

Figure 12.2   System characteristics for marketing

customer scoring, profiling and marketing management (Figure 12.2). Relatively massive computing power needs to be delivered at point of need. These criteria make selecting a suitable systems architecture difficult.

In a bureau implementation, the type of machine used in not necessarily important except for subsequent migration in-house. Issues of cost, service and function are sufficient.

A mainframe is typically less desirable as a solution unless the system needs to be integrated with other mainframe applications (and even then it is not an essential) or a large company or shared resource (e.g. bureau) needs the power.

The use of a minicomputer or workstation solution is otherwise preferable: costs will be lower. The IBM AS/400 (a system designed as a user friendly relational database machine) and Terradata (a parallel processing machine to optimize relational databases) have both been widely used, as have powerful RISC technology machines such as SUN Workstations and IBM's RS/6000. Most installations are, of course, powerful PC and Macintosh systems, which are cheapest of all if the horsepower is enough.

Business-to-business databases

These have greater complexity. There may be a more complex decision-making unit, e.g. different people with different job titles and responsibilities, belonging to departments or divisions of a company in a group. There are often many different kinds of transactions and events, projects, orders, tenders, presentations and seminars and more.

Since companies can belong to other companies, to know how much business is done with Shell you may need to aggregate across a large number of companies, departments and contacts, with both structural and maintenance implications. Typically there is a wider range of internal contacts too: sales, service, engineers, managers and process owners may need to be modelled in the database, as well as dealers or agents. It is also much more likely that a sales management system will be in use requiring integration or linking.

Customer service applications

Telemarketing users should be linked to an up-to-date and relevant knowledge base of four elements:

1. *Relevant information about customers*, including purchases and satisfaction.
2. *Product data*. A motor insurance company may hold information about all car models; a hotel company about their hotels.
3. *Problem and answer data*. Again this requires a facility to log problems as they occur, which can then be dealt with either by training or improvement of the knowledge base.
4. *Export systems*. The most obvious simple 'expert systems' are the ability to calculate a price or credit score. IBM has systems which configure computers. Depending on products, expert systems should provide an increasing level of support to operators, advising on product choice and problem resolution.

More and more companies provide customer data on screen when answering enquiries over the telephone or counter,[2] increasingly helped by Workflow or navigator software such as Lotus Notes and Unisys' Navigator software. Workflow software provides structures for administrative tasks, helping staff to follow the right procedures and giving priority to the right work.

The Bristol and West Building Society, a British financial services company and an early adopter database marketer with 100 000 customers, now uses a modified version of Logica's Vitesse software operating under Microsoft Windows to help serve customers. Their aim is that the first individual to take a call can handle the complete relationship.

The workstation screen replicates items which staff would normally have had on their desks: personal client details, calculator, customer correspondence and product portfolio. Customers are asked to give a password and PIN and the screen then displays all relevant accounts and latest transactions. The system has automated procedures for sending out client information. For example, people asking for an illustration of interest benefits on a five-year savings account can have it calculated, printed and in the post the same day.

Telemarketing, telephony systems

The telemarketing system consists of ACD, software applications and users. An ACD, or automated call distribution system, is an intelligent switchboard, or PABX. It monitors traffic, routes calls automatically and provides performance analysis. More advanced systems have links to voice or touch tone response systems, and ACDs can also be linked in a network.

The telemarketing system is a call navigation manager. This means that it is used to:

- architect or script desired conversation paths through applications;
- enable a rapid and effective response to any situation.

Telemarketing systems need to be resilient, perhaps by independence from host or server machines, but must be closely linked in real time to product and customer information. In practice, this is often done by providing copy databases of key information. They have three subelements: software, e.g. screens and data entry; telecommunications capability, including call handling and distribution; and the integration of software and telecommunications equipment.

Scripts allow a telemarketing manager to define questions to be asked, a range of possible/acceptable answers, with the answer determining the next question ('conditional branching'). Telemarketing software must be easy to use, both for operators and the supervisors setting up or trialling new call scripts. It should allow integration with external software applications, such as address generation, customer scoring or product allocation.

Power dialling is another important telephone innovation. Power dialling enables a computer program to forecast when an agent is next likely to be free and, based on ongoing statistical analysis of 'time to successful answer' (engaged, no-answer, number unobtainable), it sets up a call in time. There are two dangers:

1. People may be called before the representative is actually ready. This is unfriendly and annoys customers.
2. Telephone co-workers may be so driven by the system that their warmth, enjoyment and attitude is damaged.

Providing parameters are **carefully** set, however, power dialling can dramatically lift productivity and save co-workers from routine activities.

Computer telephone integration (CTI)

The next five years will see an enormous expansion in communications between phone systems and computer programs, enabling the sharing of information: collection *from* calls and distribution of data *with* calls. This is called CTI and its key function is allowing computers to influence phone systems and calls, and vice versa.

CTI provides low-level physical connectivity via transport-level signalling links, upper-level protocol translation, and application interfaces between computer platform digital switches to provide integrated functionality to telephone and information systems users. (In non-technical terms, CTI supports voice communications in more useful and constructive ways.) A telephone call may be influenced by information from a computer or a computer may be directed to perform functions based on a call. Crucially, the computer can also monitor a call and record additional data, such as the total time from the beginning of the telephone ringing to the end of the conversation, with outcome and process. Providers include IBM's Callpath, DEC CIT, Envoy Telelink, Novell, Microsoft TAPI.

Case study 12.1 Technology integration

A world-leading software company has been developing its own internal system based on client server architecture to:

- Provide a seamless customer interface. Callers to any part of the company enter a computer/telephone highway that measures performance, allows data and call transfer, and provides both a call navigation control system and a knowledge base for agents.
- Allow callers to direct their interest through voice response systems, with Fax on Demand for selected help documentation, automatically faxed to a number entered by touch tone or collected off the inbound call.
- Service in-house and third party telemarketing service agents, seamlessly.
- System recognize a customer (using a PIN number) and allocate to an appropriate service level based on the contracted value.
- Provide a full function text management system with a selection of standard documents for automatic editing based on conditional data factors captured during the call.
- Determine outbound communications by an event management system.
- Support a knowledge base of problems and solutions to aid service problem solving.

Advanced CTI configurations use Intelligent Networks (INs) – an architecture which allows calls to be influenced by and routed among computers in the network. Companies across Europe are implementing INs to support freephone, virtual private networks (VPNs), universal personal telephone (UPT), and other facilities likely to be made available over time, and, in the process, are catching up with a more advanced North American market.

The installation of IN allows the customer's computer system to become a node on the network providing instructions to the network on call routeing. For example, a large call centre user with many locations may continually update the availability of agents in each location. When a call destined to the user enters the network, the computer instructs the network to route the call to the call centre with available resources. This was used by Securicor to improve productivity. A major American Express service centre is sited in Finland among a community that would otherwise have found itself jobless. Trials with teleworkers from home, with video phones, could see further major demographic differences coming about as a result of this technology. The teleworker can be based anywhere.

Calling line identification (CLI) and direct dialling identification (DDI) are the two more common network attributes which affect functionality. These have proved to be key drivers of CTI-enabled call centres in the US but are just beginning in Europe. CLI provides the phone number from which the customer has dialled, enabling automatic customer selection or update of the database. DDI informs the marketer of the number dialled.

The great advantage of CTI is that it provides vastly more data for analysis of performance, perhaps 90–99 per cent of costs in an activity-based costing system at the individual consumer level.

Topic 12.3   Key CTI facilities

The facilities of computer telephone integration include:

- Screen transfer: enabling transfer simultaneously of computer-screen information and telephone call. By this method a sales department could transfer to service or management, or a call could be transferred to another specialist sales department to encourage cross-sell, or even across companies.
- Detailed customer call-management information: Agent call-performance analysis can be cross-referenced with content and result information such as product sales or enquiry interest. The length of call, process, script or action can all be captured.
- Screen pop: delivery of customer profile to an agent screen simultaneously with a call.
- Delivery of scripts and automatic detection of marketing source according to number dialled.
- Automatic detection of marketing source based on number called.
- Computer dialled number (power dialling): high-volume call processing initiated by a computer instead of by hand.
- Intelligent call routeing based on number dialled, and also via voice or touch tone responses by the caller to questions.
- Integrated information retrieval: providing an agent or caller with information from electronic, voice and fax mail systems.
- Allowing waiting callers to know how long they will probably be kept waiting based on queue length. They may then enter their telephone number for recalling by outbound telesales at a later time or, with CLI, may even automatically be recalled.
- Automated fax on demand, or text output via fax. Increased levels of home working and advanced communications will make fax transmission increasingly relevant to the domestic market.

Campaign and programme management and selection

Systems and their documentation are often not designed to help the marketing department understand what data already exists within the company.[2] There is little reason to collect data unless it can be accessed and used. So many companies across the world are like blind art collectors! The first step to restoring sight is to collect the works and display them in a gallery. This is the reason for a database.

This, however, is not enough. The appreciative collector then journeys around the gallery, inspecting and learning. So, too, must the direct marketer view the data in the database, and for this a viewing tool is required, an eye into the database.

Learning, however, must turn to action, and here the metaphor breaks down. The direct marketer needs to turn the knowledge in the database into marketing programs to selected private or professional individuals which must be stored for further analysis when results are received.

Sophisticated direct marketing requires sophisticated selection and targeting capabilities, including the ability to:

- select segments or cluster from the database using any of the data
- create campaign/programme history
- process marketing campaigns/programmes
- apply A/B split at either name or group level (this will ensure that, for example, everyone who is a customer of one dealer/retailer receives the same offer)
- perform 1 in N selections
- assign a marketing programme promotion and cell codes for inclusion in the mailing/telemarketing history
- sequence output by combinations of fields within the database
- deduplicate output of fields within the database (e.g. one record per customer name, one record per company, or one record per site).

The selection module is therefore at the heart of the second generation marketing database system and the means by which the direct marketer crafts his or her focused communication programmes, selecting customers by previous promotions, geographic region, intermediary, demographics, lifestyle, payment and buying behaviour *or any other data.*

Selection definition can become very complex. A leading American company, interested in licensing the rights to sell a leading UK supplier's database system, had a bright technician who promised the CEO that he could reproduce the function in a few weeks, and was given the authority to try. Only when the task was properly explored did the complexity emerge. (The bright technician looked considerably less bright, having made no progress in the time.)

A full customer selection may consist of many statements typically using Boolean logic in the following format:

1.1   Select those who meet *this* criteria (e.g. bought three times)
1.2   *and* this (e.g. male)
1.3   *and* this (e.g. not owing money)
1.4   *or* this (e.g. having credit risk below X)

AND

2.1   Select those who meet *this* criteria
2.2   *or* this
2.3   *and* this

Statements 1.1 to 1.4 form a group where conditions 1, 2 and 3 must *all* be met *or* 4. The second ground will *also* be actioned for conditions where 1 *or* a combination of 2 and 3 are met. Saga Holidays, mentioned in Chapter 1, had selections in the 1980s which were sometimes hundreds of statements and dozens of groups long, selecting scores of clusters of customers for testing or communication. This prompted one company to redesign its software, but is now commonplace for committed direct marketers.

Groups 1 and 2 above would both select customers. While both may go into the same mailing, marketers will want to identify each group separately – i.e. who they are, and why they were selected – for subsequent analysis.

Selections must allow for a two-part process:

(a)   the selection of all valid customers for a promotion
(b)   the subselection to a particular cell based on 1 in *N*, personal data, or a combination.

Selection should further be able to cater for:

– restrictions on use of names, including the number of uses in a period
– selection on result fields, e.g. 'take last purchase date from current date and select anyone who has not bought for more than six months'
– choice, to include any information on the database in a variety of formats and sequences in output
– ability to transfer output to selected programs to invoke further functions as required (e.g. letter printing)
– mailing/promotion history maintenance, to record which customers were output for each selection.

Campaign/programme management functions then enable marketers to set up multiple campaigns or marketing programmes with multiple subpromotions each with individual customer cells. The schematic, Figure 12.3, indicates the hierarchy, as discussed in the previous chapter.

Campaign hierarchy

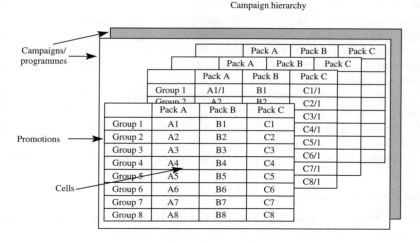

Figure 12.3 Schematic of campaign management

Campaigns or what?

Marketers commonly refer to a complex series of promotions with a unifying purpose as a 'campaign'. It is obviously a term from the military. Is it the best word for the future of marketing, devoted as it is to winning partnerships, not gaining enemies?

Perhaps it would be more suitable to call them projects or programmes. This is in fact what they are and the more neutral word also serves to show exactly what the task of marketing will be as a change agent: to attain a *goal* (retention, loyalty, satisfaction, lifetime value) through a *process*, developing the resources and history of the past.

Reporting and analysis

A variety of standard reports are typically required to control processes and understand customer profiles, e.g.:

- Data entry control
- Name acquisition/attrition
- Name and address changes
- Geographical performance
- Customer/enquirer status/performance
- Application/conversion performance
- Segment profitability.

More important analysis will come from a general-purpose cross-tabulations tool. This enables the user to set up a segment of customers, define two primary parameters for analysis, e.g. industry and size, and perform value, quantity and share breakdown analysis. More complex modelling, such as cluster and multivariate analyses, typically uses a PC package such as SAS or SPSS.

A quick count facility allows simple analysis of the number of occurrences of values or combinations of values on selected data fields. To economize processing, the system should summarize important fields into a single file, from which reports can be produced.

Advanced customer modelling by statistical routines is discussed later.

Event responsiveness

Event responsiveness (or event trigger, event management, contact management) is the installation and institution of procedures to deal with individual customers according to their circumstances. It means systematically thinking through corporate policies for service and communication, without ruling out initiative and ad hoc activity, as described in earlier chapters (First Direct, KLM, etc.). This is leading edge thinking and, at the time of writing, relatively few companies have made the journey. It is an important aspect of stage 3 database marketing systems, however.

Based on a customer's status and the last or current event, or the last series of events and their timing, a particular action would be triggered. It could be a particular response to an incoming telephone call or a personal letter or call.

It is similar to both scripting and sales contact management. All enable the computer to be programmed to action reminders or communications based on project rules, just as all service people are trained to respond in particular ways to the moment of truth confronting them.

Event responsiveness is a diary and information method that enables not only one-off activities (such as a reminder to call someone back), but also the ability to specify activities for groups of similar customers. Marketing, sales and service people can work out how they want the business to respond to different customer scenarios. What do they want to have happen; when and in what circumstances; to whom? This would involve specifying actionable policies: When this happens to one of these customers, do that! These policies would be effected by programming the system with rules.

The danger, of course, is that – just like the dangers of over-automating services or tele-services – marketers may rush like lemmings and turn their companies into machines.

Boring automation can seriously damage your wealth.

Event responsiveness is an enormously powerful tool to specify, trigger and control corporate actions, and must be used responsibly and wisely if it is not to be another junking device: to computer-aided design add computer-aided junk.

It is already difficult to keep track of all that happens in a company. Imagine the consciousness a direct marketer would need to be fully aware of every person to whom he or she was sending a letter. One hundred years from now, social or legal pressures may require just that.

Topic 12.4   Event management functions

Event responsiveness typically uses the following facilities as levers:

- A personalizing print function, for the production of personalized documents (see below)
- CTI, for selection and screening of a particular script or key questions
- The customer data
- Score cards and predictive behaviour modelling, for discrimination in selecting customers according to their profiles
- Campaign effectiveness, for the tracking and measurement of performance
- CTI, for its ability to feed the database with activity information
- Product effectiveness, for evaluating the influence that event/process character-istics have as product components.

Leading edge software packages may provide graphical user interface for ease of operation; rule definition, to indicate the basis for selection into an event; flowcharting of event sequences; marketing programme budgeting; auto-costing of activities based on parameters (or activity-based costing database); data review for decision making; and activity routeing to a fulfilment module.

Personalized printing

Friends of the Earth 'as long ago as 1989' held a text library and produced a personalized document according to the type and size of donation and the allocated activity, a development of specialist functions like insurance quotations, but now a general tool. Many advanced word-processing packages have the basic functionality to perform this. The difference is in building the business systematically around the facility.

The user can select a particular document shell from a library of documents; include or exclude paragraphs/text from a library based on conditional rules established at set-up and set-off by transferred data; include personal data in predefined locations; provide defaults for missing data; format the document; and schedule to the correct printer for a later time.

The result is personalized documents in every sense of the word: content determined by the customer.

Other functions and requirements

In addition to any service-specific access to customer data, the marketing department will need to be able to generate simple, interactive, enquiry and update functions, and questionnaire entry.

The postal service in most countries provides discounts to large mailers who pre-sort. Approved software to do this will be an important cost saver in the database.

Checklist (of fairly advanced function)

Seamless interface between people, applications and telephones:

- Telephony architecture systems for computer telephone integration (CTI)
- Intelligent networks (INs)
- User's 'hot-key' between applications, transferring appropriate data as necessary.

Rapid, reliable performance and change:

- Re-use techniques for software
- Client server architecture
- Optimized for both front end transaction performance and back end massive data manipulation
- Telemarketing resilience: independence from host
- Event architecture for action programming: event responsiveness.
- Open format data model for addition and change, including interface tool
- Extended service product format
- Ease of re-navigating customer response: GUI interface, flexible control, ease of updating scripts and knowledge base, architecture for application links
- All data open to very flexible, user-tailored analysis
- Tracking of customer groups overture is easy
- One-off targeted mailings and programmed responsiveness.

Customer contact is individual and personalized with a total commitment across the business to consistent service brand quality. Facilities which assist this include:

- Accurate name and address processing and deduplication and lookup in the national address file
- Fast name/address identification and use
- Personalized documentation: name, content and timing; reference to customer activity
- Immediate briefing to telesales/service of key customer status data
- Recognition of relationship in communication.

Telephony (CTI) and call navigation capabilities:

- Calling line identification (CLI) and direct dialling identification (DDI)
- Call-management information for customer, agent and process profiling
- Power dialling

- Intelligent call routeing for inbound service and sales including caller-initiated routeing
- Script display for telemarketing and prospecting
- Call/data transfer for cross-selling, service switches
- Automated collection of transaction and process information.

Notes and references

1. Svieby, K.E. and Lloyd, T., *Managing Knowhow* Bloomsbury, 1987.
2. 'Computers in marketing' survey by DunnHumby Associates, 1992/3.

13

Processing names and addresses

Summary This chapter examines what might seem banal, but is not: name and address processing. It will be of most interest to those with a practical interest in implementation, or curiosity about a fascinating logic problem.

Names and addresses are a subject close to 'home'. Our address intrudes into our sense of identity. Our name is who we are. We may no longer worship gods of the household, but a good address comes close to being worshipped and our name is sacrosanct. Marketers who lack such sensitivity can be rudely awoken.

(Angus Jenkinson)

Direct marketing practitioners are frequently ill-informed about name and address processing despite the fact that it remains the essential bedrock of all applied direct marketing to date. Since many companies, for example, over 33 per cent of British companies, do not have all their customer names and addresses computerized, the learning curve is still a long way from ending.[1] The efficiency and accuracy of personalization and of customer analysis depends on the prior effectiveness of name and address processing. This would be a sufficient commercial reason to focus effort in acquiring expertise, yet multi-million pound database projects – for example, in two of Britain's top high street banks – have been started and nearly completed without serious investigation of the feasibility, policy or methodology to establish the necessary processing rigour.

Beyond this commercial logic, lies a fascinating intellectual challenge for those who wish to be so stimulated. We may regard names and addresses as banal, but closer analysis shows the technical challenges of good name and address processing and deduplication as very considerable. Rigorous treatment of the imprecise makes an art of science.

Understanding name and address processing

Correct initial processing is the foundation. For example, personalization requires the definite identification of the last name. The absence of this leads to such incongruities as '*Dear Mr Phd*' and '*Dear Mr Prince, Buckingham Palace*'. Deduplication depends on like for like comparison – apples with apples. Without this, even a minor variation, e.g. a space, will throw out comparison. In order to achieve like for like comparison – e.g. surname with surname – prior identification and correction of the various component elements of a name and address are required (hygiene processing).

Clearly, data capture can be and should be disciplined, with data entered into prescribed data fields and software providing important further assistance. No software will entirely compensate for sloppy human procedures, but will help with the classic problems of human error: large volume data entry is vulnerable to boredom; telephone data entry, to mistake; and professional work, to poor typing skills. Software can also help during data entry by providing instant validation to the operator.

Generally speaking, the main software procedures and validation methods are equally relevant whether the processing is in batch or 'on-line, real time' (for example, telephone-based customer service.[2]

Hygiene processing

Hygiene processing is the preliminary to deduplication and consists of four stages: formatting, parsing, validation and correction/enhancement. Their operation is effectively intertwined as will be seen below.

The first step is basic formatting of incoming data to remove the maximum of inconsistencies and data 'noise'. Typically, therefore, the data will be read to remove all punctuation marks, all lower-case data will be converted to upper case and redundant blanks will be eliminated. This makes for a like for like comparison.

Incoming data is converted into the desired format, including sequence and, possibly, field length. A good bureau will always have quality check procedures and good hygiene software to validate assumptions and specifications such as, 'The surname is in positions 20–29'.

Long fields, e.g. 'company name', are often truncated by weak systems. Good software has plenty of space, basic abbreviation facilities (e.g. Limited to Ltd) and an audit warning.

We may recollect, from school, taking a paragraph and finding the clauses and subclauses, nouns, verbs, adjectives and so on. A similar process of parsing is undertaken by good software to identify the elements shown below (*italics* are used for business addresses):

– premise name
– flat or apartment identifier
– *company name*

- *company attribute*
- premise number
- first street name
- first street attribute (e.g. 'Road')
- second street name
- second street attribute
- double dependent locality (village/hamlet)
- dependent locality
- post town
- county, state
- postcode, zip
- (and country).

Others may include telephone number or custom details.

These elements need to be identified through situational logic (by which the answer is deduced through the relative position of the words) and key word validation and standardization. For example, 'Rd' can be identified as a street attribute and expanded to 'Road' with the help of a table of common abbreviations and misspellings.

This needs extensive tables of reference data, and checking these is important in software evaluation. Table 13.1 shows just some of the variations that can occur in the representation of 'Mr and Mrs'. Tables of prefixes (with correct salutation), first names (with gender), suffixes, villages, towns, counties, will be normal. Suffix and prefix tables should contain thousands of entries.

Table 13.1   Sample prefixes

Mrs and Mrs	Mrand Mrs	Mr andMrs	Mr/Mrs
Mr & Mrs	Mr& Mrs	Mr &Mrs	Mr Mrs
Mr and Ms	Ms & Mr	Mr + Miss	mr and msr

Advanced address-processing systems will reference the national Post Office Address files (the British PAF has about 24 million addresses) and, where available, a file of large users (companies with their own postcode). These files, typically, are neither complete nor totally accurate. New addresses and postcodes are constantly in creation with delay in updating files and software. In some countries the file is provided free or at a very modest charge. In others, such as the UK, a charge is made which does not encourage maximum use of the database to improve quality.

At the end of hygiene processing, all data will have been parsed to allocate a taxonomic value (e.g. 'this is a prefix'), will (probably) have been standardized and may have had the upper–lower-case conversion correctly reapplied (see Table 13.2). Names and/or addresses may also have been subjected to a rejection process based on invalid values. For example, good systems will recognize spurious data such as DONALD DUCK and PEPSI COLA, and will screen for Members of Parliament or Congress, the Royal Family and words in general use by pranksters. One charity had considerable difficulty getting one of its donors accepted onto the database: Donald Duck *was* his name.

With business-to-business processing software, validation of job titles may also be provided. This uses a table of common job titles and will normally both standardize abbreviations (mgr into manager) and generate codes that can be used for targeting (normally seniority and function values). Common job titles may be stored as a code (e.g. managing director, sales manager).

Some companies offer a 'competitor/customer' screening service which can be custom built for clients using the same character-scanning techniques as those to find Donald Duck. For example, a computer company may want

Table 13.2 Software processing

A. Jones	A. Jones	This requires business decisions in the
Beechmount	HOUSE NAME ADDED	use of the best software. Will you drop
109 Hivings Hill	109 Hivings Hill	Bellingdon? Will you drop Beechmount?
Bellingdon	Bellingdon	Bellingdon is actually a separate parish
Chesham	EMBELLISHMENT	from Chesham. Its inclusion is intended
Bucks	Chesham	to uprate the premise location and is not
	Bucks PRESENTATION	technically correct. Good software will
	POSTCODE MISSING	detect this and optionally drop it.
	COUNTRY RECOGNITION	Beechmount is actually not on the PAF
		file. It is a name given by the owners for
		status. The software should have post-
		coded and thereby identified these
		issues. Bucks could be upgraded to
		'Buckinghamshire' to improve
		professional appearance. International
		processing needs to recognize the
		country.
A. Jones	A. Jones	'Hvings' is incorrectly spelt. This would
109 Hivngs Hill	109 *Hivngs* Hill	be detected by some software working
Chesham	Chesham	back from the PAF file. The county is
hp52pj	COUNTY	also missing and should be included for
	HP5 2PJ	this size of post town. The postcode
		format needs correcting.

Table 13.2 *continued*

Col Jones Retd 109 Hivings Hill Bellingdon Cheshire Bucks	Co*lonel* Jones *Retd* 109 Hivings Hill CHESHAM	'Col' must be recognized as a routine abbreviation. 'Retd' must be recognized as not a surname. Good software would do this. Normally it would be dropped, but could add profile information. Missing post town, two counties however; Bellingdon is a recognized locality in Buckinghamshire and this should be enough to drop Cheshire as the incorrect county. However, the PAF file would not have Hivings Hill in Bellingdon so the address would probably by rejected by some software, posted to Bellingdon by others.
Dr Jones JONES & MARSH ASSOCS 109 HIVINGS HILL CHESGHAM HP5 2PJ	*Dr Jones* *Jones & Marsh* *Associates* *109 Hivings Hill* CHESGHAM COUNTY HP5 2PJ	Upper/lower case needs correction as does the misspelling of Chesham. (This might not be found without the postcode as Chesham is not a large place. Although 'g' and 'h' are next to each other on the keyboard, different fingers are used by keyboard operators, so although tables of misspellings are found in best packages, this may not be there.) It should be recognized as a company address through ASSOC and the name of the individual separated from the name of the company.

to look for every address with the name of another computer company (IBM, Toshiba, ICL, Bull, etc.) and/or of selected customers (look for any record containing 'Tesco'). This requires considerable processing and can increase costs, but may still be very good value.

Records with unresolvable inconsistencies (e.g. town and postcode do not match) or incomplete data will also have been rejected for separate examination. Good systems will have logic to try to resolve inconsistencies through enhancement and/or correction, and here a PAF file can help. For example, an incorrect postcode can be changed or missing postcodes added. Excellent software will also have option switches to handle issues such as:

- There is a claimed house name not on the PAF file.
- There is a claimed village or house name not strictly part of the address.
- The suburb has been adjusted to give a higher status address.[3]

Some software will flag these as an important psychographic factor. In some countries, there are files for the elimination of deceased people or 'goneaways' (nixies).

Deduplication

Once the input names and addresses are structured, standardized and enhanced, the process of deduplication may begin. Accurate deduplication is the process by which data belonging to different transactions or event items may be united for a particular customer. Most deduplication tools are proprietary and the owners are very jealous of their intellectual knowledge: the method is treated as a black box. However, general principles can be discussed.

Deduplication seeks to optimize or eliminate *overkill* and *underkill*. Overkill is the jargon (or technical term) for a set of matched records that are *not* in fact duplicates. Underkill is a set of records that have not been matched, but *are* actually duplicates. As will be shown, it is rarely possible to eliminate both entirely: improving one increases the other, so software that controls this plus some basic business decisions on priority is needed.

Five main deduplication methods are described below, of which the last two are simply modifications or tuning cases of the others:

- Matchkey
- Phonetics
- Fuzzy matching
- Weighting
- Elements selection, based on business decision.

Deduplication style and effectiveness also depends on the type of computer processing:

- *Sequential batch*, used for merge–purge processing and all traditional mailing list/database applications.
- *Direct or random access*, used by more complex, databases. Achieving a quality match without human intervention is more difficult here.

Sequential batch processing is common in direct marketing. A mailing list is input and read, record by record, to output a label. With batch deduplication processing, such as a merge–purge, the following steps are taken:

1. (Multiple) input file(s) of standardized names and addresses are read into a single file.
2. This file is sorted. This sortation is one of the most critical steps. For example, JENKINSON and ENKINSON will be far apart and are therefore unlikely to be matched on a one-by-one basis. For this reason, the best

deduplication systems go for a more reliable 'bucket', such as a postcode sector/area, and compare all records within it. The choice of particular sortation criteria will depend on the size of the input files and the processing capacity of the software/hardware system.

3. All the records belonging to a bucket are read into memory and compared using one of the techniques discussed below. Basic systems pair records. Inevitably this leads to errors:

⎧	A. Jenkins	Stepping Stones	Neither of these pairs
⎨ ⎧	R. Jenkins	IBM	is a duplicate, but two
⎩ ⎩	A. Jenkinson	Stepping Stones	of the records probably are.

In the example above, because records are only checked in pairs, both the first and second pairs marked would be correctly identified as not a duplicate. However, the (potential) match of the first and third records would be missed. More advanced systems will read large numbers of records and compare every record with every other. For example, Group 1 Software of Washington, USA, has probably the most commercially successful package in the world, which will cope well with 1000 records per bucket, provided a powerful mainframe is used. This means that approximately half a million comparisons are made per bucket and half a billion per million records.

Direct or random access computer processing finds this virtually impossible. The test now is to take a single, input record and match it against a large database file. The first problem to overcome is the one described above: to find a reasonable set of records to match against. To do this, the customer file will have one or more indices (or 'access paths'), like the index in an encyclopaedia. Good systems will have several access paths, each of which will use different sortation/selection criteria, thereby increasing the probability of finding all matches. For example, one may be built on company name, another on surname and a third on postcode and premise number. Once the process of matching begins, a matchkey technique (described below) is typically employed. Fuzzy logic (also described below) is only really available as a secondary technique.

Direct access can be used to process on-line, where a human operator can visually check the presumed or possible match(es) and confirm, or as part of a batch process, for example overnight. Different standards may need to be set up for each. For example, with human intervention, a wider tolerance may be allowed in identifying possible matches, the operator interviewing.

The availability or otherwise of human validation is a critical design element. For high-quality business address processing, it is highly recommended. IBM UK routinely paid for additional quality assurance to protect their standards.

Deduplication techniques

Matchkey processing is the traditional, and still most common, method of processing. Given the problems of 'minor' errors, such as Johnston and Johnson, matchkeys reduce the name and address element to its essential components. For example, the ends of surnames are often lost (JENKINSON and JENKINS) and vowels misheard/misspelt (BAINS and BANES). Most matchkeys consist of a code to represent the town/postcode, the premise number and an abbreviation of name and street. The particular algorithm used for input data quality and matching routine determines match quality.

For example:

A. *JENKINSON*, MANAGING DIRECTOR, *STEPPING STONES* CONSULTANCY LTD, *16 HIGH STREET, CHESHAM, BUCKS, HP5 3PJ*

may become, in a matchkey:

AJENKSTPSTN16HGH27BQR

Business-to-business marketers have particular difficulty. In addition to all the consumer complexity, business names are liable to serious deformation and job titles are often very variable. Special techniques are therefore common in processing the company name line (in particular). These include: creating a separate and additional key based on the first letters of the company's names, using fuzzy matching for this line only, and dropping out lower value elements such as 'Consultancy' or 'Services' which occur frequently but are often dropped in use (see also below).

Phonetics is another way of matching, transforming sounds into a code. Phonemes (like sounds), *a, ai, ay* and *ei* would, in certain word combinations, all be reduced to the same code.

Both phonetic and matchkey techniques risk overkill. Phonetics is particularly prone to this and therefore suitable for on-line telephone work, where mishearing often occurs. Confirmation of matches can then be sought from the customer.

Fuzzy matching is the least common deduplication method, but is most precise and controllable. It uses simple mathematical techniques to compare two names and addresses, looking for similarities and weighting difference: are the letters in the first, second, third, etc., positions the same? If not, how far apart is the first incidence of the same letter? The degree of similarity/ difference, letter by letter, is calculated and the average degree of difference calculated. Various forms of statistical method are also used. For example, letters may be weighted depending on their commonness.

Fuzzy matching is a more intensive form of processing than any other method. It is commonly used for applications such as fraud detection and other quality processing.

Weighting is used as a secondary technique to weight the impact of difference or similarity. All deduplication techniques are implicitly weighting methods. However, even if all other elements are identical (the postcode being missing), if the town is different, it is not a match, as in the example below:

P. Jones 16 High Street Oldham Notts
P. Jones 16 High Street Petersfield Notts

On the other hand, if the postcode and last name match, there is a strong likelihood of a duplicate. A different street attribute (e.g. Road/Street), all other elements being the same, is a low indicator of difference. Although uncommon in commercial practice, certain names are more common (e.g. Smith, Patel) than others. With ethnic names, there may be geodemographic trends which indicate a greater or lesser likelihood of identity.

Deduplication is normally a skilled exercise involving the practitioner in an iterative testing process tuning weighting and level of fit. With advanced (fuzzy matching type) software, there are individual parameters for each element which may be adjusted for tolerance. These enable one to select 'loose' or 'tight' matching criteria. This is a matter not just of technical judgement, but demands business judgement.

In order for the technology to play its part, the marketer must make some business decisions: What constitutes a duplicate? In Table 13.2 there are between one and four individuals present, depending on mailing or database building requirements.

There are two aspects to this:

– targeting level
– underkill/overkill preference.

Consumer marketers may be aiming at households, families, or individuals. Deduplication may therefore be made at address level, at surname level and at surname and first name level. Business-to-business marketers may be aiming at individuals, departments, locations, companies, and parent companies. This will determine the elements to be chosen for inclusion.

This generates some tough decisions for marketers; for example, bank statements are obviously sent to individuals, not households, and it is therefore vital not to deduplicate. On the other hand, charities will, in general, communicate to households as it is normal to receive only one donation per household. They must therefore deduplicate across everyone at the premise (or perhaps by family name) and make a decision about 'who is going to be left'. When should two letters be sent, and when one? Today's homes are very much more complicated: many unmarried couples live together forming lasting partnerships. Reasonable software will provide options.

Equally, a business judgement will need to be made on overkill or underkill. All deduplication is likely to produce both (at once), but any one set of parameters will emphasize one or the other. Good software enables one to tune for preference and keeps the margin of error low. A charity is likely to overkill, but this is unacceptable in the mailing of bank statements.

General and marketing program-specific quality standards are needed for deduplication. This can only be achieved by principles plus examples of records considered to be or not to be duplicates, and visual inspection of output.

One of the major trends at the moment is the creation, in the financial services sector, of customer information systems (CIS). These are intended to bring together all information about a customer against a single customer record (the warehouse or library concept). Naturally, operational and legal management will be obsessive about incorrect matching of names and addresses: they do not want to send someone a statement belonging to someone else! They will therefore set the parameters for this definition of quality. This will create major problems for some marketers. For example, when making selections for cross-selling, it may be desirable to overkill in order to avoid asking someone to purchase a product they already possess. Furthermore, in market planning and strategy setting, it is very important that a reasonably accurate assessment of duplicates (and, therefore, all the accompanying data relating to multi-purchases) is available, for which some overkill in the data used is acceptable. Given that strategic marketing decisions are often made above the level of the direct marketing department by people who may not be aware of these issues, this problem will (and in the estimation of the author, has) cost millions to the sector. Special techniques are needed to build systems under such conditions, including a marketing route to use while operational quality standards are being achieved.

Checklist Selecting software

Here is a short checklist for buyers selecting software.

1. Do not build your own. It will cost a fortune and take a long learning curve. The only way to develop great name and address and deduplication software is the technique known as 'expert trial and error', i.e. a bit of gumption and a lot of work.
2. Start choosing the software early in the database-building cycle.
3. Create quality standards. These should be shared and discussed with short-listed suppliers. All should work to a common set of standards.
4. Build trial software for your selection using real data. Do not try to construct a set. First, it will not replicate the randomness of the real world (as one client I know discovered to his cost). Second, it takes a long time. You need a lot of records (see below). Include some specific cases you are familiar with, and test for particular characteristics.

5. Plan to build some special characteristics into the processing to handle the vagaries of your data.
6. You should test several geodemographic scenarios: metropolitan suburb, small city, towns and rural. Choose areas you know. Avoid areas the supplier knows, unless the exercise is deduplication tuning. Aim for a total file of 10 000 to 20 000 records. This is large enough to give a fair spread of cases to test, and small enough to check thoroughly.
7. Be present during test runs wherever possible. You will learn a lot about the flexibility, ease of use, reliability of the software and the culture of the supplier. It takes time but it is valuable. It also prevents massaging of the results. Reputable firms do not do this, of course, but it has certainly happened ('well, *they* will do it ...'). On the other hand, the process of tuning is normal and you can participate.
8. Have an inspection output printed in several sequences (sorted on postcode and surname, surname and postcode, street and postcode, etc.). Errors will show up in different ways. Measure the errors.
9. Look separately at NAP and deduplication tools, even though you will want to get both from the same source.
10. Look for the ease of maintaining and adding to tables (prefixes, first names, misspellings of towns, etc.). This is an important opportunity to improve quality. Look for supplier commitment to ongoing development.
11. Check for reliable information on the effect of large files and more onerous matching techniques on performance.
12. Check for the usual credentials, other users, service, contracts, etc. Look for PAF update services and check the regularity and reliability of the service. Check the quality of code. Some systems are built up over many years and end up unmaintainable: if they (sort of) work now, do not do anything to change them or you never know what may happen. Endless patching and additional logic rules over the years ends up creating a sort of logical plate of spaghetti which becomes difficult to fathom.

Notes and references

1. 'Computers in marketing' survey by DunnHumby Associates, 1992/3.
2. Both of these terms are explained further below.
3. See example 1 in Table 13.3.

14
Quality development tools and ideas

Summary   There are a wide range of TQM ideas and tools which can be used to evaluate quality and design improvements continuously and for ever. All of them need quality information. This information is usually obtained from two sources: customers and employees, then filtered through systems. This chapter describes, or points the reader in the direction of, a number of such tools that have been found to be particularly useful. In some cases the tools may represent a new way of thinking about organizational performance, but based on best practice. In others, ideas introduced earlier are turned into practical methods.

A stove cannot be persuaded to heat a room by being told that it is its moral duty.
(Rudolf Steiner[1])

Quality database marketing is much more than sending a good letter to new customers. The responsive business is involved in an end-to-end business system commitment including service, telemarketing, the salesforce, fulfilment, follow-up, research, learning, staff development, marketing programme management and control, and production development in undertaking a guarantee management programme. This means *thinking* of the business as a system.

A company's productive output can be measured in four ways, as shown in Figure 14.1, one of which, function, is so broad that it includes many aspects of customer assessment of 'qualitative quality'. The other three outputs are often easier to measure. Typical inputs are also shown in the diagram. Quality is therefore a system: there are inputs, processing and outputs. Changing the inputs changes the outputs. Optimizing certain outputs affects others, possibly suboptimizing the system. The same can apply to inputs, but only where scarcity applies.

Management's responsibility is to ensure overall optimization and improvement. They 'own' the system. Professionals and workers make the system stable, working to agreed and sustainable processes and standards, and providing ideas to improve. Getting a system stable is like getting a view

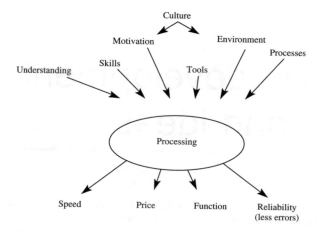

Figure 14.1 Inputs and outputs of productivity

through the car's front window: you know where you are going and what will happen and can begin a process of continuous improvement.

All too often, however, targets are set on an arbitrary basis to meet short-term goals while changes are based on the last set of results; the first is like driving blind and the second like using the rear-view mirror.

Systems thinking is vital to quality: it is one of the four cornerstones of Deming's 'profound knowledge', without which he said a manager could not be truly effective. The task of the manager is to take responsibility for the whole system, cooperating with peer colleagues in favour of the whole, and thereby approving and supporting his or her team's reliability, consistency and improvement. Doing this needs information, effective measurement and the correct tools.

One starting point is to set up a total system map, a flowchart of how the business operates. A data model also helps. The aim is to map how things actually work and then reroute and redesign to simplify and move energy up the flow stream towards right-first-time operation, customer satisfaction and key moments of value-added transformation.

Quality leader Juran argued that a business should start with information about customers; develop excellent products to meet their needs; then develop operational excellence for service product delivery. Finally, marketing and sales activity should generate the business and information, thus beginning the spiral of continuous improvement again (Figure 14.2).

Instead, businesses tend to get stuck in an established operational superstructure and the products this is capable of producing. Sales and marketing people are then given targets to move the products off the shelves

Information about customers

Marketing
and sales
quality

Information
about customers

Operational excellence

Product
excellence

Figure 14.2   Organizational development (based on Juran)

and on to the customers with little actual knowledge or consideration about customers: 'numbers thinking', which erodes relationships. This is a three-step process, which Deming described[2] as:

1. Design it.
2. Make it.
3. *Try* to sell it.

At the end of the 1970s, it was heart rending to visit companies in the Black Country in England, the industrial heartland of Victorian Britain around Wolverhampton and Birmingham. They seemed stuck in some past age, operating with machinery and production lines that had sometimes been set up 30 years previously, churning out material (that is, while the machines were working or the staff were not on strike) that sales and marketing people were tasked to sell in the new, quality conscious environment that was developing. When the recession came at the beginning of the 1980s, they fell like ninepins.

Pressure on salespeople is passed on to customers. Naturally they react by resisting the pressures, obeying Newton's third law that action breeds reaction. So this requires salespeople of a temperament capable of withstanding the contrary pressures and ever greater capacity to overcome ever more resistant customers (Figure 14.3).

Database marketing can help to break this cycle and provides the means to help at all four stages in the Juran spiral.

The cycle of continuous improvement

Continuous improvement is mainly a way of thinking. It is an attitude that improvement does not take place by aiming at some preconceived numerical goal and congratulating everyone, but by stabilizing processes, then continuously seeking out every possible improvement, implementing them

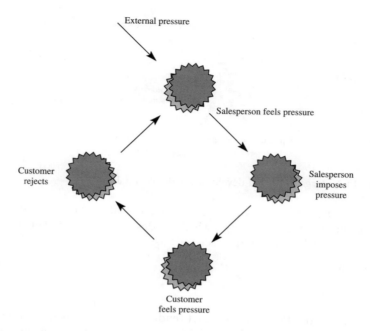

Figure 14.3 The cycle of pressure

and looking for more. There is a big difference between numerical targets and agreed, qualitative ideals. One is a whip, the other a leading vision – for a land of milk and honey, perhaps?

Whatever vision you have, progress begins with the first step and continues with the next. Plato's ideals and Aristotle's evolution meet in practical aspiration, well summed up in Deming's method.

This new environment was led by the Japanese. Deming taught an alternative four-step process to replace the traditional three-step method described above, starting from relative ignorance and building knowledge and competence:

1. Design the product.
2. Make it; test it in the production line and in the laboratory.
3. Put it on the market.
4. Test it in service, *find out what the user thinks of it and why the non-user has not bought it.*
   Redesign it for improvement.

Both the Juran and Deming cycles use the elements of the clover leaf model: information – product – process – relationship – information. There is no inconsistency between Juran and Deming. Deming too, begins with knowledge but wants to emphasize the fourth step of testing in use, which creates the information base to repeat the cycle and begins a process of continuous improvement. Deming advised the Japanese about new market research techniques. He felt that, in the West, market researchers had been taught to do research into quantitative estimates of numbers and proportions of households or businesses who are users or have problems or interests, and to identify the share of market by type of user. While this had its place he emphasized two other research topics:

1. Research into the discovery of problems such as the real reasons for dissatisfaction. This is what Bain & Co. later popularized as 'root cause analysis'.
2. Research to obtain information that will enable us to predict the consumer's reaction to a change in the product, which might only be a change in the size or colour of a package, a fundamental area of database marketing.

Deming also taught the Japanese what he called the 'quality cycle', the cycle of continuous improvement that we referred to earlier and mentioned in Chapter 10. It consists of four stages (see Figure 14.4).

1. *Plan.* See how to improve by analysing the current situation and looking for opportunities.
2. *Do.* Not what we might think, but the act of prototyping a possible solution in small scale to assess its usefulness, as quickly as possible, at the lowest possible cost and with the least disruption to present operations.
3. *Check/study.* Therefore, the next stage is to analyse the result. Did it work? Was it an improvement? In what ways? Was the implementation successful? Could it have been done a little better?
4. *Act.* Finally, any benefit is rolled out and locked into the organization before moving on to another cycle of improvement.

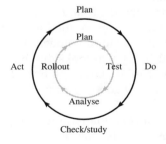

Figure 14.4 The Deming/direct marketing quality cycles

This seemingly simple and fundamental cycle was the cornerstone of Deming's work with the Japanese. It is an archetypal quality process *and precisely the discipline that underpins the whole direct marketing industry*: plan, test, analyse, rollout!

Planning means looking for a better solution to a marketing problem. It involves various techniques of brainstorming, root cause analysis, strategy making, etc., leading to an idea which is *tested*, often in the form of a particular pack, catalogue, script, sales call method or advertisement. The aim, however, should be to test it on a small scale, on a sample, to see if it really works and is really better than what we had before. After executing the test, it is then necessary to *analyse* the result. Planning and analysis need statistical techniques. Where a successful solution is found it should be *rolled out* in order to secure the maximum profit and benefit.

Direct marketers will say that the key to direct marketing is to test, test, then test again. The contribution of direct marketing to marketing is to test ideas to see if they really work. Debate is resolved in the cauldron of action.

But, the fundamental axis of *testing* is actually in planning and analysis, i.e. the vertical, not the horizontal, axis in Figure 14.4. Creative new ideas, and a carefully planned and formulated marketing project with rigorous sample sizes to test the outcomes are features of good planning. Similarly, analysis of results and operational review are the crux of improvement and rollout.

Analysis is most effective when done not just for an individual promotion or a mere transaction in the life of the relationship, but when checking effects on long-term retention.

Digging for truffles (root cause analysis)

Earlier, we noted the importance of measuring from 100 per cent down, not 0 per cent up: How do non-responders react, and why? Why did people respond? Why do customers defect? Beginning with modelling the relationship, research and problem-solving techniques are needed to probe with employees, customers and the team for the deeper layers that determine tomorrow's profit and satisfaction. A good analogy are the pigs which are trained in France and elsewhere to root under the leaves and topsoil, digging for truffles – the prize delicacy that looks dull but is worth more by weight than gold. Digging for truffles should be one of the key activities in the responsive business. It needs a good nose and a willingness to dig happily in the dirt.

Root cause analysis is a common term for the process of seeking out the real reasons why things happen. The only successful way to improve the business is to understand objectively, honestly and fully the reasons why the customers are dissatisfied or failing to buy: probing under the surface of the phenomena. For example, research has shown that most of the customers who migrate have claimed to have been satisfied with their supplier. What is really going on?

There are a number of techniques for doing root cause analysis, including focus groups, both with customers and employees. Remember, employees usually have a very good idea of what is happening. One leading American direct marketer always shows the employees in his shop his mailings before sending them, with very helpful results. In an exercise in a holiday company, employees were able to give a vast array of reasons why customers were dissatisfied, most of which management were unaware.

In addition, there are a number of techniques for analysis: for example, control charts, flowcharting, systems analysis. Other techniques include force field analysis, stratification, and the 5 Whys. The starting point must, however, be skills in separating the meaningful from the random: learning to recognize the prize smells.

The importance of variation, or SPC

This means understanding variation, the second of Deming's cornerstones for Profound Knowledge and essential to planning and analysis. It is one of the single most useful ways of improving management effectiveness and was a fundamental to the Japanese becoming world leaders in production quality. It is absolutely basic and relevant to all database marketing.

When two packs are sent out, and one outperforms the other, is it really better? Is the difference significant? Can we isolate two groups or segments of customers; are they really two groups? Any serious direct marketer uses significance in marketing planning and improvement.

A catalogue marketer should know from the way orders come in over the first few days exactly what the probable demand curve will be for that catalogue and how much will be sold over the period. Two different telesales teams/people get different results. Is one better than the other? There are many other examples relevant to process, product and marketing (relationship) applications. Ensuring that volumes tested are enough to get a statistically significant result is a big feature of planning.

British Rail made a big breakthrough when it realized that its journey lengths would always vary, but by measuring the parameters they could plan a train length that would be accurate 95 per cent (or more) of the time. Now, instead of promoting their best or average journey time, they promote what they know they can deliver, and they can often tell customers: 'Hey, we're early!' if they want to. Satisfaction leaped. It is obvious, and simple; why did they not do it before? For the same reason that your company may not give its management accounting results tests of significance.

Variations in output or results may be attributable to certain causes:

1. *Common causes*, i.e. the natural variation occurring in any system, pattern or routine – the natural variation of nature. Results within this natural variation have no significance. (One day, five hundred statisticians assembled in the annual meeting of the Institute of Statisticians. Suddenly one of them rose from his chair, flew into the air and disappeared out of the window. However, none of the statisticians batted an eyelid because they knew that one out of five hundred was not significant.)
2. *Special causes*, i.e. variation outside standard parameters, significant variation.

(See also the control chart in Figure 14.5, below, for an illustration of the principle.)

Improvement arises from:

– elimination of special causes, getting a stable system;
– improvement in consistency, i.e. reduction in variation: reliability noted as the single most important factor customers look for in a service;
– follow-up and use of repeatable, valuable special causes – i.e. improvements – once stability is achieved.

A system can first be made more stable, then more consistent – the two stages of reliability – but variation will never be eliminated. One of the first signs of a certain kind of heart failure is when the heart beat starts to become metronomic. Such a beat is unstable, unhealthy and leads to death. Natural heart beat follows a gentle, moving rhythm, independent of activity, around a stable or average point. Any company that has tried to get metronomic reliability – machine reliability – will know that it leads to death. What is needed is a stable system with modest and known variation.

Unless managers take variation into account, they are likely to get all kinds of spurious results. *Instead of just measuring, the application of statistics gives knowledge not numbers.* Advanced use of variation control techniques is called statistical process control (SPC) in quality circles.

Topic 14.1 Examples of variation in tele-business

Different phone calls will naturally have different lengths. The number of calls that a person answers will naturally vary from day to day, and from one person to another, just as human height and weight varies. How do you measure genuine effectiveness? If results or times are wildly varying, how do you begin to get order and improve?

Often bonuses are paid on sales. Yet, has analysis been done to determine common and special causes? Paying people bonuses on better common cause results is counter-productive: it costs money and it gives unrealistic expectations. It may even breed cynicism from a worker who instinctively knows they 'do not deserve it'.

A company could record the length of phone calls, or the response percentage of mailings, or the number of orders processed per hour. This can be collected in information systems, especially with CTI, or by people using, for example, tally counts to measure performance more effectively.

For example: if the computer and telephone have been linked together, then it will be possible to identify:

- the number of calls received by each person in a period
- the outcome of the call
- the length of each individual call and its outcome
- the script that was used
- the number of the inbound telephone called
- the length of time the person was kept waiting before the call was answered
- whether the call was transferred, and if so, to whom and for how long, with what result

all of which will help with root cause analysis.

As a modest digression, very few Western *systems* integrate these techniques, users having to work ad hoc. The following software might be a very big business opportunity over the next 10 years:

- Reporting all activities based on common and special cause variation ('this event probably had a special cause'): i.e. adding into all budget/ actual reporting a test of significance and including considerably more measurement of really useful activity reporting, see 'Activity-based costing' below.
- Widespread provision of software tools to produce test sample sizes and rollout range probabilities.
- Reporting on response dynamics, according to significance, e.g. comparison between test samples/cells/packs/activities/scripts, etc.

Control charts

The most essential variation tool is the control chart, a tool almost as essential to the modern professional as the six gun and lipstick were to the heroes and heroines of Hollywood's West. It is a means of recording and reporting variation in output or results, e.g. to analyse customer complaints by type, perhaps broken into simple criteria such as product, service and human problems. These can then be measured day by day or over a period and inserted in a control chart to identify trends, patterns, and standard and special causes.

It is beyond the scope of this book to fully explain control charting. However, the interested reader can turn to a wide selection of texts.[3] Figure 14.5 shows a control chart and illustrates the principles; it was generated using a standard spreadsheet package in a few minutes, although specialized

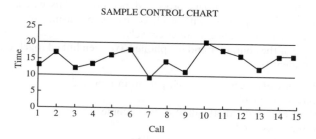

Figure 14.5   An example of a control chart

software is also available. The length of a number of phone calls was noted, taking their average or mean. Then the 'control limits' were calculated (see Topic 14.2 below). The control limits measure the amount of variation that can be considered to be 'normal', as opposed to special.

Central to the Deming method (and Shewhart, his statistics professor from whom he obtained the principle) was 3 sigma as the economically reasonable level of normal system results. What does this mean? Sigma is the name for the Greek letter commonly used by statisticians as a measure of variation: the standard deviation (see Chapter 15 and Topic 15.1). 3 sigma is chosen because it saves us running around over every single funny blip but does not hide real difference: it is a practical test. The control chart uses 3 sigma as the basis of determining what the control limits should be.

Then, *any result which appears within these control limits is a standard result, produced by the system,* i.e. common causes. Only results which appear outside the control limits have been determined by some non-standard cause, i.e. special causes, however surprising it might sometimes seem.

It is not enough to separate special from common causes. The aim is to be able to produce stable, reliable systems. Deming, following Shewhart,[4] identified four states for a system:

1. Ideal state, the process in control with 100 per cent conforming results
2. Threshold state, the process in control with some non-conforming results
3. Brink of chaos, the process out of control, with conforming results but all are determined by special causes
4. Chaos, the process out of control with non-conforming product.

Stable results mean (a) trains on time, and (b) something solid to work on. When you try to change a system that is out of control you do not know whether it is your change that had the effect, or anything else. The first rule of experiment – the nature of management – is control, one known change at a time.

It is very important to note that a fundamental aspect of the Deming/ Shewhart method is that the techniques used recognize that a system may not be 'in control'. Most statistics prefer normal distributions. Since one aim is to find out whether this is in fact operational, different methods which are robust for both stable and unstable systems are needed.

Topic 14.2   Control charts

1. *Understanding results from a series (the x-chart)*
This could be used to check on a standard mailing, phone program or other that goes out regularly: any set of data where there is a series of one at a time observations, lengths of calls, numbers of calls, etc. First measure the gaps or 'moving range' (MR) between consecutive results:

2.2	2.6	2.3	2.8	2.1 ...	(x)
0.4	0.3	0.5	0.7		(MR)

Calculate the mean (i.e. average) of these moving ranges $\overline{\text{MR}}$ and of the values. This is called x-bar and written $\bar{x}$. Then a simple and reasonably accurate measure of variation is just the size of the average or mean range. You can compute upper control limits (UCLs) and lower control limits (LCLs) using the formula:

$$\frac{\text{UCL}}{\text{LCL}} = \bar{x} \pm 2.66 \times \overline{\text{MR}}$$

Results above or below the control limits are special causes. All other results are common. (For the precise minded, 2.66 is derived by dividing 3, i.e. for 3 sigma, by a constant based on the fact that the ranges are calculated from pairs of numbers.)

2. *Discovering whether a proportional result is normal or special (the attributes chart)*
This is used whenever you wish to assess the proportion of one kind of result against another, such as defects or complaints out of the total, or orders out of the total. First, calculate the mean: divide the total by number of occurrences, e.g. total number of calls: x-bar or $\bar{x}$. Next, calculate the average proportion of errors, defects, complaints or other items per correct result. This is called p-bar and written $\bar{p}$ (some books replace $\bar{x}$ with $n\bar{p}$).

From these figures you can compute upper control limits (UCLs) and lower control limits (LCLs) using the formula:

$$\frac{\text{UCL}}{\text{LCL}} = \bar{x} \pm 3 \sqrt{(\bar{x}(1 - \bar{p}))}$$

Again, only results above or below the control limits are special causes.

Choice of chart
It will be obvious that either method could be used to calculate a series of response percentages from, say, a weekly subscription renewal or anniversary mailing by considering the response per cent as an absolute or a proportion. Sometimes it is

useful to use both methods to see if they give consistent results, or if one throws up more information.

There are six major charts, one of the most powerful of which has not been described, the $\overline{X}$–R chart which is used when data can be collected in groups. The reader may wish to follow this up in the literature.

Stability

If there are no results outside the control limits, the system is probably stable and can now be improved progressively. However, if there are many results outside control limits, it means that many special causes are operating. Effectively this is not a stable system. Changes in the parameters of the system are simply likely to add more special causes and cause more swings. Such 'improvements' would actually be 'tampering'. The first job is to remove special causes and get some reliability or stability. This can be done by checking on the 'special causes' – Why are these happening? How can we operate the current system more Reliably? – perhaps using fishbone analysis and other methods described below.

Four operating rules for detecting lack of control are:

1. When a single point falls outside three significant deviations (the 3 sigma test)
2. When two out of three successive values fall both on the same side and two standard deviations (2 sigma) from the centre or median line.
3. When four out of five values are on the same side and one standard deviation.
4. When eight successive values are on the same side.

Process thinking and flowcharting

Process thinking has already been isolated as one of the key routes to improve service, product and business. Process thinking means starting to see flow and bottlenecks, not forms and structures. It means paying attention to the arteries and not just the bony skeleton of the business.

Western organizations used to be almost exclusively goal oriented: e.g. management by objectives. Today, some people emphasize processes almost as exclusively. In fact three dynamics to think of, past present and future, or momentum – process – goal:

1. No goals, no direction: all goals are value judgements, and the value judgements which determine the most successful goals are those which are driven by work to which people can bind their commitment. (Peter Drucker once wrote, 'Management by objectives works if you know the objectives. Ninety per cent of the time you don't.')
2. How to get there: the new or improved processes needed.
3. Where we have been/come from: That which both drives us forward and preserves the good and bad habits (or processes and done policies) of the structural culture, which sustain or block us.

One useful way to understand the processes is by analysing the value chain or *value stream*. There are two key components of this:

1. Establishing the process, perhaps in terms of flowcharting (see below), or simply as a system of *customer–supplier* relationships, thereby mapping the value stream. *Everyone* serves customers (see also Figure 14.7 below). It is a question of working out who the customer is and whether the action actually adds *end* value, i.e. to the final customer or goal. For example, telemarketing serves salespeople by delivering leads, salespeople serve production by delivering orders.

2. Then the value input is analysed: (a) What is actually provided? (b) Is it useful? (c) What is really needed? Only activities which transform or change and improve data, products, etc., add value. Checking quality, for example, adds no value (the product is the same after as before). Giving poor quality leads adds negative value – rework or wasted work is generated.

Process flowcharting can help identify root causes and lead to a fundamental re-evaluation of how things could be done better. A useful method is deployment flowcharting which not only depicts the process but also who is responsible using a set of standard icons for decisions, actions, meetings, etc. (see Figure 14.6 for a light-hearted demonstration). It can map the relationship between the customer, parts of the organization and activity flow, showing where things go wrong, where responsibility may be divided, uncertain or even unknown, and where and how rework is most commonly caused, so quality can move up the line towards 'right first time'. For example, in Figure 14.6 there are four reasons why the man has to begin again.

If the business is not sure of what happens, who does it and with what expectations, then it probably is not doing what needs to be done. A characteristic of small pioneering companies is that processes are vague and re-invented, but skills and energy are considerable and the top person is close to all the action. As companies get larger this leads to chaos. Fire fighting, the greatest skill of the growing pioneer company, cannot keep pace with the raging fires. Clarity and order are required, and flowcharting helps to achieve these.

A fundamental ingredient of good flowcharting is to analyse not just what happens, but *the criteria that have to be met for success*. This is called an *operational definition*. A goal or objective without an operational definition is an undefined goal (see the Drucker quotation above).

Another flowcharting tool which is particularly useful, because it directly links with the clover leaf model of the organization and product, is shown in Figure 14.7. The diagram indicates the essential elements of the method. In addition to defining the input and output criteria for a particular process

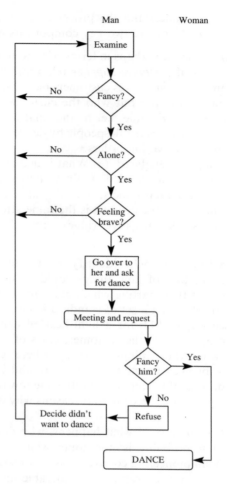

Figure 14.6 Deployment flowcharting for idle moments

step, the information/controls and resources needed are also specified, as well as feedback. This enables marketers or their assistants to describe both the product and company operation in terms of processes.

ISO 9000

ISO 9000 and its former version, BS 5750, in the UK, is an international, government-sponsored set of standards focusing on conformance to defined policy. It can therefore be contrasted with TQM, as in the words of Nigel Gallimore, a UK direct marketer: 'TQM seeks to ensure the right person

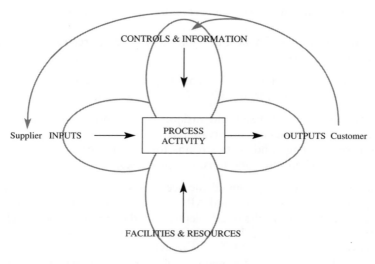

Figure 14.7 Flowcharting which links to the clover leaf

carries out the correct procedures ... while BS 5750/ISO 9000 ensure that established procedures are correctly carried out by the right person.' One could theoretically promise standards below industry norms and conform.

But, it is exacting and demands honesty: what you tell your customers you will do is what you do actually have to do, forcing standards. You cannot tell your customer, 'I promise to deliver, maybe'. It tends towards stable systems, even bureaucratic ones, thereby reducing fire fighting. The very overheads of ISO 9000 in delivering these new standards soon awaken the need to find ways of being more process efficient and cost effective.

Activity-based costing (ABC)

Activity-based costing is developing as the accounting method of the future because it is oriented to horizontal processes, not vertical functions. Instead of dividing functions into cost categories where the important issue is the convenience of the cost category, a database associated with resources is linked to process steps. This means that each process step can be costed. Especially when it is linked to CTI, this enables full customer, product and activity valuation and increases control, e.g.:

- the profitability of the individual customer based on actual costs of servicing and revenue streams;
- the actual, full project costs of a product/service given its customer

portfolio and the costs and revenues associated with serving these customers;
– interaction between a product and subsequent purchases (e.g. the 'loss leader' concept).

Traditional functional-based accounting systems do not provide this adequately. The true profitability of a customer is not available, because:

– interaction between fixed and variable costs is often not available;
– actual service costs are not available;
– complete revenue and costs streams for a customer are not available as costs are locked into functions, not processes.

Chapter 8 (Loyalty) highlighted the need for such information. Combining CTI, process reorganization and ABC is very powerful. CTI means that the time, resources and results of all telephone and computer-based work can be captured automatically, including most costs of service in the direct business. Even without CTI, however, ABC is a step forward.

Take this European financial services company, strong in personal finance through dealer networks, which experienced its leadership position and margins under threat. Dealer loyalty was reducing.

Customers were frustrated because of the line of control:

Customer – Car dealer – Salespeople – Local Office – Head Office

After analysis, it was found that core activities (client support and new business) occupied only 12 per cent of all activity. Travel used 27 per cent; noise, i.e. ineffectual activity following someone's exhortation, 12 per cent; and administration-related activity, 49 per cent.

By introducing ABC with process re-engineering, there was both a 40 per cent reduction in effort and a major rebalancing of time. New business and client support (the core activities) grew to over 40 per cent of all activities. Continuous information feedback then enabled further, progressive improvement and accurate costing/profitability evaluation.

Implementing ABC will require:

– Training in the concepts
– Process definition (activities
– Resource database definition, with cost parameters
– Automating recording of activities and therefore costs
– Process improvement and/or clarity.

Moments of truth analysis

Moments of truth analysis (see Figure 14.8) has already been shown as a fundamental exercise in analysing the customer–company threshold. It is a systematic modelling of the points and process of interaction and how they evolve over time and is a most useful key to data analysis. It consists of defining or identifying

- quality standards (operational definitions) expected by the customer, benchmarked perhaps against best practice and as potential;
- how the company wants to respond, both at the time *and later*;
- what information is needed;
- what information is captured (and who is the 'customer' for this) and what has been missed, i.e. not captured.

MOT	Key data needed to deliver quality	Key data provided by customer	Missed data	Quality standards and expectations
(List, identifying current actual and potential or desirable)	(and who is responsible/able to get it?)	(and who will be the key users?)	(How can we get it in the future?)	(operational definition: how shall we know when we have done a good job?)

Figure 14.8   Simple MOT analysis form

Other tools

STRATIFICATION

This technique separates clustered data points into meaningful categories to help determine problem causes. Stratified or categorized data can indicate significant problems and trends as well as defects and opportunities for improvement. By stratifying the data, meaningful information is presented much more immediately to the user.

Stratification data is collected either from users using such tools as *check sheets* (a tally count split out by time periods) or from a computer system if it has been collected. The computer can then produce scatter diagrams which show the distribution of data, or techniques such as cluster analysis (see Chapter 16) can be used to analyse the data statistically.

FORCE FIELD ANALYSIS

Force field analysis is a brainstorming tool to define the struggle between opposing forces: *driving forces* which move a situation towards change and *restraining forces* which hinder it. Organizational factors that either drive or block desired change are identified, and ways to move round these or change them are identified.

But the principle can be applied in many ways. For example, a force field analysis could have customer complaints as the driving force for change with the real causes of the complaints as the opposing forces. An easy way to do force field analysis is to draw a vertical line on a flip chart and brainstorm the two sides.

5 WHY'S

This 5 Why's method (Figure 14.9) was developed by Toyota in Japan. It simply means probing below the surface a number of times, digging under the leaves. They found that if you ask the question *why*? five times you are more likely to get at the real reasons and below surface noise (and excuses). It is also a wonderful technique in interviews.

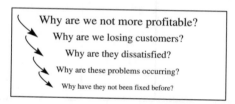

Figure 14.9   5 Why's: a questioning tool to get below the surface to the real issues

FISHBONE, OR CAUSE AND EFFECT

Fishbone analysis is a total quality technique, a group brainstorming tool which allows you to dig down, as with 5 Why's, and be able to flit about over the subject. It is a more structured form of mind mapping and can easily be converted to documentation (Figure 14.10).

Fishbone analysis selects a key question or problem, such as loyalty, response, order delay, dissatisfaction, and together the group analyses and brainstorms the root causes. By taking a simple structure of, say, five bones dealing with typical key issues, such as information, technology, customer attitudes, products and processes, causes can be identified and progressively broken down into greater and greater detail.

Having looked at the causes of the problem, the issue is then reversed from *What prevents loyalty/response*? To *What is needed to create loyalty/*

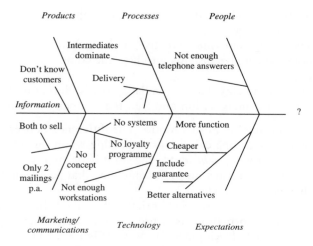

Figure 14.10   Fishbone analysis: e.g. what prevents loyalty?

response? The aim is to identify a set of possible changes which are then prioritized (perhaps by *Pareto analysis*, which is a method of sorting and identifying the most frequent or highest impact issues, say, by creating a bar chart) for investigation and testing.

IS/IS NOT

This is a very simple but useful device to analyse an issue. Ask both what 'it is' and 'is not' in two columns. You can analyse quality, operational success, performance, satisfaction, and almost any qualitative issue. It is surprising how often the asking of such a simple question surfaces great ideas, differences in expectations and ideas (which can then be resolved) or helps to create an *operational definition*.

Developing a new vision: beacon setting

In addition to analysing current systems, processes, results, etc., it may also be necessary to renew the future vision: to '*greenprint*' (less rigid, more alive blueprinting). There are several ways, including using methods already discussed:

1. MOTs from the customers' perspective, using not just dry data but as many ways as possible to let the information sing and dance its message, from graphical representation to getting customers to come and talk to executives.

2. Value stream analysis, the sources of a company's value generation and market advantage;
3. Storyboarding and other creative tools such as 'drama therapy', and cartoons, which give insights into how the company/people interact with customers.
4. Visioning using clay, colours, collage, words, drama to create ideas that can live in the imagination and lead the company forward.

'Quality is job one' is Ford's motto. The difference between greenprinting and slogans is that one can be just a passing whim, or worse, a top-down exhortation that you *ought* to do, and do it better if you want to keep your job. A greenprint vision aims to be something that people understand and in which they participate willingly.

The *beacon-setting* process briefly described in Chapter 8 under 'Marketing transformation' is a proven approach to greenprinting based on an archetypal development process (Figure 14.11). The sequence is important.

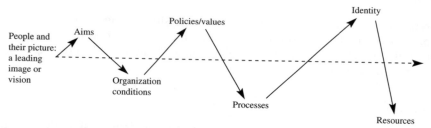

Figure 14.11   Beacon setting

It begins with developing a clear picture of the group's purpose and motivation for the initiative/company and a leading image or vision. There is then a continuous process, first, of elaborating the ideas-related content and, second, of elaborating the practical implications. *Aims* are concrete goals and objectives, detailing when they might be achieved. Then a basic *organizational framework* will need to be established, including people, ways of working, location, structure and culture to provide *how* functions, competences or faculties.

Guiding principles (*policies and values*) are established. These give us our character and personality and will be significant in determining the kind of company we are to supply, work for and buy from. Key *processes* by which the organization or initiative will operate anchor this in the planned 'behaviour' of the company.

Defining the organization's corporate identity, which also includes the brand, means identifying both the current recognition and perception of the outside world, including suppliers and customers, and the inner motivations. Who are we? Where are we based? Where do we operate (locations, markets, etc.)? What are our boundaries, the niche territory? What are the core competences? What is our name? (This can be a fun exercise even if the brand named is fixed. If we were an animal, what would we be, and why? What first name is most appropriate? What colour? What nickname would our customers give? What do we want them to give? What tone of voice do we speak with? Who are our friends? etc.)

The corporate identity of the organization or initiative becomes a sustaining principle. Wolff Olins, a top corporate identity designer, put it like this:

> In the first or heroic period of a company's development, the personality of its founder gives it its identity. In the second or technocratic phase the carefully cultivated and developed corporate identity is the major element that provides this link. It becomes the substitute for the personality of the entrepreneur ...
>
> People need to belong. They need to know where they stand, they need their loyalties underlined and emphasized, and they desperately need – we all desperately need – the magic of symbolism.[5]

The company is then grounded in the key resources necessary.

This process can either be used to start an initiative or business or to review an existing one which already has 'a biography', reviewing existing realities and playing with possibilities to decide how to change.

Commitment

Commitment is our primary tool. Part of commitment is willingness to stay the course, even when it hurts, absence of which must be the principal cause of failure. When L.L. Bean applied for the Baldridge national quality award, the judges told them that they had to fix customer problems too often rather than doing the right things initially. As a result, L.L. Bean, whose sales had been expanding 50 per cent faster than those of the mail order industry as a whole, decided to cut back on growth to improve quality of service. This meant creating the right culture and employee expectations by ensuring they had the right resources, training, incentives and policies to work consistently towards customer satisfaction.

It takes a lot of courage to cut back on growth in favour of control and quality, but it worked.

Notes and references

1. Steiner, R., *World Economy*, Rudolf Steiner Press, 1949.
2. Deming, W.E., *Out of the Crisis*, Cambridge University Press, 1992.
3. The British Deming Association (2 Castle Street, Salisbury, Wiltshire, SP1 1BB, England, Tel. +44 1722 412138) have two useful booklets, *Why SPC* and *How SPC*. Deming describes the reasoning in *Out of the Crisis*, cited elsewhere, and a detailed explanation is given in Wheeler, D.J. and Chambers, D.S., *Understanding Statistical Process Control*, Addison Wesley, 1990.
4. Wheeler, D.J. and Chambers, D.S., *Understanding Statistical Process Control*, Addison Wesley, 1990.
5. Olins, W., *The Corporate Personality*, Design Council, 1978, and *Corporate Identity*, Thames and Hudson, 1989.

PART THREE
TURNING DATA INTO ACTION

The final part explores how to turn data into knowledge – and contains a significant section on how to expand corporate creativity through its use. The basic principles of statistics – and how it helps to turn numbers into meaning – are explained in an imaginative way before demonstrating various modelling and analytical techniques which exploit statistics throughout the plan – test – analyse – rollout cycle.

The final chapter looks at the new information technologies and their potential impact on society and marketing – from the infobahn to the human challenge it creates.

15

The power and abuse of statistics

Summary This chapter explores the opportunities statistics brings to the database marketer – and their limits. It covers methodologies for planning, testing and building customer models. It aims to give a basic introduction to a few *key* statistical tools for those less familiar with them.

A numerical goal cannot increase the capability of a process. What improves results is an improvement in the process.

(W. Edwards Deming)

Statistical tools and methods have an extremely important part to play in database marketing, just as statistical process control has in TQM, being used to produce reliable, meaningful information. But in database marketing it has a far more direct role in determining and driving activity. Statistical method, however, is not devoid of disadvantages. Every light causes a shadow, and it is better if the shadow is known. Statistics is quite a powerful tool and we should be aware of its limitations and uses.

Mark Twain had an antipathy towards statistics. Once, with all the sardonic irony at his disposal, he set out to explain why. The Mississippi river, he said, was becoming shorter at the rate of one mile each year. This meant, quite obviously, that in the old Silurian Oolitic period, a million years ago, the Mississippi river must have stuck a million miles out over the Gulf of Mexico like a fishing rod, and in a thousand years time the head and the mouth of the river would meet! Fifteen or twenty years ago scientists reported another demographic trend. According to the population movements of the time, by the end of the century the population of the USA would be bald, female, six feet three inches tall and live in California. By the year 2020, so would the rest of the world.

This is deadly serious fun about the unreliability of trends. What is happening now may not have always happened and may not do so in the future. Incidentally, nearly all serious astronomical, geological and biological research presumes a steady state for all the fundamental parameters (e.g. decay rate of carbon, speed of light). What would happen if this was not true?

In business, we know that we cannot rely on tomorrow being like yesterday. When WH Smith (see Chapter 4) opened its travel agency business, it was expecting the boom in package holidays to continue. Unfortunately, instead there came first a recession and then the Gulf War.

Statistics is a blind science. It operates according to the Newtonian principle that a force will continue in a particular direction for ever until altered by another force. It can predict results, it can predict trends, it can predict trends of trends but all of these can be upset by the unexpected, and the most unexpected of all realms is the innovatory capacity of humans.

There is the wonderful story of the opportunism of Jeno Paulucci, the founder of a number of successful businesses. While still at high school and working as a fruit stand barker in Duluth, Minnesota, he one day found himself with a shipment of bananas that had become damaged during refrigeration, causing an unusual discoloration of the peel. Jeno was asked by his boss to try to sell the bananas at a discount. Instead the artful young man hit upon the idea that these brown bananas looked different and set out to exploit that difference. He set up a pile of crates and began calling to the customers, 'Argentine bananas!' Of course there are no such thing as Argentine bananas, but he made them sound exotic and managed to convert a cut price into a 100 per cent mark-up and sold 18 crates in three hours.

More and more scientists are becoming excited by the chaos theory – a theory that has enormous relevance to direct marketing because it deals with the unpredictable flows and currents that take place in complex environments. By now, we are all familiar with the principle that a butterfly flapping its wings in Sidney can cause a thunderstorm in New York. Well, is it not the case that a model flapping her arms in Paris can cause a sensation in London? A sloppily dressed group in Seattle cause a grunge wave across the world? A dictator, like Michael Gorbachev, can shake up a five-year plan and end a dictatorship. De Clerk can talk to a black 'terrorist' or a group of Norwegians can talk to some Palestinians and Israelis, and shake up our tidy world.

So database marketers must attune both their right and left brains to all trend modelling.

There is no such thing as a free lunch

The power of statistics is that it abstracts, generalizes and dichotomizes. It *abstracts* by drawing the concentrated essence out of the larger whole, but in the process abstraction loses the concrete. Abstractionism is also reductionism.

An example of simple abstraction would be to look at all the very many examples of how two cows and two cows make four cows, two boys and two girls make four children, two maples and two elms make four trees and to turn this into the mathematical principle: $2 + 2 = 4$. This is a gain, but it is also a loss of concreteness, of individuals. 'Abstraction is extraction, reduction, simplification, elimination. Such operations must entail some degree of falsification', said two mathematical philosophers Davis and Hersh, in discussing the post-Cartesian world.[1] Satisfaction can be reduced to '5' or '6' very usefully, but what happens to the experience itself? Quantitative research can never wholly replace qualitative research.

Generalization is similar to abstraction. It works from concrete examples and draws up general principles. For example: I like this advertisement so other people will too; or 100 British football fans are convicted for anti-social behaviour and therefore British football fans are yobs. Or, here is a group of people: their average age is 27, their predominant interest is football, their average income is $31 056, but one is an artist, another a Cambridge philosopher, four are coal miners, and two are salespeople. The generalization hides as much as it tells.

Geodemographics is a tool for generalizing about households. Acorn, Mosaic, etc., reducing the description of the 'household' to a number of useful variables, and probabilities, yet we have already noted the variation in each home, the so-called cellular household. Segmentation inevitably reduces the individual to a set of statistics.

We can form a number of generalizations from just a name and address. For example: Martha Smith, Holly Hedges, ... HP5 2TT. We can assume that this individual is female, and can even estimate an approximate age based on forename (e.g. the Monica program developed by CACI will do this). We can identify that there is a house name and by reference to the address file recognize that this is something that has been added by the owner and therefore draw certain lifestyle conclusions, e.g. she is status conscious. The postcode gives us a geodemographic generalization. The more we collect facts and generalize the more we are doing two things at once:

1. We are getting a sharper picture.
2. We are committing the ever greater inaccuracy of reducing the individual to the 'facts'.

The danger of segmentation is that it produces 'thin thinking'. In Chapter 17, a useful technique is described called 'prototyping', which complements segmentation and counters this tendency.

Mathematics also *dichotomizes*. For example, it separates into segments: fiveness as absolutely different from sixness, 30 year olds from 40 year olds. (Codes like 'young', 'middle-aged' and 'old' when used in statistical techniques such as CHAID are abstractions that are then used as mathematical entities.) Statistics tries to find valid bases for making such distinctions. When mathematics separates people, choosing to rate satisfaction at 5 from those rating it at 6, it tells us something very useful, but how much blurring did the customer do? How does he or she convert a feeling into a number? The world is not so simple. Seeming precision and convenience can be a source of delusion. Statistics tries to blur these harsh distinctions.

It is a method of 'controlled blurring'. We add the incomes of three people and calculate an average, i.e. a compression of data, and make a gain in knowledge at the expense of knowledge. We lose the individual, the very danger we have identified in modern businesses. We cannot exclude the individual from the picture. The challenge is to use the power of statistics for information without depersonalizing our knowledge. For, as Davis and Hersh point out,

> Whenever we use computerisation to proceed from formulas and algorithms to policy and actions affecting humans, we stand open to good and to evil on a massive scale ... this de-humanisation is intrinsic to the fundamental intellectual processes that are inherent in mathematics.

So, as a first rule of statistics, the business person should keep his or her eye and heart attuned carefully to real phenomena and people. Knowing customers is much more than mathematical prediction.

Nevertheless, statistics has a vital role in steadily improving our marketing and service operations. No direct marketer can be truly effective without having a basic grasp of statistics. Using statistical modelling, the World Wildlife Fund (WWF) reduced 2.4 million ostensibly appropriate names to 1.4 million, proving that you can commonly eliminate 30 per cent of names and still retain 90 per cent of responses.[2]

Beech tree leaves, groups and individuals

The core of statistics begins in the surprising and wonderful phenomena that we meet casually every day. It is a very empirical science. There is a beech tree wood in the Chiltern Hills of England near Chesham. It has perhaps 5000 mature beech trees growing in it. Each tree has perhaps 50 000 leaves. That makes a total of 250 million leaves. The astonishing thing is that each and every one of those leaves looks like a beech tree leaf!

This is astonishing, because each of those 250 million leaves is also unique. If we think about this carefully we reach certain conclusions.

1. There must be an active force or principle at work which tends towards making every one of those leaves identical; that is, it makes each leaf

recognizably a *beech tree* leaf. It is an active principle producing commonality, and if it worked unchecked it would produce 50 million clones.
2. There is also an active force or principle tending to make every one of those leaves unique or individual. If this force worked unchecked then the result would be 250 million leaves which could not be recognized as belonging to a single species. Each leaf would be so individual that its 'group belonging' would vanish.

It is amazing that these two principles are not more closely researched. We know that when the light blub goes on there is a force of electricity. What produces these results? Whatever it is, and I suppose the Chinese would call it the yin/yang principle, it has a great deal of relevance to database marketing. Here we see the principle of the group and the individual. Wherever we look in nature there are groups, species or families which share common characteristics. Each of these groups allows for a spectrum of possibilities by which each member retains certain individual features. The basic mathematical principles of statistics are empirical descriptives and arise from this phenomenon, in particular the basic statistical term: the 'normal' population, or the 'normal distribution'.

Ten-year-old boys in France will tend to cluster around a certain height, although some will be taller and some will be shorter. However, there will be an average (median) at about the middle and most boys will be of a height quite close to this. (See Figure 15.1.)

Figure 15.1 Normal distribution: a population is defined by its tendency to group around the middle and capacity to 'scatter' or 'spread' to individuals at the edge

The same is true for:

— the circumference of 50-year-old beech trees
— the number of invoices processed per hour
— the number of orders per month
— the height of adult women in Britain

and so on. Every regular population has this form. It is so common we take it for granted, although many fail to take advantage of it in business.

Of course not all populations are normal and regular like this. The useful

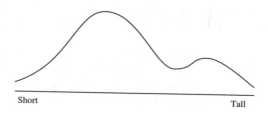

Figure 15.2 Bi-modal distribution, i.e. two groups

thing about statistics is that it can analyse a population and tell us whether it is normal or not. Whatever the answer, it will be useful and interesting. For example, let us look at Figure 15.2, which plots the heights of a group of people. What can we say about this population? What could give rise to the curve? Here are some explanations given to the author in workshops:

- A group of missionaries among some pygmies
- Male waiters during a women's convention
- Teachers in a school.

Whatever the explanation, one thing is clear: there are two different groups in this population, especially if measuring, say, income or age, we could probably draw some powerful marketing conclusions.

This is the essence of the statistical process known as clustering, which looks at populations and detects different groups. There is a graphical technique known as the scattergram which demonstrates clustering vividly. Figure 15.3 presents a scattergram of a population, showing the relationship between spend and age. The scattergram is used to illustrate visually the distribution of any population. Sometimes it is possible to see distinct correlations or population subgroups by eye, but the difficulty, which is

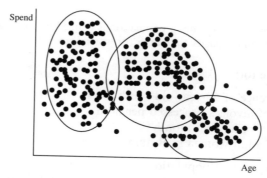

Figure 15.3 Scattergram of customers

repeated in mathematical methods, is determining where one group ends and another begins.

Figure 15.3 shows three fairly 'definite' groups:

1. Younger, more active spenders, but with a broad scatter
2. Older, less active spenders
3. Later, middle-aged, more active spenders (possibly because their children have left home and their careers are maturing).

Statistics helps to formalize and check the intuition of the eye and gives a mathematical function for the probability of 'belonging' or 'not belonging'.

Topic 15.1   A beautiful curve and the standard deviation

Marshal MacLuhan observed that, 'When producers want to know what the public wants, they graph it in curves. When they want to tell the public what to get, they say it in curves.' The fundamental curve of statistics is the normal distribution curve because it has an extraordinarily useful property. In Figure 15.1, following the curve from the centre, you will be travelling in two directions at once: across the page and down. At a certain point, the curve flips, and begins to travel mostly across the page. This is the *point of inflexion* and is the basis for powerful analysis.

Just by visual inspection, it is possible to guess approximately where it is. Obviously, therefore, it is possible for a mathematical formula to calculate the point exactly for a given curve. The property of this point is that approximately two-thirds of the population will be found between the two mirror-image inflexion points, *whatever the shape, i.e. the degree of scatter*. (See Figure 15.4 for a number of different examples of curves with greater or less scatter.)

The distance from the centre of the curve to the point of inflexion can now be used as a *standard*. Just as our bodies were once used as standards, or references for measurements – for example, the distance from the nose to the tip of the finger was a

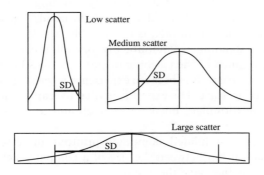

Figure 15.4   Different population curves

yard, the distance from the end of the thumb to the joint was an inch and a foot was a foot – so the distance from the centre to the point of inflexion on a particular curve becomes a standard unit of measure *for each curve or population.*

Within one standard deviation, two-thirds of the population is found. Within two standard deviations (two each side of the mean), just under 95 per cent of the population is acquired and three standard deviations gives approximately 99 per cent of the population, and the exponential process continues. This can also be referred to as one sigma, two sigma and three sigma analysis. (So the TQM object of 6 sigma performance is extraordinarily exacting, a 'normal world' zero, and not always helpful.) This is a very useful property. It means that, for example, a clothes manufacturer can make a range of women's clothing which, in quite a narrow range of sizes, will reach two-thirds of the population. The size range then has to be doubled for a return of less than 50 per cent extra.

By definition, something held in common draws groups together. Hence the tendency to cluster around a normative point. Beech tree leaves tend to the shape of beech tree leaves and 10-year-old French boys to the height of 10-year-old French boys. This is the anchor of database marketing. We identify individuals, and which group they probably belong to, based on performance data, primary research data such as questionnaires and psychographics, secondary analysis data such as lifestyle analysis and geodemographics and overlays with third party data.

Statistical techniques: regression analysis

The author's statistical journey began when he and a client would meet for lunch, and discuss multi-variate regression analysis, quite a lunchtime mouthful but a widely used and powerful statistical modelling technique used in database marketing and elsewhere. This conversation always came about late in the lunch, when inhibitions had been reduced, or rather lubricated, but never survived until morning. Truth to tell, we had no idea what it meant, just that we should do it. By morning, our *mutual fear* of looking stupid if asked, 'What did you have in mind?' prevented the idea going farther. The answer, in fact, is remarkably simple.

Lack of understanding is undoubtedly one of the key factors which prevents use, and much of the teaching of statistics does little to help. So, if what follows seems basic, it is because experience suggests that that is where many people need to start. The expert is invited to leap ahead. Other books will contain more formulae[3] but here we shall aim to show *why* and how they work.

Figure 15.5 is a simulated computer printout of a scatter diagram showing the relationship between the size of a company's clientele and the amount of business they give the company.

(Imagine any 'size' parameter that makes sense: budget, number of employees, last year's spend, and assume a correlation with the amount of

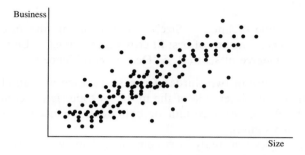

Figure 15.5   Business related to customer size

'business', again measured in any convenient variable.) Obviously, a straight line, representing the line of best fit, can be drawn and, even visually, can be estimated. The computer can work this out precisely using statistical methods. So it is possible to predict roughly the amount of business that would come from a new client, based on its size. The dotted line in Figure 15.6 shows this. Of course, it is by no means certain that the amount of business will exactly respond to the point on the *y*, or 'business' axis. In fact it will be somewhere *around* this point, given by the degree of scatter, measured in standard deviations.

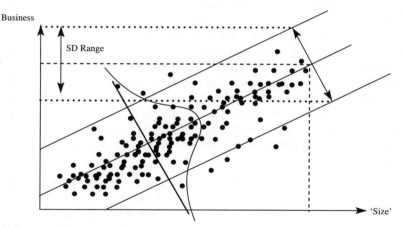

Figure 15.6   Regression analysis

This is 'all' that basic regression analysis is. It produces a simple formula or function similar to those we did at school:

$$y = ax + b \pm c.$$

Or, for example:

> Business = Slope of line × 'Size' + Given factor [the Intercept, i.e. where the line of best fit crosses the *y* axis] ± Limits of error ['Degree of scatter' × 'Desired confidence'].

If we want to be sure in two-thirds of occasions, then we can choose one standard distribution either side of the mean, or 'one sigma' confidence. If we want to be 95 per cent certain or confident, we need two standard distributions (two sigma).

In practice, regression analysis is complicated in two ways. First, it is often not a straight but a curved line that is found to represent the correlation. If we look at these two groups of numbers:

3   9
4   16
5   25

we can see that they are obviously powerfully correlated, but not on a straight-line basis. The second number is the *square* of the first. The statistician will check, using a host of mathematical functions and software, to see if any particular curve function finds a best correlation. Whichever is the best will be used to translate the data into a straight-line function. In fact, the process of preparing the data is the most important element of regression modelling. The execution itself is simple and performed by software.

Second, in the example that we demonstrated, only one input parameter was used to predict business. In practice, it is obvious that many different variables are needed to give a more accurate picture. Hence, most marketers will do 'multi-variate' regression analysis. It is easy to visually imagine two variables: a three-dimensional cuboid space in which a line would be drawn like three-dimensional noughts and crosses. It is much more difficult to imagine a 17-dimensional universe, but fortunately mathematics has no problem pretending that there is one. The resulting formula is likely to look something like this:

> Customer score relative to the average = 14.6 + [3.4 × (annual income in 000s)] + [17.2 × (average number of purchases per annum)] + [5.3 × (number of years of regular purchase)] − [7.4 × (number of months over 3 since last purchase)] ...

and so on. To interpret this: the average score is rendered as 50 or 100; the individual's score increases by 3.4 points for every $1000 of increased income and reduces by 7.4 points for very month more than 3 since last purchase; 14.6 is a 'placeholder' meaning it is a basic score given to everyone – in this case 'everyone has some chance of buying'.

Topic 15.2 Output of regression modelling

R-squared: the coefficient of determination, it explains how much of the behaviour of the dependent variable is explained by the independent or predictor variables. Its range is from zero to 1 and, in principle, the closer to 1 the better. In practice, simply loading new variables to improve it is not productive. The effect of diminishing returns sets in.

Sum of squares: the total variation which R-squared is seeking to explain.

Error: unexplained sum of squares.

F value: a measure of the significance of the independent variables. The effect of simply adding in more variables is to reduce the F value.

Intercept: where the line crosses the Y axis.

Regression coefficient: the slope of the line, or the power of the particular variable.

Testing the direct marketing proposition

Direct marketing is accountable: you can try out two things, compare them and decide which is best. Doing that accurately requires a statistical method. Here is a fundamental question: suppose your test mailing got a response of 4 per cent and one of 3.7 per cent was needed in order to break even (or exceed some minimum standard required by the company). Would you roll out?

Or, take this example. Someone sends out two packs. Pack A produces a response of 3 per cent and pack B of 4 per cent. Is pack B really better than pack A? On the face of it, it obviously seems to be so. But if each had only been mailed to only 100 people, then the decision would be rather flimsy. If the mailing volumes had each been 1000 and therefore the number of responses were 30 and 40 respectively, then confidence is more assured, *but not yet significant*. It is only just better than 50 : 50.

So, if the two responses had been 3.7 per cent and 4 per cent respectively, how many names and addresses would have been needed to be mailed before one can be statistically confident that B is really better than A? (Of course, it may not be a mailing that you are testing but a direct response advertisement, telemarketing project or other activity.)

These are not academic questions. These are the daily bread and butter decisions of direct marketing. Making the correct decisions is the difference between wealth and a stealthy retreat.

Three vital techniques are illustrated in these questions:

1. Is it safe to roll this project out? Will it be profitable?
2. Is one pack really better than another? Or, in a more complex example, are any of the mailings really better than the control? (The control is the benchmark against which other tests will be made.)
3. How many people do I need to test with my marketing proposition in order to get useful results?

Figure 15.7 illustrates how these calculations are done.

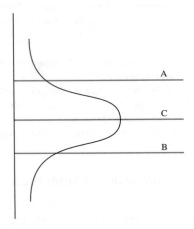

Figure 15.7 Rollout and test comparison

If the vertical line in Figure 15.7 represents a series of possible responses from low to high and the horizontal line C is a response to a mailing, the normal distribution curve shown represents the probability of responses on rollout. In a moment, we will look at why it has been drawn in this particular shape. Obviously, two-thirds of the probable rollout results will occur within one standard deviation of the test result, and 95 per cent within two standard deviations (or 1.96 to be precise). So, if B represented the breakeven response, the probability of exceeding breakeven can easily be calculated (or estimated).

The first question a marketer needs to ask is, *how confident do I want to be before I roll out?* Sometimes it is a luxury to be 95 per cent certain before we do anything. The decision will vary according to the culture of the organization (do you get killed if you are wrong?) and the size of the risk relative to resources. The more confident the marketer needs to be before acting, the more likely it is that a profitable opportunity will be missed (along with the reduced risk of failure). Confidence required is translated into a number of standard deviations (see Topic 15.3 for some examples).

One interesting effect is the so-called tendency to regress to the mean. This means that better results tend to return to a lower level and poorer tests tend to improve (because half of the test results will produce a result better than the 'true mean' and half will produce a worse result.

How is the calculation done in practice? Either the marketer calls a friendly agent or consultant, or looks it up in a book of tables, which is easily available from sources such as the local Direct Marketing Association – or the formula in Topic 15.3 may be applied in a Lotus, Excel or other spreadsheet program.

So far, we have looked at rollout results. All the tests described above use versions of a single formula in various forms according to the question (in the best tradition of mathematics, the answer we want to find is put on the left-hand side, and everything else is put on the right.): Do I mail? Is A better than B? How many shall I test?

Returning to Figure 15.7, if we now want to compare two different results and decide whether the difference is statistically significant, then let C represent the control (against which we are testing) and A the new, test pack. As we can see, A is only slightly more than one standard deviation away. This means that there is only a small chance that the higher response is statistically significant, i.e. really better.

The answer to the third question (How many shall I test?) lies in the 'shape' of the normal distribution curve mentioned earlier. Why a 'particular curve' is selected is illustrated in Figure 15.8.

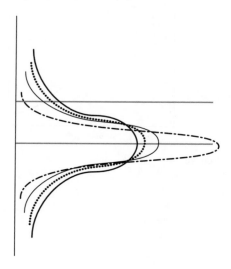

Figure 15.8 The response curve

A series of curves have been plotted with greater and greater scatter. From a very tight curve with a short standard deviation to a very loose curve with a long standard deviation. What makes the difference?

This is simply determined by the size of the mailing. The greater the mailing, the more certain the result and therefore the tighter the curve – or, in statistical language, the less scatter. A smaller mailing produces the opposite effect.

Visually, we can say that the larger the mailing the more the apex of the curve is drawn to the right along the horizontal axis and the more squeezed it becomes. Obviously, this effect is simply reproduced in a formula and translated directly into a result. The same principle applies to all the other questions we have been discussing above.

One very simple curve in a number of different formats becomes the basis for a powerful method of decision making.

Of course, it is not always a normal distribution curve that is found. Curves may be skewed in various ways, but each is revealing. For example, direct marketers know that the order response level curve takes on a skewed configuration (see Figure 15.9); after the mailing goes out, order levels generally peak quickly with a long tail until they eventually dry up. Every company or product will have its own particular curve and effective direct marketers will calculate this and apply it to their product and resource forecasts. It is usually possible within a few days to estimate the complete order cycle by applying the first few days' orders to the standard curve.

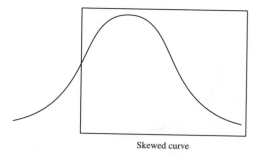

Skewed curve

Figure 15.9 Skewed curve

Topic 15.3 Formulae to calculate rollout, sample size and to compare packs

For sample size

Sample size $= \dfrac{C^2 \times R \times (100 - R)}{V^2}$

where R is the expected response rate; V is the tolerance allowable, i.e. per cent range flexibility; and, C is the standard deviation constant (based on the confidence required).

To predict rollout

Response range $= \sqrt{\dfrac{C^2 \times R \times (100 - R)}{M}}$

Where M is the mailed quantity; R is the response rate achieved; and C is the standard deviation constant (depending on confidence required).

Note, the two formulae are only rearrangements of the same elements. So, essentially, is the formula for comparing two packs:

Significant difference between results

$$= C \times \sqrt{\left(\frac{R_1 \times (100 - R_1)}{M_1} + \frac{R_2 \times (100 - R_2)}{M_2} \right)}$$

Another way to look at the comparison between packs is to assess the level of statistical difference between two results.

First, calculate a special average value R

$$R = \frac{R_1 \times M_1 + R_2 \times M_2}{M_1 + M_2}$$

Then

$$\text{Response range} = \sqrt{\left(R \times (100 - R) \times \frac{M_1 + M_2}{M_1 \times M_2} \right)}$$

Then divide the observed difference by the standard error of the difference, i.e. response range, and compare with desired confidence levels. For example, a result of 1.7 means just over 90 per cent confidence (1.64 standard deviations):

Significant difference between results

$$= C \times \sqrt{\left(\frac{R_1 \times (100 - R_1)}{M_1} + \frac{R_2 \times (100 - R_2)}{M_2} \right)}$$

How do you actually do it? Put the formula in a spreadsheet, or look it up in tables. (Most people do the latter.)

Direct marketing statisticians usually call the 'response range' the 'limits of error' or 'standard error', but since the term is so unfriendly, it was avoided in the examples. The response range in the last example is the 'Standard error of the difference'.

Similarly, C would be called the 'confidence interval'. Different lettering is also used by different practitioners.

Some useful numbers for confidence
2.33 standard deviations gives 98 per cent confidence.
1.96 standard deviations gives 95 per cent confidence.
1.64 standard deviations gives 90 per cent confidence.
1.28 standard deviations gives 80 per cent confidence.

Selecting samples

The quantity of records for a sample has already been discussed. It is equally important to be aware of the mechanics of drawing off a sample. Let us suppose that a sample of 1500 names is needed for a test mailing. How is this to be obtained? Obviously you do not draw off the first 1500 names from the database as this would produce a bias dependent upon how the database has been arranged. Even if it is arranged on something relatively random such as name, there will be some bias; for example, business names with acronyms or numerical values will be skewed. Many companies choose names that place them at the beginning or end of a list to become more obvious in *Yellow Pages* or directory advertising. In consumer names and addresses, ethnic groupings tend to cluster distribution.

Instead, names must be drawn from across the entire spectrum of the database. This is commonly done using random number software or a technique known as '1 in *N*'. The '1 in *N*' used should select sample names evenly from across the database. To get 1500 names from a 300 000 strong database, a 1 in 200 factor is applied.

It is also important to ensure that the starting point for sample selection is varied. One marketer discovered with horror that the bureau had drawn off many 1 in 20 samples, always beginning at the beginning of the database. This meant that the same names were being selected again and again without anyone noticing. Such a sample rapidly ceases to be representative. Disciplines and software are needed to control such mechanics.

In practice, a segment of the database is frequently selected for a project and then split into a number of '1 in *N*' test samples and the balance used for the mailing. The software must prevent customers being selected for more than one sample group.

While the basic '1 in *N*' sample method is quite effective in most cases, if there are strong skewing factors in the database – for example, a strong regional bias – some purists believe that these need to be handled separately. More advanced and complex databases may require the expert judgement of a statistician. Marketers should always check their bureau or internal operating group's procedures to ensure confidence and rigour.

Modelling techniques

What we have discussed are the basic tools of model building and response analysis. In addition to analysis, i.e. planning and analysing individual mailings, marketers need sophisticated models to predict future responsiveness. Models attempt to represent reality mathematically. Common tools used in modelling, in addition to cluster and regression analysis, are factor analysis and CHAID. In practice, all the techniques produce results that are much better than random activity. Statistics does not, however, replace or replicate an individual talking to an individual.

Turning models into business strategy will be discussed in the next chapter.

Neural networks

Direct marketers are making increasing use of neural networks. Putting it very simply, neural networks operate as follows: the direct marketer puts all the data in at one end. The software takes a library of curves and attempts to fit them against the data until as good a result as possible, as time allows, has been achieved.

With sophisticated versions, the software will break the data into smaller groups and use a series of curves to try to plot each one. In effect, it is looking for the groups and subgroups and clusters and microclusters within the database.

All processing takes place in a 'black box'. The system interprets the data and gives an outcome that can be difficult to assess but produces fair results.

Factor analysis

Factor analysis is in essence a very simple concept. It takes a number of different variables and aggregates them into a single factor. For example, in the illustration above during the discussion on regression analysis, the input variable was said to be 'size'. This could well be a composite factor based on a number of different variables including, for example, budget, number of employees, number of product lines and last year's spend. These are typically interacting factors, and their recognition is one of the keys to successful modelling. If you fail to recognize them you may be putting into the model several variables that are essentially saying the same thing. Not only is this redundancy wasteful, but it tends to double counting.

One of the weaknesses of regression analysis is that it cannot detect interactions, so factor analysis is often used as preparation for it.

The advantages of factor analysis in its own right is that it aggregates several variables into a single variable, by performing an abstraction. And, as we have discussed, this is a loss as well as a gain. In regression analysis, the predictor variable's correlation with the dependent variable is used to predict. In factor analysis variables are correlated and merged. In the process, each sacrifices some of its effect but the overall new factor is more powerful than any of the individual components. Furthermore, redundancy is largely eliminated.

Because factor analysis detects the interaction between parameters and clusters them, it can also be used as part of a clustering process. For example, in geodemographic analysis, factor analysis is used to define the various geodemographic cluster types, as a result of which a postcode can be assigned to the class DINKY or 'wealthy retired'. Many organizations find it useful to define and then give their own labels to clusters within their customer base.

Discriminant analysis

Discriminant analysis is another means of detecting the interaction of variables, aiming to maximize the statistical difference between groups. In practice, it is less used in response analysis because it is sensitive to numbers that are not normal distributions, which is often the case in direct marketing.

One of the classic and most important examples of this is response/null-response. A customer either buys or does not. If you are trying to predict the likelihood of response (response analysis), then you are trying to predict either the value 1 or 0 (the numeric equivalent of the variable). There is no way that this can be plotted as a normal distribution. It is skewed! Hence, discriminate analysis is rarely used for such applications, but can be helpful in cluster analysis.

Regression and logit regression for response analysis

Regression analysis has the same theoretical problem, although in practice most marketers find it quite satisfactory. Some purists, however, are uncomfortable and prefer CHAID (see below). The basic principles of regression were described above. Regression analysis works only with numeric or 'scalar data'. This means that all 'categoric' data, such as male/female or yes/no, has to be converted into dummy variables using numeric data. Alternatively, log-linear regression can be used when all the variables are categorical. Logit, or logistic regression, is used when a categorical dependent variable is to be modelled, such as the response YES or NO.

Response analysis seeks to identify the probability of a response. The 'odds of a response' is the response per cent divided by non-responders $(R/100 - R)$. Using some algebra this can be turned into a probability equation such that the natural log (logit) of a YES response can be expressed as a probability dependent on the values of a variable, X, i.e. the independent variables. This is then used in regression analysis as described above.

The result is that each customer's probability of response can be calculated as a factor between 0 and 1, effectively scoring customers. This can then be used as input into a gains chart (see p. 324).

CHAID

Automatic interactive detector (AID) is an extremely useful modelling method in direct marketing. CHAID is an improvement of AID and refers to the additional use of a chi-squared statistical method – a technique for distinguishing the difference between two or more populations. A version of particular use for marketers has been licensed and is sold by SPSS, one of the major vendors of statistical software.

The great advantages of CHAID are that (a) it works automatically with interdependent data and (b) it produces output which is particularly convenient to the direct marketer. It works only with categoric data, the reverse of regression, so scalar values must be converted to categoric. For example, age or income can be converted into bands. This might be a problem, the bands being an artificial introduction, but in practice CHAID examines the input values and will aggregate or amend them where appropriate. CHAID was initially developed as a preprocessor for regression (for detecting interaction) but is frequently used alone by modellers. It can be worth checking whether adding CHAID to regression improves the model: it often does at the margin (high and low responders). Since most of the work is in the data preparation, it takes very little extra to do another model calculation.

CHAID reads the input customer data and, as a result, identifies various groups or clusters of customers within the database. It then reports on these, showing how many such customers there are, what their characteristics are and what average response is likely to be obtained for this group. Figure 15.10 illustrates the type of output that is produced.

First, it identifies the variable that has had the greatest differentiating effect in predicting responsiveness. Thus, a charity might find that 'gender' is most important. Having identified the most important differentiating category, it automatically examines the resulting population groups and for each of these identifies the single most important factor in differentiating responsiveness. This process iterates for as long as is sensible.

As is evident, the output provides most of the information that the direct marketer needs to be able to construct a marketing programme. This includes:

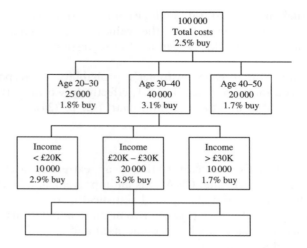

Figure 15.10   CHAID output

- the number of people or companies;
- the average or typical responsiveness, with the scatter factor;
- who this group is: i.e. the categories that define this group of people or companies (important because it enables the appropriate tone of voice and relevancy to be designed into the subsequent communication).

Credit and other scorecards

A credit scorecard is used to estimate the risk of a default and is based on a number of data variables (e.g. age, income, house ownership, etc.). Depending on the value (e.g. yes owns house, or age equals 30), negative or positive points are scored. The points values are based on statistical analysis and experience.

Behavioural scoring techniques are now widely used and do not necessarily require the use of traditional credit referencing agencies, although such organizations may also offer the service. (Agencies collect market and public data, such as court cases, defaults and bankruptcies.) Traditional scorecards look at demographic information (history at the house, neighbourhood, income, age, etc.) to score customers for risk. Behaviourial systems analyse customer behaviour.

Scorecards may also be used to weight the probability of a customer buying, or to qualify a prospect. For example, AT&T Business Telephone Systems use systems developed by O&M Dataconsult, Toronto, for lead generation, scoring readiness to buy, tracking customers at each stage in the contact cycle and allocating resource accordingly.

How a model is constructed

A great deal of the model-building process is involved in assessing and transforming the quality of data. The modeller must read through the data and look for aberrations, poor quality and other discrepancies (physically, and using statistical tools).

For example, if there is data that does not fit or make sense, this needs to be examined and possibly extracted from the database. Many systems have dummy records to process odd transactions. There may be a customer record used to process cash sales or a product record used to process ad hoc product sales. There could be a particular exceptional transaction such as a one-off export order that needs to be removed because it skews the data.

Very frequently data is missing – so-called 'holes' – and a judgement has to be made. For example, if a large segment of records have no date of birth, is this because they have come from a different source? Typically, variations in data of this kind have some significance and the modeller will need to decide whether to exclude the data or codify it.

Statistical methods are used to assess data quality, including hole counting and the assessment of *mean, median* (midpoint) and *mode* (most common occurrence) to identify whether they concur. A significant difference between them indicates that this is not a normal distribution (if it were, the average value would also be the midpoint of the curve and the place where the most frequent number of occurrences were to be found: i.e. a bell-shaped curve).

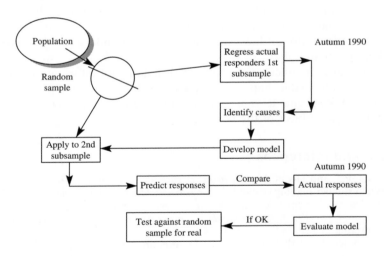

Figure 15.11   Model building

Once the data has been suitably conditioned, the model process, as shown in Figure 15.11, is to draw a sample of suitable size from the database and split it randomly in two. One portion is used to construct the model and the other to test its quality.

The new model is applied to the old data to predict what should have happened in a marketing programme that has already taken place. This prediction is then compared with what actually happened. If the model is good it can be tested in use; if not, something has gone wrong and the modelling process must be repeated. This means that models can be tested at no expense other than data-processing and consultancy time, and their probable accuracy can be calibrated before going to the expense of using them in a live project.

One potential data need for model building is customer status at the original action/reaction time, i.e. at the time of the promotion. One way of achieving this is to capture a customer status snapshot of key data with each promotion and either archive it or attach it to the promotion history record.

New software is steadily emerging which attempts to automate as much as possible of the model-building process. Neural networking is the most high profile example. A number of companies have also developed products to help the direct marketer through the process. It should be said that the process of building a model is *relatively* simple with good software *providing the data is right*, and interactions, oddities, etc., are dealt with. This is the area in which many consultants make a living.

However, it is crucially important that the person who does the modelling either understands the data or has good interaction with those who do. Data needs personal knowledge to get good interpretation, yet two-thirds of direct companies do not have statistical staff who understand database and marketing research data.[4]

Statistical techniques are the tools to turn data into information. Turning them into knowledge happens in their use by marketing people in the decision making and learning which subsequently takes place. How this happens is the subject of the next chapter.

Notes and references

1. Davis, P.J. and Hersh, R; *Descartes' Dream*, Penguin Books, 1988.
2. 'When smaller mailings mean better business', *Marketing Services* (20 May 1993).
3. Try David Shephard Assoc., *The New Direct Marketing*, Business One, Irwin, 1990, and *The Practitioner's Guide to Direct Marketing*, The Institute of Direct Marketing in Britain.
4. 'Computers in marketing' survey by DunnHumby Associates, 1992/3.

16
Data to knowledge: segmentation methods

Summary   How do we use analytical and statistical techniques for marketing advantage? This is the key content of Chapter 16.

Marketing is not about trying to persuade some faceless aggregation of customers to see it our way. It is about a dialogue over time with a specific group of customers whose needs you understand in depth and for whom you develop a specific offer with a differential advantage ... If you have something to shout about – shout. If you don't – shut up.

(Malcolm McDonald)

Segmentation is a response to both individual taste and personality and the need to provide product identity with which customers can more closely associate. Skills in brand differentiation and marketing based on the 4 Ps grew as a consequence and necessity when the stable world of traditional products was shocked by the product proliferation of the last century or so (and especially the last few decades). As craft products from guilds and local, known traders and manufacturers were replaced by relatively anonymous supply sources, the need for the establishment of brand and corporate identity became increasingly important for relationships to exist.

Products sought preference niches. People's tastes were then further shaped by new products. Ever-increasing proliferation of 'people' and 'product' personalities makes the matching process ever more critical.

The step from individual, small-scale, craft production and trade directed towards traditional, undifferentiated, slowly changing demand patterns to national or even global manufacture aimed at differentiated, rapidly changing demand requires the focus of segmentation. Mass marketing is typically too inefficient. Segmentation as differentiated mass marketing was the new solution with information as the means to achieve it.

Project reporting

Basic reporting of marketing project results is the beginning, including:

- number mailed
- costs
- number and percentage of responses and acceptances
- average cost per response and acceptance
- total value of sales
- average value of sales

and available by:

- overall campaign/programme/project
- promotion
- cell
- key product elements
- retailer/intermediary/salesperson or team
- media, including catalogues, scripts, papers, etc.

and in combinations.

This necessitates both the capture of promotion codes and maintenance of a cross reference to a programme history file, as previously discussed. The importance of methods for tracking customer activity is obvious, both at transaction level (i.e. promotion-response) and over time: i.e. what differences do different marketing programmes make to retention?

As Figure 16.1 shows, it may be necessary to keep track of customers over several cycles or seasons, measuring their product adoption and propensity to complain, cross-purchase, recommend, buy again. The aim will be to assess not just the effectiveness of single actions, but strategies. Tracking like this can be done with the aid of a system which records all promotional and other events and enables these to be used as the basis of selection, either manually or automatically, by subsequent marketing promotions.

Cross-tabulation

The most basic and therefore important of database marketing's analysis tools is cross-tabulation. This is a software tool and approach enabling the marketer to select two variables for analysis and then to define category values for the variables (so, for example, converting 'time since last order' into a number of buckets: 'up to 3 months', '3–6 months' and so on) to be reported in a spreadsheet format. It should be possible to select a customer segment for analysis and then get counts, percentage split by cell, average values by cell for some other variable, such as order value, finally subtotalling by yet another variable and set of values.

Cells

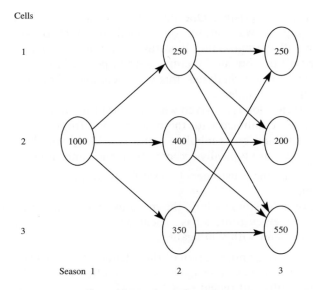

Figure 16.1 Long-term cell tracking: where the customers go

Frequency: Mail to Order Ratio

		1 to 2	2 to 3	3 to 4	4 to 5	5 plus
	0–6	325	256	1545	758	865
	0–12	450	425	1211	680	987
Recency in months	13–18	512	589	1298	542	1058
	19–24	362	615	1475	375	745
	25–30	211	412	1005	412	912

Monetary subtotal: £20–£50 spend	1860	2297	6534	2767	4567
	Total customers, £20 to £50 spend			18025	

Figure 16.2 Cross-tabulation example

Advanced systems, such as matchkey, have basic significance testing functions on the cell segments defined and are useful at giving breakdown data like average value or order size for each cell. Analysts can choose options such as leaving out records where there is a blank field (or 'hole') or keeping them in and defining that as a significant piece of data.

Cross-tabulation lets the marketer or data owner spend time getting to know the shape and profile of the data and customer base. There is no good replacement in database marketing for the intimacy that comes from spending time looking at data in many different combinations and ways.

Results are often surprising. One marketer had a life insurance product which the company was certain was aimed at 30–35 or 40 year olds. Consequently, all the marketing literature, copy and placing of advertisements worked off this premise. Pictures were of people in that age group. In fact, when the data was analysed, this was a complete illusion. The actual customers were much older.

Deeper segmentation is achieved when the best (or worst) customers from one data slice are combined with the best or worst from another. Define a segment (or 'all') and cross-tabulate using two likely variables. The most powerful variables are typically recency, frequency and monetary value:

- The longer it is since customers bought from you, the less likely it is that they will buy.
- The more often customers buy, the more likely they will buy again.
- The more money customers have spent with you, the more money they are likely to spend with you again.

This is a compulsive demonstration of the retention theory! Then choose the best cells. Do the same exercise again using two other criteria, then combine the two populations and repeat.

Earlier, it was described how, in many markets, customers have portfolio buying habits. Loyalty can be measured as the percentage of purchase given to a brand or outlet. This would be a useful factor to build into segmentation and financial modelling analysis either as a predictor or dependent factor, if known. Segmenting by portfolio percentage and value is another useful breakdown.

Gains charts

The output of regression and other modelling is often a gains chart. After scoring customers, as described, they are sorted from best to worst, rather like letting the cream rise to the top of the milk, and then grouped for reporting purposes, often using decile analysis (splitting into tenths, but any grouping is acceptable, it is an arbitrary split and the aim is convenience): see Figure 16.3.

The aim of the gains chart is to enable business decisions. For each decile, say, the score range and average response are given plus a breakdown showing the effects of marketing to different penetration levels:

- effect on average response by adding extra deciles in absolute and relative terms;
- improvement (reduction) in response over average by mailing individual deciles.

Marketers can then make decisions about profitability, profit and customer reactivation.

% of database	Score from model	Average% response of decile	Cumulative response. Marketing better deciles	% gain of this decile over average response	Cumulative gain % by marketing only better deciles
10	173+	2.80	2.8	72	72
20	143–172	2.60	2.6	50	62
30	125–142	2.40	2.4	25	50
40	109–124	2.20	2.2	12	40
50	100–108	2.10	2.1	6	34
60	91–99	2.00	2	–12	25
70	77–90	1.90	1.9	–25	19
80	59–76	1.80	1.8	–38	12
90	26–58	1.70	1.7	–50	6
100	0–25	1.60	1.6	–56	0

Figure 16.3 Gains chart

By this method you can begin to make business decisions linked to profits. Sometimes it is worth mailing unprofitable segments in order to reactivate customers or to maintain the relationship. When profits are flowing, this may be a particularly sound policy. On the other hand, if the chairman is fighting off a takeover and has promised great returns in the short term, it might make sense to keep only to the most profitable elements.

The aim of all segmentation and modelling is to try to get more discrimination: more rich cream, more really thin skimmed milk. The data and processes that pull apart results best are the most powerful.

Differential marketing

Two interesting models have been developed by Ogilvy & Mather Direct to guide the strategic development of their clients. Differential Marketing is a business philosophy with a number of conceptual and analytical techniques originally developed for FMCG and similar business sectors. Value Spectrum modelling is an analytical decision support tool which has broad application in business-to-business marketing and service businesses.

Differential Marketing particularly works for companies whose businesses have historically depended on brand image and are meeting media fragmentation and customer diversity. However, its general principles are almost universal. It began with a very simple proposition: *a minority of customers produce business out of proportion to their numbers.* The Pareto principle operates with telling force. Yet, when marketing and customer service spend is analysed, it is frequently shared equally across the customer base, as shown in Figure 16.4.

In a not untypical case, 10 per cent of consumers generated 60 per cent of sales and over 60 per cent of profit. If broadcast communication and

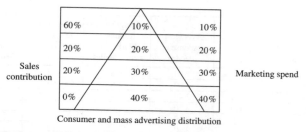

Sales contribution — Marketing spend

Consumer and mass advertising distribution

Figure 16.4 Differential marketing model (*source*: Ogilvy & Mather Direct)

relationship building is used, then 10 per cent of spend generates 60 per cent of business. That sounds like good news until you see that 70 per cent of the spend is generating only 20 per cent of the business. It is not uncommon for over half the category customers to provide no business at all. It makes economic sense to redeploy some of that expenditure to the key consumer groups to acquire or keep them, if you can. This is likely to mean a shift towards customer care and direct programmes to the top customer base, paid for by a shift in emphasis away from mass techniques, which cost more money. Since it is increasingly difficult to find good media to reach all the best customers, owing to media fragmentation, a shift to database marketing is signalled.

Furthermore, when sales promotion spend is analysed, over 60 per cent of it may be given to the top 10 per cent top spenders. Many companies, when they examine what kind of material they are giving to their most loyal customers, are appalled. The real danger demonstrated earlier is that sales promotion discounts train their customers in disloyalty.

In discussing this concept with clients it has been interesting to see how difficult it is for them to make fundamental decisions, simply because of lack of knowledge. If the question is asked of top management, 'Who are the customers that occupy the top, middle and lower tiers and what do you think you spend per head with what financial results?' there is typically a long and heated discussion, often ultimately unresolved.

Part of the problem is the lack of a good basis for assessing the profit contribution of customers. Organizations with large fixed asset bases such as railways and postal services (an increasing commercial trend with investment in machines replacing people) have real difficulty in judging how much contribution a customer makes. For example, British Rail invested resources in services to meet its peak load commuter base. These commuters are also the largest source of revenue, and provide the largest revenue per head. But how profitable are they, given the cost of idle stock during the rest of the day? The question can therefore generate fundamental re-thinking of the business.

Even when a profit contribution formula is determined, deciding which customers fall into what segments typically requires care. Marketers frequently give answers shaped by product or brand management thinking: 'The customers of this *product* are best.' This is perpetuating a product push myth. We want to know the characteristics of the people, not the product. The shift towards recognizing people clusters and their cross-purchasing patterns can be a corporate eye-opener. Similarly, recognition that spend on customers is not proportional to their contribution sometimes sparks the re-thinking required by the 'silly spiral'.

The solution is obviously quality data assisted by ABC accounting and a customer database. Customer prototyping, described later, is also useful.

Value Spectrum modelling is based on the two fundamental dynamics noted in the economics of loyalty: loyalty and worth. Value Spectrum modelling at its simplest is based on a four-box Boston matrix, although more detailed breakdowns are frequent, dividing customers according to their degree of loyalty and value (see Figure 16.5).

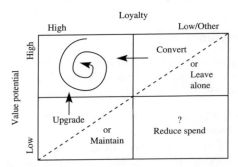

Figure 16.5   Value spectrum modelling (*source*: Ogilvy & Mather Direct)

This is useful because it helps to translate data analysis into a set of actionable programmes based on a long-term vision, typically refocusing resources from the bottom quartile of low-value, low-loyalty customers to high-value, high-loyalty customers. The aim will be to husband and develop this resource. Low-value, low-loyalty customers are frequently unprofitable. Many credit card and finance companies have many unprofitable customers with no transactions or only one unprofitable policy.

Another two crucial questions concern the opportunity to convert or upgrade boxes 2 and 3 in Figure 16.5. It is superficial simply to launch into conversion and upgrade. Not all customers can be upgraded, because resources are limited. Those in a *stable*, loyal relationship with a competitor are less likely than loyals whose relationship has become unstable.

Case study 16.1   How BAT used value modelling

BAT Netherlands wanted to improve the effectiveness of their salespeople in dealing with 2400 non-specialist tobacco outlets. Each salesperson was looking after 200 outlets on a more or less equal basis, with limited direction and focus. Salespeople were expected to call on all outlets on a regular basis and sell as much as they could.

A database was built with the help of the salesforce, who collected information on each of the outlets, including size, type and potential, as well as actual sales volumes for the different brands. Analysis of value (i.e. the total quantity of packs sold per outlet) and loyalty (i.e. the range of BAT brands carried) resulted in new mission for the salesforce affecting frequency of visit, offers and customer recruitment policy changes based on the characteristics of the high-value, high-loyalty outlets.

Low-value, low-loyalty outlets received reduced attention. Customer service quality improved for key segments. A great deal more thought went into the proposition. Instead of trying to hammer away at everything, a more selective approach based on shifting either volume or loyalty proved successful. Sales increased, for example one brand in snack bars lifted from a 19 per cent to a 46 per cent penetration. Salesforce satisfaction also improved.

Opportunity analysis

Breaking the customer base into segments or clusters is a preliminary to opportunity analysis. This seeks to identify the financial opportunity of various market approaches – obviously after testing – based on:

(a) the financial lift opportunity: the gap between current contribution potential after conversion;
(b) the probability of achieving conversion;
(c) the cost of achieving the outcome using the optimum interaction between (b) and (c) (see Table 16.1).

Opportunity analysis, which assesses *lift* opportunity, should not be confused with retention analysis, which assesses the value of keeping customers. In segment 3 in Table 16.1, the true value is not just the lift but retention. Later it will be shown how the two can be combined.

Predictive behaviour modelling and moments of truth

Statistical and segmentation analysis can help with both set-up and evaluation of computer-aided programs to leverage perceived quality, service value and sales effect based on moments of truth. The objective is to develop a predictive behaviour modelling loyalty and service knowledge base such as:

Table 16.1   Sample opportunity analysis

Segment	Current value (DM)	Potential value (DM)	GAP	Probability of conversion (%)	Cost (DM)	Net oppor- tunity (%)
1. Satisfied competitor Loyals	350	3500	3150	0.05	100	57.5
2. Unstable competitor Loyals	1250	3500	2250	0.20	100	350
3. Satisfied own loyals High value	3150	3500	350	0.6	60	150
4. Unstable own loyals High value	2400	3500	1100	0.7	150	620
5. Own loyal Mid/low value	1700	2100	400	0.5	60	(40)

- customers who buy $2x$ in the first four months are $3x$ more profitable
- customers who get this service call after two months are 20 per cent more likely to buy in the next three months
- married women respond 14 per cent better, and 23 per cent better if we give them a freephone Careline number
- customers who complain and are then satisfied with the response are 31 per cent more loyal than those who do not complain
- over 30 per cent of customers lack confidence in this service; the follow-up phone call increased subsequent purchase by 24 per cent in the first six months
- customers acquired without a discount are 40 per cent more valuable over two years.

A statistical scoring system can then be used to influence the inclusion or exclusion of customers in marketing programmes. One of the most prominent of such applications is the American Express monthly statement cycle, Relationship Billing, which responds to each individual customer's moving, lifetime and recent profile to generate a unique customer statement with a range of offers from their library. These offers are provided jointly with their retail base and target individuals based on types of activity, location, usage of card in specific establishments and desired changes.

In another example, a leading European frequent flyer programme identifies for each customer his or her monthly profile versus the anticipated profile for the month, and the trend. Based on this, a programme of automatic mailings and awards is generated to stimulate or reward behaviours.

Beyond segmentation[1]

Segmentation as differentiated mass marketing represents only the *first stage* in the response to the market phenomena. It is a first breakdown of the monolithic market into smaller units. We can go on to the individual, from share of market to share of customer through the bond of I to I marketing.

Segmentation represents an analytical reductionism. Indeed, that is its power. The essence of segmentation is the division of a presumed larger whole into smaller separate groups which may require different treatment. Segmentation adds essential *focus* which brings quality improvement and waste reduction and helps in brand building. This is a considerable development step, but how does it cope with the 'individual'? The answer is: not well enough. The next step is 'building from ones': a developmental, bottom-up approach leading to one-to-one, or I to I marketing. Many analytical segmentation techniques remain valid, but there is an important reframing which enhances brand and corporate positioning, service and 'targeting', leading to:

- a better intellectual and practical tool for dealing with the interaction between the concept of the individual and the concept of group;
- a better way to develop brand and organization positioning;
- a more significant role for marketing in the ongoing evolution of quality;
- a better value and values-related approach to the task of marketing.

In Chapter 1 we discussed communities and groups. Rather than *structure* a segment, we *identify* a group. *Segmenting* implies *dividing* a given population into portions based on appropriate factors (age, buyer or not, interests, etc.), whereas *grouping* means finding and collecting together people who share common characteristics (interests, buyer or not, age). Groups and segments are not, at first, very far apart. In practical terms we could use factor and cluster analysis, for example, to determine both. In both cases, we would create discrete programmes and products aimed at a portion of the consumer marketplace. In fact CHAID and regression are essentially grouping techniques, leading to one-to-one selection and marketing.

The difference may seem subtle, but it is the thinking that harbours important differences (see Table 16.2). It is much easier to 'segment' than to 'group', as grouping requires more intimate knowledge and relationship.

What is in a word? Ask the copy writer. Stressing grouping as a *direction* to evolve (ideas always precede implementation) means shifting thinking from a divisive mode to an integrative one – the essence of loyalty – and more in tune with the times. Thinking right is the essence of the power of positive thinking. Much of business is about managing the 'seams': finding ways to bring people and things together, effectively. Is that not the task of marketing?

It is much easier to imagine a relationship with a *group* (of people) than with a *segment*. With how many *segments* have you personally formed a relationship? Do you even want to be in a relationship with a segment? A group is a set of individuals who share something in common: a community of individuals.

Table 16.2   Characteristics of segments and groups

Segment	Group
Top down	Bottom up
What divides?	What unites?
Population based	People based
Macro-economic	Micro-economic
Class determined values	Individual values shared
[Useful] abstraction	Concrete people
Product driven	Requirements driven
Aims to generate aspirations	Aims to recognize
Targeted solutions	Tailored solutions
Targeted, focused on	Aligned with, focused on
Aimed at 'target' audience	Aimed at 'listening' audience
Selected by factors in common	Recognized as community or individuals
Transaction potential	Relationship potential

One may want to belong to a group, e.g. be an Elvis fan, a Weight Watcher, an environmentalist or an Armani client; but one does so as an *individual*, a trend that is increasing with each generation. Since the job of the marketer must surely be to sense the realities and movements at work in the psyche of society (or a relevant part of it) and to react accordingly, it is now clear that today's task demands *individualized marketing*: I∞I marketing.

The company needs to maintain a relationship with both the individual customer and the community to which he, she or it belongs by virtue of shared values (see Figure 16.6 – it will be obvious that this develops from Figure 1.1).

Interaction with the group/community provides the generalized base for investment and for the tailoring of product and service set to meet a broad base of individual needs. This is also the realm of *organization* development and relationship marketing. In the *dialogue* of individual moments of truth with the customer a unique relationship is developed: the realm of direct marketing. *Information*-knowledge is the key to both.

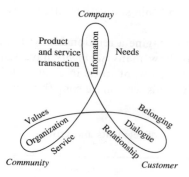

Figure 16.6 Individualized marketing

These three dynamics also correspond to the three dynamics of willing, feeling and thinking described earlier:

1. The company becomes aware of needs (thinking) and deploys resources (willing) to build an exchange, a relationship (feeling).
2. The customer *feels* a connection with its community (consciously or unconsciously) and *acts* in broad conformity, the company growing in *awareness* with each transaction.

This is an integrated approach to marketing which builds loyalty rather than an accidental discovery of a fractured customer base.

Market group description and prototyping

Market group description links the group's shared identity or outlook with the characteristics or dynamics of their response to your product or offer (see Figure 16.7). The identity and shared outlook can be defined as a function of the:

- demographics
- psychographic factors including individual personalities, attitudes of customers and their lifestyle
- geography and geographical distribution.

The consumer response is made up of the subjective measures of response which rise from the expectation and experience of perceived benefits (inner dynamics) and objective analysis of the communication or offer characteristics (outer dynamics). The latter includes factors such as:

Topic 16.1   Stages in mass market breakdown

The switch from a relatively undifferentiated 'clan market' consciousness, where large groups behave the same way, driven by traditions such as class, ethnic or cultural habits, to a highly personal market of individuals can be described in four major stages constituting a conceptual continuum: see Table 16.3.

Table 16.3   The differentiation continuum

	<—— Past ——> Outer drivers dominate		<—— Future ——> Inner drivers dominate	
	Mass	*Segmented*	*Group*	*Individual*
Grouping driver	'Class' or clan habits	'Keeping up with the 'Jones's': aspirational values	We feel recognized	I – expression
Supply dynamic	Local, traditional, with some 'monolithic', big brands	Local service and many brands, some very big	Tailored products and services of all sizes	Multiplicity
Customer attitude	I know my place	I want my place	I have my place	I am my place
Archetypal products	A Model T for everyone	This year's Buick for young executives	Virgin Records/ Harrods	Home hairstyling
	*	*	*	*
	½" screws	Brass ½" screws	Own label specialist screws	Give me your screw design today

Grouping as opposed to segmentation, represents the flip from a 'class' or 'clan' dominated society or market (where an external order imposes the sense of self and place in society) to an individually created society/market. Whether we ever want or would have the kind of society/market where individualism is totally rampant ('the customer is king') and no meaningful cohesion or tolerance exists is open to doubt. There is more than one kind of tyranny.

Figure 16.7 Market group description

- level of usage of the product
- price sensitivity
- promotional response
- loyalty to the company channel or outlet.

By linking database segmentation and clustering to market research, much richer patterns and observations can be achieved. At a simple level, if a questionnaire is sent to a group of customers and subsequently profiled, it is often possible to extrapolate the results to other customers in the same groups who did not take part in the questionnaire.

Alternatively, market research can be used to identify *reasons* for response or non-response, and the deeper psychological profile of customers. The aim must be to extend analysis from the impersonal to the personal (without intruding into the private).

Prototyping is a way to add value to segmentation and leads to improved creative treatment. Brian Wansink describes the result of several research projects which show that prototyping can significantly improve traditional segmentation.[2] Since the best small business people can mentally visualize and then describe their key customers, often as individuals, the questions are: Can the same be done in larger companies (where marketers have developed an intimate knowledge of customers)? and, How does this compare with solely data-based segmentation, particularly demographics?

The answers seem to be that prototyping is a useful tool. Customers would typically not describe themselves as segmentation describes them: i.e.

I'm a 40 to 60 year old with a high school education and 3.5 children with my own flat. I like to think of myself as a heavy user of wholemeal bread and am brand loyal on the whole although I could be persuaded if . . .

and so on. As Professor Wansink observes: 'No consumer sees her or himself as a bundle of mere statistics,' and he goes on to quote Fortini-Campbell's observation that statistics alone do as much good in describing people as a ruler does measuring a beach ball.[3]

He then carried out two particular studies of the insights and accuracy of prototyping. It is basically a simple methodology and involves recalling or imagining an ideal customer and then naming and describing him or her in detail: just as the person with the small business does. This process can then be iterated, each defining a new cluster.

According to the research, the insights were rich and fruitful. Whereas, solely databased segmentation provided only one significant variable indicating the difference between yuppies and establishment types, prototyping gave a rich differentiation. Manager's accuracy was also significantly more effective ($t = 5.5$; $p > 0.01$).

With a good database it then becomes possible to research groups, then select the right customers for an appropriate offer, text, format and so on. If key data is missing, this can perhaps be found with the help of a questionnaire.

The process can be reversed. Find customer groups in the database, then ask who they are, what their names are, describe them and decide on the appropriate tone of voice and offer. After all, most good copywriters describe how they visualize customers before writing to them. The regular flipping of the process, visualizing to database, database to visualization will be one of the useful techniques of the new marketing.

Segmenting customers and modelling products

Sixteen per cent of the British population positively dislike the telephone. Another 22 per cent prefer suppliers not to use it and 15 per cent will use it only grudgingly. So one way to segment relationships is by attitude to the telephone.

Using customer attitudes to the relative importance of the service product elements (based on a trade-off matrix) can cluster customers. One questionnaire could both cluster the customers and identify the changes needed to the product.

Product effectiveness can be modelled: first identify the various product attributes, as described in Chapter 8, then survey customer attitudes to their *importance* and *satisfaction*. Use this to map the pull per pound or dollar, weighting each attribute accordingly. For example, attributes that are of high quality but low importance may be over-invested, especially if expensive, such as 2-hour film processing. Alternatively, there may be poorer quality and important attributes that could be improved.

When such surveys are linked to long-term tracking of the database (or historic data), the value return of product attributes and their effect on retention and lifetime value can be calculated.

Case study 16.2 DHL model their product

DHL, the parcel distributor, offered their key customers in Belgium a thank-you carrot in the form of a software tool which helps to prepare shipments and gives the client information (another smart product). They wanted to know how this service was rated and which elements were adding or hitting value.

Working with the consultancy, O&M Dataconsult, and their modelling service, Quest, a client questionnaire was prepared which checked satisfaction and importance. Using a graphical mapping tool and statistics, this was displayed on a grid showing the relative positioning and importance of each feature of the software and back-up service.

The result was an opportunity to reallocate resources and emphasis productively, adding value to DHL and clients simultaneously.

Lifetime value modelling

Lifetime value modelling (LTV) is the outcome of all other predictive and testing strategies and the justification for service-based strategies. The aim is to move from analysing product profitability to modelling customer profitability.

Case study 16.3 CoreStates Financial Corporation

CoreStates Financial Corporation is the $24 billion US holding company for three banks in Pennsylvania and New Jersey. They carried out a project to analyse the profitability of individual customers and discovered some surprising results. They had always analysed profitability at product or business line level and, as a consequence, were able to identify the average profitability for account line. With the new systems they were able to do this by customer and household across product lines.

A desktop decision support system brings together all the information affecting profitability, and this is updated on a monthly basis in order to indicate trends.

CoreStates identified 174 different profitability formulae for their 58 different products, in each of their three banks. As a result, they identified that some of their most successful packages were unprofitable for certain customer groups. For example, the blue riband package for customers with substantial balances, certificates of deposit, was considered a marketing success until they found that 25 per cent of households owning this product were in fact unprofitable. Certain market segments were much larger profit contributors than expected. In one branch, 37 per cent of customers generated 59 per cent of the branch's total profit.

As a result, CoreStates were able to redevelop their products and marketing to be more effective. Product packages were adapted to meet key market communities. Branches with similar market potential and customer communities were clustered with micro-marketing campaigns focused on developing the potential. By rolling out the best marketing practices of the most successful branches, they could benefit the least profitable branches. By changing distribution channels and type of service offered to unprofitable households, they were able to make progress towards achieving profitability for all groups.[4]

When lifetime value modelling is applied to decision making, quality improves. For example, it was Kimberly Clark's realization about the lifetime value of Huggies' customers which led to their investment in recruiting and keeping new customers. It was the Vermont Teddy Bear's realization about how customers come back and tell their friends that led to their passionate involvement in the total buying and using experience.

How do you build and use an LTV model for business planning? In Table 16.4, referral revenue refers to average incremental profit contribution from referrals per customer. Additional revenue refers to cross-selling and up-selling contribution supplements to base revenue. Costs are broken down into initial acquisition, service (administration and other), 'guarantee' (i.e. the plan to keep customers with allocated careline and other guarantee resources), marketing/relationship costs (to promote the relationship and generate continued and upgraded purchases and referrals) and finally, product cost of sales. The initial base of customers reduces over time, giving a discounted net present value per initial customer.

A general mathematical expression for lifetime value calculation is:

$$\text{LTV} = \sum_{i=1}^{n} C_i \, (1 + d)^{-i}$$

where C is the net contribution from various cross-selling, up-selling, referral and base revenue and d is the discount rate.

As the sample spreadsheet in Table 16.4 shows, the principle is very simple:

1. Identify and collect revenue and cost elements for a viable cluster.
2. Compute the relationship as a cash flow estimate (initially) or forecast (based on statistical extrapolation); e.g. in Table 16.4 a relationship is assumed between service cost, guarantee cost, product cost, etc., as a percentage of revenue which varies with the length of the relationship.
3. Identify retention statistics (usually shown as the number of customers retained from an initial base of 1000 per period).
4. Calculate net present value per customer (the discounted value of future contribution streams).

The mechanics are easy. The secret is in the data, assumptions, quality of processing and willingness to try it. The effect of lifetime thinking and modelling is a willingness to invest carefully in the future, with better results and fewer short-term arbitrary decisions.

Table 16.4   Sample lifetime value model

	First period	2nd period	3rd period	4th period	5th period	6th period	7th period	8th period	9th period	10th period
Referral revenue	0.00	0.00	12.00	12.36	12.73	13.11	13.51	13.91	14.33	14.76
Up- and cross-sell revenue	0.00	10.00	10.30	10.61	10.93	11.26	11.59	11.94	12.30	12.67
Base revenue	100.00	103.00	106.09	109.27	112.55	115.93	119.41	122.99	126.68	130.48
Acquisition cost	40.00	0.00	0.00	0.00	0.00	0.00	0.00	0.00	0.00	0.00
Service cost	15.00	14.89	17.14	17.65	18.18	18.73	19.29	19.87	20.46	21.08
Guarantee costs	5.00	5.65	6.42	6.61	6.81	7.01	7.23	7.44	7.67	7.90
Marketing and relationship costs	10.00	11.30	12.84	13.22	13.62	14.03	14.45	14.88	15.33	15.79
Product costs	50.00	56.50	64.20	66.12	68.10	70.15	72.25	74.42	76.65	78.95
Profit contribution per head	-20.00	24.66	27.80	28.63	29.49	30.38	31.29	32.23	33.19	34.19
Quantity of customers	1000	880	774	681	600	528	464	409	360	316
Period profit contribution	-20 000	21 701	21 528	19 513	17 687	16 031	14 531	13 171	11 938	10 820
Net present value	− 20 000	1667	22 731	41 399	57 904	72 457	85 248	96 450	106 220	114 700

Notes and references

1. A version of this section first appeared as 'Beyond segmentation' in *Journal of Targeting, Measurement and Analysis for Marketing,* **3** (No. 1).
2. Wansink, Dr B., 'The customer prototyping technique: its validation and application', *Journal of Targeting, Measurement and Analysis for Marketing*, **3** (No. 1).
3. Fortini-Campbell, L., *The Customer Insight Book*, The Copy Workshop, Chicago.
4. Information provided by Kingdom of Marketing Dynamics Ltd.

17
Creativity and continuous relationship improvement

Summary Database marketing is clearly more than qualification. It includes creativity, business judgement, intuition, teambuilding and insight. It demands what Max DePree calls 'intimacy',[1] a profound understanding of man, machine, context and system – akin to what W. Edwards Deming calls 'Profound Knowledge'. The challenge is to blend left and right brain thinking creatively, to create a new alloy out of systemic and creative excellence. How do we do this?

Is it the bell that rings,
Is it the hammer that rings,
Or is it the meeting
of the two that rings?

(Old Japanese riddle quoted by Deming)

Barriers and breakthrough

Apart from a lack of practice, what prevents companies being creative? Is it not fear, hatred (of our weakness and of another's success), and doubt? These lead (i) to the desire to clamp control over the company; (ii) to stress and competitiveness that create barriers to competence, (iii) to panic rushing around, where people are too busy to think, perpetuating problems. This applies equally to the individual and the culture of the company. The more senior we are the more opportunity we have to shape the culture, so that personal and corporate improvement, via groups, functions and processes, go hand in hand. In each case, the way forward includes creating a more open attitude.

One of the leading models in Western society is the Roman Catholic Church. In the Middle Ages, the Pope decided, real messages were delivered in Latin and the population got a cut down KISS version. Priests, the hierarchy, controlled: the aim was improvement by overcoming sin, based on the fear of being 'cast out', excommunication and hell. Models of reality in one area tend to metamorphose or move into others, like the model of the brain that follows the latest technology: brains have been steam engines, telephones, transistors, computers and neural networks. Paradigms are built out of tradition, and if a model such as the medieval Catholic Church is transposed to where it does not belong, like business, we have a legacy of uncreative people, driven by 'protesting' revolutionaries: the dissatisfied customers (and employees). (We still have 'excommunication' and the 'hell' of unemployment, too.)

When culture and attitude is control oriented it tends to become rigid and brittle. Trying to control the world leads first to stasis and then to revolution. First the bogged down going nowhere aristocracy and then the cart heading to the guillotine. Fear of change and disruption and uncertainty brings worse. And it damages creativity. If our assumption is that our plans are right and it is the outside world that needs to be changed, then we react out of our need for control. We all know the irritable choleric who is frustrated when the outer world challenges his or her plans.

The new networking models based on open systems architecture, object level programming and the information highway are a more useful culture model which have resonances for the organization: ways of being and working and capacities in open interaction with anyone speaking a recognizable language, only people working this way can be even more productive than computers.

Furthermore, unfortunately perhaps, we have to *live with* customers, for we cannot dominate them for long, although we try. In a target-driven organization, whose interests come first? The salesperson/marketer. In a customer-driven organization, customer relationship must come first.

Yet, trying to dominate customers is built into the very fabric of our methods. As Don Peppers and Martha Rogers put it in their excellent book, *The One to One Future*,

> If you're a mass marketer, you do your job as if there is no difference between a transaction with a first-time customer and a transaction with a brand-loyal fan. Since the mass media available to you are totally non-addressable, you treat new customers as new customers, and you treat current customers as new customers, too. This irrational devotion to customer acquisition leads directly to a contest of wills between marketer and customer.

It is a win–lose, zero-sum game based on a competition between the marketer and customer to win the best deal, the best price, to win business versus to win a bargain. If your methods are wrong, then your creativity is devoted to trying to do the wrong things better. However clever you become, the pit just gets deeper. Since the wrong thing means trying to beat the customer, the only kind of creativity that makes sense is cunning and the only way the customer can respond is the same way, an adversarial contest of cunning.

One starting point, which has been mentioned earlier, is to move the paradigm towards a cooperative, win–win, joint problem-solving approach, the very way we are learning to work with our suppliers. Another is to change the language. If you talk dirty, you end up thinking dirty. If you talk slovenly, you end up thinking slovenly. If you talk aggressively, you end up in a fight trying to deploy your creativity to beat your friend. You have to guarantee all the strategy, tactics, campaigns, targets, market share wars and competition when all you want is a project to make friends and influence people.

Listening to complaints and throwing out the guarantee lifeline is a cooperative, joint problem-solving culture, a win-win build-not-break way of working. And it is not just for fun and ethics, it is the only economically viable method of the future.

IBM built its hegemony on a core business goal: to enhance customer *partnerships*. In those days customers rented equipment they could return at any time, so IBMers worried about quality and satisfaction. It threw it all away when it decided, post-Tom Watson, that it was easier to beat customers, so they decided to sell off their computers and base and lose the risk of customers saying they were unhappy. Talk about walking away from a guarantee management design. Maybe something had to change, but the manner changed culture, loyalties and focus. (For some time they even tried to be low-cost producers rather than high added value suppliers.)

The starting point of effective creativity in marketing is a big lateral jump in thinking, reframing what it is really all about. The real enemy on whom to direct our strategy is inside; it is our own lazy, competitive, cunning habits. The new creativity is flexible responsiveness.

Responsiveness is a *capacity* we need, not just an action. If we think that change is a constant and the only constant, this creates relentless demands for faster reaction. We think of change as *happening to* the organization. Should we not think of change as a living, vital, natural process arising from the whole interaction of the company with its environment? Learning, living, growing, developing, all become natural.

Imagine an organization as a strongly rooted plant, its tap root delving deep for dry spells, round rocks and stones and dust, searching for permanent water. Growth adjusts to light conditions. If another shrub grows beside it, reducing opportunity and light in one direction, it emphasizes the more open, bright area. There is a sensitive, dynamic readjustment as new plants arrive or disappear. Always an intimate, subtle adjustment to the opportunity to interact with the world of light, air and moisture.

This is a natural database marketing culture. The natural way is testing, dialogue, listening, adjusting actions, messages and products, all evolving over the years.

When we learn to live *with* the environment and *with* each other, we may go through this metanoia, this profoundly valuable change of the future, seeing things differently and bringing a new imagination to bear.

Creativity and learning

Creative improvement is inseparable from learning, and learning is inseparable from progress beyond recognized weakness, inadequacy or lack of fulfilment. Avery's observation is 'It does not matter if you fall down as long as you pick up something from the floor while you get up.' Graeme McCorkell, the Institute of Direct Marketing chairman, likes to quote Gary Glenn, a star sales trainer, who said: 'Anything worth doing is worth doing badly at first.'

The ability to acknowledge doubt, problems and mistakes is essential to learning maturity, as we saw with Parzival. In this, Socrates is the great archetype. Told that the Delphic Oracle had proclaimed him the wisest man in Greece, he was astonished: 'But I know I am completely ignorant,' he said. 'This', said the Oracle, 'is why you are the wisest man.'

Because Socrates was not content with ignorance – it was the driving force in his pursuit of knowledge – he could not remain complacent. 'Man, know thyself' was the basis of his pursuit and he spent his time exposing humbug and pushing the frontiers of his own and his friends' wisdom. Knowing ourselves and our organizations is essential in three ways, the three tools of human development:

1. What am I/the company *really doing*? The ability to be objectively and wholly conscious is not easy, but its absence is a kind of lie, a lack of honesty. Lack of consciousness quickly overcomes awareness, just as we lose a particular smell in a few minutes. Habits just become part of the situation – like the mailing that went out for eight years in one financial services company without any review, or our habitual route to work. Process flowcharts are one way to become more aware. Root cause analysis and double-loop learning are others. The database marketing discipline aims to tackle this.
2. How do I *feel* about what I am doing? Each person or group has an excellent inner sense for quality: do I feel good, or proud, about the work? Whatever it may be, conscience is a quality tool, for it is a force of judgement. Sir Montague Burton, founder of the British retailing legend, said, 'A company must have a conscience as well as a counting house.' The 'feel good' factor is a useful acid test. We cannot always do what we would prefer, but we can at least listen to our judgement.
3. We can become aware of our own *imagination*: the power to build a picture of what we would really like to do, how we want things to be, and

then turn it into reality. It is shocking to see how, when a group of people sit around a table and really decide to do something, it *happens*. Imagination is a creative force. A group of UK sales and marketing system providers decided to have an association (AIMS), to recruit members and then to have an exhibition, and so on. They met occasionally, made some decisions, and things happened for as long as the commitment lasted: a national association actually came into being just out of an idea! We may lament our failures, but surely our achievements are more remarkable. As Goethe put it:

> Until one is committed there is hesitancy, the chance to draw back, always ineffectiveness. Concerning all acts of initiative (and creation) there is one elementary truth the ignorance of which kills countless ideas and splendid plans: that the moment one definitely commits oneself, Providence moves too. All sorts of things occur to help one that would never otherwise have occurred. A whole stream of events issues from the decision raising in one's favour all manner of unforeseen incidents and meetings and material assistance which no man could have dreamt would have come his way. Whatever you can do, or dream you can, begin it. Boldness has genius, power and magic in it. Begin it now!

No one can be really creative without the active continuous weaving of these inner activities, which are the reverse of the three problems just described. They happen best between people, and including customers. Socrates did not retire into a solitary place for contemplation. He worked with others in the marketplace. What is happening to them, what do they feel, what lives in their imagination? Only in the meeting can really successful, creative responsive marketing take place. The idea may arise in a retreat, but is fed by prior experience.

Mintzberg describes successful strategy making as being like a craft activity, like a potter throwing fine ware[2]: constant awareness and alertness of what is happening, judgement and aliveness to new possibilities. It is a very 'hands on' process and includes a fine sensitivity to what is not right and to imaginative possibilities – seeing a new form emerge from the failure of an old one.

The creative side of responsive marketing is also a craft. Any poet, writer or artist will tell you that it is what has been 'left out' that makes a work.

Celebrating 'tactics'

No one seems to want to be a tactician. Earlier, 'only tactical' was used as a derogatory term, and we should now correct the balance. What is the 'tactical' approach really? Often it is used to mean short term (why do we not say 'short term', is it one of those euphemisms to hide our shame?). Does it not really mean deriving creative situational advantage? Deciding how to respond most effectively to the long-term relationship cycle (strategic) with situational creativity and learning?

Is tactics not part of the fundamental 'how to' learning cycle? When it becomes genuine double-loop learning, is not this often the basis for so-called strategy? Take the example Mintzberg gives of how Honda entered the American market.[3]

All the analysts said it was a carefully worked out strategy. Honda people said it was creative muddling through when they met the real situation. They wanted to sell big motorcycles and cars and ended up selling small motorcycles. All because the executives who were sent to open up the market began in a small downtown office and rode their own motorcycles to and from work, attracting so much interest from real customers that the penny eventually dropped.

Quality improvement: a type of pilgrimage

The Deming and Lievegoed models for improvement were described. Deming's *plan, do, check (or study), act* model served to aid the development of Japan from a shocked, bombed, social pariah with a poor reputation for production quality. Lievegoed's *plan, do, review* is archetypal and successfully proven. Do they conflict?

In fact, the continuous improvement cycle actually consists of these as two interlocking learning and improvement cycles, see Figure 17.1.

Deming's *plan, do, study* corresponds to the first stage in the process: the experimental phase. But implementation or rollout has its own *plan, do, review*, reviewing the experiment as the first phase of planning. Implementation has its own dynamics and needs planning as much as experiment and this is much of what Deming's *study* (or *check*) is about. For example, what else can we test, even at this stage? What about briefing the

Figure 17.1   Integrating Lievegoed's and Deming's models

sales and service people? Do operations need to know about volumes and any key issues? Does the telemarketing agency need to know when and how to expect Calls? How do we improve fulfilment and service? etc.

The three stages of *plan, do, review* correspond also to the three human tools mentioned earlier. Planning is an act of imagination, which is why Mintzberg is right to balance the rational view of planning with the more chaotic or 'emergent' view that he describes. Just as it took the creative imagination of Picasso to see that an old bicycle seat and handlebars made a perfect bull's head if placed together, so our creative imagination feeds off the situation. That is why database marketing should never become divorced from the people about whom information is collected.

The best modern organizations tend towards either end of a polarity: a systematic control culture, a Michael Porter style, or the never-ending spontaneous, situational response, the Tom Peters principle. Blending and marrying the two is the real challenge. The danger with database marketing is to become too obsessed with figures, numbers, analysis. It must be tempered by constant encounters with people – listening to telephone conversations, focus groups, leading letters, and questionnaires – as Marriott's chairman or Richard Branson do – and meeting the people, customers and front line, as Sam Walton did every day, or as Media Profil do with their customer panel, rather than the surprise of the direct marketer who had not even read the survey results.

The end of all profiling is to better understand real people, and this simply cannot be reduced to statistics.

The first stage of planning is therefore 'good imagination', which is creatively built out of intelligence (of both kinds), statistics, pictures, profiles, analysis, meetings and wisdom. An example is Dr Wansink's prototyping approach, described earlier.

Even at this stage we 'Do' the exercise in our minds and then review it – all mentally. When we believe we have a solution, we then *try it* (and both prototype tests and rollouts are experiments, but of different kinds): we engage and connect to the real situation: the meeting at the threshold takes place, the moment of truth.

Finally, we review. This is a kind of *listening*: What do the results tell us? Here, we have to be open to hear. Numbers will tell us one set of data, but we must still interpret this. And we need to broaden the base of response analysis, as described, into qualitative research and even intuition. Sometimes, we are too closed to hear what the world, the situation, our friends and employees, tell us.

The strength and weakness of direct marketing is its accountability. That means that direct marketers get a very loud shout, indeed, with very simple analysis:

- your mailing is NOT WORKING!
- *Yes*, your new pack *is better* than the old one!

Even these simple statements are not always listened to. Many companies do not systematically analyse and measure responses, the most basic messages by which we learn. More challenging is to listen to more subtle and difficult messages:

- Why did 92 per cent respond?
- What made those who responded do so?

Systematic testing answers many of these questions, but an increasing number of marketers recognize the need to supplement with traditional market research techniques, but using the database, as Toyota or Saga Holidays do, to direct the analysis, record results and use it for follow-up with individual customers (a feature of the Henley Centre forecast noted earlier) and thereby move from a share of market to a share of customer mode. The aim of such research has two parts (and they cannot always be done in the same step):

- fundamental analysis of the system problems, the common causes that need to be changed by root cause analysis – the left brain issues;
- identification of the individual issues that need to be repaired by empathy and an act of care – the right brain, Parzival principle.

Thinking of analysis as a 'listening' activity also helps to bring the left and right brains together: what are data and people *telling* us? Not only the logic of the result (the 'counting house'), but also how people, including marketers, front line and customers, feel about the process (the 'conscience'), thereby connecting our imagined plan with the actual response, the ivory tower with the rocks at its feet. In this way, we are more likely to avoid both junk mail and junked customers.

One Rover car marketing programme won the following astonishing result. When customers were surveyed, 4 per cent showed awareness of receiving direct mail, yet 80 per cent were aware of regularly receiving post, letters and correspondence. This is communication that has flipped its image and landed on the right side of the table with customers.

Table 17.1 shows the quality improvement or learning model in many different guises.

It can also be described as the evolution of Parzival from a state of naive wonder to maturity tested in action, attaining thereby the Grail Castle. Database marketing is sometimes presented as a boring, iterative, mechanical activity: the plan, test, analyse, rollout robotics workshop. Hopefully, another picture has been presented. Having tried that, there are, as with any craft, some basic trade skills to learn: as artists once first learnt

Table 17.1 Modes of development

Plan	Do	Review
Seeing	Touching/speaking	Listening
Imagination	Action	Judgement
Thinking	Willing	Feeling
Plan	Test	Analyse
Formulate/speculate	Form/function	Evaluate
Ideas	Actions	Lessons
Ivory tower	Rocky shore	Maturity

to grind their pigments. These are the mechanics or techniques which set free the artist.

Pausing to look below the waterline

Today companies are involved in a panic of change, looking everywhere for answers. Everyone agrees that change is disturbing. 'When the paradigm shifts we all go down to zero. Past expertise doesn't carry over', said Joel Barker in *Future Edge*. This creates exhaustion and inadequacy. If everything I know is superfluous, I become valueless. What is the point if everything is impermanent?

Yet, the most effective change and growth come about by digesting our own experience. It is easy to change by bringing in new people, but will it be any better, and what happens to the relationship values meantime? Often difficulties arise not from what is missing, *but from what is there and not seen.* When we look outside our organizations for solutions we often overlook what is inside. If we are cultivating the right customer or client relationships, will they effectively be a part of, and therefore *inside*, the organization boundary? Rather than rushing around, we could stop and pay attention.

Do we keep trying to implement things that do not work, only to keep trying to implement things that do not work? What is the pattern of frustration? Every company, like every person, has at least one. It is a social law that we must make the same mistakes until we have understood and learnt from them. Running away does not do that, it only postpones an even more vicious lesson.

Instead of trying to be like a Cortez discovering a new Pacific, should we be looking again at what we have, and renewing the business continuously in the process? ICI searched the world for a vegetable protein only to find it growing, as Quorn®, in the field outside the factory.

A starting point is to find out what employees know.

Sidney Yoshida asked a cross-section of people in a large factory to list all significant problems known to them.[4] He called the surprising result the 'iceberg of ignorance'. Of all the problems known to rank and file employees, only 74 per cent were known to supervisors, 9 per cent were known to general supervisors *and only 4 per cent were known to top management*. It is a common phenomenon.

Try asking employees how they feel about your products, service and marketing. Murray Raphael, the well-known writer on retail database marketing, describes how he never failed to pick up at least one idea from an employee. Of course, it is rather important that you take the comments seriously. At a later meeting Raphael would report what he had done as a result of their comments.

We know that employee motivation and satisfaction is highly correlated to customer satisfaction and motivation to purchase. Involving your employees in this way not only motivates them directly but provides you with valuable information about your efforts. Many of your employees are just like the people you want to buy your products.

There is the well-known story of the person who had been working for the company for 20 years before delivering a great new idea. When asked why he had never mentioned the idea before, he said he had never been asked.

Customer driven 'strategy'

Another group to ask are your customers.

Buyers in companies are starting to learn to overcome the old zero-sum power game of negotiation and working towards cooperative partnership and joint problem solving. Every such buyer is a customer and every such supplier is a seller, so perhaps this is the shape of the future. It is the essence of I∞I marketing.

Cooperative strategies are potentially more creative than 'competitive' strategies in achieving profit. Check the dictionary: before 'competition' was interpreted as competition it mean *competent*.

Despite our understandable emphasis on competitive advantage, it is a little observed fact that there is no other sphere of society than business where cooperation and associative endeavour is more vital. Without an immensely sophisticated network of association and cooperation, almost nothing would get from the ground to the consumer.

For example, Zeelandia, a flour manufacturer in The Netherlands, cooperated with WWF, the environmental charity, to co-promote a new bread mixture with eight natural grains. Each purchase produced a donation for WWF as well as providing the customer with a stamp that went towards the purchase of a small Panda bear, WWF's logo. The promotion went out to the 6500 local bakery shops inviting them to participate, and 92 per cent did. Adverts in trade magazines supported the mailing. PR and local and national radio supported the programme, the first loaf going to Prince Bernhard. A newsletter was produced to tell of the successes during the three-month project and to encourage and advise the baker. Point of sale merchandising material supported the bakery.

Awareness for the project reached 70 per cent across The Netherlands. After 12 weeks, 8.5 million loaves against a target 2.5 million were obtained. There were 12 000 new donors (from the 120 000 redemptions) and $450 000 raised for WWF. A series of print advertisements informed everyone of what had happened and thanked the bakers for their participation.

Country Charm used direct mail to enhance business through a series of customer friendly offers, such as a cooperative, reciprocal sunrise inflation sale, which meant that customers who shopped between 5 a.m. and 6 a.m. got 50 per cent off regular prices, and with each successive hour the discount was progressively reduced until finally, at 11 a.m., the sale was over. They sent customers a birthday card with the offer of 20 per cent off their next purchase on any day of their birthday month. Country Charm then approached its neighbours in the shopping mall and they put together a *joint* promotion which helped everyone in the neighbourhood.

Omaha Steaks International listens to customers. It is a mail order and catalogue business which, using toll-free telephone numbers, sells steaks and other gourmet foods. Their business began in 1952 *in response to customer requests*. Their local customers wanted to send steaks as gifts to friends and relatives across the country. Instead of throwing their hands up in despair, they built a business that continued to listen, winning the American Direct Marketing Association's annual award for customer service excellence in 1994, partly by becoming one of the first companies in the US to integrate both order taking and customer service with toll-free numbers.

By contrast, one NHS trust hospital in the south-east of England decided that patients were neither intelligent nor sufficiently informed to know best what they wanted. Nevertheless, because it was expected, they ran a survey in which patients rated clinical quality only 14th in their list of priorities. The top three concerns were length of wait, staff friendliness, and physical surroundings.

Top medical staff concluded that the survey was flawed because everyone knows that clinical quality comes first! Rosabeth Moss Kantor gives 10 tips to stifle change, and especially to never forget that 'you, the higher ups, already know everything important about the business'.[5]

Actually they had failed to realize that patients view clinical competence as an expectation. Their concerns in other areas of service are, however, rising dramatically and are the critical issues that *make the difference.*

Mystery shopper and customer survey approaches must not ask platitudinous questions. Before asking, 'How do you rate service at the front desk?' you should consider whether a front desk is even needed? Who are the best customers to talk to?

1. Spot those who complain or defect and analyse and act on the information they provide.
2. Spot new customers looking lost. Offer help and ask their impressions. Supermarkets could benefit here.

Creating creativity

If you want to enhance personal and organizational creativity, clear the conditions, support personal growth and much of the rest will follow, providing you create the dialogue opportunities for people to share their progressive ideas.

All social creation outside started inside. The unemployment in our society starts with the widespread, unemployed inner life. It is creativity that creates jobs.

Creativity comes by luck and by practice. 'It's amazing how lucky you are,' said one observer to Gary Player. 'Yes,' he said, 'and the more I practise the luckier I get.' Here are a few ideas for personal creative growth which, if followed, do work,[6] but they need to be practised, and regularly.

1. Observe the wonder of children and remember, we were all once like that and perhaps could be again, at least sometimes. Make room for wonder.
2. Change one habit, however trivial. The arm you wear your watch on, say. Overcoming one habit creates forces to overcome another.
3. Change your handwriting. It is a more drastic and powerful version of 2, because it goes deeper.
4. Learn a new language! Another version of 2.
5. Try to build up your concentration. Take a trivial object like a pencil or pin and spend five minutes each day for six weeks thinking about nothing but it and things to with it. It is easy at first. It is working when it gets boring and you still do it.
6. Imagine a simple object like a pin. Make it very big, then small. Rotate it in your imagination. Change its colour. Turn it inside out. Keep trying day after day until you can.
7. Closely observe some object like a twig and a few leaves. Observe every minute thing, without interpretation or personal reaction. Just, what is there? When you think you have seen everything, look for 10 more aspects. This makes a good game with friends, or a start-up exercise for the team each morning, with each person taking a turn. Do it again and again.

8. Observe the difference between the leaves growing up the stem of a plant.
9. When nothing is happening, look around and closely observe. How plans interact is one good example. Try to figure out how a particular odd shape in a tree, say, came to be there. What is the story? Do not speculate, be Sherlock Holmes.
10. Take some simple object like a pen, and imagine backwards (starting 'now'), the process by which it arrived as an object in your possession, for each of the different components in parallel as far as possible.
11. Decide to do one absolutely simple, useless and trivial thing, like swopping a coin between pockets, at exactly the same time for 30 days in succession: it builds commitment and willpower and may take years to accomplish.
12. Closely observe and sense or feel the difference between blooming, blossoming plants or leaves, and dying ones.
13. Do the same with the difference between sounds from living things and non-organic or artificial.
14. Carefully imagine, with a real seed in your hand, what the process or growth of its plant would be from beginning to end. Observe a flourishing plant and imagine it dying and turning into a seed.
15. Practise positivity and, equanimity. Take one not so good thing (or person) each day and see the bright side. Take one upsetting thing and observe it carefully in your mind until you accept it (could be a person).

Do several, but only one or a few at a time and do it justice. After a few weeks or months, try another. Be patient. It takes two years to learn to stand up, when we are changing fastest! The rhythm and practice of the exercise helps, and new ones get easier with time.

In the responsive company, we can expect a great increase in the use of creativity and fun programmes to stimulate, using a variety of 'artistic' means. When you have wrestled to put your shape of the future first into colour and then into clay, articulating it in speech comes much easier.

One method that excites me – which has been successfully developed in The Netherlands by Anne-Marie Ehrlich and is now increasingly being offered around Europe's banks, manufacturers and service companies by practitioners – is a movement exercise called Eurythmy, which helps to model any aspect of social and process work and is enormously stimulating and enlivening for team-building, creativity, change learning and stress reduction. Try it.[7]

Notes and references

1. *Source: Leadership Is an Art*, New York, 1989.
2. Mintzberg, H., *Mintzberg on Management*, The Free Press, 1989, pp. 25–42.
3. Mintzberg, H., *Mintzberg on Management*, The Free Press, 1989, pp 358–361.
4. Yoshida, 'Quality improvement and TQC management at Calsonic in Japan and overseas', *Second International Quality Symposium, Mexico*, November 1989.
5. Kantor, R.M., *The Change Masters*, Simon and Schuster, 1983.
6. Variety of origins including Goethean observation, but particularly exercises given by Rudolf Steiner for teachers and personal development.
7. Institute for Eurythmy in Industry, Business and Professional Life, Dedestraat 11, NL 2596 RA DEN HAAG, The Netherlands.

18
Beginning points: social and technology trends

Summary The world is suddenly full of rumour and forecast of transformation based on the new interactive communication media. What might have started this book has been left to the end. The impending social and technological changes threaten or promise a new social and commercial structure. Whether they become a threat or a promise will greatly depend on how we deal with them. The fact is, they will probably be both. If the paradigm shifts towards a world of gain–gain cooperation, which seems probable, then it is the promise that will win through. If the technologies are used to force home advantage, the customer-competitors will retreat into their defensive shells and we shall all lose as the technological and legal barriers go up in a nightmare world.

There is a declining world market for words.

(Lech Walesa)

Rumoured changes to legal rules and policies for reserves made the Spanish press decide that the lending industry was in trouble, threatening loss of business for over 100 members of the Spanish Lending Association. To respond, they got together. The association produced a campaign which each member could send to its customers with a variety of fulfilment packs, including application software on diskette for large corporate clients. The result helped to stave off the crisis and implant the right ideas. Not only does this illustrate the power of database marketing to communicate and change ideas and not only does it illustrate the technologies for communication, but it illustrates the power of affinity or cooperative marketing.

The development of affinity clubs, such as those described in Chapter 8, Air Miles, American Express, and many frequency, fundraising and other programmes is further testimony to this and justifies the underlying database marketing archetype of partnership: people and technology, customers and suppliers, suppliers and suppliers, service and sales, managers and service people, ideas and implementation.

But, the success of the partnership between people and technology will be the acid test of database marketing over the next 10 or 20 years.

New technology: a dream or a nightmare?

Communication technologies are expanding, opening new possibilities. Palm top computers, personal telephone numbers, mobile phones, mobile and colour faxes, electronic mailing of moving images and voice mail, voice interface, vast capacity through optical fibre cables and satellite transmission are some of the changes here or on the near horizon. They threaten, or offer opportunities – depending on your point of view – for massive increases in communication and messages.

A huge variety of organizations will be offering loyalty schemes with personal cards. There will be widespread use of the event-based marketing communications systems described, reacting to and initiating changes in the relationship, with hopefully appropriate messages.

Another new technology will be interactive compact disk enabling customers to receive detailed information at home in an interactive form. These could take the place of catalogues, allowing customers to determine the messages they want to look at, how and when. Technology will provide the means to search selectively, then zoom in and consult among a vast library of information and images, before generating orders at the touch of a button. Television advertisements are also likely to be much more personally profiled. This could either happen through technology in the television itself or by cable or satellite registration.

Communication over the telephone will become increasingly easy and sophisticated. ACDs are already voice responsive. IBM now has technology leaping ahead of the pen interface to understand and decode the voice. When we can turn voice into text and commands simply and easily, the power of the computer to do things will leap forward.

Electronic voice messaging and links between the company's computer, its telephone and the touch tone pad or customer palm top, already enable a variety of interactions to take place on a semi-automated basis. This could include accessing information banks or triggering requested actions or services. When the customer responsive service infrastructure is established, a customer could call up a standard shopping list, make a few changes and arrange for delivery at a particular time with the greatest of ease.

Technology means that the 'mail shot' is no longer exclusively print on paper. With the PC almost as common an item of executive furniture as the in-tray, some communications lend themselves to the computer disk, which is cheap to duplicate (as low as 40c/25p each including the disk) and can be mailed at the standard letter rate.

Cadillac used a free interactive PC diskette to promote its 1994 model range. The diskette is divided into three sections, consisting of an animated sequence showing the vehicles, a detailed and comprehensive set of information on models that can be accessed according to interest, and an interactive golf game. What is the golf game? Is this not an example of the grocer's free carrot? Potential buyers can order the diskette by calling a toll-free telephone number featured in Cadillac's off-the-page advertising as well as being mailed to people on the database, integrating media and corporate programmes.

Satellites will also be involved. Ford has a satellite TV network to its dealers which it uses to enrich the quality and speed of communication, replacing conventional mailing. Not only can it communicate with a dealer, but with customers. But this is not, by itself, a good dialogue technique.

Fax, as a multiple distribution medium, is being used to transmit several hundred faxes simultaneously, from head office to dealerships, for example, by a London firm of financial analysts sending tips.

Fax on demand is growing. There are 1.4 million fax machines in the UK compared with 34 000 in 1984 and it can cost half as much to send information by fax as by post, and it is much quicker. Advertising and service companies can provide information by publishing a telephone number that the customer can dial using his/her own fax, calling off what they want by return.

EMAP, a major UK business and leisure magazine publisher, provides this service. Advertisers use one of the EMAP telephone numbers, and interested consumers call it for further information on the product or service advertised.

A London estate agent has a computerized telephone answering system through which the caller can activate the faxing of information from a database of commercial properties. Others are the American Embassy which distributes statements from the US Government, Autosport which publishes motor racing results, and the Consumers Association provides selected '*Which?*' reports. This is obviously not unsolicited junk faxing. Vodaphone, for example, stress this point strongly, since fax costs the recipient money. The customer is invited to request information.

Users of Microsoft products can call and go through a question and answer process in order to identify a problem, automatically controlled by an expert system. At the end the customer is asked to give a fax number by pressing a touch tone and information is sent from a databank. (Unfortunately, users have experienced delay and delivery problems.)

Multi-media is another wave of technology that will change many person–machine and person–person interfaces. Rover Cars in the UK identified that customers spend 12–16 weeks before buying a new car. However, market research showed that customers loathe the idea of walking into a car showroom and waiting for the inevitable pounce by a lurking salesperson. They have therefore decided to convert their salespeople into consultants and have turned the forecourt into the first point of contact where customers can browse. A sophisticated multi-media based computer system enables customers to view and browse stills, text and videos of the cars, and to configure models in which they are interested within budget. Trade-in figures, finance programmes and delivery times can be printed.

Toyota began the process of putting computers in the forecourt. For example, its Corolla channel customers have a personal card which gives them home or dealer file access to an information system solving problems from insurance to finance to model range – and asks the customer for an information update, which they are happy to provide.

Apple Computer is piloting a new direct-selling medium in the USA that could become big. *Enpassant* is a CD ROM disk that features 21 well-known US catalogues, including Lands End, LL Bean, and Tiffany & Co., to 30 000 known CD ROM users. It is designed to interact with the user, with the catalogue marrying text, images and sound. It also allows the consumer to specify personal preferences and will prompt a range of products and gift suggestions. Editorial content includes features on fashion, children and personal finance. Buyers are able to order by calling *Enpassant* toll free. *Enpassant* then processes the transaction, routeing orders to the appropriate companies for shipping.

British Telecom is developing an information, communications and entertainment division. The first service is video on demand, which will be delivered through the telephone lines to subscribers. Other services that will follow include home shopping, information services, and video games.

Barclays Bank is introducing a range of in-house multi-media products through its network. Business Needs Analyser is a CD ROM-based PC product which uses text, graphics and video to help staff explain services available to small businesses. The system can be personalized by downloading customer details from the bank's computers. Video on demand is seen as a key technology at Barclays, including interactive video kiosks in its network and at outside locations such as airports. It is also trialling home shopping, based on the Philips CD-I system.

The British and other governments will be using the information superhighway to deliver official information to the public. They believe that widespread use of interactive multi-media services via this highway is likely throughout public sector organizations. Video-based tourist information kiosks could give information on exhibitions and places to visit, and information could be delivered to the home in response to needs.

The developing technologies will change shopping habits. Instead of picking up goods, shoppers may 'shoot' the bar code on the shelf for further information, or to order the product. In supermarkets, dietary and nutritional specifications of products would be displayed. Wandering round the displays in this manner could allow shoppers to pick up a list, check the final charge, confirm, pay and either collect or arrange delivery, all automatically. In Britain, the Centre for Exploitation of Science and Technology (CEST) is funded by a consortium of retailers to develop such products and methods.

There are even smart trash cans on the way to read the label on what we have consumed. Can-Scan is an intelligent dustbin being developed in Noston that offers to tell the consumer what has been used and it even sends a refresh order to the producer/distributor whose software will automatically determine replenishment.

The popularity of shopping channels in the US is increasing. These are specialized cable channels which act rather like an audio-visual catalogue. They provide offers on a wide range of products, any of which you can buy immediately from home with a telephone and credit card.

Interactive TV is going to be a very significant phenomenon. It is normally supplied by cable and features extended TV displays of products which the customer can then order through the TV communications device. Its sales potential was once powerfully revealed in the $1.2 million sale of Diane von Furstenberg dresses and silk separates in under two hours. Interactive TV can handle, through computer-supported communications, 20 000 orders per hour, and rising.

Users simply plug the TV into the telephone or cable outlet via an adaptor and sit back, pressing the remote control. More than 10 000 companies made applications during 1993 for franchises to make and broadcast interactive TV programmes in the nine markets initially opened in the United States. BT are trialling interactive TV in 1995 involving major UK retailers such as Thomas Cook, Sears, NatWest Bank, WH Smith and on-line magazines from IPC.

Videotron has, for over eight years, been offering interactive TV facilities to sell houses in Canada and has just started in the UK. Consumers select type, budget and location parameters and view details of the houses that suit, before going to see them. In Canada, 57 per cent of Videotron subscribers use this as first source of property information, and this will rise as the databanks increase.

Mobile and personal phones, telecommuting, videophones and integrated devices will change communication and accessibility. Barclaycard and Mercury One2One have formed a partnership to enable users to shop while on the move. Barclaycard is issuing a mobile credit card with a micro chip that will allow callers to access information about any financial or telephone service provided by Barclaycard and One2One. This will enable them to pay bills, and get access to banking services. It is expected that there will be 10 million mobile phone owners in the UK by the end of this century.

Forecasts for the increase in telecommuters across the developed world proliferate, and give different results. However, they do all agree that more and more telecommuters will be in place by the end of the century. These are people who will be working from home or local village centres using fax, telephone and computer with digital links to communicate, correspond, network, take part in bulletin board sessions, and conference calls. The increased availability of telephones with built-in videos will increase the opportunity, and so will the information highway. The US-based OVUM report identified 600 000 telecommuters in 1992 but prophesied that the number would increase to 12 million by the end of the century. This is a huge change and will signal and drive many other changes in the way that people interact, buy and organize their leisure time. They will also be a more difficult group to reach by traditional media and retailing methods.

I to I or impersonal marketing: trust or shields

The questions are: How much will be personal and 1 to 1 and how much impersonal? How will the customers protect themselves from the coming deluge?

While shopping channels such as QVC (quality/value/convenience) are proving successful, their limitation is that scheduling of products is determined by the channel programme and not by the shopper. Most people are not prepared to wait in the hope that something may appear that is of interest. This means that the success of the channel is largely driven by addicts (a rather sad indictment). Products appear at random and there is no guarantee that the one you want will arrive during the time you are watching.

Craig Evans[1] suggests the development of dedicated, specialized channels devoted to particular key product lines. For example, there could be a channel focusing on cars and another on TVs. The fibre optics being laid into the home will make up to 500 channels available, thus the dedication of 30 or so to specialized marketing channels is quite feasible. This would enable a potential buyer to become more educated in the product range available by reviewing quality, function and value through a range of 'infomercials'. These would be extended in detailed presentations on products. But, even this is not very personal.

We can imagine in the not too distant future that all television watching will be selected by the consumer from a library of classic and fresh documentaries, films and programmes, in which case the choice of infomercials and messages is likely to increase. Already, dial-up video is turning into a mega business.

The technology exists to enable targeted electronic mail catalogues to consumers and business people, the resulting 'document' consisting of text, voice, graphic and video elements, with voice interaction. Everything might be personalized: references, model sizes in clothes, content of the catalogue, text, voice messages. The buyer could 'ask' for more detail on one element and be taken into video, conferencing, a careline call, an electronics spreadsheet to calculate alternative costs or just simple text. The technology exists but is generally neither commercially priced nor commercially matched to the market, yet.

In the new world the customer will have the opportunity to be much more selective and in control.

The customers may well end up selling their data in various ways. A *Wall Street Journal* article by sociologist James Rule in 1990 proposed a customer property right over the commercial use of a consumer's data. Releasing the data would trigger royalties. Brokers may emerge who work for the consumer as the ultimate data owner, not the current list compiler.

Information technology may be used to distribute messages, and as a *shield* to protect customers from such messages. Interactive TV provides opportunities to select programme content on an unprecedented scale. So does the answerphone, and systems to screen electronic mail. As the rising tide of communication turns into a deluge, customers are and will become more and more selective. Those providing the initial technologies will have every incentive to give customers the maximum opportunity to choose the messages they wish to receive, and when.

HomeFax is a start-up US business which is establishing the new technology, new psychology market. It offers subscribers (a 'choice' word) the opportunity to have a home fax, either subsidized or even free, and all paper expenses paid, in return for completing a monthly form which itemizes their latest interests. Advertisers then send offers and information by fax, but the quantity is screened by HomeFax according to an agreement with the subscriber. So subscribers get information on subjects of current interest, but in controlled doses, and the advertisers do not know who they are sending to. HomeFax operates as a shell. The number is unlisted (although it can be given to friends, like any other unlisted number).

FreeFone is a Seattle, USA, company which offers another special private service. Again, subscribers complete forms indicating their interests and agreements and now their regular outside calls are intercepted with special offers from rival companies. The subscriber can listen, accept the offer, say, for different pizza or car hire supplier, or can ignore and complete the call. The intercepting marketers do not know who they are speaking to, unless an order is given.

Sellers, too, want a measure of security and comfort. Service mastery in the future will depend on agreements, associations between customers and customer communities and companies who plan to take care of their needs.

Already FreeFone and HomeFax are pointing the way to a new set of agreements with consumers, just as is common in the business-to-business arena. The agreement is a bond between the customer and supplier that says, you agree to buy from me and I shall give you the service you need and specify. So, in the 'wild idea' of the smart trash can above, the retailer agrees to replenish the consumer's needs automatically according to the consumer's rules. Some of these agreements will be formal, like a consumer credit agreement today, and others will be part of the Guarantee of Trust.

Instead of competing to master a share of the market, service mastery will aim to serve the needs of the whole community, one customer at a time, one individual at a time.

Will customers be retreating behind shields or will shared trust build mutual value? Will technology be a nightmare or a vision?

If you do not want your customers to disappear behind the shield, into the cave or cocoon, or under the shell, then a way will need to be found to continue to reach and touch the human being – to get past technology and impersonal communication to the human heart.

I to I.

Reference

1. Evans, C., *Marketing Channels*, Prentice Hall, 1994.

Glossary

ACD Automatic call distribution; computerized inward and outward telephone call distribution

API Application program interface

CLI Call line identification: the process of supplying the incoming telephone number as part of the telephone call

CSTA Computer supported telephony applications: integration of ACD, telephony and applications database

CTI Computer telephone integration

Data Protection Registrar Body responsible for education and policing of data privacy; all holders of computer data about people must register and abide by the laws

Database Marketing Direct marketing with systematic data collection and use

Direct response Direct response is sometimes used to mean direct marketing, but emphasizes the fact of response, as in Direct Response TV (DRTV)

EIS Executive information system

EU Directive on Data Common agreement, similar to Data Protection; the main point is that you must tell people you are collecting, and the purpose, and give them opt out (but not for your own customers where data is naturally collected, e.g. for delivery)

Merge-Purge Key industry activity: taking many mailing lists, merging them and removing any duplicates or suppression files (such as existing customers) then creating one or more output mailing files

MIS Management information system

Modelling Profiling customers, typically using such techniques as regression and CHAID

MPS Mailing preference scheme: opportunity for consumers to register dislike (or like!) of direct mail

Nixie, goneaway The addressee is no longer there

Overkill/underkill When you extract duplicates that are not really duplicates from a mailing or database file/or the opposite, when you fail to find all duplicates.

Segmentation Dividing a customer population into meaningful smaller parts in order to align activity to interest more effectively and profitably

Source code, pack code, response code Code placed on advertisement, etc., to register the marketing activity from which it came.

Through the line Integrating both advertising and direct response

Bibliography

The following material is not mentioned in the footnotes but was useful in preparation.

Service, The New Competitive Edge, Management Centre Europe, 1990.

The Impact of Computerised Sales and Marketing Systems, 4th edition, HCG Publications, Olney, UK, 1994.

'The pluralization of consumption', Editorial, *Harvard Business Review*, May/June 1988.

Block, P., *Stewardship: Choosing Service over Self Interest*, Berret-Koehler, 1993.

Berry, L., Bennett, D.R. and Brown, C.W., *Service Quality – A Profit Strategy for Financial Institutions*, Dow-Jones Irwin, 1989.

Bird, D., *Commonsense Direct Marketing, The Printed Shop 1982*, Kogan Page, 1989.

Burnett, K., *Relationship Fundraising*, White Lion Press, London, 1992.

Carlzon, J., *Moments of Truth*, Ballantyne, New York, 1987.

Carroll, P., 'Revisiting customer retention', *Journal of Retail Banking*, Vol. **15**, (No. 1; Spring 1993), pp. 5–13.

Holz, H., *Databased Marketing*, John Wiley & Sons, 1992.

Jenkinson, A., 'Automation to boost sales and marketing', *Direct Marketing International*, May 1993.

Jenkinson, A., 'Beyond segmentation', *Journal of Targeting, Marketing and Analysis for Measurement*, Vol. **3** (No. 1).

Jenkinson, A., 'Elevating the banal: understanding and selecting name and address processing software', *Journal of Targeting, Measurement and Analysis for Marketing*, Vol. **1** (No. 2; Autumn 1992).

Jenkinson, A., 'Structural changes to optimise database marketing performance', *Journal of Database Marketing*, Vol. **2** (No. 2).

Levinger, G., 'A social exchange view on the dissolution of pair relationships' in Burgess, R.L. and Huston, T.L., *Social Exchange in Developing Relationships*, Academic Press, 1979.

Lockhart, J. F., 'Chief executives define their own data needs', *Harvard Business Review*, March/April 1979.

Luchs, R., 'Successful businesses compete on quality – not costs', *Long*

Range Planning, Vol. **19** (No. 1; 1986), pp 12–17.

Rapp, S. and Collins, T., *Maximarketing*, McGraw-Hill, New York, 1976.

Senge, P., *The Fifth Discipline: The Art and Practice of the Learning Organization*, Century Business, 1993.

Shaw, R. and Stone, M., *Database Marketing*, Gower, 1988.

Voelkel, J., 'Land Rover's direct marketing programme: a case study', *Journal of Database Marketing*, Vol. **1** (No. 1).

Zemke, R., Bell, C. R., *Service Wisdom*, Lakewood Books, 1990.

Index